Giulietta Simionato

HOW CINDERELLA BECAME QUEEN

*Selections on CD**

Great Voices, Volume 4

1. LE NOZZE DI FIGARO (Mozart) *Voi che sapete...* Oct. 6, 1956 [2:45]
2. IL BARBIERE DI SIVIGLIA (Rossini) *Una voce poca fa...* Nov. 26, 1956 [5:03]
3. LA CENERENTOLA (Rossini) *Nacqui all'affanno...* Nov. 26, 1956 [5:42]
4. L'ITALIANA IN ALGERI (Rossini) *Pensa alla patria...* Nov. 26, 1956 [5:41]
5. NORMA (Bellini) *Mira, o Norma...* Dec. 7, 1955 [7:15]
6. LA FAVORITA (Donizetti) *O mio Fernando...* Feb. 25, 1959 [6:40]
7. MIGNON (Thomas) *Conosco un garzoncel...* Nov. 26, 1956 [7:11]
8. CARMEN (Bizet) Card song. Oct. 8, 1954 [3:31]
9. IL TROVATORE (Verdi) *Stride la vampa...* Oct. 16, 1963 [4:35]
10. DON CARLO (Verdi) *O don fatale...* Oct. 24, 1961 [4:28]
11. AIDA (Verdi) *Già i sacerdoti adunansi...* (duet, with Mario Del Monaco) Oct. 16, 1961 [6:31]
12. ADRIANA LECOUVREUR (Cilea) *Acerba voluttà...* Nov. 28, 1959 [4:22]
13. CAVALLERIA RUSTICANA (Mascagni) *Voi lo sapete...* (with Amilia Pini) Oct. 23, 1961 [5:21]
14. CAVALLERIA RUSTICANA (Mascagni) *No, Turiddu, rimani ancora...* (duet, with Angelo Lo Forese) Oct. 23, 1961 [4:58]

1 — NHK Symphony, Tokyo, Sankei Hall. Conductor: Gui. 2, 3, 4, 7 — RAI Symphony. Conductor: Sanzogno. 5 — La Scala Orchestra, Milan. Conductor: Votto. 6 — NHK Symphony, Tokyo, Takarazuka Theatre. Conductor: Erede. 8 — Vienna Philharmonic, Vienna. Conductor: Karajan. 9 — NHK Symphony, Tokyo, Bunka Kaikan. Conductor: De Fabritiis. 10 — NHK Symphony, Tokyo, Bunka Kaikan. Conductor: Basile. 11 — NHK Symphony, Tokyo, Bunka Kaikan. Conductor: Capuana. 12 — Orchestra of the Teatro San Carlo, Naples, Teatro San Carlo. Conductor: Rossi. 13, 14 — NHK Symphony, Tokyo, Metropolitan Hall. Conductor: Morelli.

*All performances "live."

GREAT VOICES

Volumes published in this series:

Ruffo: My Parabola
Tebaldi: The Voice of an Angel
Tito Schipa
Simionato: How Cinderella Became Queen
Corelli: A Man, A Voice

— *Giulietta Simionato* —

HOW CINDERELLA BECAME QUEEN

by
Jean-Jacques Hanine Roussel

translated by
Samuel Chase with Teresa Brentegani,
Albert and Adriana Miner

chronology and discography by
Jean-Jacques Hanine Roussel

compact disc compiled by
Bill Park

GREAT VOICES

4

Originally published in Italian as
Come Cenerentola Divenne Regina
by Jean-Jacques Hanine Vallaut, Azzali Editori, S.N.C., Parma, 1987

All photographs are from the private collection
of Jean-Jacques Hanine Roussel.

Baskerville Publishers, Inc.
7616 LBJ Freeway, Suite 510, Dallas, TX 75251-1008

Library of Congress Cataloging-in-Publication Data

Hanine-Roussel, Jean-Jacques, 1950-
[Giulietta Simionato. English]
Giulietta Simionato : how Cinderella became queen / by Jean-Jacques Hanine-Roussel ; translated by Samuel Chase, with Teresa Brentegani, Albert and Adriana Miner ; chronology and discography by Jean-Jacques Hanine-Roussel ; compact disc compiled by Bill Park.
p. cm. -- (Great voices ; 4)
Discography : p.
Includes index.
ISBN 1-880909-49-9
1. Simionato, Giulietta. 2. Mezzo-sopranos--Italy--Biography.
I. Title. II. Series.
ML420.S5628H313 1997
782.1'092--dc21
[B]

97-7714
MN

Manufactured in the United States of America
First Printing, 1997

To my adored wife Danièle

To my daughters, Stéphanie, Delphine, and Linh-Juliette

Introduction to the American Edition

AT THE BEGINNING of 1983 I decided to write a biography of Giulietta Simionato. I wanted to pay tribute to an artist who has left an indelible mark on the history of singing and on the history of opera theater. It is no coincidence that the first full-length studies of this remarkable singer were written by foreigners: a Japanese friend and admirer, Naomi Takeya Uchida, and the author of this book, which was published in the original Italian by Azzali Editori (1987).

The United States edition of my biography is not a mere translation. The chronology of Giulietta's career has been considerably increased and corrected. The list of her recordings on compact discs has been added. A great number of tributes to her life and work which were submitted by her colleagues, omitted in the original edition, have found a place here. Many books referring to our artist that have appeared all over the world since 1983 have been taken into consideration.

In short this is a new book which better showcases the immense talent of one of the greatest mezzo-sopranos of our century and attests to my sincere affection for the friend and admiration for the artist.

ACKNOWLEDGMENTS

In compiling my biography I chose to cast myself in the role of historian rather than critic and was particularly concerned that my research should document, as completely as possible, the unique chronology of this artist's career — a great artist who unfortunately never kept a diary.

The photographs that Signora Simionato made available to me and the meetings she agreed to in Milan provided the basic outline of the book. However, I was unable to derive enough material from them to create the book I had in mind.

To do that I proceeded to contact the archivists of every theater in which Giulietta Simionato had sung. I interviewed many of her former colleagues and asked the help of many friends who owned critical and photographic material. To all of those whose invaluable assistance helped to enrich my text I wish to extend my deepest gratitude:

Iris Adami Corradetti (Padua), Antoine Arrighi (Marseille), Walter Baldasso (Turin), Roberto Baldi (Milan), Fernando Battaglia (Forlì), Anna Bergera (Turin), Paola Bernardi Rugiù (Bologna), Enrico Erasmo Bonavera (Turin), Francisco Bueno Camejo (L'Alcudia), Nini Castiglioni (Milan), Matteo Cavalcoli (Ravenna), Mario Cavriani (Rovigo), Anne Marie Chalbos (Paris), Eraldo Coda (Milan), Christian Colombeau (Chernex), Viorica Cortez (Paris), Giuseppe Damiani (Bologna), Masako Deguci (Milan), Ina Del Campo (Milan), Mario Delgado (Boulogne Billancourt), Esperia De Rosa Couetoux (Paris), Henry Dumoulin (Lyon), Bruno De Franceschi (Imola), Carlos Diaz Du Pond (Mexico City), Juan Dzazopulos (Santiago, Chile), Gastone Fara (Turin), Georges Farret (Marseille), Giorgio Feliciotti (Rome), Dominique Feron (Paris), Enzo Gamberini (Bologna), Anthony Gasson (London), Daniele Glaise (Paris), Valeria and Giorgio Gualerzi (Turin), Télémaque Khavessian (Vincennes), Rita Koch (Vienna), Jean-Fernand Le Guellec (Paris), Carlo Marinelli Roscioni (Rome), Simonetta Marchi (Bologna), Angelo Mercuriali (Milan), Vittorio MezzoMonaco (Forlì), Moises Miguel (São Paulo), Paolo Montarsolo (Rome), Santos Muscas (Montserrat), Rosetta Noli (Genoa), Paulo Padoan (Chioggia), Ennio Pezzi (Russi), Michaele Raffaeli (Forlì), Emma Rossi Tegani (Milan), Jean-Jacques Rouveroux (Limoges), Ornella Rovero Dezza (Vittorio Veneto), Daniele Rubboli (Milan), Vincenzo Quattrocchi (Turin), Lore Salzburger (Salzburg), Carlo F. Semini (Breganzona), Gilberto Starone (Voghera), Italo Tajo (Cincinnati), Naomi Takeya Uchida (Osaka), Frédéric Thiebaut (Bois Colombes), Romano

Travan (Gradisca), Claude Vacherot (Paris), Paride Venturi (Bologna), Lanfranco Visconti (Cagliari), Pierre Vogelweith (Strasbourg), John Wustman (Urbana) and the entire Interpreters' Office of the Paris Police Department who were completely at my disposal.

I want to thank the many theater managers and librarians who responded to my inquiries:

Austria: Salzburg, Salzburg Festival (Hans Jaklitsch); Belgium: Brussels, Théâtre Royal de la Monnaie (A. Rousseau); Brazil: Rio de Janeiro, Théâtre Municipal (Antonio José Faro); France: Lyon, Opéra (Jean-Pierre Brossman) - Paris, Bibliothèque de l'Arsenal (Valentine Faure, Mademoiselle Giteau); Théâtre National de l'Opéra (M. Ruffo) - Strasbourg, Opéra du Rhin (Bernadette Wendling) - Toulouse, Théâtre du Capitole (Gérald Van Ham); Germany: Hamburg, Hamburg State Opera; Japan: Tokyo, Nippon Hoso Kyokai; England: Glyndebourne, Opera Festival (Helen O'Neill) - London, Royal Opera House, Covent Garden (Francesca Franchi, Lynne Kinnerley, Harold Rosenthal); Italy: Bergamo, Teatro Donizetti (Francesco Invernici) - Bologna, Teatro Comunale (Pierpaolo Sabattini) - Brescia, Teatro Grande - Carpi, Teatro Comunale (Mario Bizzoccoli) - Catania, Teatro Massimo Bellini (Antonio Scrima) - Como, Teatro Sociale - Livorno, Teatro La Gran Guardia (Paolo Bassano) - Merano, Teatro Comunale (Peter Abram) - Milan, Teatro alla Scala (Edoardo Bossi, Patrizia Biffi, Dino Belletti, Elena Fumagalli, Renato Garavaglia, Silvia Suighi) - Modena, Teatro Comunale (Alfredo Guidi) - Naples, Teatro San Carlo (Francesco Canessa) - Novara, Teatro Coccia (Pietro Rogati) - Palermo, Teatro Massimo (Ubaldo Mirabelli) - Pesaro, Teatro Rossini (Gilberto Calcagnini) - Piacenza, Teatro Municipale (Antonella Peruffo) - Roma, Teatro dell'Opera (Giovanna Megna) - Rovigo, Teatro Sociale (Claudio Zerbinati) - Treviso, Teatro Comunale (Lucio De Piccoli) - Trieste, Teatro Verdi e Politeama Rossetti (Grazia Bravar, Adriana Zonta) - Venezia, Gran Teatro La Fenice (A. Busetto); Malta: Valletta, Teatro Manoel, Royal Opera House (A. Agius Ferrante); Mexico: Mexico City, Palacio de Bellas Artes (Carlos Diaz Du Pond, Ignacio Toscano Jarquín); The Netherlands: Amsterdam, Holland Festival (Ivonne Valk); Portugal:

Lisbon, Teatro Sao Carlos (Vasco Eloy Nunes Cardoso); Spain: Barcelona, Gran Teatro del Liceu (Luis Andreu) - Bilbao, Teatro Coliseo Albia (Mikel Viar Bilbao); Switzerland: Geneva, Grand Théâtre (Georgette Rostand), Bibliothèque Municipale (A. Galetti) - Lausanne, Théâtre Municipal (Albert Linder); Hungary: Budapest, Magyar Allami Operahaz (Pal Fejer); United States: Chicago, Lyric Opera (Jina Vergeer) - New York, Carnegie Hall (Gino Francesconi, Mark Hayman), Metropolitan Opera (Richard Delheim, Kenneth Schlesinger, Robert Tuggle) - San Francisco, Opera (Robert Robb); Tunisia: Tunis, Bibliothèque Nationale (Azedine Bachaouch).

In addition I would like to thank the individuals who generously contributed the tributes which serve as the book's opening chapters: Dr. Jean Mongrédien, Professor of Eighteenth and Nineteenth Century French Music at the Sorbonne, Maestro Marcel Landowski, Secretary in Perpetuity of the Académie de Beaux Arts, Maestro Giampiero Tintoni, Director of the La Scala Museum, and the eminent critic Roland Mancini, whose introductory tribute expresses the feelings of a true connoisseur.

Finally, grateful mention must be made of my sister Marie-Michèle Santini Hanine, who made my research easier.

Jean-Jacques Hanine Roussel
March 11, 1996—Paris

Contents

Giulietta Simionato

HOW CINDERELLA BECAME QUEEN

—*A Voice of Burnished Metal and Velvet*—

by Roland Mancini

IF THE ABOVE formulation has been heard before, it's because it applies to the woman as well as the artist. Her voice is so flexible, so easily led, never forced, always present, while its extent and force is hidden behind a smile — the smile of a woman, who with charm and courtesy masks a silent, internal rebellion... All of which no voice had revealed to me before I had the pleasure of approaching Signora Simionato Frugoni.

I had wanted to title my modest homage: "She of whom no one ever spoke ill." Then an annoying article came into my hands — a discography of *Il trovatore*, a work of two voice aficionados which appeared in a French opera magazine over ten years ago, where it was presumptuously stated that La Simionato was never in any way a good Azucena. In the first place the authors of this article invite ridicule by ignoring what this artist accomplished at Salzburg, among other places, and yet a pretext for their absurd judgment might be found in the arc of this unique singer's career. Her art surprised the tastes of an entire generation after the last world war, a generation subjected to "malcanto"— wretched singing full of screams and strident notes: a transitional generation, then, of which a remnant may still be found today, the illegitimate spawn of a past which lives on in its young admirers.

In fact, if this sort of snap judgment had consecrated the ephemeral imprint of the Barbieri mirage (without doubt an authentic contralto, who soon deviated toward the heroic mezzo-soprano repertory), it points up a true generation gap which has always existed: on the one hand are the old fans who in good faith find themselves siding with the too-young admirers of bel canto in thinking that the crown of reigning Italian mezzo-soprano should have passed directly from the venerable Stignani to the head of the young Cossotto (who was just debuting when Simionato was retiring from the stage), thus giving the thirty-year career of La Simionato short shrift; on the other hand the generation in the middle, for whom La Simionato has had absolute primacy, have been compensated for all that they missed in Stignani, qualities that the young Cossotto, wielding her voice like a flaming sword, was unable to recall. In fact the signatory quality of the mezzo-soprano, whose voice is midway between soprano and contralto, resembling the former in the splendor of its upper register, in the way the sparks fly, in its inherent charm, and the latter in the deep resonance of its human spirit and sensuality, may only be heard in the middle register.

Quietly secure in the universality of her approach Simionato was less susceptible to the events of one evening when she was the darling of the press. For more than thirty years she had known how to exploit the whole range of her sensitivity and her voice, lending her rosy velvet to Santuzza while she was still young. In addition she was one of the first of her time to do justice to the nearly forgotten Mozart repertory, then to Cimarosa, Donizetti and above all Rossini, at the same time as she was able to shine in the more dramatic Verdi repertory, so that she was able to incarnate characters as diverse as Leonora in *La favorita*, Charlotte, Romeo and Adalgisa, and then, in her fifties, Karajan's Azucena. In one year at La Scala she was Valentine in *The Huguenots*, flaunting a superb high C; then Arsace — a role for contralto coloratura to follow the role of a full-fledged soprano — after which she made her "debut" at the Paris Opera as much to celebrate her fifty-five years as to say goodbye to her public with the Mozart opera with which she had begun her career. This might be a small list, but it has no equivalent in the century for singers in her voice category.

If Jean-Jacques Hanine Roussel has kindly opened the door

to the temple that he has erected in honor of his goddess, probably because some years ago he discerned in my writings a well-founded admiration for her art, and not just a run-of-the-mill enthusiast of the sort so common in opera circles, it behooves me once again to use the first person to better delineate the state of mind in which this appreciation of her rare talent is being written.

I had scarcely attained adolescence when her voice was revealed to me, as it was to others, as Mamma Lucia in a recorded performance conducted by the composer. I was surprised that such a modest part could fall to the lot of a singer of the first rank, and from then on I never missed a repeat performance on the Italian radio. Instrumentalist that I was (and particularly attached to perfection of tone and to the aesthetic catharsis caused by beauty), the voice of this "new" artist immediately entered my private paradise, already inhabited by the likes of Galli-Curci, Ponselle and Besanzoni, De Luca and Pinza, and presided over — in perfect cohabitation, it goes without saying — by the immense Gigli and the incomparable Schipa. Today this paradise has been repopulated without displacing the original occupants.

Anyway, after my adolescence, one evening in 1957, in fact, in a box seat at the Théâtre Sarah Bernhardt in Paris, I heard a voice arise from the shadows that was like no other, a voice that was singing "There once was a King...": the voice of Cinderella-Simionato, seemingly fragile in the vast hall, though able to take possession of it, even so, with scarcely three phrases which easily made her bright presence felt: a voice that was never forte but never insufficient.

Then, in the midst of so many memories, there were those twenty minutes of applause that greeted her exit as Eboli at the Salzburg Festival of 1958, and then her Azucena, and certainly her Adalgisa which was practically a farewell performance for the ill singer at her side, Maria Callas, who had shared her first international triumphs ("And that was why," she would tell me later, "I decided to retire from the stage at about the same time.").

And so it went until the day when I found that velvet feminine presence sitting across from me, cloaked in impenetrable affability, where we were to sit for some years on the jury for the international singing competition at Treviso. In the beginning I was struck by her charming but distant smile, and we exchanged no more than a few words of no particular moment. There was nothing in this comparable to the confidence I enjoyed with great stars like Magda Olivero and Rossi Lemeni, to name a few of the big names. Then one night at perhaps two in the morning, at the end of a long consultation, or perhaps between two plates of perfumed Montello mushrooms, "It's strange," I told her, "we never vote for the same candidates." "I've been noticing that myself for quite some time," she replied serenely, her smile turning to laughter. The ice was broken. Then later, when I wanted to give greater authenticity to my biography of Maria Callas and asked her to write several lines in remembrance, her response was even more spontaneous: "Fifteen years of friendship can't be summarized in a couple of lines. Come to Rome." It was an offer I declined with much regret.

All my personal impressions about the artist and the woman are bound up in her infinite kindness and great sensitivity, dominated by so much strength; by the sudden rages which interrupt her Olympian smile for a moment and give proof of a personality which is more complex than it might seem. So it is that her singing brings home to us evidence of a power and a temperament that has been severely disciplined by hard-won technical mastery. Of course it was this hard work that was responsible for the extension of her range and the increase in amplitude, and the sweet timbre which makes you forget the size of her voice.

Even so, might we not find the secret to her method in the revolt which she had to learn to subdue during her long years in the "galleys," a time when fate had consigned her to a sort of anonymity while true professionals had already recognized in her the first among Italian mezzo-sopranos? Can we not discern here the reason for the discretion that stuns us to this day when we hear her fantastic interpretation of Jane Seymour in La Scala's revival of *Anna Bolena*, a part which she brought back from obscurity just ten years before, in Barcelona? It had been a royal interpretation which passed unnoticed in the eyes of the paparazzi, who were uniquely preoccupied with Callas, and only began to notice her in the revival of the following year, when the majority of journalists had decided to dethrone "la divina." Many only became aware of her "serene mastery," her "quiet power," when she decided to retire from the stage, and when a succession of mezzo-sopranos were obliged to receive only a part of her heritage, which was too heavy for only one of them.

Of course her universal appeal is controversial. There are those who would deny her the Superstar's ability to dazzle us with vocal fireworks, but what Superstar can sing Amneris? As for those who deny her the tartness of Barbieri as Laura: how long did that star maintain the integrity of her instrument? And for those who prefer the steel of a Cossotto, did Cossotto ever achieve the sensuality of Simionato's Dalila, the loving tenderness of her Charlotte, or her greatness in Rossinian trouser roles? For those who bemoan the lack of Stignani's vocal opulence, did Stignani ever portray a Dido or Marguerite back to back with Donizetti and Bellini heroines? And for those who would prefer the sensuousness of a Bumbry — certainly the most apt of all to inherit from Simionato — could Bumbry get anywhere near Mozart or Rossini? Or when people reprove her for a Carmen that is essentially "too lyrical," were Ebe Stignani or Fiorenza Cossotto ever her equal in it? No one has ever thought of comparing her to Horne, so different are their voices in timbre and emotional charge (the great Horne never came close to Verdi without running a certain risk) — above all because a Simionato born in 1929 would be something else again, as would a Horne who had been born in 1910.

In the forties it was only Giulietta Simionato among the mezzo-sopranos who was capable of responding to the richness of Mozart during her early career, and to Cimarosa's, having recorded his *Orazi e Curiazi*, and above all to Rossini's. Until 1948 at La Scala, then in 1952 at the Maggio Musicale in Florence and then on all the stages she took on three Rossini roles, adding Arsace in the 1962 Scala season and Cenerentola in 1964. Only Simionato, we have said, but not without the hard work of having to impose her image as a mezzo-soprano who knew how to make her career, as she said in a witty interview in *Discoteca*, "in the parts that until then had been reserved for singers with a generous bosom" — and in fact her physique did permit her, on the stage, to give a marked verisimilitude to Amneris's amorous rivalry with Aida or with Elisabeth of Valois, and above all to be believable in *travestie* roles from Siebel to Mignon, all the way to Tancredi and Arsace by way of Isoliero and Romeo, Cherubino and Orfeo (at Salzburg with Karajan), without forgetting a furtive but nevertheless noteworthy stint as Zanetto at La Scala.

Finally, since "live" recordings have triumphed in spite of the hostility of the big recording companies, one is obligated to regret her aberrant "official" recording career which made her the victim of the incompetence (or the self-interested subterfuges) of those who controlled the record market. No testimony of her Adalgisa survives from studio recordings, or of her Eboli or her Charlotte or her Leonora or her Rossini parts, mutilated by cuts, and so forth... Fortunately, however, we are able to relive in all their true theatricality her interpretations of Leonora, Charlotte, Eboli, Adalgisa, Bouillon, Azucena, Dalila, Carmen, Margherita and so many other characters offered as live interpretations, in all their immortal splendor, which satisfy the desires of the most discriminating music-lovers of our era.

—The Ideal Interpreter—

by Jean Mongrédien

EVERYTHING, OR NEARLY everything, has been said a thousand times about the magic power of the human voice, which is capable, in the words of Balzac, of "so profoundly moving our souls." And yet, reading these pages, we go back to dreaming: all the critics are unanimous in praising the exceptional gifts of a woman, whose passage through the artistic world has left an indelible imprint. As a matter of fact it is the privilege of exceptional beings, all too rare, who have the power to transmit happiness, pure happiness, generously and without stint.

Giulietta Simionato, then, was fortunate to be a messenger sent from another world — but from which gods? — to make humanity conscious of that "call from the beyond" that so profoundly influenced Marcel Proust.

Always seeking to perfect herself, and doubting herself, even when she was enjoying the fullest success, this artist gave a great lesson to future generations about energy and courage. She felt herself invested with a duty to obtain absolute and constant mastery of technical control as the only means of reaching artistic perfection. Opposed to scandal and cheap publicity, which she considered beneath the notice of a true diva, she was, in fact, in every sense of the word, the ideal interpreter: able to translate for us the language of the gods.

Having opened this book, the fruit of a passionate biographer's research, from the first page you will be immersed in one of the most beautiful fairy tales of our time.

–A Fable–

by Giampiero Tintori

PERHAPS BOOKS ABOUT singers have always been written, or singers have written autobiographies, articulate texts of all kinds. From pure hagiography, which is by definition void of critical sense, to observations about the world that the subject had known, books useful to understand a period or an epoch of the melodrama, but also useless books of pure vainglory.

To write a book on Giulietta Simionato means to single out a conspicuous period in operatic history. The historian never tires of putting her center stage, surrounding her with what befell her during some golden operatic moments. And the reader in the detailed descriptions of Hanine Roussel cannot succeed even today in understanding the fact that Simionato had to work so hard amid so much ignorance of her true merit at the beginning of her career to achieve the exalted position the place in her art that was rightfully hers.

The first period of her career must have cost her a lot of bitterness, especially as she realized that no one understood her merit.

When the Simionato "phenomenon" finally came to be recognized for what it was, these same audiences found themselves confronted by an artist they imagined had developed overnight. The hard work and suffering silences were obscured by resounding triumphs that must have been utterly beyond their comprehension.

This is not only a book about a singer, but a book about all great artists who are able to continually renew their art by renewing themselves. It is the eternal fable recited by an enchantress night after night reaching into our imagination and weaving together all our stray thoughts of the immortal. And for Giulietta Simionato, night after night, performance after performance, the fables to be sung were endless, running the gamut from classicism to *verismo*, from Carmen's subtle malice to Dalila's ardent sensuality to the classic nobility of Adalgisa — and let us not forget the performances of Mozart along the way.

This book, then, is not only the story of a great artist, but it is a fable. The fable of a magical moment that will never happen again.

–Voicing Our Hopes–

by Marcel Landowski

GREAT HUMAN VOICES and their mystery are one of the most admirable paths upon which the music of the spheres can choose to travel. This is a thought that composers and great interpreters should never neglect.

For nothing is ever certain, nothing is ever new: whether we like it or not we come from somewhere and we are going towards an end, and our reason for being is to sing our experience, and the eternity of our human condition: love and death.

These two themes, indissoluble, with all the possible variables, mark our basic need to overcome our ego, complete and mortal, to direct ourselves toward something transcendent which is higher than ourselves.

Homage should be paid to Giulietta Simionato, who knew how to lead us on such a lustrous, sublime path.

1

–A Star Is Born–

Giulia (or Giulietta, as she was nicknamed practically at birth) was born in Forlì on May 12th, 1910, the third daughter of Felice Simionato and Giovanna Maria Truddaiu Barroccu. Her father originally came from Mirano in Venetia and her mother from Bortigiadas in the province of Sassari, Sardinia. The couple already had two children, both of whom were born in Tempo Pausania: Regina (on May 15th, 1901) and Carlo (August 10th, 1903).

Giovanna Maria was already expecting Giulia when Felice Simionato, a civil servant, was transferred from Sardinia to Forlì in the Emilia-Romagna region of the mainland. Everyone, including her doctors, believed Giovanna's fatigue and chronic ailments were due to her pregnancy instead of a severe form of migraine, which was never diagnosed. After Giulietta's birth her father, believing that the climate of her native region would be beneficial to his wife's health, requested a transfer back to Sardinia; his request was granted and Giovanna and her three children went ahead of him, making the trip only forty days after Giulietta's birth.

Giovanna Maria does not seem to have been very extroverted and was excessively strict with her children. To this day Giulietta does not recall ever having been kissed or embraced by her mother. Instead she remembers growing up, along with her siblings, in an atmosphere of almost military discipline, which influenced her children in ways that were both positive and negative. To punish her children's mischief the mother did not hesitate to ply the rod — in this case a sort of cat-o'-nine-tails made especially by her for the purpose, with lots of fine cords, that she applied liberally to the legs of her small children. To avoid these corrective measures as much as they could, Regina and Carlo talked Giulietta into throwing the dreaded whip into a well. They knew full well that she would be spared the inevitable punishment because of her tender age. Giulietta went along with the children's plan and then when their mother, after looking about in vain, asked what had happened to the thing, Giulietta opened her eyes wide and kept mum. Without batting an eye, Giovanna Maria made another whip right away and resumed punishing the little culprits. The harshness of the children's treatment was such that, at one point, Regina, a sensitive and intelligent child, was driven to go to the local town hall on the pretext of asking them to issue a document, but in reality to find out if Giovanna might have been her stepmother and not the woman who bore her. Regina was a feisty, energetic young girl, who suffered markedly from her mother's severity and repeatedly tried to stand up to it, but without much success.

Felice Simionato was exactly the opposite. His sweet nature was almost incompatible with his profession, and may even have incited his wife's intransigence. He was the youngest of *twenty-four* children and, almost from the time of his birth, his parents had decided he would become a priest. At the appropriate age he was sent to a seminary in Venice, but at the moment he was to pronounce his vows, he escaped from the college and took refuge in Sardinia, where he did all sorts of jobs, including that of prison guard. However, he continued to study, at the cost of great personal sacrifice, and managed to obtain a law degree. Then, winning a competitive examination, he was named director of the same prison where he had been working as a simple guard, where the meekness of soul he had demonstrated had been proverbial. In prison riots he was the one responsible for restoring order, because he alone knew how to placate the most hardened prisoners.

However, Felice's good nature was not an indication of weakness. Sustained by great tenacity it had been his sole support throughout his youth and by itself had kept him at his studies. His strong will, moreover, was a gift from his family, because Giulietta demonstrated that she had it in abundance throughout the course of her life.

She who would later become a great singer passed her childhood in Sardinia. In her free time, together with her maternal grandfather, she visited the estates of the Truddaiu in Limbara or in Caraddu. There she amused herself by tormenting — or feeding — voracious leeches, and by riding Pariggeddu, the pony that her grandfather had bought for his young relations; she climbed trees to pick fruit or made long swims together with the farm workers' children. Then, as a consequence of the rash comportment of some of her contemporaries she decided to give up swimming, just as she did, later, the high jump and long jump, which she enjoyed as much (skiing, which she tried in 1932-33, was another experience of short duration).

From the time she was a baby Giulietta loved to play and was happy only when she was out of the house. When she came home to her own four walls she gave the impression of being in a cage. There her favorite pastime was to repeat the little songs her sister Regina would sing, eliciting her protests, however, since she considered Giulietta's voice too strident. But Giulietta never gave up, shutting herself up in some room, closing doors and windows, continuing fearlessly to issue her own version of the singer's art.

In 1918 Felice Simionato was transferred to Rovigo near Venice on the Italian mainland, and took his family with him, hoping that his wife's health would not be affected by the Venetian climate as it had been earlier in Forlì. In Rovigo Giulietta attended the Silvestri Institute, a boarding school run by the Sisters of the Infant Maria, where she completed her first studies, receiving lessons in embroidery, art, cooking and piano from outside teachers whose job it was to round out her basic instruction. Her teachers immediately recognized the young girl's vocal and artistic gifts and taught her to recite poetry and learn dramatic monologues.

Whenever her kindergarten teacher, Sister Giulia, was called away, "Little Giulia" was made class monitor. Following her mistresses' example the new substitute would instruct the class in the correct recitation of simple poems. At boarding school Giulietta also received her first voice lessons. The good sisters taught her how to open her mouth correctly, and since she had become used to singing with clenched teeth, in the manner of Sardinian grape-pickers, they obliged her to hold a cork between her back teeth, which made her jaw ache for a time.

The lay teachers of the Institute also arranged concerts to benefit the school and through them Giulietta came to the attention of one Maestro Cremesini, director of the local music school, the Francesco Venezze Liceo. The maestro was sure that this robust voice was well suited to the choir that he was forming for a performance in the church. Admitted to the second soprano section, the little girl distinguished herself by producing a perfect high G, which none of her fellow choir members was able to achieve. At rehearsal when Giulietta realized she was the only one who could hit the high note and hold it as required by the music, she became alarmed and stopped singing. She refused to sing it again, in spite of the maestro's thoughtful urging, as if she might have been embarrassed.

Cremesini, a first-rate chorusmaster, recognized the child's gift and urged Giovanna Maria to start singing lessons for her daughter. Her crisp response admitted of no reply: "I would kill my daughter with my own hands rather than see her become a singer." Singing was never spoken of again while Giovanna Maria was alive.

In 1924 Giovanna Maria became seriously ill with bronchitis. She kept to her bed strictly for over a year and a half, refusing medication or treatment of any kind, and finally died on May 31st, 1925.

After her death Maestro Cremesini, who had never relented in his determination to have Giulietta trained in the art of bel canto, repeated his request to Felice, who refused out of respect for his wife's wishes, whose body was scarcely cold in the ground.

In early 1927 the Workmen's Club of Rovigo organized a small musical season. The two works programmed were *Nina, no far la stupida* by Arturo Rossato and *Ostrega, che sbrego* by Arnaldo Fraccaroli. The producers could find no voice of sufficient quality to take the leading roles and once again Felice Simionato was asked to allow his daughter to participate. Since his acceptance could not be seen as sanctioning his daughter's pursuit of a singing career, but rather giving her the chance to participate in two productions that alternated spoken recitation and real singing, he relented. His only condition was that he be allowed to accompany his daughter and be present at the rehearsals, which were held at the Teatro Sociale in Rovigo. It was during one of these rehearsals that the baritone Albanese, who had been engaged as Rigoletto at the opera during this period, heard Giulietta and predicted: "With proper training this is a voice that will bring down all the houses with applause. You'd best keep her in mind!"

Giulietta's first important public debut took place at Rovigo's Teatro Sociale on May 14th, 1927, when she was seventeen, in the title role of Nina in *Nina, no far la stupida.* Also participating were the founder of the "Friends of the Drama" of Rovigo, Giuseppe Padoan, a lawyer, his wife Carla, and the tenor Duilio Mazzetto in the role of Lelio, Nina's lover. A few days before the performance the drama society of Rovigo in its entirety went to Padua to see a performance of *Nina* being given by Gianfranco Giachetti's touring theatrical company in the city of Santo. The purpose of the Rovigo company's trip was twofold: to improve the cast's familiarity with the work, but more importantly, to borrow a score and have it copied.

The premiere of *Nina, no far la stupida* in Rovigo was sold out and the warmest and most sustained applause was for young Giulietta, who enjoyed her first triumph.[1] In reviewing the opening night performance the critic Eugenio Ferdinando Palmieri, journalist, critic, as well as a playwright and sometime actor, wrote that the production of *Nina* had proceeded "in an admirable way... not a misstep or a slip of the tongue. Everybody agile, quick, secure."[2] Passing the performers in review he said of Giulietta "La Simionato has a beautifully flexible voice, a quick intelligence. She was a delicious Nina."

The second performance, which took place on May 20th, was a huge success and, because of the acclaim in the press,[3] resulted in a tour by the company of the entire province of Padua that took them to Montagnana, Piove di Sacco and Monselice (all in the province of Padua). On October 22nd there was a repeat performance of *Nina* which featured Ferdinando Palmieri in the role of "Peocina, Malcontenta's barber" and a review termed the evening a success and Giulietta as a "most charming Nina."[4] On October 5, 1927, the comedy *Ostrega, che sbrego!* was mounted, again in the Teatro Sociale. Simionato and Palmieri both figured in the cast and the review by Gida in the *Voce del Mattino*[5] praised the company as a whole for giving a "superb performance" and singled out as "skillful and sympathetic in their interpretations" both Duilio Mazzetto as Fiorello and "la Signorina G. Simionato in the part of Amalasunta... and as a female tenor!"

What had happened? In *Ostrega, che sbrego!* Giulietta played the sister of a tenor who has suddenly lost his voice. To save the performance an actor has to mime the brother's part, while an offstage singer — Simionato, in this case — sings an aria. Thus Simionato made her debut as a tenor singing "*Ecco, ridente in cielo.*"

After her successes with the Rovigo amateur company, first Cremesini and later Maestro Lucatello (director of the local band, as well as a teacher of singing and various instruments, whom Simionato to this day considers a genius) insisted that Felice allow his daughter to study singing. Felice finally relented and entrusted her to Lucatello, who proceeded to train her in the placement of her voice without altering its characteristics. Once he said to her: "Don't be fooled. Someday someone will tell you you are a soprano but, even though your voice has a wide range, you are not a soprano. You are a mezzo." Giulietta was always grateful for this advice. Unfortunately, Lucatello also counseled her to stop studying piano and solfeggio because, according to him, she learned so quickly by ear that she had no need of other help. Today Giulietta thinks she made a grave mistake in following Lucatello's advice in this matter.

In the meantime Lucatello was getting her singing engagements in the environs of Rovigo, as she needed to gain confidence before an audience. When he was appointed to a new post in Crespano del Grappa he left her in the care of Guido Palumbo, a voice teacher and chorusmaster in Padua. Twice a week for a year and a half Giulietta went from Rovigo to Padua for voice lessons, and afterward studied alone for a short time. While with Palumbo in 1932 she appeared in the role of Maddalena in *Rigoletto* at the Montagnana Theater (both Pertile and Martinelli were natives of Montagnana) and as Lola in *Cavalleria* alongside Rosina Sasso as Santuzza. Finally she went to Venice where she read through certain scores under the guidance of Signorina Tandura.

In 1933 Giulietta read in a newspaper that Florence's Teatro Comunale would sponsor a vocal competition, which was scheduled for June, at the closing of the first Maggio Musicale Fiorentino.[6] She discussed entering the competition with Palumbo and wrote to Lucatello as well. Palumbo advised her not to enter, while Lucatello eagerly urged her to, convinced that she would win. Encouraged, she entered as one of three hundred and eighty-five entrants, eighteen of whom were mezzos. She successfully passed through the first two rounds but, during rehearsals for the third, came down with a sore throat. Remembering that castor oil was favored as a remedy by another Palumbo pupil, the tenor Malipiero, she swallowed a considerable amount of the odious liquid. The following day her voice sounded clear as a bell but Giulietta was never again tempted by such a cure.

The competition finals consisted of three concerts in which eleven singers performed two arias apiece. Three mezzos were left to compete, one in each concert. Giulietta sang an aria from *Mignon* and one from *La favorita*. The president of the illustrious jury was Giordano; panelists included Salomea Krusceniski, Rosina Storchio, Alessandro Bonci, Tullio Serafin, Riccardo Stracciari, and Amedeo Bassi, all luminaries of the lyric stage, past and present.

Bassi, upon hearing the young Simionato, could not restrain his excitement and applauded loudly. This provoked a response from Serafin reprimanding Bassi for "playing favorites." (The critic Ugo Ojetti, was covering the event for the magazine *Cose Viste*, wrote of Giulietta's appearance: "...la Simionato from Mestre..." sic! "...tiny under her bushy black hair..."[7])

Storchio too was lavish with her praise. Giulietta had scarcely finished Mignon's aria when the great diva sprang to her feet, causing the bouquet in her lap to fall to the floor. After retrieving it she presented the flowers to the young girl (she was 23), telling her in a sweet voice that Giulietta remembers to this day: "Always sing like this, dear one."

As a competition winner Giulietta received a certificate and a check for 5,000 lire. She sent her sister a brief message: "I've won! I'm on top of the world!" Other winners included the tenor Aldo Sinnone, the baritone Pietro Sopransi, the bass Giulio Neri and the sopranos Marisa Merlo (who would use the stage name Marisa Morel), Olimpia Quarantacinque (known later as Di Ruggeri) and Gianna Catania.

The foundations of a great career had been laid. However, it would take two years before the young singer would appear on the Comunale's stage as the young mother Cate in Pizzetti's *Orseolo* on May 4th, 1935.

In fact, immediately after the competition victory Tullio Serafin, through the artistic director of La Scala, Piero Fabbroni, invited her to La Scala for an audition. They judged her voice immature and undeveloped and advised her to study more and come back in two years.

In the meantime, the management of Mestre's Toniolo Theater signed her, as a competition winner, to give two performances of *La favorita* on the 17th and 18th of October with the tenor Malipiero. Unfortunately a throat infection prevented her from singing and the performances had to be canceled.

Still in Florence Giulietta took the part of Maddalena in *Rigoletto* at the Pergola Theater on January 5th, 1934 and Lola in a *Cavalleria* which featured Sara Scuderi at the Comunale in Treviso (May 19, 1934). Then the bass Dante Sciacqui convinced her to settle in Milan where she would have better chances of making a career.

With this goal in mind, in 1934 Sciacqui arranged for Giulietta to meet the Faruggia family, owners of a large brewery in Malta. The Faruggias planned to organize an opera company that would tour Malta, Libya and Tunisia and had come to Italy to engage young singers. So it was that on the occasion of a matinee organized for the centennial of Bellini's death, January 13, 1935, Giulietta interpreted Adalgisa in *Norma*—without benefit of a rehearsal, since she was only covering for an indisposed singer. Conscious of the role's demands, and of her responsibility, she wasn't able to sleep a wink on the eve of the performance.

As if her anxiety over Adalgisa were not enough, when La Pollini, another colleague, fell ill she was also called upon to sing the roles of Teodoro, Marina and the hostess in *Boris Godunov*, with the bass Cirino.

The tour lasted from November 1934 to March 1935. During this four-month period the young mezzo appeared in *Ballo in maschera*, *L'amico Fritz*, *Madama Butterfly*, *Andrea Chénier*, *Adriana Lecouvreur*, and *Mignon*, among others. At the end of March the company sailed to Tunis. During the voyage Giulietta fell ill (it was at this time that she began to suffer serious attacks of migraine). Her illness notwithstanding, she was a success as the Princess of Bouillon in a performance of *Adriana Lecouvreur* on March 3rd, 1935. The critic of *L'Unione* wrote: "We found that the Principessa di Bouillon possessed a formidable elegance in the way she looked and sang. She was played by Giulietta Simionato, of whom it easy to predict a bright future, because she has a voice that is far from ordinary."[8]

The same critic, reviewing *Cavalleria rusticana* days later, singled out Simionato's work: "The excellent Lola was Signorina Giulietta Simionato, who sang with lively coquettishness and a beautiful soft voice." These were the words used by the critic in *L'Unione* in his review of her performance, which gave rise to "real explosions of enthusiasm."[9]

While still in Tunisia Giulietta heard of Tatiana Menotti for the first time. Menotti was touring with the Schwarz Company in operettas like *Il cavallino bianco*. A few years later the two singers would become colleagues and dear friends.

The company's next stop was Tripoli, a trip by Pullman car across the desert. Licia Albanese, wrapped in a large scarf that made her look like an Arab, was also a passenger, as were Bruna Castagna's sister, the mezzo Marù Falliani and the great baritone Afro Poli. Maestro Cordone and Maestro Santarelli alternated as conductors. This tour provided Simionato her first earnings as a singer.

Before she left Italy, through the bass Sciacqui she had been given the part of Azucena at the Politeama Rossetti Theater in Trieste. Simionato considered herself too young and her voice too immature for this demanding role, but sang it anyway on October 17th, 1934. A year later (October 16th, 1935) she would sing it again in Turin at the Vittorio Emanuele Theater.

It was a daunting task. Rehearsals were on Friday, the first performance Saturday and matinee and evening performance on Sunday. Manrico (the tenor Lois) was in the habit of giving three encores of *Di quella pira*; a young American soprano, Della Benni (née Bening) was making her debut as Leonora, a rather exotic occurrence at the time. During this performance she met the Emilian baritone Giuseppe Monachini who would later become her husband.

Less than a month before, on the occasion of the opening of the Teatro Comunale in Adria, Simionato had been called upon to perform the roles of Marta and Pantalis in *Mefistofele* under Serafin. Her costars were Pampanini, Scuderi, Pasero and Malipiero. The weekly *Polesine Fascista*, speaking of the artists involved before the performance had actually transpired, praised Simionato, who "in such a short time has established herself as a lyric mezzo of the first rank," whose Marta and Panalis "would be played with real art and bravura."[10] Giuseppe Cordella, reviewing the performance, says pointedly: "Giulietta Simionato was truly the devil's mistress to come by a role that suits her as well as this. As Pantalis she framed Elena's noble aria in a perfect way."[11] The same newspaper carried a review of the second night performance on September 26, singling out *Marta*'s and *Mefistofele*'s second act duets as receiving "the most heart-felt ovations."[12]

At the end of 1935, finally, Simionato went back to audition at La Scala. She was hired and required to sign a contract for the 1935-36 season which she thinks of today as more of a harness than a contract. She was obliged to learn any role that might be assigned her without right of refusal, and had to be prepared to replace any singer, without complaining, at a moment's notice.

Advertised at the time, besides a *Suor Angelica*, was a *Parsifal*, with Maestro Gino Marinuzzi conducting. "According to that contract," Simionato says today, "I had to be ready as an understudy for any comprimario part without the right to protest. I had to be at all the piano rehearsals, and all the calls for the rehearsal hall, as well as stage, orchestra and full dress rehearsals."

Her first appearance at La Scala was as the Mistress of Novitiates in *Suor Angelica* on January 29th, 1936, and then as Giovanna in *Rigoletto* (February 22nd) alongside the tenor Sinnone (who had also been a winner of the prize competition in Florence). Then came the *Parsifal* (March 25th) mentioned above. The La Scala contract provided for three month's employment during the first season and six months for the second; the salary was 2,400 lire a month — enough to live on, provided you saved your money during the winter — in order to have enough money to get through the summer when the theater was closed.

As Simionato recalls: "I could have asked for advances on my fortnightly pay but I was too proud. Thus I received deferred earnings when I was paid, but to do so I sometimes had to skip meals on the twelfth or thirteenth of the month.

"When payday finally did roll around it was time to celebrate. Serene and cheerful, I would go and collect my pay. As soon as I had the money I would rush downstairs to the nearest coffee shop and wolf down a cappuccino and a brioche before I literally fainted from hunger."[13]

At that time Giulietta was self-conscious about being short and thin. She took insulin injections and ate bananas to put on weight, and she wore very high heels to add inches to her diminutive frame.

During the rehearsals of *Parsifal* Maestro Fornarini, substituting for Marinuzzi, though he didn't care much for Simionato, took note, nevertheless, of the ease with which she produced her top notes.

When the summer months arrived and La Scala was dark she went back to Crespano del Grappa to resume studies with her old coach, Lucatello. She lived in his house and payed him a token rent, passing happy hours with the Maestro's youngest daughter.

In January, 1937, she returned to La Scala where a long list of secondary roles was waiting, some of which were not very gratifying [the reader will find them in the Chronology and list of roles in the back of this book]. The next season saw no change. She was the slave in *Francesca da Rimini* in Merano, September 1938; the Tsarevitch in *Boris* (Teatro Donizetti, Bergamo, October 8th) with Tancredi Pasero, for whom she had the very highest regard. In Bergamo she met Giuseppe Valdengo who was also at the beginning of his career. In November she was Maddalena in *Rigoletto*, then for the first time Preziosilla (with the bass Sciacqui), and again, Lola, at the Politeama Theater in Palermo. Reviewing her performance as Preziosilla the critic for the newspaper *L'Ora* wrote that "in this part Simionato had the opportunity to display her vocal agility and her musical and interpretive intelligence."[14]

In November 1938 the singer received a letter from Tullio Serafin, whom she had not seen for some time. He invited her to meet him in Montecatini where he was enjoying a rest cure at the Hotel Pace. The moment he saw her he asked her to take off her shoes. In fact he wanted to give her the part of Puck in *Oberon* and needed to reassure himself about her stature. Giulietta was surprised and a little humiliated that she hadn't been asked to sing; but Serafin told her he didn't think it necessary. Shortly afterward Simionato received a contract to perform Puck (March 26th, 1940).

In the meantime she was too busy to stop for breath. In December 1938 at Bologna's Teatro Comunale Simionato sang Siebel in *Faust* and Beppe in *L'amico Fritz*, a role that she reprised in Fiuggi under the baton of the composer himself. Of this last performance Simionato remembers the maestro, already aged and exhausted at the time, imposing "exasperatingly slow tempos."[15]

That same year she sang a *Rigoletto* in Fiume, where the Gilda was Tatiana Menotti, whom she had met in 1934 and with whom she had since become good friends (as mentioned previously). Rigoletto was portrayed by the baritone Enrico De Franceschi, the son-in-law of Giulietta's old teacher Palumbo. Giulietta received eighty lire for each performance.

In 1938 a defining event occurred in her life that she remembers all too well today.[16] At a performance of *Mignon* at La Scala, Simionato was cast as Federico, an important role for someone still at such an early stage of her career.

Giulietta remembers: "The second act was especially important. I sang my aria and felt enormously relieved. I went back to my dressing room and made a big mistake! Instead of putting on my costume for Act Three, I put on my street clothes and went home. At home, as I started taking off my makeup, I turned on the radio to hear the broadcast of the third act from the theater. I was horrified to realize that my part was missing. I literally thought I was dying; all the fear even gave me a fever. In the third act I had to sing two or three phrases alone.

"The next day I was ashamed to go to work. I was reproached by everyone, even the doorman. Then I remembered something that had happened when I was a child. The nuns at my school in Rovigo, having decided that I had vocal and artistic talent, had arranged for me to sing a little song at a festival. It was to be my 'debut!' I had to wait backstage a long time to go on and, being eight years old, got bored with the wait. Then the caretaker of the school came up to me and said that my parents had come to pick me up. You see, I hadn't told them that I was going to sing in a theater because my mother did not approve of me performing in public. So I went for a walk with my parents, never thinking the good sisters would be alarmed to discover that their leading player had disappeared. A week later at a repeat performance, with all the other boarders' parents present, not to mention the local authorities, I was locked in a room so I couldn't run away. The night after my 'involuntary' absence from La Scala I remembered that strange episode from my childhood. It never occurred to me that, nine years later, in 1947, I would sing the leading role in the same opera, *Mignon*."

In the course of the following years Simionato kept performing without respite. Flora in *La traviata* in Turin (June 1939), Dimitri and The Little Shepherd in *Fedora*; Maddalena in *Rigoletto* and Beppe in *L'amico Fritz*, both at the Comunale in Florence (October 1939). Simionato's appearance in this last role two months later at La Scala is the stuff of legend. The singer who had been entrusted with the role of Beppe, a recitalist, renounced the role because she believed herself incapable of bringing it off. The part was then offered to five mezzo-sopranos and the conductor Antonio Guarnieri chose Giulietta, who was a success.

Also in 1939 Simionato was asked to stand in for Cloe Elmo for a Saturday matinee performance of *Hänsel und Gretel* (the matinees were especially for recreational clubs). Management was worried that Elmo couldn't hold up after the matinee to perform an evening performance of *Adriana* on the same day and asked Simionato to study the part of Hänsel. She met the challenge by learning the part in a week, but nothing came of it: Elmo decided to fulfill her obligations and sing both roles.

Early in 1940 Mariano Stabile had occasion to hear Simionato's singing and was deeply impressed. He exerted himself to persuade the management of the theater in Trieste to cast her as Cherubino in *The Marriage of Figaro*, a role Simionato had been regularly contracted to sing that year at the Teatro Comunale in Bologna. But once again, the performance in Bologna hadn't come off. Another mezzo, quite celebrated for her Cherubino, had not been engaged because of a commitment with the Rome Radio in the leading role of Zandonai's *Conchita*. This mezzo managed to get the Rome performance postponed so that she could sing at the Comunale. This time around Giulietta had been paid, according to her contract, but hadn't sung a note.

She had to wait until January 16th, 1940, for her first performance of Cherubino. She sang it under the baton of Vittorio Gui with Stabile as Figaro and Pierisa Giri as Susanna. The critic of *Il Popolo* was enthusiastic about the performance: "Giulietta Simionato, who sang Cherubino for the first time with the very best vocal resources, is certainly on the road to perfection. Her interpretation of the character seems to be just what it should be, based on vocal and dramatic study that has unearthed his essential traits of character: a young man in love who, though frightened and troubled, is charming and likable."[17]

This exhilarating Cherubino was the first of a long series.

Also in 1940 La Simionato took part in a *Suor Angelica* with Magda Olivero in the title role at the Donizetti Theater in Bergamo. In November there was an *Otello* at Bologna. Then in 1941, more small parts.

However, during the summer the press had special praise for her appearance at Bologna's Third of July Music Festival. In a review of the opening night of *L'amico Fritz* in *Il Resto del*

Carlino[18] this premonitory judgment appeared: "La Simionato not only has a beautiful voice, but the vast resources as a singer and interpreter that will enable her to take on more important roles." In fact, this production of *L'amico Fritz* was a glittering success: at the premiere there were 35 curtain calls!

A few days later, seeing Simionato clad in Suzuki's kimono alongside the Sharpless of Tito Gobbi, the same critic extolled her voice as "excellent in every respect."[19] In the next performance of the Puccini opera Giulietta earned the highest laudatory judgment in one word ("*benissimo!*") and in the part of Maddalena in *Rigoletto*, she was called "a valuable singer, with an expansive style and a rare sense of proportion."[20]

Giulietta then traveled to Pesaro where in August 1941 she appeared twice in *Hansel and Gretel* and, in September to the Teatro Metastasio di Prato, where she was Suzuki again. The local newspaper expressed the following opinion: "What to say of Giulietta Simionato? Prato audiences know her quite well by now, and find her closer to perfection this time. A studious artist, secure in her voice and her interpretation, last night she made Suzuki into a character of the highest order. A Suzuki for La Scala..."[21]

For Simionato the last part of 1941 was most eventful. *Villon* at the Teatro Donizetti in Bergamo (September the 24th), *Maria d'Alessandria* by Ghedini on Turin Radio (September 30th), *La forza del destino* at the Teatro Verdi in Ferrara (October the 2d), *Andrea Chénier* again in Ferrara (October 11th), *Madama Butterfly* at the Municipale of Reggio Emilia (October 25th), *La morte di Frine* at the same theater (November 1st), *Butterfly* again in Ferrara (November 4th) — before taking the road back to La Scala. Of course these performances gave Simionato much satisfaction, particularly the *Forza* she sang in Ferrara on October 2 and 5, 1941, and about which *Il Corriere Padano* wrote: "Public interest is very intense regarding the last performance of *La forza del destino*, which is being given in the most highly decorated style. Castellani, Momo, Tagliabue, Nerone, Ghirardini and Simionato are a great opera cast."[22]

At La Scala in February 1942 Simionato took the modest role of Emilia in an *Otello* which starred Maria Caniglia and

Giacomo Lauri-Volpi. Twenty-seven years later the great tenor recalled Giulietta's debut: "These first appearances demonstrated her innate musicality, the flexibility of her voice and her artistry. She was also clearly aware of the true value of her gift and of the destiny that had assigned it to her. In a concert she gave at the home of Dr. Sigurtà, a Milanese businessman, she demonstrated the extent of her promise, and showed her determination to achieve the place in her profession that corresponds to it."[23]

Reviewers were speaking enthusiastically[24] about the loan of Simionato for Lola in *Cavalleria* in Forlì (May 7th, 1942) in which Lina Bruna Rasa, the greatest Santuzza of the day, appeared opposite a young tenor making his debut as Turiddu in the first performance — Mario Del Monaco, who was badly received. "Simionato's recitative, on the other hand, was greeted with great outbursts of applause *a scena aperta* [in the middle of the scene]. Her vocalism was intensely expressive and luminous throughout her range, dominating the score; the quick thrust and incisiveness of her phrasing gushed out fulsomely, shining with a brilliant light through the entire course of the opera."[25]

L'amico Fritz was staged for the first time in Rovigo on May 21st. The performance, under Giuseppe Podestà, starred Simionato, Pia Tassinari, Ferruccio Tagliavini and Afro Poli, and was a huge success. The reviewer for the local *Gazzettino* had this to say of Giulietta:[26] "The audience welcomed our brilliant local prodigy with great affection. In Beppe's aria our fellow citizen revealed herself to be a first-rate artist in every sense of the word. Hers is a powerful and harmonious voice, and her vocal gifts complement a rare sensibility that enables her to produce a more than intelligent portrayal of her character."[27]

The next performance took place on May 23rd. Reactions in the press were again highly favorable: "...a singer of undisputed value... warmly welcomed by the hometown crowd, she gave another brilliant account of herself even though the part confided to her was rather small. Audiences in Rovigo want her to come back soon so they can again admire her interpretations."[28] Giulietta was not to return to the Teatro Sociale for thirteen years.

She did return to Rovigo, however, on May 7th, 1943, to perform at the Francesco Venezze Liceo in a concert that was to conclude the 21st musical season organized by the institute. (Simionato had sung at the institute once before, when it was directed by Maestro Cremesini, on February 9th, 1934, a few months after winning first prize in the Florence vocal competition.) The music critic of the *Gazzettino*, recalling Simionato's triumphal appearance in *L'amico Fritz* the previous year, wrote: "Giulietta Simionato, through careful study and strict discipline, has matched her natural gifts to the technical demands of the music. This plus the exquisite sensitivity of her style have placed her in the top rank of Italian bel canto singers. She possesses a warm and melodious mezzo-soprano voice, seamlessly equalized through the range, which makes her perfectly suited for both dramatic performance and more intimate chamber music."[29] Then a day later the same reviewer augmented his earlier praise: "Once again Madame Simionato has demonstrated her artistry and, with it, a maturity and experience that enable her to combine her rich vocal gifts and deft technique in portrayals of ever-increasing refinement."[30]

In February 1944 the La Scala company appeared at Bergamo's Donizetti Theater for a series of performances of *Falstaff* featuring Mariano Stabile in the title role. Giulietta in the minor role of the gossipy Meg was judged by the press to be "precious." Later, in June, Giulietta, along with Afro Poli and Angelo Mercuriali, took part in a concert of sixteenth-century music in Milan at the Teatro del Popolo. The first half of the program alternated "ancient" arias with excerpts from period ballets. After intermission the three artists presented Monteverdi's *Combattimento di Tancredi e Clorinda*. The critic of *Il Corriere della Sera* called the participants "skilled and confident" and ended his review speaking of an enjoyable success.[31]

Late in 1944, during the war, the Scala season was being given at the Teatro Lirico. The announced program included *Werther*, *Mignon*, and *The Marriage of Figaro*, which featured Simionato as Cherubino, a role she had been assigned at the urging of Stabile. During this cycle of performances she was asked to substitute for an ailing Gianna Pederzini, singing Charlotte in *Werther*. Believing she was not well enough prepared, Giulietta refused, showing some courage. Meanwhile Tancredi Pasero, who had once before unsuccessfully tried to have Simionato engaged as Siebel at Verona's Arena, advised her that Pederzini had been scheduled to sing only four of the five *Mignons*. Pasero strongly urged Giulietta to audition for the fifth, since he felt it was a role she was comfortable with and knew well. Giulietta agreed, but the outcome was not as might have been expected. The Lirico's management stated that the conductor Guarnieri was reluctant to cast a singer he didn't know very well, and that, furthermore, Madame Pederzini would have no objection if she were asked to appear in the fifth performance. So nothing came of it.

On May 23, 1945 Simionato went to Bellinzona for a music conference given by Maestro Carlo F. Semini, in which she took part by singing arias by Verdi, Gordigiani, Tosti, Martucci, Pizzetti, Respighi, Tocchi, Persico, Nussio and Maestro Semini himself (a rather wide-ranging program!). Maestro Semini accompanied her on the piano. The newspaper *Popolo e Libertà*[32] reported that "Signora Simionato has paid her dues in a superb manner and has received full favor from the audience, who applauded her very warmly. Her beautiful and soft voice, both full and strong, along with her confident and profound acting, bear witness to a mezzo who has been gifted with exceptional resources, and one who knew how to win her audience from the very first notes she sang."

After the Allied Army arrived in Venice in August 1945 an operatic season was organized jointly by the 56th London Regiment and the Delfa Organization, featuring the orchestra and chorus of La Scala under the direction of Maestro Alfredo Simonetto. The program in the "*Giornale Alleato*" called for performances of *Cavalleria rusticana* and *Rigoletto*, among others, to be presented in the small northern town of Gradisca d'Isonzo and Campo d'Isonzo. In the premiere of August 18th, Cloe Elmo, Mario Del Monaco and Giulietta Simionato (as Lola) sang *Cavalleria*. In the archival record of Gradisca (*Vicende storiche gradiscane*)[33] the performance is described as "a clamorous success... The beauty of the scenery and play of light was indescribable, so much so that it will remain forever in the minds of those lucky enough to be present." From the same source, a *Rigoletto* of three days earlier with Carlo Tagliabue as the main protagonist is described as "a success beyond all expectations..." Giulietta had her share of the applause for her performance as Maddalena.

The year 1945 proved to be a turning point in Simionato's career. Marisa Morel (an anagram of Merlo), one of the winners of the Florence competition, and someone Giulietta had not seen in the intervening eleven years, proposed that Giulietta leave La Scala and join the company that she had formed in Switzerland in 1941 and had directed since then: the Grand Théâtre de Genève (Geneva). She wanted Simionato for the role of Dorabella in *Così fan tutte* in October of the 1945 season.

Dorabella proved to be what might nowadays be called Simionato's first great success. Overwhelmed by the audience's response and afraid to step out of character she was hesitant to acknowledge the applause that erupted in the middle of a scene. Merlo, who was also singing, urged her take a bow, and thus the performance was briefly interrupted.

With Merlo's company from 1945 to 1947 we find the artist as Dorabella and also as Fidalma in Cimarosa's *Il matrimonio segreto*—almost always opposite the debutante Suzanne Danco and with the conductor Otto Ackermann— in Geneva, Turin, Lyon, Paris, Bologna and Barcelona. In the same years, in Geneva and in Paris, she was interpreting Mistress Quickly in *Falstaff* and Ulrica in *Ballo in maschera*, parts that she had refused at an earlier time because she wasn't sufficiently sure of her low register. (In Geneva in May, 1946, she sang Ulrica with Mario Del Monaco, who was just then embarking on an international career).

To convince Giulietta to sing Quickly and Ulrica, roles that were not in her repertory, Morel did all she could, and was lavish with advice: for example, to take a good long nap each afternoon before a performance, and to speak as little as possible.

Giulietta has remained grateful to this influential colleague, who gave her her first chance to sing major roles and helped her to have confidence in herself. Her last appearance with the Grand Théâtre de Genève was on November 8th, 1950, in *Il matrimonio segreto*, a performance conducted by Gianandrea Gavazzeni.

But let's go back to April of 1946 when, still with Morel,

Giulietta had debuted in Paris in the part of Dorabella. The elite of Paris were present at the Théâtre de la Gaîté Lyrique and her interpretation was a success. The composer Louis Beydts, a friend of Sacha Guitry, wrote in a signed review in the magazine *Opera*: "La Signora Simionato as Dorabella, along with an altogether praiseworthy cast, seems to be the best example of a style of singing entirely favorable to the voice's freedom to develop. Her ample mezzo-soprano voice, with dark highlights, isn't afraid of the high notes, while the middle is rich and the low voice is very attractive and very pure, though she has clearly not had the chance to consistently employ all of her opulent resources."[34]

The late Henri Sauguet, the esteemed composer who was a member of the Institut de France and president of the Académie des Beaux Arts, was also in the audience that night and was impressed by the singer's "wondrous voice and truly beautiful tone."[35]

In his review of the performance the musician Antoine Goléa spoke of the "particular coloration of the timbre in the low range as well as in the high F."[36]

In his *History of the Opera*, René Leibowitz describes the three Paris performances of *Così* as the most exciting in living memory. He goes on to express his disappointment that they were not as successful as they should have been (only the second was sold out!). It should be noted that, in 1946, Mozart's masterpiece had not been presented in the French capital for over thirty years. Leibowitz underlines this omission by stating that "performances of this caliber (are) seldom seen anymore in France, therefore no praise can be too high for these artists, heretofore unknown to the Parisian public, for the remarkable evening they have given us."[37]

During 1946 Simionato sang several concerts in the Ticino. *Il Corriere del Ticino,*[38] commenting on her May 21st concert in Lagan, noted that Simionato, who had offered a wide-ranging program, similar to that of her 1945 concert in Bellinzona, "had shown a voice in which pleasing musicality and ample volume were allied with uncommon flexibility, vigor and purity in the upper register." On September 10th the concert tour ended with a program given over the Swiss Italian Radio. *Illustrazione*

Ticinese related that Simionato "was maintaining Italian vocal tradition at a high level."[39]

Only thirteen months later Giulietta sang again before a Parisian audience, in the same theater, this time in *Falstaff*.

Naomi Takeya, in her biography of the singer, records an amusing incident related to this appearance. All over Europe at the time there were still reminders of the War. Young singers of many different nationalities made up the Merlo company — a Czech, a Rumanian and an Iranian, among others. But, as usual, customs officials, on the lookout for smugglers, were most likely to regard an Italian with the deepest suspicion. Giulietta, sporting a fashionable swept up *chignon* was commanded to take down her hair to prove that nothing valuable was hidden beneath. Traveling with the group was an unfortunate Italian bass who was ordered to take off his shoes. Both were suspected of smuggling jewels. Of course no contraband was discovered, but in the process the unfortunate bass lost the lifts that had been disguising his small stature.

In 1947 Simionato was engaged to appear as Mignon at the Grattacielo Theater in Genoa. Opening night was January 8th and the cast included, in addition to Simionato, four debut artists: the tenor Agostino Lazzari, the Neapolitan coloratura Fernanda Basile, the bass Giuseppe Modesti, as well as Gianandrea Gavazzeni as conductor. The opening night performance took place on January 8th and proved to be a stunning achievement for Giulietta. Of all the cast she alone, because of her long experience, needed no cues. She recalls today that she knew the part as if she had lived it herself in another life. The opera was adapted perfectly to her physical and vocal possibilities. Thus Simionato, always seeking a role in which all her vocal talent could be displayed, gave her all to Thomas's heroine. She would repeat her success a few months later at La Scala where Tullio Serafin had become artistic director.

During rehearsals of *Oberon* in 1940 Maestro Serafin had repeatedly advised her to learn *Cenerentola*. When Giulietta saw that *Hänsel und Gretel*, *Così fan tutte* and *Cenerentola* were being programmed at La Scala, she remembered the maestro's words of years past, and emboldened by her successes in Geneva, thought she would be entrusted with the interpretation of the first-named. Arriving at La Scala she was disappointed to discover that these roles, except for *Così*, had gone to Fedora Barbieri. So once again she had to be content with *Così fan tutte*, which she had already had the chance to sing in previous years at Geneva, under the baton of Maestro Franz von Hoesslin, and which she now sang at La Scala, in April of 1947, alongside Tatiana Menotti and Suzanne Danco.

The reviews of *Così* were highly favorable. "Giulietta Simionato, whom we used to strain to see in the last row is now in the front, which is where she belongs," the reviewer for the weekly *Candido* wrote. And in *Il Tempo*: "Of all the singers onstage, the best acting and the most beautiful voice belonged to Simionato. This is an artist who has been neglected for too long and consigned to secondary roles. She should now be given leading parts."[40]

After the first performance of Mozart's masterpiece, Serafin visited Simionato in her dressing room and declared that she had not only improved, but had taken "a giant step." "Listening to this Dorabella I hear a voice of enormous potential." He then offered Giulietta the role of Carmen, which she declined, since she didn't feel that she was ready for it. She was conscious that the notes in her low register didn't lie as comfortably for her as they should, and she needed a deeper technical understanding to be completely sure of them.

Instead, in May 1947, Giulietta was off to the King's Theater in Edinburgh, which was hosting the Glyndebourne Festival. There she appeared again with Tatiana Menotti, but also with Italo Tajo, John Brownlee and Eleanor Steber, among others, in nine performances.

Five weeks later she was back at La Scala where, finally, after having endured so much discouragement, she scored a resounding triumph in *Mignon*. It would be no exaggeration to say that her Mignon at La Scala on October 2, 1947, was "historic." Then on the 28th of October, again as Mignon, and again with Giuseppe Di Stefano, who had been in the cast of the Milanese production, she held audiences spellbound in Turin. Press accounts of the time report Giulietta as "achieving the most profound results with the utmost simplicity."

[1] Giulietta's first success is reported in the "Il Gazzettino" of July 7, 1975.
[2] "La Voce del Mattino," May 15, 1927.
[3] Ibid., May 21, 1927.
[4] Ibid., October 23, 1927.
[5] October 7, 1927.
[6] See Leonardo Pinzauti, *Storia del Maggio*, Libreria Musicale Italiana, Firenze, 1994, p. 23.
[7] Ugo Ojetti, *Cose viste*, 1921-1943, with a prose work of G. D'Annunzio, Florence, 1960, p.126.
[8] In: Naomi Takeya, *La strada di una primadonna: Una mela e due biscotti per Giulietta Simionato*, Tokyo, 1977 (with the kind permission of the author).
[9] March 7, 1935.
[10] September 24, 1935.
[11] September 25, 1935.
[12] Ibid., September 27, 1935.
[13] In: N. Takeya, op. cit.
[14] Ibid.
[15] In: "Rassegna musicale Curci," December, 1975.
[16] In: N. Takeya, op. cit.
[17] Ibid.
[18] July 31, 1941.
[19] August 8, 1941.
[20] "Il Resto del Carlino," August 5, 1941.
[21] In: N. Takeya, op. cit.
[22] October 4, 1941
[23] In: "Musica e dischi," April 1969.
[24] Michele Raffaelli, *Il teatro comunale di Forlì nella vita musicale italiana*, S. Sofia di Romagna, 1982, p. 298.
[25] Ibid., p. 300.
[26] May 22, 1942.
[27] Giulietta was considered a citizen of Rovigo by adoption.
[28] "Il Gazzettino," May 24, 1942.
[29] May 7, 1943.
[30] May 8, 1943.
[31] June 4, 1944.
[32] May 24, 1945
[33] Marino Di Bert, *Vicende storiche gradiscane*, Gradisca d'Isonzo, 1982, p. 389.
[34] April 24, 1946.
[35] "La Bataille," April 17, 1946.
[36] "France Théâtre," April 17, 1946.
[37] René Leibowitz, *Histoire de l'Opéra*, Paris, 2nd edition, 1987, p. 49.
[38] May 22, 1946.
[39] September 21, 1946
[40] In: N. Takeya, op. cit.

2

–Three Honeymoons–

While at La Scala in 1939 Giulietta met the violinist Renato Carenzio, who was to become her first husband. Carenzio had been a member of the well-known Poltronieri Quartet before he won a competition that resulted in a chair with the La Scala orchestra. Giulietta saw him at the theater every evening because as one of the understudies she was obliged to be present in the box provided them at all the run-throughs and rehearsals, orchestra rehearsals and stage rehearsals, as well as all the performances.

When Carenzio began to court her Giulietta was very wary and reserved in response, without realizing that her attitude made her all the more attractive to her admirer. Carenzio made her feel fear more than love, since in order to convince her of his passion he not only resorted to threats, but pointed a gun at her (nothing more than a toy pistol, she found out later).

Giulietta turned to Carenzio's brother for advice, who happened to be a lawyer. She learned that the family was opposed to the marriage because they considered Carenzio entirely too young and immature. Besides she learned that Carenzio had a "fragile nervous system" and was a compulsive gambler who rarely won at cards and, if that was not enough, a spendthrift. All of this frightened Giulietta, but she decided to take the attorney's advice and see if the relationship could survive a year. After the year Giulietta decided to marry him, mostly out of fear, even though he was an attractive man.

The marriage ceremony took place on May 3rd, 1940 and the bride cried throughout the ceremony. The couple found an apartment in Milan (11 via Desiderio da Settignano). Carenzio played with the orchestra, Simionato continued performing in secondary roles.

In October 1944 the first air raids on Milan began, and they so terrified Carenzio that he decided to join his family at their country home in Ortisei... Without Giulietta, who began commuting between Milan and Gorgonzola, where her sister and two children lived.

One day after the first air raid Giulietta went to the theater before the scheduled time for her rehearsal. While she was chatting with the doorman, Cibea, the Scala archivist Semprini, a member of the Fascist Secret Police, arrived dressed in his finest uniform. Unable to control herself Giulietta asked Semprini: "After what happened yesterday, do you really think you should be dressed for a celebration?" Semprini stared at her, said nothing and left. A short while later she was called to the porter's office. Two men were waiting for her. They whisked her to a house near via Vincenzo Monti. There four or five members of the secret police subjected her to an exhausting interrogation. Semprini had denounced Simionato as a "subversive." She was released late that night, and Semprini was shunned thereafter by the La Scala staff, who would spit on the floor whenever he walked by one of them in the theater.

One unlucky day a new bombardment destroyed Giulietta's apartment in Milan, and she had to commute daily between Gorgonzola and Milan until the end of the La Scala season. In the summer, free at last of her engagements, she rejoined her husband in Ortisei and returned to Milan with him that fall.

That same fall, however, to flee the Germans, Simionato and Carenzio decided to move to Como. They stopped along the way in Verona and Muronico and finally settled down in Carate Urio with Carenzio's mother. Carenzio found work in the Monte Ceneri Radio Orchestra in Switzerland and Giulietta was once again a commuter, this time back and forth between the lake and Milan.

By now the singer was conscious that she had, indeed, married the wrong man, who was still gambling and going into debt. Nevertheless, she remained with him for eleven years, and today she claims that she never betrayed him, even in her thoughts.

In 1949 Carenzio — who had given up the violin for the viola, the only open chair, in order to be taken by the Monte Ceneri Radio orchestra — decided to resign even so in order to become his wife's secretary. Giulietta was not without reservations about her husband's decision.

It was Carenzio, then, who introduced Giulietta to the bass Mario Petri, whom she was to meet again in 1949 in Catania, where they were both singing in *Mignon*.

Seeing him again she felt an emotional upheaval that was new to her. Petri, some twelve or thirteen years younger than she, had his charm. However, when they were making the return trip together and he asked her to stop with him in Rome, where he lived, La Simionato told him no quite plainly and continued on to Milan.

Giulietta saw Petri again, not long after—in February, 1950—in Turin, where both were singing in the Donizetti *Requiem*. Carenzio decided to join her, without telling her of his intention. He arrived in the evening and couldn't find his wife in her room, since she had left her room for Petri's, on the floor above, to borrow some newspapers. When she reentered her room she found her husband waiting.

The following day Giulietta made an extreme but necessary decision. With Petri's agreement, they would continue their friendship until such time as her husband, believing he had been betrayed, would accept an annulment of their marriage. This arrangement continued from 1950 to 1952. Carenzio returned to Lugano[1] and Giulietta finally felt free. When their separation finally became a *fait accompli* in 1954 she left the Roman apartment where she had lived until then with Petri's mother and brother.

Since childhood Giulietta had suffered from migraine, without knowing the precise nature of her illness. The ailment was diagnosed variously as cervical arthrosis or a form of rheumatism. In Catania in 1951, before singing *Sansone*, she suffered an attack more severe than usual. She attributed it to the fact that, following a suggestion made to her by the tenor Penno, she had eaten raw meat with one of her meals. When she donned her wig that evening in the theater she felt as if she were wearing a crown of thorns, and she went through the performance in a pitiable state.

Later she realized that every time she underwent a change of climate her condition was exacerbated. When she returned to Rome she consulted a number of doctors but none of their remedies gave her any help.

In that fall of 1953, while in San Francisco, where she was appearing under Serafin in *Boris*, *Barbiere di Siviglia*, and *Werther*, the attacks escalated in intensity. For this reason when she was back in Rome in 1954 she determined to get the opinions of two specialists, the endocrinologist Nicola Pende and the clinical physician Cesare Frugoni. She wrote their names on two pieces of paper and picked at random to decide who to see first. She drew Professor Frugoni, and was able to get an appointment for St. Stephen's day at 2:00 in the afternoon.

Cesare Frugoni was born in Brescia on May 4th, 1881 and moved to Venice before he was twenty-five, where he became a resident at the Santa Maria delle Grazie Hospital. When later he was appointed director of the Institute of Pathology at the University of Florence he had already been famous since 1911, when he identified the first case of an illness resulting from rodent bites. In 1926 he was invited to join the faculty of Clinical Medicine at Padua University, where he remained until 1931. His research in cures for bronchial asthma was considered definitive and had been widely published, as were his "clinical lectures," which had been collected in three volumes which appeared simultaneously. He left Padua for Rome, where he taught for twenty years, becoming Director of the Institute for Clinical Medicine, and he retired from the teacher's life at the end of the 1951 academic year. As a physician he enjoyed a great reputation, which impressed Giulietta.[2] From his student days, Frugoni had been a passionate opera fan who never missed a performance. He even knew some libretti by memory. Then his work had smothered his enthusiasm.

At their first meeting, which was going to be decisive in her life, Giulietta was excited at the thought of meeting this great man and showed up in an agitated state. But the professor seemed to radiate a gentle serenity that immediately put Giulietta at ease, so that she could respond sincerely to all of his questions. She admitted she was high-strung, and that when she was getting ready to sing, red blotches would sometimes come out on her chest. The visit, at the end of which the famous physician offered a detailed therapeutic regimen, lasted more than an hour. Before his patient left he told her: "You see, my dear, you're as fit as a fiddle, but you suffer from a migraine that you've inherited from your mother. Unfortunately, a migraine isn't a simple headache, as many people believe; on the contrary, it's a malady unto itself, and one of the most refractory. You're going to have to have a lot of patience to cure it." It was agreed that Giulietta would return soon for a checkup.

Frugoni was then seventy-three, though he looked no older than sixty, and spoke to her like a father; saying goodbye to her he made her the gift of an oval box inlaid with pearl and had promised to go hear her at the theater. He kept his word and went to hear her in *La forza del destino*. At the end of the performance Giulietta received a bouquet of one hundred roses with a note inscribed: "After seeing you jump like a cricket from one seat to another onstage, you certainly didn't look as exhausted as you say you always are!"

In 1956 Giulietta, performing in Brazil, was again stricken severely by migraine attacks. She sent a letter to Frugoni, who immediately telephoned, advising her what she should do for relief and whom to consult for medication. From Brazil Giulietta went to Bilbao, and from there, in August of 1957, got in touch with the professor once again, who convinced her to come to him as soon as she returned to Rome. This was exactly what Giulietta did.

The moment she found herself in front of the great doctor she threw herself in his arms, revealing an emotion which Frugoni quickly reciprocated. This was the spark that gave rise to feelings of love that would endure for years in spite Giulietta's scruples; she knew that he had been married for some thirty years, even though he was separated. His wife, a manic-depressive, lived as a recluse in her villa with two servants and wanted to see no one, not even her two children, who remained with their father.

On the 2nd of September Giulietta went to Florence to make a recording of *Il barbiere di Siviglia* and the professor joined her there. It was their second romantic encounter and both gave full expression to their newfound feelings. Then Simionato left for Japan. While she was there Frugoni wrote a passionate and sincere letter. He spoke of his character, of his relations with his wife, and he confessed that his heart was full of tender feelings for Giulietta, the only woman with whom he could imagine spending the rest of his days. Giulietta appreciated his sincerity and was happy when he was able to join her wherever her work took her: in Japan, Chicago, Paris, Vienna. Still, the fact that they were unable to marry made her suffer. On the other hand, the professor didn't dare ask for a divorce because of a sense of respect for his wife, by now incapable of exercising free will, and for his children. Simionato understood the reasons for his behavior, but it continued to cause her pain.

At the wedding of the daughter of one of Frugoni's colleagues (where Frugoni was best man) Giulietta happened to meet an attorney who had represented the groom, who had already fathered two children, in the annulment of his first marriage. [In Italy at the time annulments were not a simple matter, especially when children were involved. Ed.] This attorney was Gino Sotis, and Giulietta would turn to him later when she was preoccupied with her own annulment. Alas, nothing could be done on that occasion — in the meantime the attorney Sotis had died.

Giulietta consulted another attorney, one Angelo Angelini Rota, who finally succeeded in the undertaking, freeing her from the burden of a connection that had made her very unhappy. Giulietta was always grateful for his help and later described this attorney as an angel in name and in fact.

By now the professor, too, was free to tie the knot with a new wedding ceremony, for his wife had finally passed away. But with characteristic delicacy he wanted to wait for a year to pass before legitimizing his relationship with Giulietta.

The wedding finally took place in Rome on November 18th, 1965, in the church of Santa Maria della Pace (open only an hour each day for mass) with only the witnesses present: Professor Scimone and Count Vittorio Cini for the groom, the currency exchange agent Campos Venuti and the lawyer Angelini Rota for the bride. Against all those friends and relations who had argued against the step he was taking Frugoni had opposed his polite but iron determination to go ahead.

On the morning of the great day the professor went to the clinic the way he always did, then left shortly after on the pretext of going to a consultation. He went immediately to the church to wait for the arrival of his witnesses, who were coming by plane. Right after the ceremony the couple separated: Frugoni went back to work and Giulietta to La Scala. No one noticed a thing. The priest had assured them news of the wedding would not be posted in Campidoglio for two months, which reassured Giulietta, who had decided to put an end to her artistic activity during that time.

She sang Preziosilla in *Forza* without great enthusiasm or her usual vocal and psychological commitment. After the performance she was struck with the recollection that February 1st marked the thirtieth anniversary of her debut at La Scala. Reflecting on this history she confronted Luigi Oldani, the Theater Manager, and learned that all they had for her was the cameo role of Servilia in *La clemenza di Tito*.

Very demoralized Simionato remembered Marinuzzi's words of thirty years before: "You cannot reenter La Scala by the front door once you have entered by the back."

At her hotel, meanwhile, in secret, she began to prepare the wedding announcements which she intended to mail on the eve of the last performance of her career. But unexpectedly a bomb went off on the 25th of January: she learned from Signorina Castiglioni that on the next day an illustrated magazine would release the news about her marriage, naming the precise date. Alarmed by this news she arranged to expedite the mailing of the wedding announcements, to save what could be saved. And on the 1st of February, after having trod the boards for the last time, having interpreted her unimportant role in *La clemenza di Tito*, she said a definitive goodbye to the world of opera, joyfully and without regret or nostalgia, as they say today.

On February 2, to flee the journalists, she took a plane to

Rome early in the morning, where the news of her wedding had raised a chorus of protest from Frugoni's family, who had learned of it from the press. The professor's son and sister wrote him to say that they would never accept Giulietta in the role of his wife. He, on the other hand, appeared confident that when his family knew Giulietta better, they'd come to love her.

Mr. and Mrs. Frugoni embarked on a life of high style: numerous servants, princely gifts for their friends. To maintain this standard of living the professor, once he had given up his medical practice, had to sell the lands he owned in Montecatini and his apartment on via Bruxelles. But Giulietta was happy with him, and had everything she wanted. And the world of theater, from which she had won so much deserved acclaim, was now part of a past that no longer interested her.

Professor Frugoni died at 96 years of age in the Sanatrix Clinic in Rome, where he had been a patient for two months, on the 5th of January, 1978, attended by his wife. Frugoni's will stipulated that his death not be announced until his funeral, but the news of his passing was divulged sooner than he had hoped.[3] This death was an enormous shock for Giulietta, though it wasn't unforeseen. She strongly felt the effects of this loss, and was more deeply saddened by it than she had expected; so much suffering promised a tough time ahead.

She left her home in Rome (the heirs had come into possession of everything that was left), and took refuge with her nieces, living for two years "like a vegetable." Life had lost its meaning. She didn't want to see anyone and she didn't take care of her appearance. During this period Dr. Florio De Angeli was affectionately supportive; in 1973 he had lost his own spouse, Adriana, who for twenty years had been a very dear friend of Giulietta's.

Born on the 15th of January in 1905, and a graduate in chemistry and pharmacy, Doctor De Angeli came from an old, noble Italian family from the Val di Non, and his father had been a pharmacist in Milan. Along with his brother, a year younger and a graduate in industrial chemistry, Florio De Angeli had started a pharmaceutical company. During World War Two, and very rapidly thereafter, their firm had experienced notable growth. In 1931 he married Adriana Brunelli, by whom he had two children.

Adriana De Angeli was an impassioned lover of opera and had an unconditional admiration for Giulietta Simionato.

In 1951 the two brothers decided to separate their business interests to avoid possible dissension among their children, who would be taking over management of the firm. Florio De Angeli took over the Italfarmaco firm, while his brother Carlo stayed with the Istituto De Angeli.

In 1969 Adriana De Angeli passed away, struck down by a cerebral hemorrhage. The loss was terrible for the husband, who had been very much in love with her and held her to be the most extraordinary woman, with the very best character, lively and full of optimism.

After his wife's death De Angeli frequently telephoned Giulietta in search of a little comfort. After the death of Simionato's husband, De Angeli found opportunities to visit her at home, though her house had lost its power to console him, now that she in her turn was bereft. Then one day he suggested that they end their solitude with a relationship. La Simionato wavered, still too overcome by sadness. In the end, however, confronted with the insistence of this stimulating man, she relented, on condition that the marriage take place soon, before she might think better of it and go back on her decision.

The nieces took care of the documents. The couple's witnesses were Tatiana Menotti and Nini Castiglioni. The brief religious ceremony took place on the 9th of July, 1979, in the Via Monte Napoleone church in Milan. The groom wept throughout the ceremony while the bride remained impassive, distant.

When she found herself in the Milanese house on via Gesù, and the full significance of having a new husband came home to her, she understood that she had to react. She had lived for so many years close to a gentle man, understanding, delicate; now she was at the side of an industrialist who had become habituated to command, and wasn't inclined to indulge her. But he was also sensitive; if during the first years together there was some conflict, Giulietta recognizes today that her present husband is a person of the highest caliber, who helped her to love life again. "I was like a blind woman," she says now, "and he gave me back my sight."

He still remembers with vivid emotion the time when his feelings revealed themselves. The day of Adriana's funeral Giulietta came expressly to Rome and, embracing him, told him: "Try to be brave, the way she would have wanted." Then Florio De Angeli thought: "This is the only woman who could take the place of my Adriana." If today La Simionato feels fulfilled, and she says she does, she owes it to her husband.

For his part Florio appreciates his wife's loving nature, innate goodness and sensitivity, loves her very much, and hopes to be at her side for all the years of life that remain to him.[4]

[1] Professor Carenzio died on September 5th, 1988, in Lugano.

[2] Cesare Frugoni's career is remembered in *Il Resto del Carlino*, January 7th, 1978.

[3] In the *Paese Sera*, January 7, 1978.

[4] Florio De Angeli passed away in Milan on the 22d of September, 1996.

3

—Chronicle of a Success—

In the Spring of 1947 Giulietta sang the leading role in *Mignon* at Genoa's Grattacielo Theater. As a result of her success in Genoa she was offered the same role at La Scala with a promising new tenor named Giuseppe Di Stefano. Di Stefano had made his debut that season in *Manon* with the celebrated soprano Mafalda Favero. The audience that had come to hear Favero's legendary interpretation of Massenet's heroine was astounded at the discovery of a young tenor with a stupendous voice. A few months later the audience that returned to hear their new-found favorite discovered yet another star singing alongside him in *Mignon*. The first performance took place on the 2nd of October and was a resounding triumph for Simionato as well as Di Stefano.

In Naomi Takeya's 1976 biography Simionato confessed to the author that if she closed her eyes she could still hear the applause. "I went to my dressing room after the Act II Styrian aria and the faces of everyone around me were covered in tears: the dressmaker, stagehands, stage director, electricians, everyone, in tears! While I was changing my costume the audience was still applauding. The performance was interrupted... I don't know for how many minutes. At La Scala singers were forbidden to take bows at the end of each act. When the audience would not stop applauding at the end of the scene, the conductor Guarnieri came backstage while I was changing costumes to admonish me for not breaking the house rule on taking bows: "Can't you come out to thank the public? All this time I've been waiting for a chance to continue the performance and I'm going to freeze to death!"

Simionato went on to tell Naomi Takeya that after that night's performance she was too dazed to comprehend her success because she had sung as if in a trance the whole time.

"You know I was like a mistreated dog that shrinks away when a hand is extended to pet him. He is so used to being slapped that his instinct takes over to protect him. I was like that dog. I could not believe that my career would take such a turn. I was afraid. I kept telling myself: 'This can't continue; tomorrow will bring a setback.' It was a good thing that didn't happen."

The following day Eugenio Gara, writing under the pen name Bardolfo, published an article in the review *Candido* punningly titled "*Laurea a Giulietta.*" ["Giulietta gets her degree."] The renowned music critic wrote: "Did Giulietta Simionato graduate at La Scala last night? We are accustomed to her being a principal about as often as she is a stand-in. She did not have a title. Now the full grade has come, cum laude. And very deserved. Unlike the many primitive souls who wander through the world of opera as if it were a forest, Simionato is a shining example of highly evolved civilization. Everything she does is in the service of the music. The constant dominion of intelligence over the voice, the nobility of expression, the delineation of character without resort to stereotypes. True, nature has imposed some limitations on this singer, but her talent will enable her to escape them — more than once."

Fourteen years later, in an article in the April 1951 edition of *L'Europeo* Gara recalled that extraordinary evening, October 2nd, 1947 when "Giulietta graduated with highest honors."[1] The eminent critic confirmed his earlier evaluation in these words: "The tone color of unequaled purity and incisiveness, a flawless style and sophisticated musicality — all made a big impression that evening; but more important still was the dominion of intelligence over the voice, her delicate taste, the nobility of her phrasing, finally the interior resonance and disdain to trace expected stereotypes and reproduce the mannerisms that are so annoying in opera."

In *Il Corriere Lombardo* Vice wrote: "The principal reason for the opera's success is Giulietta Simonato, whose power of voice and interpretive intelligence recall its greatest interpreters, and even surpass some of them. The ovations that crowned the famous rondeau of the second act had an eloquent insistence that was quite extraordinary."[2]

The reporter for *L'Umanità* stated emphatically that since the beautiful "rehearsal" of *Così fan tutte* last spring, the singer "obtained an honest-to-God triumph last night, and it couldn't have been more well-deserved. Simionato works with a great and terribly acute musical intelligence, and constantly makes use of a civility, a sophistication in her singing that is all too rare these days. Is it clear to you, gentlemen of La Scala? La Simionato must never return to the secondary roles to which she has been relegated for much too long."[3]

In the newspaper *Buonsenso*[4] it could be read that Giulietta had "sung with a clear voice, soft and lustrous at the same time, which is hard to find in a Mignon. An interpretation not easy to conjure. Beautiful harmonious singing. In her acting she could have gone a little deeper into her character..."

The interpreter who, according to the *Italia*,[5] was "the absolute master of her vocal resources and always sang with grace and meaning," was judged "excellent," "truly praiseworthy" in the *Gazzetta dello Sport*."[6]

The reviewer for *L'Avanti*, Vice, judged Giulietta's "a composed and moving Mignon."[7]

The *Corriere della Sera* had this to say: "Giulietta Simionato had the evening's most important success as Mignon, and she deserved it by reason of the beauty of her high notes, dazzling but secure, and the perfection of her passage work, and above all by the intelligence of her acting."[8]

The review in *Il Mattino d'Italia* expressed an opinion quite similar to Eugenio Gara's: "Giulietta Simionato, with her healthy and ample voice, easy and secure, which she uses with great technical mastery and sustains with a vivid and intelligent temperament, has graduated and takes her place with the most prestigious leading ladies."[9]

Giulio Confalonieri, writing in *Il Tempo*, observed: "Giulietta

Simionato sings with great warmth and perfect intonation. Her voice is flexible yet equalized throughout its range. Her interpretation is both intelligent and convincing."[10]

Il Popolo: "Taking a leading role for the first time, at least in our memory, Giulietta Simionato demonstrated qualities of the highest order, as she did for years in bit parts or secondary roles: a powerful voice, clear emission, and an ability to take over the stage. These are the talents which, managed by her ever-present intelligence, have enabled her to earn such fervent applause."[11]

Teodoro Celli recalls the October 2, 1947, with these words: "She was wearing rags onstage, a diminutive figure who seemed crushed by the weight of some mysterious sorrow, and could have been once again the bit player we had seen so many times. But in her innermost being she was surely telling herself 'Now or Never!' This was her big chance. And she did sing. She sang with the consuming sadness of a prima donna who for a lifetime had been denied her importance; she sang with the dignity of a queen, returning from unjust exile to the throne that was rightly hers; finally, she sang the way Giulietta Simionato sings today. The journalists present wrote about her 'graduation' with a certain astonishment."[12]

Giorgio Gualerzi remembers: "I heard her Mignon two months later at Turin's Carignano Theater with a delicious young tenor named Giuseppe Di Stefano, and was very impressed. The timbre of her voice was at once pure and sweet. She had perfect breath control and an exceptional sense of style, all brought under control magnificently by her artistic temperament, in which there was, as Rodolfo Celletti put it, a certain kind of lyric sensibility which is particularly well-suited to express sorrow."[13]

Months later Giulietta was to make her debut at La Scala as Rosina, singing the role in the original mezzo-soprano key.

Reviewing that performance in *Il Corriere della Sera*, Franco Abbiati invoked the memory of Gertrude Giorgi-Righetti, the first Rosina, to help the surprised public understand that the role was for a contralto, not a soprano. The critic refused to speculate as to what motivated the changes in tessitura, but left no doubt that "La Simionato, an artist with a sense of humor, has known how to create a mischievous and seductive Rosina, vivacious and disarming — a Rosina with perfect pitch, secure and convincing in the florid passages."[14]

The reviewer for *Giornale d'Italia* had this to say: "Beautiful, elegant, Giulietta Simionato has been able to extract all the lightness to be found in her sumptuous voice, thus happily overcoming all the fearful virtuoso writing the role contains."[15]

The reporters for *Il Popolo*[16] and *L'Unità*[17] both felt that La Simionato was "an excellent Rosina."

The *Milano Sera* held that "Simionato as Rosina gave very convincing proof of her bravura, her confidence, her intonation."[18]

In a similar vein, the *Mattino d'Italia* felt that "Simionato, after having fully established her credentials last October as Mignon, has now risen to the challenge of Rosina, performing the role as originally written for mezzo-soprano. She has given the part everything it could possibly require. Besides making a convincing rascal of Rosina she has sung the part according to the highest performance standards, reproducing note for note all the flying roulades, the stratospheric scales and florid passages. After passing this test I think a favorable opinion of La Simionato could become definitive."[19] Thus Teodoro Celli.

It should be remembered at this point that at the last La Scala production of *Barbiere* Gianna Pederzini had played Rosina opposite Ferruccio Tagliavini and Gino Bechi, and Milan audiences had noted a young singer named Giulietta Simionato in the bit part of Berta. In only six years that bit player had become the heroine of the opera.

The judgment of Emilio Radius in *L'Europeo* was more severe: "Simionato's acting certainly does not have enough brio to equal her beautiful vocal agility."[20]

The reviewer for *Il Sole*, on the other hand, was moved to compliment Simionato for the beautiful performance she had turned in thanks to "hard study and real passion."[21]

Giulio Confalonieri in *Il Tempo* added: "Simionato possessed a beautiful tone, a confident and careful delivery, an unflagging security in the part, convincing diction and a consummate mastery of dramatic aspects of the role. This combination of qualities along with those inherent in the color of her voice made Rosina a deeply human character. She was never a chirpy bird in a cage or a flute executing a trill."[22]

During these same performances of *Barbiere* in 1947 Simionato learned that Toscanini had expressed an interest in casting her as Rubria in the performance of *Nerone* he was preparing to celebrate the thirtieth anniversary of Arrigo Boito's death. She felt tremendous personal emotion as she prepared for the audition the Maestro had requested.

Piano rehearsals took place at Toscanini's apartment in Milan. The Maestro had developed knee pains which caused him to limp, and was therefore loathe to be seen in public. Antonino Votto was Toscanini's assistant at the piano rehearsals. Other members of the cast included Siepi, Prandelli, Guarrera and Nelli. The latter two (Nelli spoke no Italian) had accompanied Toscanini to Milan from the United States. Simionato was very nervous but Toscanini reassured her by telling her to stand by the window against the light so that she could feel the essence of Rubria's otherworldly character. He went on to explain that Rubria's love for Fanuel was so pure that the voice must express an otherworldly serenity, attain tones of intense spirituality. After rehearsals Toscanini complimented Giulietta on her voice's unusual beauty in a paternal manner that moved her, and may have been the reason she had been able to give her best with him.

In fact she became so involved in the role that, at one point, despite the discomfort it caused, she held onto a chair and knelt to sing the death scene as if required to do so by the score. She sang with such religious passion that Toscanini's eyes shone with tears as he told her: "This is how poor Arrigo would have wanted to hear his music sung!"

Votto, accustomed to the famous conductor's reputation for stoicism, was clearly amazed by Toscanini's reaction. Toscanini himself, taken aback by his lapse, hastily dried his eyes and continued with the rehearsal.

Tullio Serafin's brother, who held the first oboist's chair in the La Scala orchestra at the time, was astonished by Simionato's audacity. During orchestra rehearsals for *Nerone*, Simionato stopped the proceedings by raising her hand and pointed out that in one scene her position onstage prevented her from seeing the conductor. Contrary to all expectations, Toscanini did not lose his temper, but calmly advised the stage director to remedy the situation by adding some fake boulders to the set.

Leandro Serafin remembers telling Giulietta: "You know, you could have been fired!" Such was the fear everyone had of Toscanini...

The evening honoring Boito was that of June 10th, 1948. Nine days later it was immortalized in a cover photo (allegedly taken from the prompter's box) in *Il Tempo*. Toscanini, of course, appears in the center; Simionato stands to one side of him, and on the other, but cropped almost entirely from the picture, stands the soprano Herva Nelli. The caption reads "Maestro Toscanini before the curtain with the soprano, Herva Nelli." To this day Simionato expresses outrage at the misattribution.

In 1949 Toscanini returned to Italy from America and made inquiries about Simionato, who was singing in *Cavalleria* at La Scala. When the Maestro learned this he made a face.

A few days later the conductor and singer ran into each other in one of the corridors behind the box seats. They discussed the opera she was singing, which Toscanini considered a "voice-ruiner." Simionato countered by insisting she loved the character because "she is tremendously emotional." Toscanini persisted in his negative judgment.

A year later Toscanini and Simionato met again at La Scala. Upon hearing that she was still singing *Cavalleria*, this time in Genoa, the Maestro rebuked her indirectly, perhaps somewhat amused: "As for *that opera*, the less said, the better."

At the start of 1949 Simionato was back at La Scala singing Hänsel in *Hänsel und Gretel*, an opera in which she had appeared for years in cameo roles. This time she sang Hänsel at a children's matinee under the baton of Maestro Sanzogno.

The reviewer for *L'Umanità* called her "a self-confident and daring Hänsel."[23] Franco Abbiati in *Corriere della Sera* referred to her "vocal fervor and willingness to take risks."[24] A production of *La forza del destino* that month found her singing alongside Elisabetta Barbato, Mario Filippeschi, Paolo Silveri and Boris Christoff; De Sabata conducted. *L'Umanità* pointed out that: "Giulietta's portrayal gives us a rich image of Preziosilla: an ample, cheerful voice enhanced by appealing gestures."[25] On the other hand Teodoro Celli's view of the performance certainly does not reflect a unanimity of judgment: "Giulietta Simionato, a fine artist we have all heard and enjoyed many times, does not have the voice to project Preziosilla's character, and maybe comic roles are not her strong suit. The result was a Preziosilla who was a rather pitiful gypsy."

We find this judgment somewhat surprising because the author of it had had the chance to interview some of Simionato's colleagues about performances in Brussels and Lausanne in 1950 and was assured by them that Giulietta's Preziosilla had made the entire cast laugh heartily.

Franco Abbiati, writing in the *Corriere della Sera*, felt that "Simionato's vocal resources were such that she never missed a beat or went off the slightest bit in her modulations, though her volume was sometimes inadequate to the requirements of a role like the gypsy Preziosilla,"a remark similar to Celli's, and one which is somewhat perplexing, not for what is being said about the volume of her voice, but for the feeling that Preziosilla was an unsuitable part for her. By then, after all, she had been performing it for more than ten years.[26]

In April, 1950, Simionato replaced Fedora Barbieri as Marfa in a revival of *Khovanshchina*. Writing this time in *Il Corriere Lombardo* the critic Celli found her Marfa "not very intense but pure in style."[27] Likewise the reporter for *Il Sole* endorsed her "forceful musical shaping of phrases."[28] The review in *L'Avanti* referred to "Simionato's always vivid but perfectly controlled interpretation."[29] Elsewhere she was referred to as "an exquisite singer, always a pleasure to listen to, who has powerfully brought to life Marfa's difficult character."[30, 31]

1950 was a busy year. After *Khovanshchina*, Giulietta's next appearance at La Scala took place a week later when she sang in a production of Rossini's *Mosè* with the great Tancredi Pasero in the lead role.

"Impressive in the solo arias but not up to the demands of the recitatives (which were always of noteworthy beauty and structure)"[32] wrote a reviewer in *Italia*.

Many other critics singled out Pasero and Simionato for praise,

Roberto Leydi among them.[33]

In the 1951 season Giulietta once again took the part of Carlotta in *Werther*, this time with Ferruccio Tagliavini in the title role. Tagliavini was returning to La Scala after five years of absence.

Bardolfo described Simionato in this performance as "vocally unexceptionable, though perhaps because of the contrast to Tagliavini, she lacked a realistic conception of her character and her diction seemed muddy."[34]

Celli was of the same mind writing in the *Corriere Lombardo:* "Simionato sang Carlotta well, with intimacy and melancholy accents, as well as the required dramatic eruptions. We would only recommend a more succinct diction which would make her lines easier to understand."[35]

In *Milano Sera* il Vice reported that "Simionato's remarkable vocal abilities were enhanced as usual by equally remarkable dramatic skills" and judged her performance excellent.[36]

Franco Abbiati found her "very good indeed, attentive, sure, though somewhat more endearing than anguished; more stylized than profound."[37]

Abbiati's colleague at *Il Popolo* ventured: "Signora Simionato did not seem convinced, in fact seemed almost uncertain how to put her extraordinary gifts to the best use."[38]

De gustibus non est disputandum!

According to the reporter for *Italia* Simionato lacked "that special virtuous and silent aptitude which creates the most intimacy and is hardest to express."[39]

On the other hand the reviewer for *L'Avanti* wrote that Simionato once again affirmed her "high standing as a thoroughly prepared singer and natural actress who establishes herself as the true protagonist of the opera."[40] This opinion was shared by the reviewer for *Il Sole*.[41]

In Milan's *Il Tempo* the critic Giulio Confalonieri observed that "Giulietta Simionato again gives us evidence of her great talents, her intuitive dramatic ability, her preparation and her care in constructing a character."[42]

Throughout this overview of journalistic response it seems that Simionato's vocal interpretation of Charlotte isn't as prominently mentioned as her dramatic interpretation. This is to be expected, anyway. Since dramatic interpretation is generally more susceptible to change according to the singer's personality, it lends itself to being evaluated differently by different critics.

April of the following year, 1952, found Giulietta with Ferruccio Tagliavini in a *Barbiere* conducted by De Sabata in which Gino Bechi and Nicola Rossi Lemeni were also featured. Giulietta finally had the opportunity to refine her conception of the cunning Rosina after having sung the role in several theaters since the 1948 La Scala production.

Because of Simionato, Bechi, Rossi Lemeni and the other brilliant cast members this 1952 Barbiere came to be considered one of La Scala's greatest productions, "a performance worthy of export," as Giulio Confalonieri wrote.[43]

The press was unanimous in its praise. The *Corriere della Sera* judged Simionato "an admirable artist; very intelligent regarding the dramatic projection of her character; faultless for her style, which is of the purest bel canto kind, and notable also for the exceptional range of her voice."[44]

In *Il Tempo* Confalonieri made special note of Simionato's "invariably true intonation, her healthy and focused vocal timbre, her melodic and rhythmic accuracy."[45]

In *Il Corriere Lombardo* Teodoro Celli spoke of "the rare beauty of her singing."[46]

The reviewer for *Il Sole* judged Simionato "a very fine artist (mistress of a precious, flexible voice which easily reaches the exalted heights of the upper register and at the same time makes use of a stupendous middle register) and furthermore, a cunning and intelligent actress."[47]

In *L'Italia* Luigi Gianoli described a Rosina who was "at the same time pleasant, courteous, capricious, flighty and anxious — all the while remaining within the limits of tasteful, gentle comedy."[48]

In *Il Popolo* she was said to be an "excellent singer and pleasing actress who easily overcame every obstacle the role presented to create her character confidently and correctly."[49]

The 1953 La Scala production of *L'italiana in Algeri*, in which Simionato took the leading role, was directed by Corrado Pavolini, and marked Franco Zeffirelli's first work at La Scala as set and costume designer. It was during this production of *L'italiana* that Zeffirelli got to know Simionato and a deep, lifelong friendship began. The cast, in addition to Simionato, included the bass Mario Petri, tenor Cesare Valletti and baritone Sesto Bruscantini; Carlo Maria Giulini conducted. The production was a great success and La Scala management decided to mount it (with the same cast) at the Holland Festival the following year.

Reviewing the production in *Il Corriere Lombardo*, Teodoro Celli wrote: "Giulietta Simionato proved again what a perfect stylist she is."[50] In *Il Corriere della Sera* Franco Abbiati commented thus: "Simionato is an exceptional Isabella. She overcomes the difficulties of the musical figures which go whirling past and conquers the killing trios without compromising the lively and impudent dramatic essence of the character."[51] The critic Vice of Milan's *Il Tempo* likewise was impressed: "Confronted with the virtuosity of Rossini's writing, this artist is undaunted, able to deliver the most difficult passages with remarkable ease, and give an excellent demonstration of her vocal technique and her warm, full tones."[52]

In March 1954 Simionato was featured as Angelina (Cinderella) in a production of *Cenerentola* mounted especially for her. It would remain in chronicles of the theater as the performance that would henceforth cause her to come to mind at the mention of Cinderella's name. Staging and direction were by Franco Zeffirelli.

An anecdote about Zeffirelli's choice of costumes (costumes were always of great importance to Simionato) serves to illuminate the relationship between these two professionals. The singer who prided herself on never having argued with her set designers recalls that on this occasion she found it necessary to have an amiable discussion with Zeffirelli. He was convinced that the story's original author, Perrault, had imagined his fable as taking place in the Seventeenth Century. Costumes would therefore resemble renderings of Rubens. Moreover, in Zeffirelli's view, the breast didn't matter, so Simionato's costume was so tight that she was worn out trying to breathe. So as not to upset the director Simionato decided to try to make do with the costumes, saying that she would manage as long as she could. However, during rehearsals she became so constricted by the costume that she couldn't continue to sing. Still, she was able to work out a compromise with Zeffirelli: the costumes would be let out — but only a little! For her part Giulietta yielded to him in tolerating a bonnet which went over her ears and actually covered them, making it very uncomfortable to sing.

The press decreed this *Cenerentola* a great success. Teodoro Celli did not hesitate to declare that the opening of the show on March 14th marked "Simionato's finest accomplishment since the Mignon she gave us some time ago, which has not been forgotten." He added: "We are especially taken with this Cenerentola thanks to the precision and virtuosity of her voice, the balance and style of her overall presentation, for the splendid equalization of registers throughout her range."[53] In fact Simionato herself found the role Cenerentola extremely sympathetic and was an instinctive interpreter of it.

In the cast with her that evening were the tenor Nicola Monti making his La Scala debut, the bass Mario Petri and Sesto Bruscantini, baritone; Giulini again conducted. According to the critic Claudio Sartori, the other singers were "at a noteworthy remove from the magic that was being created by Simionato as Cinderella... a splendid interpretation." The Milanese critic was also moved to point out: "In Simionato's hands the character becomes a memorable and unsurpassable creation because of her consummate vocal accomplishments — their clarity and smoothness — as well as her affecting dramatic portrayal. Here her petite frame gives her certain advantages to begin with, but she has built on them with the grace of her attitudes, gestures, glances, always intelligently observing accents and inflections; with the clarity of her diction; finally, with a vocalism that is not only perfect from the standpoint of emission, in its solid technical foundation and squillo, but in the exact measurement of how much voice to give, the bite of her florid passages, the concealment of artifice. I can think of no other singer working today, Italian or foreign, who has such a complete talent, and can give us such intense emotional and musical fulfillment."[54]

In *La Patria* Giulio Confalonieri called Giulietta "an admirable leading lady, vocally and musically secure, rich in virtuosic capacity and expressive intensity, immersed in her portrayal."[55]

Luigi Gianoli in *L'Italia* noted that "Simionato brought the skills required for chamber music to the role, along with a great vocal richness. She was once again dramatically and vocally delicious."[56]

In the *Corriere della Sera* Abbiati directed attention to "the elegance of the singing in respect to the prickly *fioriture*; singing that softly capitulated to warm, expressive phrasing."[57]

The audience that evening clearly registered the success of her performance by demanding fifteen curtain calls. The La Scala management decided to take this production of *Cenerentola* to Amsterdam and The Hague for the Holland Festival of 1955. The role was performed so often by Simionato, more even than her Mignon, that it soon became linked to her name.

In May 1954 Dimitri Mitropoulos conducted Ferruccio Busoni's rarely performed *Arlecchino* at La Scala. The composer's son Raffaello designed the costumes and sets for this brief farce and Simionato sang Colombina and, once again, was lavishly praised by the critics. Abbiati found her "excellent,"[58] and il Vice referred to a "winning and vivacious Colombina."[59]

Her La Scala *Carmen*, performed in January, 1955, constituted another milestone in her career. It was conducted by Herbert von Karajan and sung in the original French. A sort of dress rehearsal had taken place three months earlier in Vienna, on October 8th and 11th, 1954. A concert version of Bizet's masterpiece was presented, in French, at the Grosser Musikvereinssaal, again under the baton of von Karajan. Giulietta was the cigarette girl, Nicolai Gedda was Don José, Hilde Güden was Micaela and Michel Roux, Escamillo. In attendance were Antonio Ghiringelli and Luigi Oldani, directors of La Scala, who had come expressly to hear Simionato and were enough impressed to sign her on the spot for a future production in Milan.

Giulietta sang Carmen more than three hundred times throughout her career, but the 1955 La Scala *Carmen*, even though it left the audience somewhat baffled, remains in her memory as one of the most important in her life. The cast was as brilliant as the one in the Vienna concert version, in fact it was much the same, with La Simionato and Michel Roux in principal parts, and the same comprimario artists — Sciutti, Ribacchi, Carlin, Del Signore and Sordello. Gedda's and Güden's roles were taken over by Giuseppe Di Stefano and Rosanna Carteri. Thanks to live recordings those memorable evenings were documented.

Not wholly won over, Eugenio Montale, who had attended the opening, commented as follows in the *Corriere d'Informazione*: "La Simionato, desperate in her contortions, has the voice to sing Carmen. She is particularly affecting in the card scene when, under a purple light giving her a Wagnerian Fricka-like aspect, she takes advantage of the low notes (low notes that she might have put to good use earlier in the Act One *Habañera*), but she lacks the bit of spice that would justify the fact that a brave dragoon of the *Guardia Civil* has fallen head over heels in love with her."[60] Giorgio Gualerzi shared Montale's opinion.[61]

It seems that Giulietta, by nature somewhat introverted, did not want to go beyond what she considered the bounds of good taste.

Teodoro Celli, writing in the *Corriere Lombardo*, had this to say: "Giulietta Simionato, whom we all know as a fine artist, demonstrated her usual impeccable style but lacked sufficient volume to project the tragic character of Carmen; in particular her low register seemed a bit thin."[62] Rodolfo Celletti's opinion was that "her Carmen, although vocally impeccable, was excessively lyrical."[63]

One of her La Scala performances, that of January 18th, 1955, was broadcast and recorded. Carlo Marinelli, in his book "Opera on Disc," has said of that evening: "Mocking and indolent, wriggling or flighty, Giulietta Simionato at forty-four years of age is a Carmen who is by turns sad and listless, patient and irritated, but rather ponderous in the first two acts. The turning point, the revelation of character, comes toward the end of the second act when Carmen sings a veritable "cradle song," wherein the image of the mountains seems to promise a passage back to the freedoms of her childhood. The contralto from Forlì tends to rely too much on shadings of color and volume in her warm, velvety voice to convey Carmen's tragic nature. The voice is sensuous and fascinating but so dark and gloomy that there is some danger of vulgarizing the character."[64]

A few months later Mascagni's *Cavalleria rusticana* and his little-known opera *Zanetto* were given to commemorate the tenth anniversary of the composer's death. (Originally the more familiar *L'amico Fritz* was to have shared the program with *Cavalleria.*) *Zanetto* had not been performed since 1930, on the occasion of the International Exposition of the Decorative Arts in Villa Reale di Monza. The glittering opening night audience included Maria Callas and her husband Meneghini who had come specifically to hear and applaud Giulietta Simionato.

The performances, presided over by Antonino Votto, were very well received. Rosanna Carteri figured in the cast of *Zanetto* and Giuseppe Di Stefano and Giangiacomo Guelfi in *Cavalleria.*

Franco Abbiati in the *Corriere della Sera* called *Zanetto* "altogether likable and spontaneous. Credit for its successful revival must go to the exceptional cast. Giulietta Simionato, in particular, gave a passionate and insinuating interpretation in the trouser role. Rosanna Carteri's Silvia was delicate of voice and physically convincing. Simionato's Santuzza (in *Cavalleria*) was a special attraction, distinguished by her purity of tone and sweet timbre. In the ardent words of this young girl who has been seduced and has become extremely jealous Simionato's voice displays a progression of fiery accents and brilliant colorings."[65]

Writing elsewhere Carlo Marinelli compared the evening to the excitement generated by the first Cetra recording of 1950. "At forty-four Simionato brings her considerable experience to bear upon the role, not only in the ulterior enrichment of the characterization by adding psychological notes, but also in a more definite delineation of the character proper. This is a Santuzza who is strong and sad, tender and violent; who doesn't beg or implore but merely asks, very nearly demanding and admonishing, at the same time as she is reconstructing what happened as a vivid image in the present. She is asking for something more than a memory, for a genuine return to the past as opposed to an evocation, reliving her seduction and the passion that had overwhelmed her. Her pride is determined by her awareness of her devotion and loyalty, and also by her awareness that she truly loves. She clings to her pride in fear and trembling, and with a deep intensity, and with hidden anxiety, though she never manages to deny the light of hope as well as a desolate certainty that in hope she will not capitulate. Indeed what is growing in her, as she takes stock of her situation, is bewilderment rather than rage — and it is this which makes her menacing. Anguish rather than jealousy, love more than the desire for revenge are fueling the desperate actions of someone who believes she has lost everything. Simionato makes Santuzza's outpouring to Alfio a truly tragic epitaph for a memory that is diminishing and finally destroyed by absence."[66]

In *La Notte* Vice said that Carteri and Simionato in *Zanetto* "displayed a wealth of voice and interpretive efficacy" but was less convinced by Simionato's Santuzza, feeling that "in the service of Santuzza's pain and anger her vocal resources weren't always up to the demands of the character."[67]

Eugenio Montale thought that in *Zanetto* "Simionato simply did not succeed in becoming a troubadour who would bring down bolts of lightning, though she did bring some beautiful modulations to the part," while he felt she had given a "touching and vigorous accent" to her Santuzza. Teodoro Celli in *Corriere Lombardo* dealt primarily with Simionato's Santuzza: "It's clear that this singer just does not have a big enough voice to displace the Santuzzas of recent memory. However, she is a true artist and makes us aware of the fact with the intelligent accents and the tremendously pure singing style with which she has constructed this character."[69]

The same mixed reactions were expressed in *24 Hours*.[70] But the writer for *L'Unità* qualified Giulietta's Santuzza as "a magnificent interpretation — dramatic, incisive and moving, ringing."[71]

We will have more to say later about these two Mascagni operas, which, because of their diversity, she had been hesitant to take on (even though the Rome Opera had also asked for them both) in one evening performance.

Giulietta twice had the honor of inaugurating the La Scala season by singing beside Maria Callas — two great occasions in their careers that must be remembered. On December 7th, 1955, the season began solemnly with *Norma* in the presence of the

President of the Republic, with Antonino Votto conducting. Mario Del Monaco was singing Pollione for the first time in his career and the distinguished bass Nicola Zaccaria was Oroveso.

Franco Abbiati in *Corriere della Sera* submitted that "Simionato's performance (was) warmer and more sensual" than Callas's, though "perhaps not as proficient or well constructed." Even so he proclaimed her a "lively and spontaneous Adalgisa and almost aggressively effectual."[72]

Giulio Confalonieri, writing in *La Patria*, credited Simionato with a successful creation. "Her Adalgisa is a deeply moving character thanks to the beauty of Simionato's timbre, the elegance of her phrasing and her instinctive musicality."[73]

Il Corriere Lombardo's Celli wrote that "Simionato, who was vocally rich, stylistically irreproachable, being most attentive to the juvenile chastity of her character, can stand comparison to the most celebrated prior interpreters."[74]

Rubens Tedeschi of *L'Unità* said: "Giulietta Simionato was truly impeccable. Year after year she improves and grows. She rendered the delicate character of Adalgisa with magnificent purity and warmth of voice."[75]

Alceo Toni of *La Notte*: "Simionato allayed our reservations that her natural tendency to pathos and sweetness in her singing would prevent her from identifying with Adalgisa. She kept up with Callas from a vocal as well as a dramatic point of view, and perhaps surpassed her at times. Her singing was animated with an amorous and sad sweetness, with an Italianate expressiveness, abandoned and yet artistically composed."[76]

Luigi Pestalozza in *L'Unità*[77] felt the need to point out the audience's participation, especially during the Third Act duet, which was given with "the utmost style, to Simionato's credit, who as Adalgisa gave another sample of her artistic gifts." This is precisely the duet that for many years has enabled us to compare the voices of Simionato and Callas singing together in perfect harmony. This beautiful page in the Bellini canon became an interpretive milestone for both singers (as did the duet in *Anna Bolena*), unforgettable moments, in my opinion, which to our great good fortune recordings have conserved for us.

As Eugenio Montale put it: "With a beautiful low voice that

gave just the right contrast to Norma's (an effect that is often lacking in the best performances), and with her excellent diction, Giulietta Simionato was an Adalgisa worthy of the highest acclaim."[78]

The Piccola Scala grand opening took place on December 26, 1955, with Cimarosa's *Il matrimonio segreto* which was conducted by Maestro Nino Sanzogno and directed by Giorgio Strehler. In it were "a group of singers that was exceptional":[79] Simionato, Ratti, Sciutti, Alva, replaced by Monti, Carlo Badioli and Calabrese. Together they created what was called "an enchanting performance."[80]

Engaged for *Il barbiere di Siviglia* in Rome, whose premiere was four days later, Simionato had to go back and forth between the two cities several times, alternating the roles of Fidalma and Rosina. These days she is often heard to say that the title of Cimarosa's masterpiece well suited her second wedding, celebrated in such mysterious circumstances.

In May of 1956 a performance of *Samson and Dalila* replaced the originally scheduled *Parsifal*, canceled because of the sudden death of Erich Kleiber. Simionato appeared as Dalila opposite the eminent Chilean tenor Ramón Vinay. Reviewing the first performance the critic for *Il Popolo*[81] had this to say: "The female star of the evening was Giulietta Simionato, whose high vocal art and expression created Dalila in a masterly manner, making her just what she ought to be: a skilled plotter, a master of double-dealing, as it would be called today, bent on revenge, but perfectly disguising her quest in her loving devotion. Yet another towering performance by an artist who has by now achieved the peak of her powers."

The reviewer for *L'Avanti* declared that Simionato "...as usual gave her character an aspect, an emotion, a clarity even when it hardly seemed possible,"[82] while his colleague at *L'Unità* described "the dramatic warmth of her great interpretation, with the vibrant colors and passion of her voice rivaling any of the greatest interpreters of the past."[83] Abbiati in the *Corriere della Sera* felt that Giulietta "stood out because of the fluidity and brilliant luster of her vocal means, which made her a proud and enchanting Dalila."[84] According to Eugenio Montale, Giulietta "surpassed even her most celebrated interpretations thanks to the beauty of her voice and her lofty and accurate realization of this character. Her timbre was a marvel, and her diction was what we have come to expect of mezzo-sopranos and contraltos generally, and we may as well resign ourselves to what Nature has decreed."[85]

In the *Corriere Lombardo* Teodoro Celli spoke in more measured tones of Simionato's Dalila: "As always, her style is never less than admirable as is her strength of voice at the extremes of the scale. However, it is in the middle range that the voice thins out and it is precisely in the middle range that Dalila's role mainly lies. Having noted this we must go on to say that Simionato's performance is yet another example of an authentic artistic nature."[86]

Alceo Toni maintained that Giulietta had surpassed all expectations and was the greatest Dalila ever to have graced the stage of La Scala. "Such is the balance of her voice; such is its round, joyous potency. Her singing is so pure, that without expressive mannerisms, without conceding anything to the usual easily obtained effect, her voice is always vibrant with intense expression."[87]

At the same time as she was a triumphant Dalila at the main theater Giulietta was also appearing in Alessandro Scarlatti's *Mitridate Eupatore* at the Piccola Scala, where the production featured, along with Simionato, Victoria de Los Angeles, Jolanda Gardino and Ferrando Ferrari. Nino Sanzogno was the conductor. Emilio Radius, commenting in *L'Europeo*, found the performance "a gourmet dish."[88]

The Scala season that year was launched with a new production of *Aida* conducted by Maestro Votto and featuring Antonietta Stella, Giuseppe Di Stefano, Giangiacomo Guelfi, Nicola Zaccaria and... Simionato as Amneris, who appeared to Franco Abbiati "dazzling as usual with her warm, polished vocalism; a grand actress but one capable of heartfelt emotion."[89]

According to Eugenio Montale, Giulietta dominated the cast: "Though she lacks the exact coloration and declamatory power which defines Amneris's regal character, yet Simionato is continuously a miracle of balance, intonation, and of clear and faultless musicality."[90] To Luigi Giannoli, Giulietta was "perfectly focused, never excessive, a model of balance."[91] Rubens Tedeschi maintained that Giulietta Simionato was "one of the very rare Italian singers who knows how to make every note tell with just the right accent."[92]

Riccardo Malipiero admitted being enthusiastic to the point of ecstasy, celebrating Giulietta's "splendid voice, her secure emission, her perfect technique, her style, combined with her stagecraft, which have made of our marvelous singer a perfect Amneris."[93] In *Il Giorno* Beniamino Dal Fabbro noted that Simionato was "lavish with art and experience." [94]

Massimo Mila's beautiful words may best sum up the general reaction: "The accepted hierarchy for listing the cast of this opera would have Simionato (Amneris) mentioned third, but her place is at the top. The stylistic mastery of this mezzo-soprano has reached such a degree of refinement, together with her vocal means, that for some years now she has been writing the book on how to sing."[95]

Gloria Davy was present at the premiere, the African-American soprano who had to substitute for La Stella "out of rotation" in January 1957. She was never Giulietta's colleague, really, at La Scala, but she would meet her again in New York in 1958 when she was Anna Bolena in a concert version of the opera which was making the rounds of American cities, while Giulietta would portray her rival several months after the revival at La Scala, of which we will have more to say shortly.

Three days after the *Aida* premiere on December 11th, 1956, Giulietta, who had scarcely had time to breathe, appeared as Cornelia in Händel's *Giulio Cesare*. The conductor was Gianandrea Gavazzeni and the cast included Nicola Rossi Lemeni, Virginia Zeani, Franco Corelli and Mario Petri. Franco Abbiati judged her to possess "the only superlatively Handelian voice. Her Cornelia was impeccable in respect to the sedate staging and her singing was both moving and convincing."[96]

In *L'Italia* Luigi Gianoli wrote: "The indefatigable Giulietta Simionato, just out of her costume as Amneris, has with just as much bravura become a capable and robust Cornelia, with just the right notes of grief. One might say that the best arias in the opera fall to her lot, and that she knew just how to make the best of them."[97]

The production traveled to Vienna the following year. There was a reception at the Italian Embassy following the first performance. During the reception the Ambassador stepped up to the much honored star of the evening and asked matter-of-factly: "Signora Simionato, are you doing anything interesting in Vienna?" A gaffe of such monumental proportions could not fail to get people talking!

December 7, 1957 saw two familiar figures from a certain 1955 *Norma* together again to open the Scala season with a production of Verdi's *Un ballo in maschera.* Gavazzeni conducted; Di Stefano and Bastianini returned in the parts they had taken the year before. The critic of the *Corriere della Sera* wrote: "We enjoyed the singing of Giulietta Simionato, who was a superb Ulrica, completely worthy of the impression that Stignani has left among us."[98] (Stignani had taken the part of Adalgisa in the preceding year's production.)

In the *Giornale d'Italia* Luigi Gianoli described Simionato as "a little hoarse, but she overcame her difficulty in an admirable way, singing with beautiful intensity and acting with instinctive theatrical resources as the gypsy."[99]

In *L'Unità* Rubens Tedeschi noted that "The part of the sorceress requires a darker timbre than Simionato possesses but she overcame this difficulty by means of the admirable intelligence with which she employed her vocal means."[100] Eugenio Montale, this time in *Il Corriere d'Informazione*, called her Ulrica "infallible."[101] *La Notte*'s critic found her "wonderful,"[102] while Giulio Confalonieri in *La Tribuna* was amazed by the "concentrated fire" of her interpretation.[103]

Only a few months earlier in that same year (1957) an incident took place at La Scala which became famous in the annals of opera theater. During the rehearsals for *Anna Bolena* Callas, who was only horsing around, amused herself by giving Giulietta a few slaps on the back. At one point the force of her unexpected blows caused Giulietta such sharp pain that she instinctively slapped Callas's cheek—hard enough to leave the imprint of her five fingers.

Luchino Visconti happened to witness the incident and was shocked. According to him, Callas, with tears in her eyes, said: "No one ever hit me that hard, not even my mother, who hated me." But the friction between them didn't last; in fact they were seen arm in arm only a half hour later.

This production of *Anna Bolena* was a resounding success, as is well known, and Callas and Simionato shared it in perfect harmony without a shadow of envy; indeed, between the two there was a kind of friendly rivalry by the terms of which each tried to give her character an interpretation that would stand up to the other's.

The first performance took place on April 14th, 1957. Maria Callas was the ill-fated queen with Simionato as her pitiless rival. Nicola Rossi Lemeni and Gianni Raimondi rounded out the cast. But it was the two women who drove audiences wild. Callas as the protagonist shared the audience's excitement with Simionato. Mario Morni recalls that on that evening "Simionato was celebrated as much as Callas, if not more."[104] The testimony of Luigi Oldani, published elsewhere, confirms this version of what happened.[105] It was a gala performance given on Nations Day. Among others present were Carla Gronchi, wife of the President of the Republic, the royal family of Liechtenstein; nearly the entire foreign diplomatic corps of all major governments recognized by Italy as well as the actors Marcello Mastroianni and Paolo Stoppa. There were no fewer than thirty-four curtain calls, with twenty at the end of the third act alone! At the opera's end the two *prime donne* embraced each other onstage, causing renewed cries of acclamation from the audience: this was nothing less than a triumph.

In *La Notte* Alceo Toni spoke of "an undoubtedly superior display of virtuoso vocalism," admiring Simionato's "treasure of a beautiful voice."[106]

In *L'Italia* Luigi Gianoli noted the "full splendor of Giulietta Simionato's vocal endowment, displayed in its maturity as well as the intelligence revealed by her dramatic persona," calling her voice "sincere, thick, round, full."[107]

In *L'Unità* Rubens Tedeschi praised the "resources of an enchanting voice, deep and thrilling" and an amazingly mature musical and artistic sensibility."[108] According to Gian Galeazzo Severi "the evening belonged to Simionato. The great Callas has shared some of the laurels, and not the least important, that had been reserved for her, and she did so very gallantly. Giulietta Simionato, tackling a role whose tessitura lies dangerously high for a mezzo — and is besides alternately impassioned or impetuous, in the grand manner — offered her spellbound audience the fruits of her superb and dependable artistic maturity. She was acclaimed without respite and called again and again to the footlights and even applauded in mid-scene."[109]

Eugenio Montale wrote that besides Callas "La Simionato also triumphed with her powerful voice, her style and the authority of her dramatic portrayal of Giovanna, which was beyond compare." The famous poet and critic, after considering Callas's merits, was moved to say of Simionato's: "In the part of Jane Seymour, the mezzo held her own wonderfully, demonstrating a power and *class* which was in the end acknowledged by everyone."[110]

These opinions were shared by Teodoro Celli[111] and Beniamino Dal Fabbro[112] writing respectively in *Il Corriere Lombardo* and *Il Giorno*.

Rodolfo Celletti's words about this famous performance should not be forgotten: "She has proved herself a more beautiful singer by purely vocal criteria and probably, from the 1957 performance of *Anna Bolena*, can be said to be competing much more closely with the leading lady, La Callas, by reason of her security, her verve and her virtuosity."[113]

Among all the critics there wasn't a single discordant note: this production of *Anna Bolena*, the premiere of which was fortunately recorded, elicited nothing but praise.

Anna Bolena was staged again on April 9th, 1958. The performance was eagerly awaited because Maria Callas was appearing at La Scala for the first time after her famous "walkout" in the Rome Opera House the previous season. The *Bolena* cast was identical to the earlier one except that Cesare Siepi had replaced Rossi Lemeni as Henry VIII.

Once again Giulietta Simionato received praise from critics and public alike. Franco Abbiati, writing in the *Corriere della*

Sera, felt that "for her part, La Simionato seemed to be a worthy rival of the soprano lead on her own turf whether in the regal magnificence of their portrayals or, if nothing else, in the fiery, sun-like expansiveness of singing that was radiant, vivid, rich."[114] In the *Corriere Lombardo* Celli qualified Giulietta as "invaluable for her vocal splendor, and a passionate character."[115] Alceo Toni said that "La Simionato was without equal, insuperable: one of the greatest vocal phenomena of our time, an artist who is suited to her roles to a very rare extent."[116]

Nor was Luigi Gianoli sparing in his praise this time: "As far as Simionato is concerned she has not given any sign that there are limits to her bravura. A year ago we thought we heard her at the height of her powers. This year she appears to have gone further. She is a great singer, musical to the highest degree and most generous with her talent, as well as a persuasive and intelligent actress, who succeeds miraculously in blending her voice and gestures with those of La Callas — in blending so many personal characteristics as to astound anyone who considers the technical difficulty of being so skillful at the same time as she is required to be so humble and sensitive."[117] This miraculous "competition of bravura" between the two performers was also praised by the reviewer writing in the *Corriere d'Informazione*.[118]

The public was wildly enthusiastic at the end of the first act, and even more at the end of the second when Callas kissed Simionato. There was no end of the applause for the two *prime donne*.

Today when Simionato is asked which of her many performances with Callas was dearest to her in memory she answers without hesitation, "The La Scala *Anna Bolena*. It was a performance which defined an era. The cast was extraordinary. Visconti directed. Staging and sets were by Benois. The conductor, Gavazzeni, made cuts in the score like a great surgeon and this reexhumed opera was made to sound fresh and new. And then, he conducted like a god and had all of us in a state of grace."[119]

It is worth mentioning that Simionato was unfamiliar with the score even though ten years earlier, in 1947, she had sung the opera at the Gran Teatro del Liceo in Barcelona with Sara Scuderi and Cesare Siepi (the king). Asked about that performance today

Giulietta admits she remembers practically nothing. Incidentally, this opera had been readied to celebrate the centenary of the Liceo which opened on April 17, 1847 with *Anna Bolena*, which hadn't been performed again after that for seventy years. We will have more to say of it later, but in passing we should note that Cesare Siepi who, as noted above, appeared with Giulietta in that anniversary presentation in Barcelona, is convinced that that production should have launched Simionato — who was the perfect Seymour — on a major international career then and there, but her performance did not have the impact of the Scala *Bolena*.[120]

On the 4th of January, 1958, the 1953 production of *Adriana Lecouvreur* was mounted at La Scala with Pierre Bertin's stage direction (the eclectic French actor was already a member of the Comédie Française and the friend of Cocteau and Apollinaire), with the set design of Jean-Denis Malclès. In the cast, along with the Adriana of Clara Petrella, were Giuseppe Di Stefano, Ettore Bastianini and La Simionato, under the baton of Antonino Votto. Signora Rosa Cilea, the composer's widow, congratulated all the singers by telling them: "I can't remember a more beautiful performance!"

In *La Notte*[121] Alceo Toni had this to say: "Dramatically and vocally Simionato's voice blazed forth, imperious in its endurance and meaningful beauty." After Giulietta sang the *romanza* at the beginning of the second act, '*O vagabonda stella d'oriente*,' the audience, until then only moderately excited, began to applaud the singer. (There was a curious incident during the duet between Simionato and Di Stefano in this same act: a cat crossed the stage. Fortunately it was gray, which reassured the singers.)

In *L'Unità* the reviewer heard "the smalto of a royal voice,"[122] while Giovanni Carli Ballola has this to say. "Giulietta Simionato, a stupendous interpreter of the Princess of Bouillon, scored the most significant triumph of the evening. Once again the great mezzo-soprano has been able to find truthful accents and dramatic impact that would seem to have been lacking in the modest score."[123] The writer in *24 Ore*[124] judged Giulietta "perfect in her robust and well-schooled singing, as well as in the pertinence of her gestures." Il Vice in *L'Avanti* found her "absolutely impeccable,"[125] while Beniamino Dal Fabbro[126] felt that she had sung with "great clarity and vigor in her diction and tonal emission which gave plausibility to her otherwise rather conventional character." In the *Corriere d'Informazione* Eugenio Montale described her Princess of Bouillon as "probably unsurpassable today."[127] Il Vice in the *Corriere Lombardo* was of exactly the same opinion.[128]

At the end of January 1958 Giulietta celebrated the tenth anniversary of her memorable performance in *Mignon* in a revival of the opera at La Scala with Gavazzeni conducting. For the critics this was a "spectacular triumph," as Alceo Toni put it in *La Notte*. For the occasion Giulietta had several small gold medallions made to present to her friends and colleagues at the theater as a token of her appreciation for their support. Her signature appeared on one side of the medallion while on the other side the first notes of the aria "*Non conosci il bel suol*" were inscribed on a musical staff.

The audience was unusually restive on opening night. The coughing and general din were such that Gavazzeni became very annoyed, stamped his feet on the podium and had the orchestra begin *da capo* and at breakneck speed. All this energy from the orchestra was greeted by applause from the audience.

Reviewing *Mignon*, the critic for *L'Italia* referred to "the luxurious depth of the main character, whose bravura expressed itself in vocal exploits, bursts of bel canto and virtuoso display of the most elegant and controlled sort. Simionato's voice is strong and velvety at the same time, so that she is able to pass with the greatest of ease from the demands of Amneris to the very different ones of Mignon, never insensitive to the contrasting stylistic requirements of each. On the contrary, between her costumes and gestures she has been able to confer a rustic freshness to her character, simulating a marvelous adolescence."[129]

The following brief excerpts from reviews will provide a panorama of commentary.

The *Corriere della Sera* called her "not just excellent, sublime!"[130] Alceo Toni in *La Notte*: "Though she was not at her best vocally in the dress rehearsal, she took command of the role yesterday evening whether by reason of her simplicity together with the suitably bizarre aspect of some of the action, whether by the beautiful tones in her soft singing, which she colored and animated with the most exquisite artistic feeling."[131] In the *Corriere Lombardo* Teodoro Celli declared Simionato's performance of the evening before "another triumph. The physical grace of her character, the pathos of her singing, secure but interlaced with sadness, her robust inflections in the dramatic moments and her impeccable agility in the more amusing, girlish sections qualify her once again as the ideal Mignon."[132] Eugenio Montale in the *Corriere d'Informazione*: "La Simionato, who is entering the happiest phase of her career, has imbued her Mignon with splendid vocal accents, culminating in the garden scene, in which, as performed yesterday, we are not likely to see her equal. The dramatic aspects of her performance, as well, are continuously deepening."[133]

On the 1st of June, 1958, La Scala mounted a new production of Verdi's *Nabucco*. Attention focused on the Scala debut of the young soprano Anita Cerquetti, fresh from her last-minute substitution for Callas in the notorious Roman *Norma*. Simionato's first exposure to the role of Fenena in the Verdi opera took place at the full dress rehearsal, without any other preparation and without ever having heard the opera! Only able to appear for two evenings due to engagements in *Falstaff* in Vienna, she received excellent notices, starting with Alceo Toni in *La Notte*: "In mentioning Simionato's Fenena it is only possible to use the adjective 'stupendous.'"[134] Beniamino Dal Fabbro called her "incisive,"[135] and the reviewer for the *Corriere Lombardo* found her "splendid, as usual."[136] In the *Corriere d'Informazione* the reviewer asserted that "Giulietta Simionato was an exceptional Fenena."[137]

Opening night contained a moment of high drama not included in the score. At the end of the opera a stage prop, an idol five or six meters high, was struck by Jehovah's lightning. All very well, but this evening, it fell outward, resting on the brink of the orchestra pit, frightening members of the orchestra and the audience. However, the fear was disproportionate to any actual damage.

On July 8th, 1958, *Adriana Lecouvreur* was given a revival at La Scala with Magda Olivero as Adriana (which had become closely associated with her name) and Gavazzeni conducting. Reaction to Simionato's Princess of Bouillon ranged from "singing of exceptional clarity" (*Corriere della Sera*),[138] to "By now it has become useless to say it, because everyone knows the resources of her artistry — she is always magnificent" (*Il Corriere Lombardo*),[139] to Alceo Toni's writeup in *La Notte*, wherein he found Simionato's performance no less imposing than Olivero's, whom he justly considered the ideal Adriana.[140]

In December of the same year Simionato sang Sinaide in Rossini's *Mosè* with Boris Christoff and scored another big success. "This La Scala production of *Mosè* has but one exemplary singer, who reigns over all the others as some of the fabled golden throats of yore by the beauty and power of her voice as well as her mastery of singing; a uniquely potent force that we would gladly see multiplied: Giulietta Simionato." Thus Alceo Toni in *La Notte*.[141] Giacomo Manzoni, writing in *L'Unità* judged her "excellent"[142] while Eugenio Montale discerned "a veritable prodigy of agile singing: her light stream of sound traversed her entire range with surprising facility and the actress was no less important than the singer."[143]

On April 9th, 1959, was once again Bizet's heroine — "half gypsy, half smuggler, deploying the beauty of her urgent and expressive voice. She has changed her characterization a great deal since her last interpretation on this stage a few years ago; some might accept her characterization fully, some might find much to discuss in it. If, from the first act, she was able to find suitable poses to portray the hidden instincts of a temptress, in the second the qualities of a capricious seductress are not lacking; in the last two acts incisive dramatic power is indicated, and she supplies it." Thus il Vice in *La Notte*.[144] The same critic judged Simionato's Carmen to have been perfected and more fully realized than her characterization of 1955. "Vocally, then, she is magnificent," he went on, "but we do not see such a disparity between her vocal interpretation and her stage deportment. It's all of a piece, that is to say, in which there is a logical unity between the drama and the music."[145]

According to Eugenio Montale, Giulietta gave the best of herself, even if "in the first scenes Simionato's voice might be a little too beautiful to express the protagonist's gypsy background."[146] This time, though *Il Giorno*'s critic found her "more moody than passionate and more French than Spanish or Italian," he felt she "displayed the very best of her voice and her diction."[147]

A month later Simionato had to portray another famous gypsy, Azucena, a part in which she was able to display "her natural resources of great artistry, intelligence and magnificent voice as never before."[148]

For this *Trovatore* Franco Corelli (who had been her Don José in some of La Scala's recent *Carmen*s) was Manrico; Ettore Bastianini was Count di Luna and Margherita Roberti, Leonora. In *L'Italia* Luigi Gianoli defined Simionato's Azucena as "the cornerstone of the opera."[149] Alceo Toni writing in *La Notte* felt that "Simionato has a clear, mezzo-soprano voice that one might justifiably call 'lyric.' This is not a gypsy with a cavernous voice, grim and excessive, according to certain theatrical traditions, and Simionato hasn't tried to make her this sort of creature, but has nevertheless delineated her character with strong lines, singing the way she sings best: with the mastery of artistic expression for which she has become justly famous."[150]

Finally Giacomo Manzoni weighed in with the following ideas: "Giulietta Simionato has given us a passionate, dishevelled Azucena who is consequently quite uneven vocally, expressing a kind of exasperation sometimes, but never the real Azucena, who is cold and calculating; this is not to say that, above all in her low and middle voice, the evenness of her admission is not very much to her credit, but perhaps it stands out because of the attempts to force certain melodic phrases and exaggerate certain accents."[151]

On June 5, 1959, Giulietta took the part of Ifigenia in Gluck's *Ifigenia in Aulide*. The cast included Boris Christoff, Adriana Lazzarini, Pier Miranda Ferraro and Nicola Zaccaria. In *Il Corriere d'Informazione*[152] Eugenio Montale noted that among the singers there is "the admirable Giulietta Simionato, here playing one of the roles which best suits her, a role which requires an extremely fluid, almost incorporeal, style of singing." Another success for Giulietta, whose appearances were always greatly appreciated by La Scala audiences. Much later Giulietta declared to Lanfranco Rasponi[153] that in the classic repertoire *Orfeo* and *Ifigenia in Aulide* had given her great satisfaction.

On July 21st, 1959, *Carmen* was revived at La Scala with Giuseppe Di Stefano, replaced by Angelo Lo Forese, Ettore Bastianini, and Lovro von Matacic in charge of the orchestra. Critical reaction to the rest of the cast was varied but Simionato was "a great Carmen with dense, luminous passions which emanated from her splendid vocal domination of the role, proceeding in turn from an interior musical and dramatic attitude that is completely free from the tinsel of convention."[154]

Ernest Blanc, the French baritone, made his La Scala debut in the next *Carmen* given on February 1st, 1960. Di Stefano was Don José. It was Simionato's 173rd appearance in Bizet's opera.

Said Alceo Toni: "Her voice is always beautiful and perfect. I say this not only of her singing, which has lost none of its harmonious classicism, but I must also affirm that she is more the mistress of her characters, which have now been enriched with more incisive gestures. To be sure, she hasn't given us a loud-voiced, erotic or overly sensual gypsy. And who is to say that Carmen should be otherwise? We can even say that she doesn't dance, but what a great artist she shows herself to be in so many ways!"[155]

The *Corriere Lombardo* praised Simionato as "The greatest Italian singer of our time! She sang the whole opera with the warmth that has become characteristic and with passionate variation of tone color dictated by the mastery she has achieved, without letting go of her character for the merest instant, without letting the lightest of veils obscure her great interpretation."[156]

Eugenio Montale defined Giulietta as a Carmen who was "always more persuasive," and found that "no other artist surpasses her in the purity of her sound."[157] Eugenio Gara writing in *L'Europeo* said that "La Simionato, the protagonist, has enriched with beautiful tone colors an interpretation that might otherwise have seemed a little hollow. More artists should emulate her. She disdains the easy routine, choosing instead to refine and to find something new in each role. In short, she is not the sort of phenomenon, as it is said of so many others, that time will forget."[158]

Two months later, in April of 1960, Giulietta returned to her role as the Pharaoh's daughter Amneris in an *Aida* that was conducted by Nino Sanzogno. The cast included Birgit Nilsson, Pier Miranda Ferraro (taking over for Mario Del Monaco), Nicolai Ghiaurov, Cornell MacNeil and Agostino Ferrin. In the *Corriere della Sera* Franco Abbiati described Giulietta as "an exemplary singer in every respect, luminous as well as vigorous, fiery or sinuous with a resplendent ring in her voice or polished modulations according to the demands of the part."[159] For Eugenio Montale "Giulietta Simionato has shone again with the purity of her voice and given a vibrant force to the figure of Amneris. She had a personal success after the Judgment Scene."[160] For her work in the Fourth Act she was singled out for being "an artist of the first rank,"[161] and "magnificent, as always."[162]

"This wonderful interpretive artist, who has recently given us some performances, to tell the truth, of debatable merit, has convincingly demonstrated that she is back at the top of her vocal form, completely in possession of optimal vocal equipment and consummate dramatic ability, which enabled her to dominate completely a role that is particularly apt to display her talents," concluded the reviewer for *L'Unità*.[163]

In May 1960 Giulietta took on the role of Dido in Berlioz' *Les Troyens*. Luigi Gianoli found Simionato's Dido "passionate, tremendously human, tormented and vocally superb."[164] He noted that her "stupendously impassioned Dido"[165] had a particularly intense success, as did Mario Del Monaco's Aeneas, in the colossal diptych of Berlioz, with Rafael Kubelik conducting. In the *Corriere Lombardo* Riccardo Malipiero singled out "the part of Dido, played by Giulietta Simionato, which turned out splendidly thanks to the human warmth with which she was able to imbue the character."[166]

In December 1960 Simionato sang a number of performances of the restored five-act version of *Don Carlo* together with Antonietta Stella, Flaviano Labò, Boris Christoff, Ettore Bastianini and Nicolai Ghiaurov. The opera was conducted by Gabriele Santini, who was returning to La Scala after an absence of many years.

In the opinion of Eugenio Montale Simionato obtained "a very vibrant sort of success in one of her greatest roles..."[167] Alceo

Toni also thought that the role was "tailor-made for her," and found her "stupendous."[168] Franco Abbiati was reminded of "Stignani, whose unforgettable performances in the role have been equalled by Simionato."[169]

The chronicler for *L'Unità* added: "Her Eboli is not only a proud but a generous spirit. She never spared her vocal gifts, which were always superb."[170] "There was always something of the phenomenal in her strength and confidence,"[171] wrote Giulio Confalonieri. And in *L'Europeo* Eugenio Gara summarized the critical response: "Her voice is more beautiful than ever, her modulations and accents are unrivalled, and her mode of singing and pose of body are always wonderfully simple and human."[172]

A month later Giulietta was Preziosilla under the baton of Maestro Votto in a production of *Forza del destino* dating from 1955 which had already been revived once in 1957. Antonietta Stella and Giuseppe De Stefano, who were the leads in the last revival of the show, were replaced by Floriana Cavalli and Flaviano Labò. Alceo Toni wrote that La Simionato, in the part of Preziosilla, "brought a fresh, shining vivacity to the role that was unprecedented."[173]

On April 5th, 1961 she was once again Dalila. As Eugenio Montale saw it[174] she outdid herself, earning a triumphant success, along with Mario Del Monaco. The *Avanti* critic praised her as "proud, haughty, fearsome and vocally impeccable."[175]

In *24 Ore* she was hailed as "the best Dalila anyone could ever wish for: this great singer gives vocal and acting lessons while on stage. Unconditional bravos!"[176] Franco Abbiati admired Simionato for "the plastic and fluid emotion of her impeccable phrasing..."[177] The critic in *L'Unita* praised in Simionato "not only her worthy vocal resources, but her outstanding dramatic ability, which enabled her to perfectly unite passion and perfidy in her character." In *La Notte* Alceo Toni declared that Simionato was "unsurpassable, still a miracle of pure singing, miraculous in everything she does, especially in her psychological immersion in the role and for the touchingly emotional and thrilling expressiveness with which she brings her character to life. Who could ever forget her?"[178] Everyone knew that Giulietta's personality was a far cry from Dalila's. She had been obliged to create this character out of whole cloth, transforming herself into a creature who had no precedent in private life. Yet her artistic ability enabled her to be "warm, persuasive, truly bewitching."[179]

On the 11th of December, 1961, Simionato sang Neris to Callas's Medea at La Scala in a revival conducted by Thomas Schippers where public success and critical reaction were comparable. Franco Abbiati called Giulietta a "splendid Neris, for the abundance of her rich, flexible, beautifully modulated singing, as exalted as her famous colleague's."[180] In the journal *24 Ore* il Vice wrote that "at Callas's side Giulietta was a Neris of the highest class. She sang the second-act aria '*Solo un pianto*' so well that the enthusiasm of her audience reached a high point for the evening."[181] In Italia Luigi Gianoli put it this way: "Next to Callas Giulietta Simionato as Neris was the perfect foil, a delicate, sweet figure, carried away to the high summits of song and suffering. Her aria concertante with bassoon was given with immense bravura and the sweetest possible intimacy." According to Guido Pannain[182] Giulietta "shaped Neris's stupendous aria with pointed singing and the highest possible style." Piero Santi thought her "An anxious, moving figure as Neris, who sang the second-act aria magnificently."[183] Giulio Confalonieri shared this opinion: "Giulietta Simionato, favored with a voice that is always absolutely dependable, even and perfectly in pitch has given us an outstanding Neris, singing the maidservant's aria in the second act in a spectacular manner."[184]

In *Il Resto del Carlino* Duilio Courir observed: "As Neris Simionato was the exceptional singer she always has been, who projects all the details of the characterization and makes every note telling thanks to her infallible stage presence."[185] He went on to convey the "sense of an event" that this revival of *Medea* had excited in the public. The box office had been deluged with seventy thousand requests for seats. For the December 10th and 11th performances there was a long line of spectators hoping to snap up the last available tickets."[186]

Riccardo Malipiero found her "marvelous"[187] and Giacomo Manzoni felt "she has always possessed an innate dramatic sense."[188] To many reporters this *Medea* became the "second season opener," superseding the official opening four days earlier

1. Santuzza in *Cavalleria rusticana*. Tokyo, 1961.

2

3

2. *Cavalleria* with Lo Forese. Metropolitan Hall, Tokyo, 1961.

3 and 4. *Cavalleria* at Metropolitan Hall. Tokyo, 1961.

4

5

5. *Cavalleria rusticana* with Jan Peerce. Metropolitan Opera, New York, 1959.

6

6. *Cavalleria* with Carlo Bergonzi, Piero Guelfi, Masini, Villani. Piazza San Marco, Venice, 1957.

7. *Cavalleria rusticana*. Verona Arena, 1960.

8. *Cavalleria rusticana*. La Scala, Milan, 1963.

9. Metropolitan Opera debut as Azucena in *Il trovatore*. New York, 1959.

10. *Il trovatore* with Bastianini. Verona Arena, 1959.

11. *Il trovatore* with Carlo Bergonzi. Bolshoi Theater, Moscow, 1964.

12. *Il trovatore*. Salzburg, 1962.

13. *Il trovatore* with Tucci and Vishnevskaya (guest). Moscow, 1964.

14

14 and 15. Ulrica in *Un ballo in maschera* with Maria Callas. La Scala, Milan, 1957.

15

16. *Un ballo in maschera*. La Scala, Milan, 1957.

17. *Un ballo in maschera* with Bastianini, Callas, Di Stefano, Ratti, and Gavazzeni (conductor). La Scala, Milan, 1957.

16

17

18. As Federico in *Mignon*. La Scala, Milan, 1937.

19. In the title role of *Mignon*. 1947.

20. *Mignon*. Studio photo. Barcelona, 1950.

21. *Mignon* with Italo Tajo as Lotario. Teatro San Carlos, Lisbon, 1954.

22. *Mignon*. La Scala, Milan, 1958.

23. *Mignon* with Ricciardi, Zeffirelli, Ratti, Maestro Gavazzeni, Gianni Raimondi, Malaguti and Modesti. La Scala, Milan, 1958.

24. As Adalgisa in *Norma*. La Scala, Milan, 1955.

25. In *Norma*. Paris Opera, 1965.

26. In *Norma* with Del Monaco and Callas (up stage). La Scala, Milan, 1955.

27. In *Norma* with Callas. La Scala, Milan, 1955.

28. As Adalgisa in *Norma* with Gencer. La Scala, Milan, 1965.

29. In *Norma* with Callas. Paris Opera, 1965.

30. Accepting plaudits with Callas after *Norma*. Paris Opera, 1965.

31. *Adriana Lecouvreur* with Ettore Bastianini. La Scala, Milan, 1958.

32. *Adriana Lecouvreur* with Olivero and Maestro Gavazzeni. La Scala, Milan, 1958.

33. As the Princesse de Bouillon in *Adriana Lecouvreur* with Magda Olivero in the title role. Naples, 1959.

34

34. As Preziosilla in *La forza del destino*. La Scala, Milan, 1965.

35. In *La Gioconda* with Maestro De Fabritiis, Martinis, Prandelli. Rio de Janeiro, 1952.

35

36

36. In the title role of *Fedora*. Mexico City, 1950.

37. As Cherubino, quite convincingly disguised as a girl, in *Le nozze di Figaro*, with Italo Tajo as Figaro. Teatro San Carlo, Naples, 1954.

37

38. As Rosina in *Il barbiere di Siviglia*. La Scala, Milan, 1952.

39. *Il barbiere di Siviglia* with Gino Bechi. La Scala, Milan, 1952.

40. *Il barbiere di Siviglia* with Tito Gobbi. Chicago, 1958.

39

40

41. *Il barbiere di Siviglia* with Baccaloni. War Memorial Opera House, San Francisco, 1953.

42. *Il barbiere di Siviglia* with De Sabata (conductor), Bechi, and Tagliavini. La Scala, Milan, 1952.

43. *Il barbiere di Siviglia* with Guarrera, Serafin (conductor), Baccaloni, Valletti, Rossi Lemeni, and Moudry. War Memorial Opera House, San Francisco, 1953.

44. As Dorabella in *Così fan tutte* with Badioli, Morel, Papazian, Danco, Maestro Ackermann, and Cortis. Théâtre de la Gaîté Lyrique, Paris, 1946.

45. As Melanto in *Il ritorno di Ulisse in patria*. La Scala, Milan, 1943.

46. As Mistress Quickly in *Falstaff* with Tebaldi, Gobbi, Canali. Lyric Opera, Chicago, 1958.

47. As Fidalma in *Il matrimonio segreto* with Poli, Carosio, Valletti, Rovero, and Tajo (seated) from the Teatro San Carlo of Naples. Strasbourg International Festival, 1951.

48. Simionato's first performance as Jane Seymour in *Anna Bolena*. Teatro del Liceo, Barcelona, 1947.

49

49. *Anna Bolena*. La Scala, Milan, 1958.

50. Rehearsing *Anna Bolena* with Visconti and Siepi. La Scala, Milan, 1958.

50

51. *Anna Bolena* with Rossi Lemeni. La Scala, Milan, 1957.

52. *Anna Bolena* with Siepi. La Scala, Milan, 1958.

53

53. After the performance of *Anna Bolena* with Callas. La Scala, Milan, 1957.

54

54. *Anna Bolena* with Rossi Lemeni and Callas. La Scala, Milan, 1957.

55. As Leonora in *La favorita* with Bastianini. La Scala, Milan, 1962.

56. In *La favorita* with Gianni Raimondi. La Scala, Milan, 1962.

57. In *La favorita*. Verona Arena, 1958.

56

57

58. As Charlotte in *Werther*. La Scala, Milan, 1951.

59. As Isabella in *L'italiana in Algeri*. La Scala, Milan, 1953.

60. Cinderella before the transformation in *La Cenerentola*. Teatro dell'Opera, Rome, 1954.

61. *La Cenerentola* with Tajo, Susca, Maestro Branco, Bruscantini, D'Angelo, and Canali. Teatro São Carlos, Lisbon, 1955.

62. Cinderella arrives at the ball in a production of *La Cenerentola* by Franco Zeffirelli. La Scala, Milan, 1954.

63. *La Cenerentola*. La Scala, Milan, 1954.

64

64. As Sinaide in *Mosè* with Boris Christoff.
La Scala, Milan, 1950.

65. *Mosè* with Piero Guelfi (Pharaoh).
La Scala, Milan, 1950.

65

66. As Amneris in *Aida*. Palacio de Bellas Artes, Mexico City, 1950.

67 and 68. *Aida*.
La Scala, Milan,
1956.

67

68

69. *Aida*. Metropolitan, New York, 1960.

70. *Aida*. Mexico City, 1950.

71. *Aida*. Tokyo, 1961.

72. *Aida*, with Bergonzi, Maragliano, and Colzani. Teatro San Carlo, Naples, 1965.

73. *Aida*. Covent Garden, London, 1964.

74. *Aida* with Corelli during the Metropolitan tour of 1965.

75. *Carmen*. Palacio de Bellas Artes, Mexico City, 1950.

76. *Carmen* with Aldo Protti. Teatro Coliseo Albia, Bilbao, 1954.

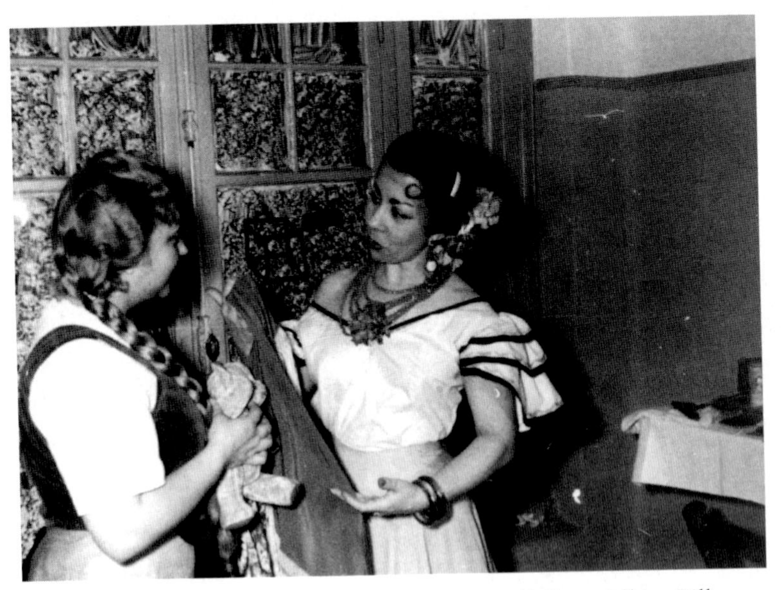

77. *Carmen*. Offstage with Noli at the Teatro Coliseo Albia. Bilbao, 1954.

78. *Carmen*. La Scala, Milan, 1955.

79. A consultation with Maestro von Karajan during *Carmen*. La Scala, Milan, 1955.

80. *Carmen* with Di Stefano and von Karajan. La Scala, Milan, 1955.

81. *Carmen* with Di Stefano. La Scala, Milan, 1955.

82

82, 83. *Carmen* with Di Stefano. La Scala, Milan, 1955.

83

84

84. *Carmen* with Corelli. Teatro Massimo, Palermo, 1959.

85. *Carmen*. Verona Arena, 1965.

85

86. *Carmen* with Mario Del Monaco. Tokyo, 1959.

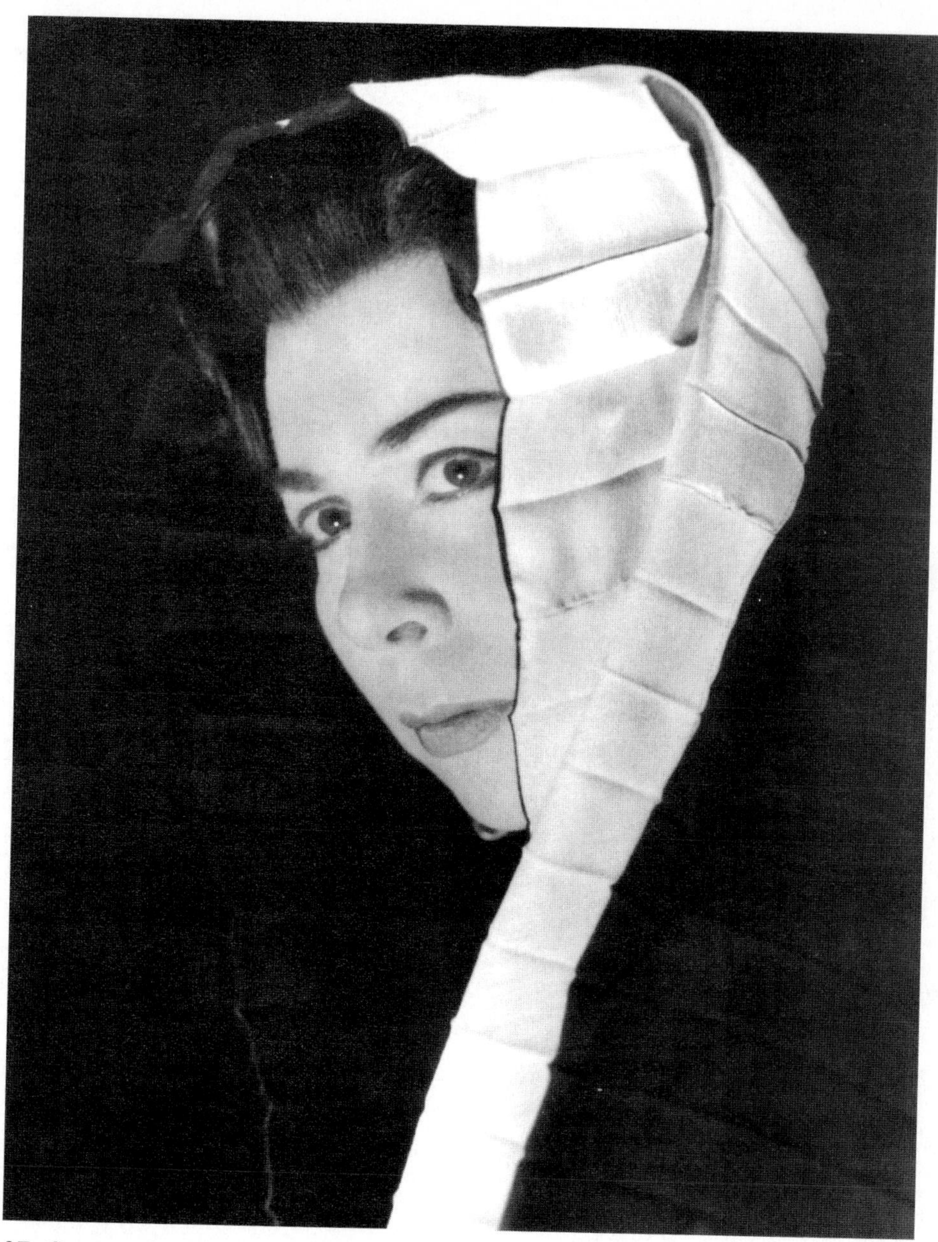

87. *Carmen*. State Opera, Vienna, 1960.

88. As Dalila in *Sansone e Dalila* with Del Monaco. La Scala, Milan, 1961.

89. As Cornelia in *Giulio Cesare*. La Scala, Milan, 1956.

90

90. As Dulcinea in *Don Quichotte* with Monachesi, Tajo and Viana. Teatro São Carlos, Lisbon, 1954.

91. As Eboli in *Don Carlo*. State Opera, Vienna, 1958.

91

89. As Cornelia in *Giulio Cesare*. La Scala, Milan, 1956.

90

90. As Dulcinea in *Don Quichotte* with Monachesi, Tajo and Viana. Teatro São Carlos, Lisbon, 1954.

91. As Eboli in *Don Carlo*. State Opera, Vienna, 1958.

91

94. An offstage celebration with Tucker, Gobbi, Christoff, Roberti and Maestro Votto during the run of *Don Carlo* at the Chicago Lyric Opera. 1960.

92

92. In *Don Carlo*. Magyar Allami Opera House, Budapest, 1961.

93. In *Don Carlo* with Tito Gobbi as Rodrigo. Lyric Opera, Chicago, 1960.

93

with *La battaglia di Legnano*. This was surely because of the presence of Callas and Simionato as female leads supported by the tenor of Jon Vickers and the bass of Nicolai Ghiaurov. Among the luminaries in the audience many colleagues joined the ovations, among them Franco Corelli, Ettore Bastianini, and Gianni Raimondi. The performance was followed by a banquet held by the "Friends of La Scala" to honor all of the performers and everyone else who had contributed to the production of *Battaglia* and *Medea*. At the head of the table sat the *Begum*, surrounded by Gavazzeni, Schippers and Wally Toscanini.

On May 14th, 1962, her voice was at the service of Gluck's *Orfeo*, a role for which she had been celebrated in a lead performance with Karajan, three years earlier, at Salzburg. In *L'Italia* Wiaroslaw Sandelewski wrote that Giulietta had played her part "in an impeccable manner," "always splendid and infallible."[189] The same judgment was to be heard in *Il Giorno*: "Vocally La Simionato gave a splendid account of the role."[190] Franco Abbiati in the *Corriere della Sera*[191] had this to say: "As expected, Giulietta Simionato dominated the stage by means of her wealth of vocal means and the authority of her moving dramatic attitudes. She dominated with singing that was miraculous for its polished splendor and its expressive ardor, and otherwise made an impression with the lordly dignity of her interpretation, pleasing us with the seductive naturalness of her stage personality and also with the precise way she has stylized her mythical character." (An opinion almost identical to that expressed in the *Corriere d'Informazione*.[192])

The press was unanimous in finding that Simionato's performance "couldn't have been more effective vocally (*L'Unità*)," and that she was "a first-rate Orfeo, with a perfectly integrated style."[193] In *Il Popolo* she was credited with having given "an excellent example of her seemingly unlimited resources"[194] and in *La Notte* it was said that she brought to the part of Orpheus "extraordinary musicality and resources of beauty in her singing that never cease to amaze."[195]

The historic revival of Meyerbeer's *Les Huguenots* was presented in Italian toward the end of the same month. Five of the world's leading singers were engaged by La Scala's management.

In addition to Giulietta, the cast included Joan Sutherland, Franco Corelli, Nicolai Ghiaurov and Fiorenza Cossotto.

Rodolfo Celletti[196] had this to say: "La Simionato was driven to excel not only because of her well-known, professional standards but because she was appearing for the first time in a soprano part, though Valentina is written for a "falcon" soprano,[197] which is to say the very highest mezzo-soprano voice. All by way of saying that La Simionato found herself in her element, and gave an exemplary performance. Her voice was soft, sonorous, moving, with full and easy high notes; in her interpretation she was a Valentina who was impassioned and aggrieved, certainly to be ranked among the very greatest portrayals she has given us in the span of her career." The critic for *L'Avanti*[198] thought Valentina had been "miraculously portrayed by Giulietta Simionato," and in *Stassera*[199] Luigi Pestalozza wrote: "Giulietta Simionato, charged for the first time with the interpretation of a soprano role, was a revelation — wholly magnificent. Her singing was secure, clear, classical, and seemed to be enriched by warmth, by generous expressiveness, purity and intensity."

Les Huguenots had not been heard by Scala audiences for sixty-three years and opinion was unanimous that the 1962 presentation was magnificent.

A short time afterward La Scala planned to mount Rossini's *Semiramide* — a production which hadn't been ready since 1881. Giulietta, singing at New York's Metropolitan Opera, was approached to sing the role of Arsace. She turned it down as being too demanding and La Scala dispatched an emissary, Maestro Ventura, to New York to persuade the great mezzo to change her mind and assist her in preparation. Their goal was achieved when Simionato was convinced and accepted the part. When she appeared in the La Scala production it was with Joan Sutherland. The two became great friends and were destined to sing together another time.

Except for some reservations to be noted later, the performance of *Semiramide* was another success for Giulietta. However, the miraculous mezzo-soprano appeared to have been "rigorously tested in the low contralto part."[200] In *La Notte*[201] Alceo Toni entitled his review "A Performance Worthy of an

Oscar." After praising Sutherland's bravura he praised Simionato's singing, which was "always of the noblest, with a sound that made her the composer's violin." However, Alfredo Mandelli,[202] along with Gianni Raimondi and Wladimiro Ganzarolli, found that Simionato was giving less than usual, feeling certain that the part of Arsace, which was pure contralto, wasn't as congenial as others in the repertoire of a singer with such a brilliant second octave and high notes that came so effortlessly. Still, these critics did not fail to acknowledge her perfect musical artistry.[203] Eugenio Gara, an admirer of La Simionato since 1947, expressed another opinion: "Naturally an artist like Simionato achieves the impossible as well as the possible. With her outstanding diction, the soft cantabile singing, her incisive accents she succeeds in creating a vivid and human Arsace. And yet in some places, for example in the proud cabaletta '*Si, vendicato il genitore*' (her *pira*, in some sense) a sound that was more aggressive and resonant at the core would have been more suitable to the exigencies of her situation."[204] According to the critic of *La Notte*[205] her "florid passages were dulled by too much rigidity in her throat, which diminished the size of her voice," even though she was "an Arsace of the first order." Anyway, the interpretations of Sutherland and Simionato in this opera, as with those of Caballé and Horne eighteen years later, constitute an important page in the history of operatic performance.

On December 7, 1963, Simionato had the honor, which she shared with Franco Corelli, of again opening the La Scala season with *Cavalleria rusticana* on a double bill with *L'amico Fritz*. It was the 100th anniversary of Mascagni's birth. A bust of the composer was unveiled in the La Scala foyer a few hours before Maestro Gavazzeni gave the downbeat. At the evening's end Corelli and Simionato shared an ovation which lasted several minutes while red carnations rained on them from the box seats.

At the Press Club after the performance Giulietta — "a Santuzza with passionate dramatic accents,"[206] "with warm but controlled vocalism, and with mighty dramatic accents"[207] — was also to receive an honorary title from the Republic at the hands of Mayor Cassinis and in the presence of the opera's leading players and many dignitaries.

Abbiati spoke of "a stupendous Simionato who, in the trembling accents of a seduced and jealous woman of the people, displayed in a gradually developing arc a splendid expressive intensity, not in the least troubled by the 'calculated risks' of the extremely high tessiture."[208] Beniamino Dal Fabbro, always more critical in every sense of the word, thought Giulietta had great expressive gifts that weren't always well adapted to Santuzza's pathetic despair, which is sharper, more lacerating, more hysterical than dramatic."[209] Riccardo Malipiero found her "too classical..."[210] Alceo Toni's striking observation was that "Simionato's voice doesn't suit the role of Santuzza," but he recognized that "the only fascinating, artistically exciting artistic emotions came from Simionato... Who will ever forget her dragging herself on the ground, clawing Turiddu's hands — ah, those hands she loved to caress — and the tender way she told him, 'Your Santuzza is crying and begs you...'? Who wasn't terrified by her curse? Who didn't feel joy to hear her intimate, inspired singing?"[211]

Objectively one has to acknowledge that Simionato could be Santuzza or Cinderella just as Maria Callas could be Medea or Norma.

Another milestone in Giulietta's career was the La Scala *Cenerentola* of March 17, 1964: as a character Cinderella was as dear to the mezzo-soprano as Mignon.

Alceo Toni in *La Notte* observed with lots of humor that "Cinderella made sparks fly!... Giulietta Simionato, again Cenerentola? Who would have thought it. In better voice than ever, she is a singer and artist so immersed in her character that she casts a spell with her beautiful voice. And all of us opera fanatics were standing there listening to her (Giulietta, our Giulietta) like so many Romeos."[212]

Eugenio Montale wrote that Giulietta Simionato, "even though she doesn't have notable gravity of sound, really owns '*la corda di mezzo*' [the mezzo notes] and... has given an exquisite musical interpretation."[213]

For Riccardo Malipiero Giulietta had a voice that was a little less polished than the one we're used to," but it was "always sure and laudable."[214] In the *Europeo* Eugenio Gara wrote: "As for Giulietta Simionato, the lead, it is enough to say that here she reaches, in full flight, the highest peaks of expression. It is not only a matter of vocal prowess (in the final rondo downright incredible for the pearl-like *fioriture*) but in the perfect design of a creature who through her admirable interpretation appears to us as Bacchelli describes her: 'the sweetest, most chaste, most lovably innocent of all the *ingenues* of opera theater.'"[215]

In September 1964 Giulietta journeyed to Moscow on a La Scala tour. She sang Azucena in *Trovatore* with Bruno Prevedi, Gabriella Tucci and Piero Cappuccilli, and participated in various concerts. In the RAI's film library in Milano they have preserved a film of this tour:[216] the most remarkable part of this film is the *"Stride la vampa"* (perhaps a rehearsal). Although it is rather short, it gives an idea of the dramatic realization of the gypsy and the art of Giulietta Simionato, who immersed herself perfectly in that character.

In the course of this tour *Turandot* was also given with Birgit Nilsson and Mirella Freni (Liù). The latter interpretation struck Nikita Khruschev with particular force. Moved by the lot of the poor slave he had words of praise for her. Other singers (Giulietta among them!) had the impression of having been upstaged: because of this misunderstanding a controversy arose with organizers of the tour, who were interested above all in the political advantages of this cultural exchange, and would therefore meet every day with the Russian Minister of Culture, Ekaterina Furtseva.

Back in Milan the La Scala company revived the 1955 production of *Norma*. Simionato and Nicola Zaccaria again played Adalgisa and Oroveso, respectively, while Leyla Gencer and Bruno Prevedi succeeded Maria Callas and Mario Del Monaco in the roles of Norma and Pollione. Maestro Gavazzeni took over from Maestro Votto. "Anyone who sees this *Norma* will become ten years younger," wrote Piero Santi,[217] who did not fail to observe that "compact, penetrating, manipulated with the usual style and finesse, we again discover Giulietta Simionato's voice, though the audience even in her case insistently wanted to stress every deviation in her emission or incidental effort."

In *L'Unità* Giulietta was said to be "always convincing and expressive visually and dramatically, even though she was a little tired vocally."[218] In *Il Giorno*[219] Giulio Confalonieri compared this 1965 production to the famous inaugural of 1831 which featured Pasta (Norma), La Grisi (Adalgisa) and Donzelli (Pollione). The 1965 model Giulietta [Alfa-Romeo makes a model called the Giulietta. Tr.] was able to stand comparison with the 1831 model. That is, undaunted by the harsh demands of the tessitura, Simionato was always composed, dignified and most effective."

In the *Corriere della Sera*[220] Franco Abbiati also had a positive opinion. "For her part Simionato has reached another peak in a career that looks miraculous. Always impressive as Adalgisa, particularly in the middle and lower registers, her rich and vibrant voice was resplendent with emotion, both sweet and penetrating, whose warmth communicated a humanity to the even effusions and recitatives as well as a seductive fascination."

Writing in the *Corriere d'Informazione* Eugenio Montale was more restrained, noting that Simionato "was in good voice, though not without some harshness that might be avoided if she would break herself of the habit of adding difficulties to a score that is already full of them. Even so, Simionato renewed the success she achieved ten years ago as Adalgisa."[221]

In the *Corriere Lombardo* il Vice wrote the following review: "Giulietta Simonato delineated her character with the greatest art and refinement, in every affective emotion, bringing to life the entire range of sentiments that unfold in Adalgisa's dramatic trajectory. Simionato's vocal mastery is no longer what it was, above all in revealing from time to time a less than perfect control of her low register. However, it seems to us that one particularly unclean high C among so many clean ones was without significance and should not have been whispered about, as it was most unjustly, by some in the audience."[222]

To round out this sampling of journalistic reaction, Alceo Toni, writing in *La Notte*, noted that "her high B-flats were not always loyally there when she needed them."[223]

For the first time an article in the press provoked a reaction from Giulietta (who never wanted to read what was written about her, sensible person though she was, for fear that it would be a negative comment). She felt she should point out to the critic that, since her appearances with Callas, she was used to singing Adalgisa in the original key, and when she was singing this opera, and the duets with Norma in particular, she was driven to emit certain notes and for this reason found herself ill at ease when Adalgisa's part had to be transposed down.

Simionato opened the La Scala opera season on December 7th, 1965, in *La forza del destino*, the opera with which she planned to make her final appearance before the public. In the cast were Ilva Ligabue, Carlo Bergonzi, Nicolai Ghiaurov, Renato Capecchi and Piero Cappuccilli, who was replaced by Carlo Meliciani after the first act when a fever prevented him from continuing. Between acts and especially at the beginning of the second act there were disturbances precipitated by the throwing of flyers from the loge seats in support of Minister Corona and against the "enti lirici" (the opera board). The police had to intervene so that the performance could continue.

The press commented on Simionato's performance with the usual warmth. Some reservations were put forward by Duilio Courir in the *Resto del Carlino*: "Giulietta Simionato, one of the greatest interpreters of Italian opera, has asked too much of herself in undertaking the ungrateful part of Preziosilla."[224]

But Eugenio Montale wrote that Giulietta had "again imposed her class in the quickwitted character of the gypsy Preziosilla."[225]

We have had occasion in due course to comment on her state of mind as she confronted this opera, how she had made up her mind by then to retire. However, instead she chose to say farewell to the stage with a small role in the *Clemenza di Tito*. The press gave much importance to the event and Eugenio Montale in *Il Corriere d'Informazione* observed that Simionato was "always a singer from an excellent school."[226]

The eve of her farewell a group of fervent admirers organized a small party at the Marino Hotel, where she was staying, at the end of which they presented her with a medallion to commemorate all of her triumphs at the Teatro alla Scala di Milano, Milan's temple devoted to lyric art, where she had opened only two months earlier.

This last performance took place February 1, 1966. Interviewed before the show Giulietta confessed to being as excited as she had been at her debut.[227] Pier Maria Paoletti remembers that her dressing room "turned into a nursery. A gigantic basket of bright red roses had been sent by her supporters from the Metropolitan Opera in New York. On the coffee table there were hundreds of telegrams..."[228] Giulietta's last performance was indelibly inscribed in the memories of those who witnessed it. As Paoletti recalls, "As soon as she entered the stage wearing Servilia's classic attire, an interminable ovation interrupted the "*mio ben*" she was starting to sing... At the end of the opera, Giulietta Simionato was loudly called back onstage alone several times, under a fantastic tempest of flowers."[229]

Giulietta received many, many letters from colleagues and opera directors expressing regret at her departure from the stage. Francesco Siciliani, at the time La Scala's Artistic Director, wrote: "Your thirty years in the theater are a rare example of artistic accomplishment and professional integrity. Applauded and loved in the greatest musical centers of the entire world, you will be remembered by everyone with gratitude and affection."

The following emotional words were written by the great Mafalda Favero, who never hid her admiration for Giulietta. "Tomorrow you will begin a new life, a serene life. But your many friends will have you in their hearts, and your voice will remain within their souls."

Mario Del Monaco sent this moving farewell: "My modest tribute cannot express my heartfelt regret over your decision to let the curtain fall for the last time on one of the most glorious careers yet seen in the centuries-old history of our art."

Giampiero Malaspina had this to say: "A few hours ago Mario Del Monaco confirmed a rumor that I would not have credited until today. So it's really true, Giulietta Simionato will bid farewell to the stage. As a colleague and a great admirer I want to extend to you my regret for your decision and my sincere gratitude for everything beautiful and good which you have given to the Italian opera without presumption, without excessive ambition, and with humble love. Please accept these lines as an expression of my thanks, and allow me to speak for all your devoted admirers in expressing theirs."

Floris Ammannati, manager of Venice's La Fenice, had this to say about her: "Her singing, together with her intelligence and sensitivity, not only made her famous all over the world but brought honor to the Italian Lyric Theater."

Not a day went by without receiving some show of support. Suzanne Danco, her colleague from the old days, expressed her best wishes thus: "You have been a Queen of Bel Canto and like a queen you knew when to leave and to start a new life beside another great person worthy of you. Please accept all my admiration and best wishes."

Alessandro Ziliani sent this message: "In the papers I learned both that you are getting married and leaving the stage forever. I was happy with all my heart for the first bit of news, and I congratulate you for a choice that could not have been better, and I send you the most sincere best wishes. For the second, I join with millions of your admirers who would like you to remain on the stage, not only for the joy you bring your public, but also to be an example for a new generation of singers. Again my best wishes to you and the illustrious professor."

From New York Tito Gobbi, Ferruccio Tagliavini and Pia Tassinari sent their best wishes. Giambattista Meneghini, Herbert von Karajan, and Margherita Wallmann were among the many who sent telegrams. The last-named wired her as follows: "Remembering you today with the greatest admiration I want to thank for your artistic collaboration, which was always wonderful, and which many times consoled me in my tiresome work and increased the success of my management. I embrace you and wish you unlimited happiness."

Giorgio Gualerzi showed his affection and admiration for Simionato with these words: "The moment you made your decision to retire from the stage the Italian lyric theater, the entire opera world lost a great singer and an exquisite interpreter, one of the most authoritative of the last thirty years, as well as a true, irreproachable professional. Please accept my grateful and deferential homage as one who has repeatedly had the pleasure of following your career. While expressing my ardent hope that our opera theater will not be deprived of the precious assistance of your thirty years of experience, I want to thank you for the unforgettable emotions you were able to give me and assure you that your interpretations of *Anna Bolena*, *Gli Ugonotti*, *Mignon*, *Cenerentola* remain as memorable occasions of a renewed golden age of melodrama."

A little later Magda Olivero sent the following letter: "Your memory and the memory of your art is in my heart. Nothing and no one will ever be able to blur the thought of your unsurpassable grandeur. You will also remain a luminous example for your iron discipline and sense of duty toward the theater. May God grant you as much happiness as you have given to suffering humanity."

Lawrence Kelly, director of the Dallas Civic Opera, wrote: "Only two lines to tell you how beautiful you are and how sad you made us with your retirement."

Massimo Bogianckino, artistic director of the Rome Opera, sent this affectionate farewell: "Your decision to end one of the most brilliant careers of these last years in the history of our opera is a cause of great regret for all of us. For myself and for all those here at the theater I warmly wish you every possible happiness."

More tributes are not necessary here to show the general and unconditional nature of esteem for Giulietta and her contributions as an artist.

In 1980 Giulietta returned to La Scala on another mission: as a "technical consultant." She gave master classes in singing (and I had the good fortune of attending such a class in March of 1986). More than actually teaching young people she tries to direct them towards a path that they will follow on their own, in the manner of someone directing traffic who can indicate the way without taking one by the hand. According to Simionato (and this was also true of Callas) you can guide someone to singing, you can educate them, but you cannot teach them to sing. With her "technical consultations" Giulietta enjoys offering the fruits of all her years of experience, and of giving, as she puts it, some direction, and in particular, lessons in life. She follows her students with all possible attention, and she intervenes by singing whenever she has to correct the defects of a mezzo-soprano/contralto; but she avoids facing the high-soprano register, remembering a tragic episode involving her husband's first wife in 1973. Adriana De Angeli (a good friend of Giulietta's), though 63 years old, was taking singing lessons for pleasure. One day in class she forced herself excessively in order to sing an aria with a rather high tessitura. Having returned home she retired to her room where a few minutes later she was joined by her husband, who was surprised not to have heard any sign of her presence. He actually found her lying lifeless on the bed. The strain of her singing had provoked a major cerebral hemorrhage.

On the 6th of May, 1986, the "Friends of La Scala" celebrated the fiftieth anniversary of Simionato's debut in *Suor Angelica* in the same theater. Visibly moved, she was surrounded by Wally Toscanini, Leyla Gencer, Giuseppe Di Stefano, Marcella Pobbe, Giampiero Tintori, Alberto Litta Modignani, Filippo Crivelli, Rina Malatrasi, Nandi Ostali and Benedetto Austoni and many other past and present fans.

Without giving a prepared speech Giulietta only delivered a few words of thanks.[230] Afterwards she informed the press that, far from Milan, a Parisian university professor was preparing her biography.[231]

Nine years later (May 12th, 1995), again at La Scala, another ceremony took place to celebrate Simionato's 85th birthday with the mayor of Milan and the Superintendent of La Scala attending. In "her" theater Giulietta is still remembered with great affection.

It would be useless to expatiate on Giulietta Simionato's role in Milanese cultural life. However, one episode stands out. On February 14, 1982, Giulietta was asked by the late Maestro Siciliani to try to placate the fury of the La Scala audience which was reacting furiously to the announcement, just prior to the premiere of a revival of *Anna Bolena*, that Montserrat Caballé would be unable to go on. This was the deluxe production of Nicola Benois and Luchino Visconti in which Giulietta herself had obtained one of her most brilliant personal successes. The fact that La Simionato was called upon to intervene was therefore appropriately symbolic.[232]

[1] In the article "La carriera su misura." ("The made-to-order career.")
[2] October 3, 1947.
[3-11] Id.
[12] In the article "Il pubblico la conosce come Giulietta," published in "Oggi."
[13] In: "Opera," February 1964, p. 87 ff. (in English).
[14] Cf. Mario Morini, "La storia di Giulietta Simionato assomiglia a quella di Cenerentola," in: "Libertà" December 14, 1955, and "A Wiesbaden la chiamarono 66 volte alla ribalta," in "Orizzonte," January 22, 1956.
[15] March 4, 1948.
[16-22] Id.
[23] March 6, 1949.
[24] Id.
[25] March 31, 1949.
[26] Id.
[27] April 9, 1950.
[28-29] Id.
[30] In "Italia," April 9, 1950.
[31] In "Il Corriere della Sera," id.
[32] April 17, 1950.
[33] In "L'Avanti," id.
[34] "Candido," April 29, 1951.
[35] April 19, 1951.
[36] Id.
[37] "Il Corriere della Sera," id.
[38-42] April 19, 1951.
[43] In "Il Tempo di Milano," April 25, 1952.
[44-49] April 25, 1951.
[50] March 5, 1953
[51-52] Id.
[53] In "Il Corriere Lombardo," March 15, 1954.
[54] In "Il Tempo di Milano," March 16, 1954.
[55-56] March 15, 1954.
[57] March 16, 1954.
[58] In "Il Corriere della Sera," May 26, 1954.
[59] In "Il Resto di Carlino," id.
[60] January 19-20, 1955.
[61] See his contribution in the chapter "Tributes."
[62] January 19-20, 1955.
[63] In *Enciclopedia dello spettacolo - voce Giulietta Simionato.*
[64] Carlo Marinelli, *Opere in disco*, Florence, 1982, p. 272.
[65] May 18, 1955.
[66] Op. cit., p. 448.
[67] May 11, 1955.
[68] In "Il Corriere d'Informazione," id.
[69-71] May 11, 1955.
[72] December 8, 1955.
[73-77] Id.
[78] In "Il Corriere d'Informazione," id.

[79] Giuseppe Barigazzi, *La Scala racconta*, Rizzoli, Milano, 1991, p. 571.
[80] Id.
[81] May 9, 1956.
[82-84] Id.
[85] In "Il Corriere d'Informazione," id.
[86] May 9, 1956.
[87] In "La Notte," id.
[88] May 20, 1956.
[89] In "Il Corriere della Sera," December 8, 1956.
[90] In "Il Corriere d'Informazione," id.
[91] In "Italia," id.
[92] In "L'Unità," id.
[93] In "Il Popolo di Milano," id.
[94] December 8, 1956.
[95] In "L'Espresso," December 16, 1956.
[96] In "Il Corriere della Sera," December 11, 1956.
[97] December 11, 1956.
[98] December 8, 1957.
[99-102] Id.
[103] December 16, 1957.
[104] "Giulietta Simionato, artista di classe e autentico fenomeno vocale," in "Musica e dischi," July 1958.
[105] Cf. the chapter "Tributes."
[106] April 15, 1957.
[107] Id.
[108] April 16, 1957.
[109] In "Settimo Giorno," April 27, 1957.
[110] In "Il Corriere d'Informazione," April 15, 1957.
[111] April 15, 1957.
[112] Id.
[113] In the *Enciclopedia dello spettacolo*, op. cit.
[114] April 10, 1958.
[115] Id.
[116] In "La Notte," id.
[117-118] April 10, 1958.
[119] Interview with Franco Attardi in the "Rivista Musicale Curci," September/December 1981.
[120] Cf. the chapter "Tributes."
[121] January 6, 1958.
[122-125] Id.
[126] In "Il Giorno," January 5, 1958.
[127] January 6, 1958.
[128] Id.
[129] January 23, 1958.
[130-133] Id.
[134] June 2, 1958.
[135] In "Il Giorno," id.
[136-137] June 2, 1958.

[138] Of July 9, 1958.
[139-140] Id.
[141] December 19, 1958.
[142] Id.
[143] In "Il Corriere d'Informazione," id.
[144] April 10, 1959.
[145] In "Il Corriere Lombardo," id.
[146] In "Il Corriere d'Informazione," id.
[147] April 10, 1959.
[148] "Così il Vice" in "Il Corriere Lombardo," May 12, 1959.
[149-150] May 12, 1959.
[151] In "L'Unità," id.
[152] 6-7 June, 1959.
[153] *The Last Prima Donnas*, Alfred Knopf, New York, 1982, p. 382.
[154] July 22, 1959.
[155] In "La Notte," February 2, 1960.
[156] February 2, 1960.
[157] In "Il Corriere d'Informazione," id.
[158] February 14, 1960.
[159] April 15, 1960.
[160] In "Il Corriere d'Informazione," id.
[161] Alceo Toni in "La Notte," id.
[162] Riccardo Malipiero in "Il Corriere Lombardo," id.
[163] April 15, 1960.
[164] In "Italia," May 28, 1960.
[165] Alceo Toni in "La Notte," id.
[166] May 28. 1960.
[167] In "Il Corriere d'Informazione," December 15, 1960.
[168] December 15, 1960.
[169] In "Il Corriere della Sera," id.
[170] December 15, 1960.
[171] In "L'Epoca," December 25, 1960.
[172] December 25, 1960.
[173] In "La Notte," January 11, 1961.
[174] In "Il Corriere d'Informazione," April 6, 1961.
[175-176] April 6, 1961.
[177] In "Il Corriere della Sera," id.
[178] Both reports are dated April 6, 1961 (in "L'Unità," signed G.M.).
[179] Riccardo Malipiero in "Il Corriere Lombardo," id.
[180] In "Il Corriere della Sera," December 12, 1961.
[181] December 12, 1961.
[182] In "Il Tempo," id.
[183] In "L'Avanti," id.
[184] In "L'Epoca," December 31, 1961.
[185] December 12, 1961.
[186] Callas hadn't sung for a year at La Scala and this performance constituted both her return to that great Milanese theater and her farewell.
[187] In "Il Corriere Lombardo," id.

[188] In "L'Unità," id.
[189] May 15, 1962.
[190-195] Id.
[196] In the liner notes of the Fonit Cetra CD case of "Documenti."
[197] According to Henry Wisneski, Maria Callas had refused it (cf. the book cited in the following chapter).
[198] May 29, 1962.
[199] Id.
[200] Franco Abbiati in "Il Corriere della Sera," December 15, 1962.
[201] December 15, 1962.
[202] In "Oggi," December 27, 1962.
[203] A.F. in "Il Sole," December 19, 1962 - see also Beniamino Dal Fabbro in "Il Giorno," December 18, 1962.
[204] In "L'Europeo," December 30, 1962.
[205] December 18, 1962.
[206] Giacomo Manzoni, in "L'Unità," December 8, 1963.
[207] Piero Santi in "L'Avanti," id.
[208] In "Il Corriere della Sera," id.
[209] In "Il Giorno," id.
[210] In "Il Corriere Lombardo," December 9/10, 1963.
[211] In "La Notte," id.
[212] March 18, 1964.
[213] In "Il Corriere d'Informazione," id.
[214] In "Il Corriere Lombardo," id.
[215] March 29, 1964: "Miss Cenerentola ha vinto anche l'ultimo Festival!" (Miss Cinderella has also been the hit of the last ball!")
[216] Unfortunately without a sound track.
[217] In "L'Avanti," January 10, 1965.
[218] January 11, 1965.
[219] January 10, 1065.
[220] Id.
[221] January 11, 1965.
[222-223] Id.
[224] December 8, 1965.
[225] "Il Corriere d'Informazione," 8-9 December, 1965.
[226] 25-26 January, 1966.
[227] Cf., among other, the article of G.P.T. (Gian Piero Tintori?) in the "Gazzetta del Popolo," February 1, 1966: "Oggi Giulietta Simionato dà il suo addio alle scene"; and the article in the "Stampa," February 2, 1966: "Feste alla Simionato per l'addio alla Scala."
[228] *Quella sera all Scala*, Rusconi, Milan, 1983, p. 126.
[229] Op. cit., p. 126 and 127.
[230] Cf. "Il Corriere della Sera," May 8, 1986, and the "Giornale," May 7, 1986.
[231] In "Il Giorno," May 8, 1986.
[232] This episode was quoted in Robert Pullen's and Stephen Taylor's fine book, *Montserrat Caballé, "Casta Diva,"* Victor Gollancz, London, 1994, p. 253.

4

– *Around the World* –

As we have already observed, Simionato's international career began in 1945 in Geneva when she had her first real recognition in performances of *Così fan tutte.* The beginnings of that international career are really evident in 1947, a year in which she took the part of Mignon in Genoa and then at La Scala, then participated in the one hundredth anniversary of the opening of the Teatro Liceo in Barcelona and not long after sang Cherubino at the Glyndebourne Festival. An encyclopedia could not encompass her appearances in Italy and abroad between 1947 and 1966. In the space allowed we will attempt to chronicle only the highlights of that singular career.

In 1947 the centennial season of the Gran Teatro del Liceo of Barcelona was celebrated with great pomp. Napoleone Annovazzi, artistic director of the Liceo at the time, signed La Simionato — in addition to La Scuderi, La Caniglia, La Stignani, La Pederzini, La Rovero, Cesare Siepi, Gianni Poggi, Antonio Annaloro and many other Spanish artists — for appearances in productions of *Falstaff*, *La forza del destino*, *Marta* and, for the first time, *Anna Bolena*. These appearances began only a month after her La Scala *Mignon*. Besides, she had to substitute for Ebe Stignani, who had developed bronchitis and could not go on as Azucena in *Il trovatore*. (We will discuss this episode later.)

A long time afterward Annovazzi confessed to his wife his astonishment that La Scala had cast Simionato in second roles for such a long time — when "with that splendid voice" she had been able to take on the most important principal roles in other great theaters.

Among the performances of Simionato on the great Catalan stage, her singing in *Anna Bolena* along with Cesare Siepi received a very special critical welcome. In the *Vanguardia*[1] one could have read "Giulietta Simionato was very good. Her dramatic temperament and her singing, full of expression, gave the part of Jane Seymour a unique dimension." And in the *Correo Catalan*[2] that: "this mezzo-soprano, always displaying impeccable artistry, gave the performance a distinctive touch very adequate to the opera's lyricism." Yet in spite of these highly laudatory judgments, which were comparable to what Cesare Siepi remembers of her performances (see the testimonials in the last chapter of this book), these performances didn't generate the same resonance as those Giulietta gave in 1957 and 1958.

We can see why in reading the fine book by Roger Alier i Aixalà and Francesc M. Nata, *El Gran Teatro del Liceo (Historia Artistica.)*[3] Whereas Giulietta was singing a part that was perfectly suited to her voice, being "in the early stages of a glorious career," the critical establishment was reticent because they were ignorant of the Donizetti opera. Quite simply, there was no recording of it available at the time which would have better enabled them to explore it. One Catalan critic even wrote that Anna Bolena should be left in peace according to the Latin formula, R.I.P.! Incredible, but true. A dim understanding of Donizetti's masterpiece on the part of public and critics alike was, in our opinion, responsible for the fact that Giulietta's 1947 *Anna Bolena* didn't start people talking the way her La Scala performances did ten years later.

In November of 1948 Giulietta sang Marina in *Boris Godunov* for three performances in Bologna with Nicola Rossi Lemeni, who was much appreciated by the Bolognese critics in the title role. After lauding the bass the reviewer in *Emilia*[4] made particular note of Simionato's contribution as Marina.

In June of 1949 Giulietta made a disastrous trip to Mexico City. She was still bound by her relationship to Carenzio, who had a mortal fear of flying, so that she was constrained to take a train to Cerbères in France, and from there to embark on the Queen Mary for New York, and once there, to take yet another train all the way to her final destination, which she reached in a state of exhaustion.

When she arrived in Mexico City Giulietta suffered from the altitude. Trying her voice for the first time she realized that she lacked enough breath to sing. This was precisely why the directors of the Palacio de Bellas Artes had insisted that the singers arrive in the Mexican capital a week prior to the beginning of rehearsals in order to acclimate themselves. Simionato realized very quickly that management had set down their rules for a good reason!

During that season she was singing with Giuseppe Di Stefano, at the time a newlywed who was insufficiently prepared in *Mignon, Barbiere, Favorita, Werther.* In *Favorita* Di Stefano had such difficulty that Giulietta turned her back on the audience to try to feed him the right words. Yet the great tenor had such a pronounced musical sense that, his scant knowledge of the libretto notwithstanding, he was able to reconcile words and music perfectly.

The day after the Mexico City premiere of *La favorita* (July 12th, 1949) the Italian ambassador arranged a meeting with Simionato to congratulate her on "the exceptional quality" of her singing. In a letter dated 14 July he wrote: "You sang with the exceptional skill which everyone by now acknowledges; but there was something unforgettable in your performance the other night besides talent and skill, something that moved me deeply. I felt the responsibility you had undertaken to make everything you could of your difficult role. You wanted to present to your public here a perfect example of Italian vocal tradition, and in this you succeeded perfectly. In doing honor to the art of singing you have also brought honor to your country. Thank you, dear lady, for what you have given the Italian community here. Please accept my best and sincere good wishes for the future and the future of your art."

In Mexico her audience's acclaim reached such heights that it could only be called fanaticism. Carlos Diaz Du Pond, remembering her debut in the Mexican capital, described her as "tiny, winning and an amazing singing actress."[5] In the part of Mignon (June 28th, 1949) she had such "an enormous success," that it was necessary to add a third performance to the schedule.

Back in Italy Giulietta sang Santuzza at the Augustus Theater in Genoa (September 8th, 1949) where the public welcomed her with an enthusiastic tribute, mindful of her *Mignon* in 1947 and of her recent *Forza del destino* and *Adriana Lecouvreur*. In the journal *Secolo XIX* the composer Vittorio Rieti spoke thus of the Mascagni's heroine: "Giulietta Simionato has obtained the warmest sort of personal success with *Cavalleria rusticana*, which establishes yet again the personality of this singer, who has been so richly endowed, who is so intense yet measured and thoughtful in her expression, so supple in her excitement and rich in sound. This was a Santuzza that was vocally perfect in accent, phrasing, and vocal finish, and most effective theatrically thanks to an intuitive and experiential coherence that one seldom hears."[6]

On the 28th of January, 1950, at the Teatro Grande in Brescia, Giulietta took the part of Carmen opposite Mario Del Monaco, her favorite Don José, in a cast which included Rosetta Noli and Raimondo Torres. This version of Bizet's masterpiece excited the Brescian public's enthusiasm and the interpretation of the title part was highly praised by critics. "The centerpiece of last night's acclaimed production was the mezzo Giulietta Simionato. Those fortunate enough to remember her *Mignon* from last year will have noted with satisfaction last night that this young interpreter has chosen her role intelligently and given us a Carmen full of zest: insinuating, provocative, mocking, tender and dramatic, adapting her superlative vocal equipment to all these aspects of her high-spirited character."[7]

Two months afterwards Simionato went to Cagliari, where on March 19, 1950, she sang Fidalma in *Matrimonio segreto* at the Teatro Massimo. Another great success. We quote the review that appeared in Cagliari's *L'Unione Sarda*:[8] "Spice was not missing. Tullio Serafin was the agile animator of the very successful performance, and we certainly must not neglect to mention the six singers, of whom we could not have expected anything better. The trio of women (Giulietta Simionato, Elena Arizmendi and Ornella Rovero), whether chirping away or singing passionately, was coordinated to resemble an aunt and daughters from the same family. The same goes for the male trio (Vito de Taranto, Boris Christoff, Cesare Valletti)..."

April 1950 found La Simionato in Brussels celebrating the 250th anniversary of the Théâtre Royal de la Monnaie with La Scala's touring company. Three extraordinary performances were given by a company which included not only Simionato but Mariano Stabile, Sesto Bruscantini, Marco Stefanoni, Cesare Valletti, Afro Poli, Giuseppe Nessi, Alda Noni, Ornella Rovero, Anna Maria Canali and the conductor Mario Rossi. In the first night's performance Simionato took the part of Fidalma in *Il matrimonio segreto*, which she had interpreted many times before in preceding years. Queen Elisabeth was in the audience.

The critic of *Libre Belgique*[9] was moved to say: "The warmly-timbred, steady and flexible voice of Signora Simionato amazed us." His colleague Paul Timel went on to say: "Finally we hear a true mezzo-soprano! The fine metal in her voice resonates superbly in the part of Fidalma, Geronimo's sister." In the same year she recorded this opera with the above cast under the direction of Maestro Wolf Ferrari. In speaking of this recording Rodolfo Celletti proclaimed Simionato "a splendid Fidalma, not only for the quality of her voice but for her vocal line,"[10] and Carlo Marinelli said that "Simionato is an all but incomparable Fidalma. Her mature vocal agility is completely at the service of youthful hopes and expectations."[11]

Less than a month after her success in Brussels Giulietta returned to Mexico with La Callas, which whom she would sing in *Norma*, *Aida*, and *Trovatore*[12] (her other operas there were *Cavalleria*, *Falstaff*, *Carmen* and *Fedora*). On the way she and Callas stopped off in New York where Callas wanted to pay her parents a visit. Only her father came to meet them at the airport because her mother had been hospitalized for an eye operation. At her house Callas offered Giulietta a glass of 7up. No one suspected that the bottle contained roach poison that Callas's mother had prepared before her hospital visit. Simionato became desperately ill. Callas's father, a pharmacist, immediately understood what had happened, but he didn't think of remedying the understandable mistake with the administration of an antidote specific to this type of poisoning, with some milk at least, and instead made her drink some water, which worsened her condition.[13]

During their stay in Mexico the two singers spent a lot of time together. Giulietta remembers Callas's eccentric way of dressing and some episodes involving her that were most amusing. Giulietta herself was no longer as serious and sad as she had been the year before, but rather a vivacious and rejuvenated young woman — as Diaz Du Pond has remembered her.[14]

Callas wasn't hiding her contempt for the tenor Kurt Baum, who reciprocated her feelings, being jealous of her ability. At the general rehearsal of *Norma* the soprano did in fact demonstrate a perfect knowledge of the opera while the tenor, who was singing Pollione for the first time, was obliged to refer to the score in his hands almost continually.[15] Their mutual hatred found expression at every opportunity. For example, in the third act of *Aida* Baum, out of spite, put his foot on the train of the long cloak the soprano was wearing in such a way that she couldn't move freely. While this opera was still in rehearsal the house manager, Carazza Campos, was asking Callas to sing an interpolated E above high C in the concertante, as La Peralta, the celebrated "Mexican nightingale," had done. La Callas maintained that the insertion of such a note would be in very poor taste, which would certainly displease Maestro Serafin. However, given the insistence of the house manager and the opportunity to cause Baum some displeasure, she decided to deliver the famous high E. And it was a huge success!

The rest of our artists' stay of about two months in Mexico was not without incident. One day, after having eaten some tropical fruit, they gave signs of not feeling well, especially during the great duet in *Norma*, and their malaise didn't pass unnoticed. Henry Wisneski (a reviewer for one of the city's leading dailies) commented: "Although the Norma-Adalgisa duets were well sung, neither Callas nor Simionato was at her best on the first night, which was carried on the radio."[16]

There were further complications when La Callas received a visit from her mother who was asking her to let her sister Jackie have some of the jewelry that Meneghini had given her. Fortunately the visit didn't last long (it was during the time that

Cavalleria and *Trovatore* were being performed) because the mother and daughter quarreled the whole time.

During this period La Callas and La Simionato were sharing a small apartment which had become practically submerged by flowers their wellwishers had sent them. Giulietta took care of them, and since she was suffering from insomnia, spent her nights reading and writing. Callas on the other hand, in a communicating room, did nothing but sleep.

In the 1950 season Callas's contract provided for five operas, *La traviata* among them. However, she refused to sing the role of Violetta, claiming that she had not been sufficiently prepared. As an alternative the Palacio de Bellas Artes announced *Cavalleria rusticana*, with Giulietta Simionato and Mario Filippeschi in the part of Turiddu. There was a technical mishap during the first performance when the electric organ was short-circuited by a passing tram.[17] And the problems didn't stop there. In *Falstaff* Leonard Warren and Maestro Cellini were so demanding that some other artists, and among them La Simionato, were quite upset. According to Diaz Du Pond, moreover, Giulietta did not please the public in *Carmen*, but she did have a real triumph in *Fedora*, in which she helped Diaz Du Pond with the production (he was substituting for Désiré Defrère).[18]

In September of 1950 Giulietta played the role of Cherubino in *Le nozze di Figaro*, performed at the Teatro Donizetti in Bergamo. *Il Giornale del Popolo* wrote that she had "delivered a Cherubino of unsurpassable vivacity, which was beautifully true to Mozart."

A short time afterward, in November of 1950, Giulietta took part in two performances of *Il matrimonio segreto* at the Municipal Theater of Lausanne; this was her last appearance with Marisa Morel's company. The first performance took place on the 8th of November. Just as the train that was transporting the company to Switzerland approached the border Angelo Mercuriali suddenly realized that he had forgotten his passport in Milan and it was feared that the cast was about to lose its Paolino. But the tenor made a rapid round trip and the full cast amazed their audience in Lausanne. The critic of the *Nouvelle Revue de Lausanne*[19] observed that this was nothing less than a cast of the very highest order, the like of which had rarely been seen in that city. In his words Giulietta revealed "a contralto voice of great fullness, and a comic sense of the highest quality. Quite simply, Signora Simionato was perfect."

On December 10, 1950, Giulietta returned to the Teatro Liceo of Barcelona for *Carmen*. The management was very nervous and let Simionato know that the success of this *Carmen* depended on her: if the production of this opera was not successful, it would never be mounted again, at least not at the Liceo! They also stipulated some particulars regarding costumes, refusing to allow Giulietta to use her personal wardrobe. In spite of their concerns everything went smoothly and in the *Correo Catalan* the following review appeared: "Giulietta Simionato, as the central character, was nervy and confident, displaying a magnificant mezzo-soprano voice which, in the lower register, proved to be opulent and vibrant."[20]

In their history of the Liceo, Alier i Aixalà and Francesc M. Nata relate that Simionato was "a spectacular leading lady."[21]

In May of 1952 La Simionato attended the Maggio Musicale Fiorentino singing three Rossini operas one after the other, all of which had to be learned in a very short time: *Il Conte Ory* (May 10), *Tancredi* (May 17) and *La Pietra del paragone* (May 29). Of the second opera the music reviewer Leonardo Pinzauti wrote that "La Simionato in her trouser role was obviously wonderful."[22]

On December 13, 1952, Jules Massenet's *Don Quichotte* was mounted for the first time in Bologna with Italo Tajo in the title role as Cervantes' hero and with Giulietta as his Dulcinea. The audience much appreciated her interpretation and the critic for *Emilia* had this to say: "Once again La Simionato, in the part of Dulcinea, makes us admire her for her well-known vocal quality as well as her elegance onstage."[23]

In April of 1953 La Simionato went to Lisbon for the first time, where she had been signed to sing *Don Quichotte* and *Sansone e Dalila* at the São Carlo. This is what the *Diario de Noticias* said about the *Don Quichotte*:[24] "Giulietta Simionato was Dulcinea and was notable as a singer with an ample and beautiful voice. She will remain in the audience's memory forever." In *Sansone* she was considered "an incomparable voice which imposed itself by singing with a good volume and expression."[25]

In June 1953 Giulietta and Callas sang together again at Covent Garden as participants in the ceremonies surround the coronation of Queen Elizabeth II. Three operas were scheduled and the first was *Aida*. Ramón Vinay (who ought to have been taking the part of Radames) was replaced by the tenor Baum, who would have to confront Callas again. As for Giulietta, she had her share of rave reviews: "A moving Amneris, and a vocally splendid one, certainly one of the best to be heard in London until now."[26]

The reprise of *Norma*, in which Callas had Simionato as a kind of rival (Ebe Stignani had been the Adalgisa in the preceding autumn's version of the opera) was considered by the British press the main attraction of the season. In the *Daily Mail*[27] Stanley Bayliss wrote: "We were fortunate... to have Maria Meneghini Callas in the title-rôle and Giulietta Simionato as Adalgisa. Both were in good form and provoked tremendous enthusiasm." Andrew Smith in the *Daily Herald*[28] praised the quality of Simionato's acting and the "devastating depth" of her voice. The critic of the *Evening News* further defined her voice as having an "exquisitely melting quality which she uses with a sure appreciation of Bellini's melodic design."[29] The *News Chronicle* noted "the pure, round tone and flawless production of the contralto, Giulietta Simionato,"[30] and *The Star* described: "...a great personal triumph for Maria Meneghini Callas and Giulietta Simionato. Their perfect sympathy in the duets brought them prolonged cheers and a dozen curtain calls after the first scene of the second act."[31] In the *Daily Express*[32] Andrew Porter noted that Giulietta had "scored a few points over her rival — for distinctness in one or two rapid passages." In the *Manchester Guardian*[33] Philip Hope-Wallace didn't hesitate to say that "the Adalgisa (Mme. Simionato) has a much more naturally beautiful voice" than Callas's, while the critic for the *Times* heard "a voice of expressive color, but her singing is marred by too wide and slow a vibrato — especially in the quieter passages, which is unusual. It has the darker shades of mezzo-soprano tone as well as brilliance at the top of a big compass. The two voices were well attuned in the florid duets."[34] The *Observer*[35] felt that Giulietta was truly a noteworthy artist even though she hadn't achieved the sovereign authority of Ebe Stignani.

Il trovatore was the final presentation of the season. Michael Langdon was the Ferrando in the premiere but a sore throat forced him to bow out of the succeeding performances and he was replaced at the last minute by Giuseppe Modesti. According to contemporary reports the mood of the cast during these performances was not good. In fact, according to Cecil Smith (of the *Daily Express)*[36] Callas was irritated with the conductor, whom she considered to be of mediocre ability, and was displeased with the production as a whole. In *Musical Opinion* one might read that the tension between the performers was in danger of becoming a contagion that would infect the public, and that Maestro Erede gave the impression of conducting a sort of battle with orchestra members. Indeed the entire production was compromised and a number of critics did not hesitate to point this out. As for the Azucena of La Simionato, it was felt to be "restrained, almost entirely undemonstrative... a curiously detached performance" (*Musical Opinion*),[37] or even "tentative and unsteady," at least in the first scene (*Times*),[38] while in "Stride la vampa" her voice seemed to Desmond Shawe Taylor, writing in the *New Statesman and Nation* to be "cruelly exposed."[39]

Yet a number of other critics were more complimentary. In the *Star* one might have read how "rarely has London heard a better Azucena than Giulietta Simionato. Her tone in the more heavily dramatic passages was never forced and in the dungeon scene she sang with memorable delicacy and sweetness,"[40] a judgment in which the critics of *News of the World*[41] and the *South Wales Argus*[42] fully concurred. But in *Opera* Cecil Smith wrote that the role didn't seem completely congenial to Simionato, although the artist had known how to invest it with the greatest musicality and stage presence.[43]

Giulietta debuted in the United States on September 19, 1953, singing *Werther* in San Francisco, followed by *Boris Godunov* and *Il barbiere di Siviglia*. Afterwards she also took part in a tour with the San Francisco company to Sacramento, Los Angeles and San Diego. She was also supposed to sing in *Carmen*, which was instead sung by Claramae Turner. In his history of the San Francisco Opera Arthur Bloomfield wrote that "Simionato's talents were brilliantly used in the Rossini opera, which was sung in the original mezzo key. The virtuosity of her fioritura, which were executed very cleanly, as well as her stage presence, made a wonderful impression."[44]

In April 1954 Giulietta returned to Lisbon with a pleasing program: *Nozze di Figaro, Don Quichotte, Don Carlo* and *Mignon*. The audience of the Portuguese capitol reserved a warm welcome for her which was reflected in newspaper reviews. Of her interpretation of Cherubino the *Diario de Noticias* wrote[45] that Simionato was "truly remarkable. We liked her very much for her generous voice and her skill in using it. She highlights the words and gives great expression to her phrases." Of *Don Quichotte* the Lisbon paper said that "Giulietta Simionato had another opportunity to show her classy talent and her total mastery of the role, enchanting the audience thanks to her voice and her perfect school."[46] Simionato's performance of Princess Eboli was greeted with yet another laudatory review: "She was magisterial from the first to the last scene. Her rich vocal quality (color, volume and emission) was accompanied by a perfect style. The audience applauded warmly and at length."[47] The last role Simionato took on in Lisbon was her warhorse, *Mignon*. The review in the *Diario de Noticias* read as follows: "In the title role Giulietta Simionato was extraordinary both from a vocal and a dramatic standpoint. She was able to give value to all the resources of her very rich voice, of her singing art and of her dramatic rendering. Without ceasing to be a very great singer of the Italian school she was able to imbue the tunes of Ambroise Thomas with French atmosphere. She achieved a great success and gained enthusiastic and prolonged applause."[48]

On June 30, 1954, in the context of the Holland Festival, Simionato played the role of Cenerentola in two performances. (Two more performances took place in Amsterdam.) In the *Dagblad Haagsch*[49] the review spoke of an enchanting performance and qualified the artist as "truly unique." His colleague of *Het Vrije Volk*[50] wrote that "among the solo singers Giulietta

Simionato was, as the main character, the revelation of the day. What a deliciously golden sound, dark but not gloomy, and what a sparkling stream of vivacity for such a low voice. With her performance, simple and musical, even simpler in the action and of convincing finesse, her creation of this character is admirable in all of its aspects." In the *Het Vaderland*[51] the local reviewer came up with the following words of praise: "As for the rest, the Dutch reviewers are left speechless. We would not know how to describe Simionato's voice. There is only one of them in the world, and there is nothing it could be compared to. What can we say of its frankly unique, fantastic and perfect timbre, of its lightness and vivacity, of the beams of silver light in its upper register and the organ tones in its lower?"

At the end of the month of October 1954 Giulietta returned to Mexico where she was to sing *Mignon* and *Werther.* In the words of Diaz Du Pond, her Mignon was "absolutely extraordinary."[52] He did not hesitate to qualify Simionato as "one of the greatest mezzos of the century."[53] Alongside Simionato, Gianni Raimondi was making his Mexican debut, while Ernestina Garfias was interpreting the part of Filina for the first time. After two performances — and then a third, gratis, to benefit the employees and workers of regional industry, under the aegis of the *Comité de Opera de Monterrey*) she had to get *Werther* ready. Giuseppe Di Stefano did not attend a single rehearsal while Giulietta didn't miss one, as Diaz Du Pond recalls in his history of the Teatro di Monterrey.[54] He has left us a very picturesque record of one episode:[55]

"Di Stefano had become a great friend of Dr. Fumagallo. In the afternoon he and the good doctor would go off to the beautiful spots outside of town and he was never present for the rehearsals of *Werther*, which was the next opera on the schedule that season. Giulietta was enraged with Pippo for his lack of responsibility, being herself quite a scrupulous professional. When it was almost time for the performance there was considerable anxiety among those in attendance, since the audience was aware of the successes the two artists had enjoyed in Mexico. They got through the first act with ease... Except that Humberto Pazos, who was playing Charlotte's father, without thinking of the consequences, closed the door of the onstage house so that Giulietta was unable to enter. When I saw what had happened I ran under the stage, but it was too late! The curtain fell and La Simionato remained alone on the stage. She was furious about this.

"Along came the second act wherein Di Stefano, in the middle of Werther's beautiful *romanza*, stopped singing and went behind the scenery, saying to me: "With an orchestra like that, this is impossible! I'm going home!" Morelli, who was the Alberto, and Betty Fabila, who was playing Sofia, stood dumbfounded. I yelled at them: 'Go onstage and continue! You can't leave the stage empty!' Poor Maestro Picco stopped the orchestra and waited. Some anxious minutes went by, during which Signora Simionato ran the risk of a nervous breakdown. Finally I convinced Pippo, who gave an explanation to the maestro in Italian, which only they could understand. Then he sang the romance and the performance resumed.

"When the third act came along, Simionato sang the letter aria magnificently, then an exquisite '*delle lacrime.*' I was very moved, but the public didn't applaud, and this was natural, because they weren't crowd-pleasing arias. Then Pippo came on to sing '*Pourquoi me réveiller*' and was obliged to repeat it. Finally the moment for the final duet arrived and Simionato practically had to sing it solo because Pippo, whether it was because he was nervous or because he'd missed so many rehearsals, was letting whole phrases go by without singing. When the curtain fell Simionato went into hysterics, and it was the real thing this time: she began to cry and scream, picking up books from the table, props of all kinds, and flinging them every which way. Di Stefano went to his dressing room and neither of the two went onstage to accept the frenetic applause of the audience, completely ignorant of everything that happened.

"The next day Simionato came to lunch with me, asked to be excused, and, charming as usual, left for New York."

Simionato's sensitivity and professionalism explain her reaction, which wasn't surprising!

For the first season of opera organized at the Teatro Degollado in Guadalajara the management would have liked to ensure the collaboration of Giulietta Simionato and Giuseppe Di Stefano, but they were already engaged in Monterrey, so this dream could not become a reality.[56]

In the 1954-55 season Giulietta was signed by Rudolf Bing for the Metropolitan Opera in New York. Among other operas she was to appear in *Orfeo* under the direction of Pierre Monteux. A serious form of exhaustion prevented her from accepting this engagement.[57] (Gluck's masterpiece went onstage February 24, 1955 with Risë Stevens as Orfeo.) As a consequence Rudolf Bing, not persuaded of the seriousness of Simionato's reasons, punished her by not including her on the roster until 1959. Nevertheless, in one of her first appearances in the United States, at the Lyric Opera of Chicago in 1954, Simionato, as Adalgisa, had obtained a greater success than Callas, proving herself to have the sort of discipline, fire and vivacity that would arouse public enthusiasm, according to the account of the American critic Irving Kolodin.[58]

In April of 1955 Giulietta was back at the São Carlos in Lisbon for *Cenerentola* and *Carmen.* She was written up as an exceptional performer in the first-named opera. "She sang and acted in such a spontaneous manner, and seemed so at ease, that the role's most difficult parts sounded as if they had been improvised."[59] As Bizet's heroine she "emphasized all her qualities as singer and actress, conveying everything required from the point of view of musicality and absolute mastery to a role already enacted by many famous singers since 1875. We won't quote any scene in particular, as Simionato defined the part with perfect unity."[60]

In July of 1955 the artist returned to Verona to sing in *Carmen.* The arena was packed (the papers there were talking about more than 20,000 people). When a thunderstorm came on near the middle of the second act Giulietta continued interpreting her part, until the persistence of bad weather would not oblige her to follow the example of so many — artists, orchestra members, and the public — who had felt it necessary to abandon the arena. The confusion was such that three ladies, crushed by the crowd, passed out. A little later, when the weather had cleared a little, the performance resumed, Carmen concluded her dance and Mario Del Monaco sang the famous Flower Song, to the satisfaction of the very large number of spectators who had been waiting for the opera to conclude.[61]

The critic of *L'Arena*[62] wrote that "Giulietta Simionato literally dominated the stage, offering a furiously energetic rendition of Bizet's character; with her singing and dancing she showed herself to be a complete artist from every point of view thanks to her exceptional and thorough experience."

A little later the Simionato-Del Monaco couple were the principals at the inauguration of the Teatro Duse in Bologna, where they were greeted with heavy applause and critical unanimity. *Il Resto del Carlino*: "Giulietta Simionato's realization of Carmen puts her in the category of the very greatest interpreters of this wonderful opera."[63]

In November of the same year Simionato sang at the Teatro Comunale in a *Forza del destino* directed by Maestro Olivero De Fabritiis, with Antonietta Stella, Roberto Turrini, Giangiacomo Guelfi, Boris Christoff and Renato Capecchi: a dream cast! Her interpretation was praised thus in the *Resto del Carlino*:[64] "A lively Preziosilla, Giulietta Simionato enjoyed a frank success with the confident vivacity of her singing; the warmest manifestations of approval followed just after the celebrated 'rataplan.'" This judgment was seconded in the *Avvenire d'Italia*:[65] "Giulietta Simionato was the very best Preziosilla imaginable. Added to her vibrancy, which is flexible enough to encompass all shades of meaning, is the enchanting vivacity of her stage business."

In Bologna, which still remembered the 1940 version (with the unforgettable trio of Favero-Pederzini-Gatti), Giulietta took part, the following week, in a rendering of *Nozze di Figaro*, once again under the baton of De Fabritiis (and had another big success). After each act the audience wanted the conductor and the entire cast in front of the curtain (besides Giulietta the cast included Alda Noni, Marcella Pobbe, Italo Tajo and Sesto Bruscantini).

In the *Resto del Carlino*[66] Lionello Levi was generous in his praise: "As Cherubino Giulietta Simionato has shown us her pure, refined art. As she interprets him he is one of the most surprising and interesting characters of the eighteenth-century theater." In addition *Avvenire d'Italia* published a long review of this performance, calling it "the warmest possible success": "Giulietta Simionato was a Cherubino who sparkled with comic energy, who also gave unforgettable proof of her extraordinary artistic versatility: she was a superb actress, a first-rate singer, who has no equal today for the evenness of her voice, for intonation, for knowledge of vocal style. She is a truly precious exponent of our operatic theater."[67]

Let us return to the month prior — the 29th of October, 1955, when the first of two performances of *Werther* took place at the Teatro Sociale in Rovigo. In the *Gazzettino*[68] Dino Fogagnolo observed that La Simionato had given "superb relief to the character of Charlotte, once again confirming her worth as a great artist with an absolutely clear vocal emission, with incisive accents and such a high level of stagecraft that it should truly serve as a model for other singers." This success was renewed the following day, when the critic judged that the female protagonist of the opera "could not have been better from the standpoint of the stylistic and interpretive qualities of her voice."[69]

In early 1956 Giulietta traveled back and forth from Rome to Milan by Pullman car no fewer than eleven times in fifteen days to sing nine performances and three general rehearsals, one right after the other: *Norma* at La Scala, *Il matrimonio segreto* at the Piccola Scala and *Il barbiere di Siviglia* at the Rome Opera.

During March and April, 1956, as she had done in previous years, Simionato went to Lisbon. Scheduled at the São Carlos were *Don Carlos* and *Cavalleria rusticana.* The Portuguese press talked of her in the role of Eboli as "a singer and actress of the highest quality," their reports echoing the great acclaim she had received at the theater.[70] Her interpretation of Santuzza was also praised, and it was observed that "the artist was gifted with a supremely beautiful voice, and has acquired a supreme knowledge of singing and dramatic art. Her singing has restored all its original vitality to the musical text as well as the libretto."[71]

At the end of the month of July, 1956, in Rio de Janeiro, Giulietta returned to the *Barbiere di Siviglia*, but in what a condition! In fact she was sick for three days and three nights. The impresario, Barreto Pinto, wouldn't listen to reason and demanded that she be taken from her bed and carried to the theater, so great was his fear of public outrage over a possible cancellation. So it was that Giulietta arrived at the theater in her nightgown and dressing gown, and was made up, dressed in her costume, and told that a chorister would sing behind the scenes for her in the first act. When she began the second act they made her lean on a chair and told her: "We need for the audience to see you. Begin to sing and see what happens!" Scarcely had Giulietta opened her mouth to sing the famous aria, "*Una voce poco fa*," than the notes came pouring out with surprising clarity, and she went on the with the role in spite of the impresario's exhortations to hold back, since by now the public realized her condition. She carried on thus till the end of the opera, when she was again carried in arms back to her bed.

In September of 1956 La Simionato went to Japan for the first time, singing *Aida* and *Nozze di Figaro* in Tokyo and Osaka. On July 14th, 1995, an article by Professor Naomi Takeya Uchida appeared in the Japanese review *Mainichi* almost 40 years after Simionato's performances, in which Giulietta recalls the premiere:[72] "At a time when the flight one way took us 36 hours, around the Haneda Airport there was an odor of fish. We began to ask ourselves if our music would be accepted in such a far-off, Oriental country, with a culture and habits of life so different from ours. When the curtain was finally raised at the premiere we were surprised at how many Japanese were wild with enthusiasm, even more so than their counterparts in America and Europe. The learned Japanese professor quotes one of her compatriots, a taxi-driver, saying to Giulietta, "I was so moved by your voice, you don't owe me a thing!"

In June 1957 a season of Italian opera was organized under the auspices of the Théâtre des Nations, hosted by the Théâtre Sarah Bernhardt in Paris. Three operas were on the marquee: *Cenerentola*, *Il turco in Italia* and *Lucia di Lammermoor*. At the season premiere Giulietta took the part of Cinderella accompanied by the chorus and orchestra of the Teatro Verdi in Trieste. The press was unanimous in its praise. René Dumesnil in *Le Monde*[73] had this to say: "La Simionato in the part of Cinderella is dazzling, accomplishing feats of skill with such ease that her vocal powers are magnified, and so is the perfection of her art." In *Figaro*, under the pen name Clarendon, the great music critic and organist Bernard Gavoty[74] felt that La Simionato had one of the most beautiful Italian voices and added that the performance should have been recorded to serve as a model of perfection. In the journal *Combat*[75] Marcel Schneider wrote that "Simionato was simply perfect in the part of Cinderella. She knows how to link the resources of her dazzling technique to the quality without which all those resources would be in vain: that is to say, poetry." The critical reception of the third and last performance was just as good. *Paris Presse*[76] contended that "the part of Cinderella requires an exceptionally gifted performer. La Simionato has become a specialist in this acrobatic feat and enjoyed a complete triumph last night." Finally the critic of the *Express*,[77] considering the mezzo-soprano parts of *Barbiere* and *Cenerentola*, felt that "the excellent Giulietta Simionato is the only singer today who has what it takes to interpret these roles."

The review *Artaban*[78] was also lavish in its praise of La Simionato "who surprises us with the extension and agility of her voice," and judged her better than Conchita Supervia. "With La Simionato the finale of the opera became a miraculous display of vocal fireworks," wrote the critic of the magazine *Les Arts*.[79]

We will conclude this panoramic view of French journalism in its response to the Simionato phenomenon by citing the review of Hélène Jourdan Morhange who, in speaking of Giulietta's performance in *Lettres françaises*,[80] felt that her "'falcon' voice was able to tackle every difficulty in the score, from the lowest notes to the highest." There is no need to enlarge upon the impression she made on Parisians that season. Sadly, they would not hear her again for eight years, on the occasion of the performance organized by the Paris Opera for Maria Callas, who insisted that Simionato be the Adalgisa — nine months before Giulietta would retire from the stage. This *Norma* was much appreciated by the Paris public for Giulietta's appearance, but Callas's caused a great deal of sadness because of her obvious vocal decline. In fact Callas, who had been admired as Norma at La Scala when she was at the top of her form, was now a mere shadow of herself. We will take up the matter again somewhat later in this book.

On July 18, 1957, Giulietta helped to inaugurate the season of the Verona Arena, again in *Norma*, with a magnificent cast: Anita Cerquetti, Franco Corelli, Giulio Neri along with the conductor Molinari Pradelli. The press judged this to be one of the best productions ever in the Veronese amphitheater. Carlo Bologna has this to say about Simionato in the *Arena*:[81] "The voice that clearly dominated all the others was that of Giulietta Simionato, a mezzo-soprano who has been conspicuous heretofore as one of the most classical and competent of singers. Surely it is difficult to bring together beauty of timbre and color, intonation and theatricality, a wide range and concise accents. In this woman a unique musical intelligence has been married to exceptional vocal gifts." In the *Gazzettino*[82] Giuseppe Pugliese had this to say: "The Adalgisa of Giulietta Simionato was already a classic operatic interpretation. Stylistic rigor and exceptional security of voice and virtuosity, expressive and dramatic coherence, and the intensity of her singing have made this Adalgisa a very great interpretation."

Simionato went to the Salzburg Festival for the first time in August of 1957, with a company from La Scala that included Tito Gobbi, Rolando Panerai, Luigi Alva who alternated with Giuseppe Zampieri, Anna Moffo, Anna Maria Canali, Mario Petri. In addition the services of Elisabeth Schwarzkopf supplemented those of the Scala company.

Four performances of *Falstaff* were given, conducted by Maestro von Karajan, who wanted to do homage to the memory of Arturo Toscanini with this production. The first performance took place on the 10th of August. Alice Gervais of *Midi Libre* of Montpellier noted that of the cast "the exceptional, splendid contralto Giulietta Simionato... shone," and she was "a picturesque Mrs. Quickly."[83] Pierre Sabatier in *Artaban* had this to say: "The contralto Giulietta Simionato, whose low notes were astonishing for their unique timbre, and the baritone Tito Gobbi gave to the parts of Mrs. Quickly and Falstaff a dimension and comic intensity that was infinitely watchable without once sacrificing the quality of their singing."[84] About a month later Verdi's masterpiece was repeated with four performances by the same cast at the Vienna State Opera.

On October 1, 1957, Simionato performed in *Carmen* in Lugano with Angelo Lo Forese, whom she met again two years later at La Scala in the same role. In a review that had the title "The triumph of Giulietta Simionato in *Carmen*," *Il Corriere del Ticino*[85] wrote that Simionato "rendered the opera's stormy heroine with an emotion that made use of her own personality, with the result that the audience was moved to very warm acclamations. An exceptional mezzo, she displayed a total mastery of her expressive means: her voice, now strong and thick, now enchanting for the transparent luminosity of the high notes, is at the service of a sensitivity which is the gift of a privileged few."

Giulietta debuted in New York on October 7, 1957, singing *Anna Bolena* in a concert version at Town Hall under the baton of Maestro Arnold Gamson, with a cast which included Gloria Davy, Richard Cassily, Kenneth Smith and David Smith. The most influential New York critics, the biggest artistic personalities and the directors of the Metropolitan Opera convened at the prestigious theater for the occasion. Her welcome was called "triumphant" in the press; after Seymour's aria the applause was so loud and long that the performance was interrupted for five minutes. In *The New York Times*[86] Howard Taubman wrote that "Signorina Simionato is a singer of dramatic temperament. Even in this modified concert version she gave the impression of tension and action. Her voice is big and expertly used; in the first half she sang constantly at the full, and the tones seemed to spread. But as she warmed up, she managed to control and focus them. She began also to add refinement to power, and at the end of her scene with the King in the second act the audience yelled as if Mantle had hit a home run." The success of the program was such, in fact, that it was necessary to program another performance of Donizetti's masterpiece at Carnegie Hall.

In the 1957-58 season Giulietta was once more the guest of great foreign theaters in a series of what turned out to be painful performances. In November 1957 she sang in *Adriana Lecouvreur* at the Chicago Opera with Renata Tebaldi, Giuseppe Di Stefano and Tito Gobbi. During one of these evening performances she fell onstage and sprained her ankle, so that she had to finish the performance in a wheelchair.[87]

On November 22, 1957, the day after the magnificent concert given by Maria Callas there, Giulietta sang with the Dallas Civic Opera in *L'italiana in Algeri* with a glorious cast: Nicola Monti, Paolo Montarsolo, Giuseppe Taddei. In reviews which appeared the following day the Dallas *Times Herald* described Giulietta as "a mezzo with the technical agility that one ordinarily associates with... Louis Armstrong's trumpet!" The Dallas *Morning News* observed that "Miss Simionato is one of those stage geniuses of limitless illusion, being as tall or as small as she wants, as beautiful as the Mustafa desires and as mischievous as the role is." John Rosenfield added that "Miss Simionato's trill... is the one you read about in the annals of Pasta, Grisi and Sontag."

Giulietta set foot on the stage of the São Carlos in Lisbon for the last time in March of 1958, as Cenerentola. The *Diario de Noticias* praised "her illustrious technique and the perfect manner in which she created her character from the vocal and dramatic point of view. The audience responded with enthusiastic and repeated plaudits."[88]

On the 16th of July, 1958, in the course of an artistic event organized by the city of Lyon to celebrate its two-thousandth anniversary Simionato once again performed as Adalgisa at the Fourvières theater opposite Mario Del Monaco, Maria Curtis Verna and Plinio Clabassi. During the premiere bad weather forced the company to reschedule the open-air production three times. When the performance finally took place Henry Dumoulin had this to say in the great Lyonnais daily *Le Progrès*:[89] "In the thirty years I've been going to the theater, Simionato's is the most beautiful mezzo-soprano voice I've ever been privileged to hear. This artist's voice has a miraculous quality all the way through its two-octave range and her duets with Norma were among the greatest moments of the performance. It doesn't seem possible that one could go any further in the art of singing!" The day after the third and final performance Giulietta was picked up and taken by automobile to Salzburg where Maestro von Karajan was waiting for her to perform Eboli in *Don Carlo* without preliminary rehearsals. In September the artist was to record *Norma* in Rome under the direction of Maestro Gavazzeni opposite Anita Cerquetti in the title role. Regrettably, however, this recording session did not come about. This was a real shame because it would have served as the last word about the outstanding vocal gifts of these great interpretive artists, and of the bravura of the conductor from Bergamo.

In February of 1959 Giulietta again took on the role of Carmen at the Teatro Massimo in Palermo alongside Franco Corelli, Mirella Freni and Giangiacomo Guelfi. Carlo Marinelli commented[90] that "Von Karajan would surely not have permitted Giulietta to create such a woman of the people, for that matter someone even a little vulgar and impudent, seething with desire and expectation, rather heavyhanded in her irony and wit, never sparing the beauty of her full, rich voice, powerful, robust, with strongly accented phrases that were supple in articulation but rich with inflections and not lacking touches which projected easygoing finesse and shadings of humorous confidence."

In August of 1959 Simionato conquered the international public at Salzburg with her interpretation of Gluck's Orfeo. This was one of the most important moments of her career, recorded by Franz Endler in the *Illustrierte Kronenzeitung* with these words: "La Simionato reigned supreme on the stage, her marvelous voice filling the hall and the soul." Mag Kaindl-Hönig in *Salzburger Nachtrechten* said: "We have had in Giulietta Simionato a stupendous interpretive artist with a magnificent dark-timbred voice of dramatic power, ripe with interior color, so that the famous aria in the last act went straight to the hearts of everyone present."[91] For Mario Morini Giulietta's interpretation was triumphant in every aspect, so much so that it achieved "such an exceptional standard in vocal execution that all her competition was forgotten."[92]

Giorgio Gualerzi wrote thus: "Giulietta Simionato, now pushing fifty, never gives the slightest inkling that she bears the burden of her long and intense career. True, she doesn't have the amplitude, the full contralto color and hieratic dignity of her great colleague Kathleen Ferrier, who was born to play Orfeo, but by the same token she was able to resolve quite decorously all the difficult problems that were put to her, betting on the nobility of her accent and the purity of her legato, without sacrificing the vocal and expressive essence of the character."[93] And Carlo Marinelli: "One must imagine that von Karajan must have seen in Giulietta Simionato, now forty-eight years old, a vocal timbre that is warm, dark, dense, almost gloomy, which would be perfect to point up what Orfeo feels as the heavy weight of destiny. This would be an Orfeo so oppressed by interior melancholy that his sad condition is second nature, so that it no longer upsets him or causes him surprise, but makes him more acutely sensitive to the situations that surround him — so it is in his anguished passion in the first act as in the urgent protest of the scene with the Furies, and so it is with the resignation of the aria '*Che puro ciel*,' that does not succeed in consoling him (a perfectly successful symbiosis between a soul-state and the appearance of nature which reflects it) as it is with the desperate (almost violent in the absence of a future perspective) isolation of '*Che farò senza Euridice*.' The character of Simionato's Orfeo is in some sense fixed or unchanging in the way one is changed by fortune, nor does he progress the way one matures; but in the uniform color and absolute homogenization of timbre (which, by the way, signifies the absolute security of a voice functioning at the very highest level) the mezzo-soprano from Forlì is able to introduce the sudden thrusts which give the character life and movement, always paying close attention to the conductor's indications."[94]

The foreign press in general (although with the inevitable reserve) spoke of the exceptional success Simionato had obtained with her Orfeo. In *Piccola Sera*[95] Bruno Tosi actually reported that the critics of Salzburg and Vienna "had stressed the marvelous prodigality of her voice in a way that has come to be frowned upon in music criticism, praising all over again the beauty of her sound and the magnificent style of her singing. Such a satisfying success is all the more remarkable in that La Simionato has never sung Gluck's masterpiece before." The Swiss critic Gilbert Chapallaz praised her surprising vocalism,[96] while Titta Brunetti (in *Il Messaggero Veneto*) commented that next to von Karajan, the other great triumph of the evening belonged to Simionato.[97] For the critic of the *Dépeche du Midi* of Tolosa[98] she was the most beautiful Orfeo he had ever heard: "Her splendid, true contralto voice projects miraculously and has accents of an extraordinary dramatic intensity." In the French review *Musica*[99] it was felt that: "Giulietta Simionato doesn't in fact have the true dramatic contralto necessary for the part of Orfeo: she is a mezzo-soprano of the Italian type, who vocalizes with stupefying lightness; she would be an ideal Rosina in the original version of *Barbiere di Siviglia* or even the Cinderella by the same composer which she has already sung in Paris. But she substituted vocal art for vocal force and only fell short in trying to disguise her difficulties with the *forte* notes at the top of her range." The critic of the *Times*,[100] who preferred Kathleen Ferrier's interpretation at Glyndebourne in 1947, still acknowledged that Giulietta had a voice that was "rich and beautiful." In the Belgian journal *Métropole*[101] Paul Scapus wrote: "The glory of the performance was Giulietta Simionato, a perfect Orpheus from the point of view of voice, art of singing, stagecraft and emotion. This singer's voice has exceptional power, flexibility and warmth. She guides it with an absolute science, uniting the three registers without the shadow of a seam and crowning her art with communicative emotion."

In this period La Simionato alternated performances of *Orfeo* at Salzburg with those of *Trovatore* at the Verona Arena, subjecting herself to fast trips between the two cities. As Rita Koch remembers: "When Herbert von Karajan decided to do Gluck's *Orfeo e Euridice*, first in Salzburg and then in Vienna, his original plan was to perform the German version of the opera, thus meeting the demands of the Austrian public, who had seen their language banned from the operatic stage. Giulietta agreed to try to learn the German text for her one engagement. But things didn't go well for her. Bathed in sweat she was up at night, walking to and fro in her room with the libretto in her hand — the memorization of which was giving her nightmares. Finally she had to tell Karajan: "Maestro, excuse me, I'm very sorry, but if you really want to do this opera in German I'll have to bow out." The maestro gave up on the German version.[102]

In 1959 Giulietta returned to the United States. It was probably the success of *Anna Bolena* at the Town Hall which drove Mr. Bing to request her services again for the 1959-60 season of the Metropolitan Opera. He announced her engagement to the press on 10 November, 1958, and *The New York Times* immediately published the announcement. Finally Giulietta, who had sung in Chicago, in San Francisco, in Dallas, in the Town Hall and at Carnegie Hall, would be able to show what she could do on the boards of the famous "Met"!

She debuted in *Trovatore* on the 26th of October, 1959, beside Carlo Bergonzi, Antonietta Stella and Leonard Warren, under the baton of Fausto Cleva. In the dressing room reserved for her she found a mountain of telegrams wishing her an auspicious debut; among the first were those of Renata Tebaldi, Victoria de Los Angeles, Mario Del Monaco, Ferruccio Tagliavini, Pia Tassinari, Franco Zeffirelli, Leonard Warren, Jan Peerce, Mario Sereni, Clara Petrella and Bianca Maria Casoni. We are stopping with these names because to mention the entire list would take much too long. The press was unanimous in considering Giulietta's "the most fervid personal affirmation," and in stressing "the public enthusiasm," happy finally to be able to hear the artist that American newspapers had not hesitated to call the greatest mezzo-soprano in the world. Mr. Bing went to join her, beaming, after the end of her debut performance to congratulate her on her "magnificent interpretation." Irving Kolodin wrote[103] that "for the first time within recent memory the anticipation of the opening night audience at the Metropolitan was magnetized not by a soprano, a tenor, or a baritone but by a mezzo. For Giulietta Simionato, the Azucena of the new production of *Il trovatore*, this was neither new nor unusual."

Simionato's first Viennese concert took place on the 26th of March, 1960, at the Musikvereinssaal and obtained fulsome praise from the press, who gave an idea of how much the singer was appreciated in the Austrian capital. In the daily *Die Presse*[104] the following article appeared, signed K.R., and given here in its entirety:

"Giulietta Simionato's evening of song in the great hall of the Musikverein is one which we wish to keep in our memories as one of the most beautiful concerts of the season. In truth there was no question of a an 'evening of song' or *liederabend*, and the definition 'an evening of arias' doesn't appear to be appropriate, either. The only way to describe the evening would seem to be 'an evening of Simionato.' In fact this artist has reigned on the stage in an absolute, unconditional way, and everything about her has charmed us: her singing, her artistry, the woman herself, her voice, her ability, her charm, her sense of humor, her seriousness, her petulance, her naturalness in performance, the confidence of her elegance, her style (which expresses itself in everything she does) which determines the way she performs, walks, stops to sing, smiles, salutes the public, wears her costume. The program of her concert contained fifteen names of composers and eighteen pieces, to which she added as an encore Rosina's aria in *Barbiere di Siviglia.* The variety of her performance adhered to a well-calculated program: at the beginning a group of classical arias: Gluck, Pergolesi, Händel, Mozart; another group included the names of the masters of Italian opera: Cimarosa, Spontini, Bellini, and it culminated in a "Stornello" of Verdi... In keeping with the dignified and serious character of this part of the program the artist was wearing long white gloves to complement a black dress which was as simple as it was elegant. After the interval she appeared without gloves, using a silk handkerchief to allude to the characters in this part of the program, who were a little more free and easy, and ranged from the impressionistic style of Pizzetti and Respighi to the popular pieces and those in dialect of De Falla, Granados, Favaro-Mistretta, Tomasi, Bellini and Donizetti. Eighteen or rather nineteen variously colored examples of the song literature, one more beautiful, more attractive than the next and every one rendered with fascinating sweetness and perfect artistic charm, in a style of natural simplicity, without affectation or ostentation, without pretense. The music we heard was as fascinating as the artist who interpreted it. Giorgio Favaretto also participated in this concert at the piano, playing with an original way of fingering; expert, however, and perfect in style, technique and musicality..."

In the daily *Osterreichische Neue Tageszeitung*[105] the following review appeared signed by Dr. Walzel: "Giulietta Simionato, greeted as soon as she appeared with long applause, sang arias of Gluck and Händel and some living Italian composers. All of the fame of this singer who is known all over the world was proven to be deserved when she went before the particularly demanding audience of the Musikverein, which had packed the house. With the size of her voice, already exceptional and singular, there is a corresponding facility and naturalness. Her technique, which is perfect beyond comparison, is completely at the service of singing and expression without equal. Just as impressive was the rather contained and formal 'penetration' of certain authors: Mozart (Cherubino's aria from the first act of *Nozze di Figaro*), Cimarosa, Donizetti, Bellini, Spontini, Verdi. Each phrase, each accent was perfect and grounded in a personal interpretation of these pieces that the singer has made hers, that she feels are most suited to her way of being. This opinion was borne out by the fact that only one aria ('*Voi che sapete*' from the first act of *Nozze di Figaro*) did not succeed perfectly and convincingly. Even in terms of the impression she made with her appearance, her face, her dignified restraint, the absence of the airs put on by so many 'stars,' of '*prima donna* behavior,' contributed to the seriousness and uplifting nature of this artistic event. New for Vienna were the delicate lyric of Pizzetti, full of atmosphere, inspired by the poetry of D'Annunzio's '*I pastori*' and the piece by Respighi entitled "Clouds" — inspired by the poetry of Ada Negri, full of clear southern light. Let it be noted that with these little works of art — as with, for example, the most pleasing, richly Italianate song of the composer Tomasi, who is still living, '*O Ciucciarella*' — provoked quite a bit more applause than the pieces by the old masters. Excellent also was Maestro Giorgio Favaretto, whose hands expressed his pianistic taste with infinite delicacy in *piano* and *pianissimo* passages, and with energy in those more *forte*. This was a superb evening, signalling a triumph for the southern Italian music of three centuries. And Signora Simionato responded to the warm enthusiasm of her audience with much charm and several encores."

In the *Express*[106] Karl Löbl wrote: "She came as a diva and sang with exceptional artistic intelligence, also conquering her audience with her considerable personal charm: Giulietta Simionato's first Viennese night of song, which took place Saturday at the Musikvereinssaal before an enthusiastic and cheering public, was a great success and a true and proper pleasure. A pleasure not only because of the contralto's magnificent voice which, in a state of grace, she exhibited for an entire evening, but also because of the ability of the artist, who succeeded in giving meaning to a program that was as various and colorful as a mosaic. Clearly, the principal scope was that of bringing her voice to light in all possible "positions," and her temperament in all of its shadings. The naturalness of her singing lent the performance exceptional distinction. One could admire her artistic refinement from moment to moment. And still her knowledge and ability combined to help her achieve a single goal: to express in music with all possible simplicity every kind of sentiment and disposition of the soul, and together to offer an incomparable example of bel canto. Thus La Simionato demonstrated that she knew how to render magnificent baroque arias just as perfectly as Sicilian songs, the romantic and the impressionistic, the serious and the silly. Maestro Favaretto, the most eminent Italian accompanist, followed the singer in an impeccable manner."

The performance was spoken of as "unforgettable,"[107] "a virtuoso display."[108] In the *Neuer Kurier*[109] Rudolf Neishappel wrote: "It goes without saying that Simionato's singing is founded on phenomenal knowledge and study. The delicate legato filatura in the Händel aria, a suspenseful and skittish parlato in Cherubino's lines, dramatic animation in the Italian aria; all these are elements of a supreme singing technique. But they are brought together with such security into the context of art that they seem never to have been wished for, but always understood, obtaining thus a natural and spontaneous effect. This is great art ennobled by simplicity." In this way we see how a concert by Simionato was a real event, as much for her admirers as her critics.

Of the *Cavalleria rusticana* which took place July 28th at the Verona Arena it is enough to say that the newspsper *Il Borghese* wrote that "it was sustained by the superb art of Giulietta Simionato."[110]

The productions of *Aida* and *Don Carlo* in October 1960 at the Lyric Opera of Chicago, conducted by Maestro Votto (who was appearing for the first time before the American public) represented a great moment in Simionato's artistic career in the United States. The Italian press picked up the echo of the laudatory welcome that had been reserved for *Aida* and did not fail to stress the fact that the biggest applause had been roused by their singer.[111] An American journalist covering the same event, after having observed how Simionato galvanized her audience with a performance that reached its high point in the fourth act, wondered if anyone had ever heard her in a poor performance.[112]

As for *Don Carlo*, Italian journalists picked up the story in American papers that Maestro Votto's performance had been received with enthusiasm.[113] Great praise went to La Simionato, naturally, about whom Robert Marsh wrote in the Chicago Sun Times: "There is no finer mezzo in the world today, and the richness of the Simionato voice carried the third act to triumph."[114]

On the 1st of November, 1960, Giulietta took part in a performance of Gluck's *Orfeo* at the Town Hall. The opera was given in the Paris version of 1774, whereas it was more customary in the United States to hear the version orchestrated by Berlioz. The judgment of Harold Schonberg, the famous critic for *The New York Times*,[115] was as follows: "Giulietta Simionato, that fine Italian mezzo, sang the role of Orfeo. A stylist, a musician of taste, a singer of skill, she sang with great albeit restrained feeling. Perhaps she didn't make as much of the great opening phrase as she might have. This, of course, is a cruel test for a singer coming 'cold' on the stage — a long, sustained, rich-colored phrase that swells and releases. But once she warmed up, Miss Simionato was in full command of her considerable vocal resources."

On the 26th of May, 1961, she played Amneris at the State Opera of Budapest. Rita Koch related[116] how the artistic director described the arrival of this diva in the Hungarian capital, where she was singing for the first time: "When we heard that Giulietta Simionato would be coming to us to participate in a performance of *Aida* we were all electric with joy and emotion. The morning of the first rehearsal the entire theater was gathered onstage. All the other soloists were there together, the members of the orchestra, the chorus — as well as all the technical and administrative personnel, in fancy dress and in costume, everyone was waiting, tense and full of enthusiasm and impatience. All at once we saw a small woman enter, very modest in her plaid skirt which went well with a dark turtleneck sweater and accentuated her simplicity. We remained taken aback for a moment. Astonished and almost disappointed we asked ourselves: 'This, then, is the great Simionato?' But then the orchestra began and at the first note of the music we saw the singer grow and raise up like a column into heaven!"

On the 27th of July, 1961, Giulietta returned to the Verona Arena to sing a *Carmen* with Franco Corelli and Ettore Bastianini. In a Veronese daily paper[117] Carlo Bologna wrote: "More than ever we admired Giulietta Simionato's great lesson in style (in singing and stagecraft) — a style by means of which she makes time stand still. For her this French opera is like an elixir of youth."

That same month in New York Rudolf Bing announced that because of a dispute between the Metropolitan Opera and the American Federation of Musicians the upcoming Met season would have to be canceled. Besides Simionato, Renata Tebaldi's engagements had to be canceled as well as those of Sena Jurinac, who was to have made her debut in that theater.[118]

In August of 1962 Giulietta returned to Salzburg for a new staging of *Trovatore*, conducted by Karajan. This time her colleagues were Leontyne Price, Franco Corelli and Ettore Bastianini who, with her, constituted "one of the most beautiful vocal quartets in the world" according to the French journalist Claude Samuel.[119] The critical piece in the important Paris daily, *Le Monde*,[120] by Jacques Longchampt, spoke of "vocal and orchestral fireworks" and said of Giulietta that she "knew how to give life to her part and revive the generosity of Verdi." In *France-Soir*[121] Nicole Hirsch called Giulietta "sublime," while in *La Croix*[122] Carl de Nys wrote that she was part of a "cast of stars of the first order, one of those constellations that comes but seldom and makes us dream..."

In October of 1963 she took part in some performances of *Aida* at the Vienna State Opera (whose director was still Karajan). In the *Wiener Zeitung*[123] there was the following notice: "Her Amneris constitutes a primary event, it is a blessed star in the annals of Italian lyric art. Her high notes shone as never before."

Rudolf Weishappel in the *Kurier*: "Speaking of singers, how is it possible not to begin with Giulietta Simionato? We often hear about her compelling Amneris. But the miracle of Simionato is her consistency in reproducing this charm. Never have I noted a momentary lapse in this artist, who always gives everything of herself: intensity and tension never let up, not even for a moment. For this combination of talent and artistic spirituality we have to earnestly thank her."[124]

Some days after she went to Japan for the last time, where the Japanese Broadcasting Corporation had organized its fourth season of Italian lyric art. Giulietta was Azucena and Rosina in Tokyo and Osaka, receiving warm accolades from the critics.[125]

In the beginning of February, 1964, she returned to Covent Garden for *Aida*. In the cast were Jon Vickers, Galina Vishnevskaya and John Shaw, and the performance was conducted by Bryan Balkwill. Asked in an interview with the *Evening Standard* "if there were any ambitions unfulfilled," she replied, "Just one. I want to be the one who says good-bye to the public—and not the public say good-bye to me." So it was evident that she was already thinking about retiring from the stage two years before she did. On that occasion, too, she remembered how during the opera season of 1953, the year of the coronation, London had seemed a sad, cold place (on the first of June there was a pouring rain...). On the subject of repertory she said that she was no longer available for the role of Carmen, she had already sung it some two hundred times. (She did sing the part of Bizet's heroine one more time, though — at her farewell appearance at the Arena of Verona in 1965.)

For the most part reviews of her Covent Garden performances were favorable, although some reviewers voiced reservations, as will be shown in the following panorama:

Martin Cooper in *The Telegraph*[127] felt that she was a regal Amneris and praised the equalization of her high and low registers, though he felt that her middle register lacked weight. Nevertheless he applauded the distinction of her vocal style and her moderate but telling use of gesture. Philip Hope Wallace rendered a similar judgment in the *Guardian*:[128] Giulietta had more or less magnificent high and low notes for the part of Amneris, but her middle register was weak, which explained why the judgment scene was not interpreted with sufficient power.

For the *Daily Worker*[129] this was a "thrilling Amneris with a strong, vibrant tone;" in the *News Daily*[130] John Clitheroe found her to possess "a wonderful voice both in size and quality throughout its range." The *Times*[131] termed it "wonderfully tender as well as authoritative," while in the *Sunday Telegraph*[132] it was felt that "the role was magnificently sung and interpreted, rich, noble of tone, dark and menacing in aspect, full of intensity, passion and dramatic fire." In the *Observer*[133] it was said that "Giulietta Simionato offers a staid, even starchy Amneris, who, perhaps understandably, rarely moves more than a pace or two on the highest lifts I've ever seen. Like... those seeded players who cunningly husband their resources and strike only when their opponent is worn out, she at first used her voice with a restraint that came close to parsimony. But nothing ever caught her on the wrong foot, and in the last act she was able to unloose a series of volleys so formidably and unerringly placed that her opponent was outclassed..." The critic of the review *Opera*[134] had this to say: "Giulietta Simionato, who had not been here since the Coronation Season, was welcomed back with great warmth, and gave a fine performance. Her Amneris still seemed to bear the imprint of Karajan's Vienna *Aida*; Peter Busse, producer of that version, finds in Amneris the pivot of the drama, the still centre round which the action turns. The three leading Amnerises today are Simionato, Gorr and Resnik. Gorr's is vocally splendid, dramatically conventional. Resnik's is very vivid and exciting: one's own flesh burns, yearns, flinches and quivers in sympathetic response whenever she touches Radames, Aida or the High Priest. Simionato's is quite different. She is an untouchable princess who masks her longing for Radames beneath imperial composure. She moves little, gestures sparely — only the eyes smoulder — and when suddenly her passion abreaks out the effect is thrilling. She is not merely majestic and dignified in a Stignani-like way, but positively eloquent in her stillness.

"(She) might well discard (her) thick 'lifts': she has the presence to dominate the stage from any height. And the voice. Well into her fifties, she retains the timbre of a young, warm, impulsive dramatic mezzo-soprano. Her clear delivery filled the house."

According to the *Daily Mail*[135] Giulietta "sang with unfailing brilliance and superb ease." In the *South Wales Argus*[136] Kenneth Loveland wrote that "Giulietta Simionato sings with great power and the bitterness of Amneris' final tirade was wonderfully revealed." Finally, according to the *Sunday Times*,[137] "The most secure sense of style was shown by Mme. Simionato, whose Amneris won a deserved triumph."

On the 20th of February Giulietta was constrained by bronchitis to stay in her hotel for a day and the theater management was fearful that their artist would have to cancel tomorrow's performance (the protagonist herself, the Russian soprano Galina Vishnevskaya, was also down with bronchitis, and should have canceled, but agreed to go on anyway). Anyway, on the night of the 21st, La Simionato went on stage. Writing of the performance of the 26th Harold Rosenthal felt that "Giulietta Simionato was a dramatically rather dull but vocally a beautiful-sounding Amneris."[138]

In April of 1964 Giulietta took part in a concert organized by UNESCO of which we have already had the opportunity to speak, and which took her to all the principal European capitals. The Hungarian Philharmonic was directed by the Greek conductor Miltiades Caridis. Soloists included the Israeli violinist Shmuel Ashkenazi, the English guitarist Julian Bream, the pianist Julian von Karolyi, and the tenor from Bologna, Paride Venturi—who was called in to substitute for Carlo Bergonzi—Astrid Varnay and Lisa Della Casa. The Dutch press, who presented the concert that took place at the Concertgebouw of Amsterdam, called Simionato "legendary,"[139] though she hadn't been to the capital of The Netherlands in nine years (since *L'italiana in Algeri* in 1955, during the Holland Festival).

Her program at London's Royal Albert Hall on April 12th, 1964, included "*O don fatale*," "*Una voce poco fa*," and the duet from the fourth act of *Trovatore* with Paride Venturi. The *Times*[140] called her "the aristocrat of mezzo-sopranos." The Norwegian *Aftenposten*[141] found that Simionato's talent surpassed that of all the other artists and spoke of "her incredibly wide and warm range."

The Danish newspaper *Berlingske Tidende*,[142] in reference to a concert which took place at Falkoner Center in Copenhagen on the 17th of April, judged Giulietta to be the only "star" among all the soloists: "Giulietta Simionato is that rare prototype of a certain kind of singer, and it might be said, of all Italian opera singers, thanks to the color of her voice, her timbre, and to her rare musical intelligence." There is no question that Giulietta — either as Eboli, Rosina or Azucena — was the artist on the tour who made the greatest impression on audiences by virtue of the range and richness of her voice.

In July 1964 Simionato recorded *Trovatore* for the second (and last) time for EMI in Rome. The cast included Gabriella Tucci, Franco Corelli and Robert Merrill. Carlo Marinelli's review was highly favorable: "In the EMI edition we encounter the Azucena of Giulietta Simionato, a character that has matured lately, with a voice that shows some sign of the passing years. The character has been made still more tragic and sad. The memory that obsesses her assumes something like a mythic sense, at the very limit of ritual evocation, but at the same time has an element of personal emotion, a palpable concreteness of imagery. The obsession has even skirted the borders of hallucination, but on the whole the character has deepened above all in her human dimension: pity for the weak, the tenderness and passion of maternal love, the force and ferocity of filial love compelled by revenge, the affirmation of a freedom that assumes the dimension of spiritual wandering, the suffering which is of the soul more than the body, the premonition of renunciation of approaching death, and in the end a yielding to the tension that has been borne for too long in a desire for peace and abandon, in an almost infantile dream of drifting away, of an extraordinary sweetness.[143]

In *The New York Times*[144] Howard Klein dedicated half of his long article to Simionato's Azucena, inlcuding the following: "The breadth and power of her acting, not to mention just her vocalism, is astonishing... But Simionato has always had a fine voice, even a beautiful one, and used it to act... What is so surprising is the endurance of the splendid, full voice... The opera is a stunning showcase for (her) high-voltage singing, which helps make it a bright and exciting performance."

Rodolfo Celletti was more difficult to please, observing that "the voice of Simionato has become a little weaker in this recording, especially in the middle and low notes."[145]

In the beginning of November 1964 Simionato went back to Covent Garden, once more to take the part of the King of Egypt's daughter, this time opposite Charles Craig, John Shaw and Suzanne Sarroca. The last-named singer was a last-minute replacement for Margaret Tynes, who was to have debuted at Covent Garden in the part of the protagonist (La Sarroca was used to this kind of thing since, already by 1959, she had substituted for Gloria Davy in the same part in the same theater).

The reviews were not as favorable as they had been in February. "Giulietta Simionato, who is usually an Amneris of ideal authority, although her performance was a model of style and musicality, was not in great vocal shape." Thus Frank Granville Barker in the *South Wales Argus*.[146] This was a conclusion shared by the other newspapers: the *Stage* (with more reservation),[147] the *Worker* (reviewer Matthew Quinn),[148] the *Standard* (reviewer Sydney Edwards),[149] the *Telegraph*,[150] the *Financial Times* (David Cairns),[151] the *Times*,[152] and *Opera* magazine (more harsh).[153]

On the 19th of November, again at Covent Garden, *Il trovatore* went onstage directed by Luchino Visconti, with La Simionato and Gwyneth Jones (replacing Leontyne Price, who was indisposed). There were eight performances, the first in the presence of the Queen Mother.

The criticisms of her *Aida* were again levied against her *Trovatore*. Thus in the *Telegraph*[154] Martin Cooper wrote that "Giulietta Simionato suffered from weakness in the middle register, but her chest tones and high notes were still powerful, allowing her to create an intense Azucena, which made for a memorable performance." In the *Financial Times*[155] David Cairns rendered a similar judgment: "It would be an exaggeration to say that it's all style now and no voice. The low register under the staff is strong and vibrant and her high register will still produce good, resonant notes. The breath is weak... but her rhythm, her phrasing sense, her magnificent spirit and her energy are holding up." The critic then remembered that Giulietta had so superbly interpreted the gypsy in the *campo di Luna* scene that she had excited much applause.

The *Bristol Evening Post*[156] called the interpretation of

Azucena a "baleful caricature"; the *Liverpool Daily Post*[157] had this to say: "It is over ten years since Giulietta Simionato last sang as Azucena here, and it must be admitted that her voice is now a trifle past its prime. Nevertheless the artistry and dramatic power of her performance remained most striking." In the *Times*[158] it was felt that "Giulietta Simionato as Azucena was at first in uncertain voice, and her musical phrasing of '*Stride la vampa*' could not altogether compensate for some weak tone and awkward changes of register. Later she gained in power, but it was her characterful phrasing (above all in '*Ai nostri monti*") and involved impersonation which were especially compelling." The following notice appeared in the *South Wales Argus*:[159] "It was left to Giulietta Simionato to carry off the vocal honours with her superbly dramatic Azucena. The middle of her voice may not be what it was, but her lower notes have all their old vibrant magic and she invested every phrase—every word, indeed—with meaning. Each time she stepped on to the stage the dramatic temperature soared."

For the most part this opinion was shared by the *Stage*[160] reviewer, by Charles Reid in the magazine *Punch*,[161] by Sydney Edwards in the *Evening Standard*,[162] by Philip Hope Wallace in *The Guardian*[163] and by David Cairns in *The Spectator*.[164]

The English critic of *Opera* magazine, present at the performance of November 23, 1964, observed:[165] "Azucena's character does allow a certain psychological depth, and here Visconti — with the aid of that resourceful artist, Giulietta Simionato — evidently went hard to work. (Her) deliberately pale, anguished tone in '*Ai nostri monti*' was beautifully appropriate. But it seemed ... against the spirit of the piece that she should turn her back on the audience in delivering her first '*Mi vendica!*', and should keep her voice soft at her shattering final revelation to Luna that he has killed his own brother ('*Egli era il tuo fratello*')."

On the eve of the first *Norma* at the Théâtre National de l'Opéra in Paris on the 14th of May, 1965, articles and interviews appeared in the press which were meant to make the singer better known to those who had never seen her onstage or heard her records.[166] This one and only appearance of our artist in the greatest Paris theater was all the more eagerly awaited because in March the press had broken the news of a serious illness that had obliged her to cancel her engagements in Palermo and New York.[167] When Bellini's masterpiece came to be performed in Paris, Maria Callas herself was feeling none too well, and it was known that she was singing the title role against her doctor's advice (the fifth and last performance, where the Shah and the Empress of Iran were present, could not be completed).

After the performance La Callas told the music critic Jacques Bourgeois that "the essential thing for me was to have sung the duets with Adalgisa well. I didn't want to ruin Simionato's Paris debut."[168] On this point the critic had this to say: "Surprising as it may seem Giulietta Simionato, the greatest contemporary Italian singer, is appearing for the first time at the Paris Opera. At this stage of her career it is obvious that the dramatic roles such as Amneris or Azucena are more congenial to her great mezzo-soprano voice than the "coloratura" part of Adalgisa. Her passage work, though impeccably precise, could seem a little heavy today. However, she gave to her aria in the first act and to the duet that followed it an interest that we are not used to seeing." In *Paris Presse*[169] Claude Samuel commented: "Simionato's voice is perhaps a little heavy for the part of Adalgisa, but what marvelous art she displayed in her singing, and what emotion in her acting! The only regret is that such an artist should come to the Opera in the shadow of Callas."

Samuel's words were badly chosen, but it needs to be said that it was extremely odd that the management of Paris's most important theater had never thought of signing Simionato before Maestro Georges Auric. Anyway, better late than never! In the magazine *Opera 65*[170] the French critic Roland Mancini dedicated an article to Simionato's debut in the great French theater, expressing an opinion quite like that of his two colleagues: "With Giulietta Simionato's debut the Opera has finally remedied an incredible oversight. It has finally given one of the four or five greatest singers of modern times her due, after a career that has already lasted thirty years, fifteen of which have transpired on the international level. It would have been better to applaud her today in a role requiring broad lyric declamation — Eboli or Amneris — rather than Adalgisa. Having reached this point in her career La Simionato has slowly moved away from parts written for mezzo-soprano coloratura (*Cenerentola*, for example, in which she was magnificent eight years ago at the Sarah Bernhardt Theater) to establish herself in contralto roles, while today Adalgisa would seem to be the highest part, the lightest, and the most demanding in virtuosity, of any romantic roles that are still fashionable for mezzo-sopranos. Let us bear in mind, also, the long illness from which Giulietta Simionato has just recovered, which would easily explain an apparent uneasiness in the tessitura of the medium-high register, while her high voice remains intact. (Simionato suppresses a high C that La Stignani herself began to omit when she was younger.) But her interpretation here still offers authority, temperament, and the style and class of the greatest international artists of the day. Her breathing may be a little heavier but her voice is intact. If thirteen years ago, in the same part opposite Maria Callas, the audience at Covent Garden heard her sing the duet of the third act one tone higher (in keeping with the original tessitura which had been abandoned in the middle of the eighteenth century), today's audience can discover a full, low tone from the chest — intense and sharp — that the artist was not using on the prior occasion, and also a totally new volume."

The majority of opinions in the press took Mancini's into account: as in *Le Monde*,[171] Georges Léon in *Humanité*,[172] Marie Brillant in *La Croix*.[173] The "refined" Clarendon in *Figaro* observed that the duets between La Callas and the "marvelous Simionato brought rare moments to life."[174]

At the beginning of 1966 everyone thought that Giulietta would fulfill all the engagements on her contract, which committed her to sing the role of the Princess of Bouillon in *Adriana Lecouvreur* at the Rome Opera in May, commemorating Cilea's centenary. But Giulietta did not accept. During the last two years of her career she had also turned down other very attractive offers: for example, a *Trovatore* conducted by von Karajan in October 1964, a *Norma* in Lyon, in January of 1966, and a series of recitals at the Metropolitan, and on tour with the same company in 1966 and '67 (*Gioconda*, *Aida*, *Trovatore*).

Offers continued to come to Giulietta till more recent times. In November of 1979 the director of the Vienna State Opera,

Professor Seefehlner, proposed that she sing the part of the Princess in *Suor Angelica* on the 8th of June, 1980, in celebration of his seventieth birthday. Giulietta didn't sing in Vienna, but in the same year, in celebration of conductor Karl Böhm's eightieth birthday, she wanted to make her own contribution by singing in his honor Cherubino's aria "*Non so più cosa sono, cosa faccio*" but... one octave lower! It was one of the most moving moments of the tribute, as Albert Moser, president of the Salzburg Festspiele, recalls. During the same evening Giulietta also conducted a children's chorus which was accompanying Mirella Freni, who was also present to pay tribute. They sang a famous Italian art song, a little modified for Giulietta on this occasion: "*Caro mio Böhm.*" This was the last time Giulietta ever sang in public.

[1] December 31, 1947.
[2] Id.
[3] Edicions F. X. Mata, Barcelona, 1991, pp. 204 and 205.
[4] November 20, 1948.
[5] Carlos Diaz Du Pond, *Cincuenta años de opera en Mexico (*Fifty Years of Opera in Mexico*)*, Mexico City, 1978, p. 138.
[6] September 9, 1949.
[7] In the "Giornale di Brescia," January 29, 1950.
[8] March 21, 1950.
[9] April 29, 1950.
[10] Rodolfo Celletti, *Il teatro d'opera in disco* (Opera theater on records), Milan, 2nd edition, 1978, p.100.
[11] In: *Opere in disco*, op. cit., p.39.
[12] C.f.: Giambattista Meneghini, *Maria Callas, mia moglie* (Maria Callas, My Wife), Milan, 1981, p.125.
[13] For a critical evaluation of the Mexican performances of Callas and Simionato, see *The Callas Legacy* by John Ardoin, 4th edition, Duckworth, London, 1995, p. 10 ff.
[14] Op. cit., p. 144.
[15] Op. cit., p. 145.
[16] Henry Wisneski, *Maria Callas, the Art behind the Legend*, New York, 1975, p. 43.
[17] C. Diaz Du Pond, op. cit., p. 148.
[18] Id., p. 151.
[19] November 15, 1950.
[20] December 11, 1950.
[21] Op. cit., p. 223.
[22] *Storia del Maggio*, Libreria Musicale Italiana, Florence, 1994, p. 23.
[23] December 16, 1952.
[24] April 11, 1953.

[25] "Diario de Noticias," April 25, 1953.
[26] In: "Music and Musicians," July 1953.
[27] June 16, 1953.
[28-30] Id.
[31] "The Star," id. Also see "The News of the World," June 21, 1953.
[32] June 16, 1953.
[33] June 17, 1953.
[34] June 16, 1953.
[35] June 21, 1953.
[36] June 27, 1953.
[37] August 1953.
[38] June 27, 1953.
[39] July 4, 1953.
[40] June 27, 1953.
[41] June 28, 1953.
[42] July 6, 1953.
[43] August 1953, p. 508.
[44] *The San Francisco Opera*, Comstock Editions, Sausalito, 1978, p.134.
[45] April 9, 1954.
[46] "Diario de Noticias," April 11, 1954.
[47] Ibid, April 23, 1954.
[48] Ibid, April 30, 1954.
[49-51] July 1, 1954.
[52] C. Diaz Du Pond, op. cit., p. 191.
[53] *Opera en Monterrey 1953-1988,* Carlos Diaz Du Pond and Jorge Rangel Guerra, 1990, p. 11.
[54] Ult. op. cit., p.12.
[55] Ibid. See also by the same author, *Opera en Monterrey*, op. cit., pp. 12-13.
[56] *15 temporadas de opera en Guadalajara* (Fifteen seasons of opera in Guadalajara), Carlos Diaz Du Pond, Guadalajara, Departamento de Bellas Artes, 1987, p. 15.
[57] In *The Miracle of the Met*, New York, 1968, p. 344, Quaintance Eaton says she broke her contract because of a "weakness of the heart," as it was then put.
[58] In the article "Great artists of our time: Giulietta Simionato," in: "S.R. Recordings," October 31, 1959, p. 37.
[59] "Diario de Noticias," April 25, 1955.
[60] Ibid, April 30, 1955.
[61] In "L'Arena," August 14, 1955.
[62] Ibid.
[63] September 21, 1955.
[64] November 18/20, 1955.
[65] September 18/20, 1955.
[66] November 25/27, 1955.
[67] November 1955.
[68] October 30, 1955.
[69] In the "Gazzettino" of October 31, 1955.
[70] "Diario de Noticias," March 24, 1956.
[71] Ibid, March 28, 1956.

[72] The article refers to another written by Masui Keyi in the review "Ongaku Geijutsu," June, 1995, which examined the influence the performances of Italian opera had had upon Japan since their inception in 1956.
[73] June 16, 1957.
[74] June 17, 1957.
[75] Id.
[76] June 20, 1957.
[77] June 21, 1957.
[78] June 28, 1957.
[79] June 26, 1957.
[80] June 20, 1957.
[81] July 19, 1957.
[82] Id.
[83] September 18, 1957.
[84] August 23, 1957.
[85] October 2, 1957.
[86] October 8, 1957.
[87] C.f.: Carlamaria Casanova, *Renata Tebaldi, la voce d'angelo,* Parma, 1987, p. 85.
[88] March 23, 1958.
[89] July 17, 1958.
[90] Op. cit., p. 275.
[91] These reviews in the Austrian press were reported in Mario Morini's article published in "Musica e Dischi," October 1959.
[92] Ibid.
[93] In the presentation (jewel case) of the CD "Replica."
[94] Op. cit., p. 33.
[95] August 26, 1959. See also the article by the same journalist in "Avvenire d'Italia," August 11, 1959.
[96] In: "Feuilles musicales et courier suisse du disque," October 1959.
[97] August 29, 1959.
[98] August 28, 1959. See also the article of Destrac in "Midi Libre," August 30, 1959.
[99] November 1959.
[100] August 12, 1959.
[101] Id.
[102] From: "Artista ed essere umano" (Artist and human being) in "Die Gemeinde," October 7, 1974.
[103] C.f. note 39.
[104] March 29, 1960: "Serata Simionato nella sala dei concerti: affascinante liederabend di Giulietta Simionato al Musikverein." (Simionato performs in concert halls: fascinating evening of song by Giulietta Simionato at the Music Society.)
[105] Id.: "Il debutto trionfale di Giulietta Simionato sul podio del concerto." (Triumphant debut by Giulietta Simionato on the concert platform.)
[106] March 28, 1960: "Alla fina della settimana nel Grosser Musikvereinssaal, Simionato." (At the end of the week in the Grosser Musikvereinssaal, Simionato.)
[107] In "Illustrierte Kronenzeitung," March 29, 1960. See also the article in "Neues

Osterreich," March 29, 1960.
[108] In the "Arbeiter Zeitung," March 31, 1960.
[109] March 28, 1960.
[110] August 11, 1960.
[111] "Il Corriere della Sera," October 20, 1960.
[112] Don Henahan: "Aida triumph will have to wait."
[113] "Il Paese," October 22, 1960; "La Nazione," id.
[114] October 15, 1960.
[115] November 2, 1960.
[116] C.f. note 102.
[117] "L'Arena," August 5, 1961.
[118] In: C. Casanova, op. cit., p. 119.
[119] "Paris Presse," August 25, 1962.
[120] August 4, 1962.
[121] August 14, 1962.
[122] August 25, 1962.
[123] October 8, 1963.
[124] October 10, 1963.
[125] C.f.: C. Eland in the English review "Opera," February 1964.
[126] February 8, 1964.
[127] February 10, 1964.
[128-129] Id.
[130] February 11, 1964.
[131] February 10, 1964.
[132] February 9, 1964.
[133] February 16, 1964.
[134] April 1964.
[135] February 10, 1964.
[136] February 28, 1964.
[137] February 23, 1964.
[138] In "Opera," April 1964.
[139] C.f.: Lee Riemens in "Tijd," April 10, 1964.
[140] April 13, 1964.
[141] April 14, 1964.
[142] April 18, 1964.
[143] Op. cit., p. 180.
[144] August 15, 1965: "Recordings: The Simionato Powerhouse Takes on *Trovatore*."
[145] Op. cit., p. 555.
[146] November 6, 1964.
[147] November 5, 1964.
[148] November 4, 1964.
[149] November 3, 1964.
[150-152] Id.
[153] December 1964.
[154] November 24, 1964.
[155-158] Id.
[159] November 25, 1964. See also in "News Daily," November 25, 1964, the

article by John Clitheroe.
[160] November 26, 1964.
[161] December 9, 1964.
[162] November 24, 1964.
[163] Id.
[164] November 27, 1964.
[165] January 1965.
[166] See among others "Paris va découvrir demain dans *Norma* avec Callas l'inégalable Simionato" ("Tomorrow Paris will discover the unsurpassable Simionato in *Norma* with Callas"), in *Aurore*, May 13, 1965, and "Vingt ans de gloire et dix ans de patience" ("Twenty years of glory and ten years of patience"), in *Combat*, May 13, 1965.
[167] In "Figaro," March 6, 1965.
[168] "Les Arts," May 19, 1965.
[169] May 16, 1965.
[170] May 15, 1965, p. 9.
[171] May 16, 1965.
[172] May 18, 1965.
[173] May 23, 1965.
[174] May 15, 1965.

5

—Giulietta and Maria—

In 1948 while she was at the Teatro Fenice in Venice for *Carmen* Giulietta met La Callas, who was singing in *Die Walkyrie*, having replaced La Carosio in *Puritani* with a resounding success. Maria was then quite plump, but had a beautiful face. Two years later, in 1950, La Simionato and La Callas would go to Mexico, as we know, both under contract for a series of performances. And they would sing together on other occasions in their turn: at Catania in *Norma*, for the Bellini centennial; in London, in 1953, for the coronation of Queen Elizabeth (*Norma*, *Trovatore*, *Aida*).

One evening, in London as it happened, after the fourth act of *Aida*, Giulietta had to take seven or eight curtain calls to thank her clamorous public. When she got back to her dressing room, through the flimsy walls that permitted one to hear everything that was being said by someone adjacent, she heard Callas grumbling to Meneghini about Giulietta's triumph: "For a few notes in the fourth act you'd think it was the end of the world, but they haven't even got a glance for me, smeared with black paint, who's been singing all evening!"

These words, naturally, didn't much please the subject of them in the next room, but they were fully redeemed when, a little later, La Callas told the press that very few singers could have conquered, as Simionato had, the "thorny" British public. It is in fact well known that a mutual respect existed between the two artists, who had become a couple in people's minds, which is easily understood after hearing the perfect blending of their vocal qualities.

They always showed each other a mutual liking and respect on stage as well. For instance, during a performance of *Medea* in 1961 when La Callas, as required by her part, fell prostrate under her immense red cloak, Giulietta, who was playing her maid, Neris, knelt beside her to begin her rather difficult aria. Maria took her hand then and under her breath wished her good luck. ("*In bocca al lupo, Giulia!*")

On another occasion, during a performance of *Norma*, when in the third act Simionato had to go toward the tenor to urge him to explain himself, she wanted to cross the stage behind the protagonist, Callas insisted that she cross in front of her, with the explanation that Giulietta was the protagonist at that moment in the action.

It is interesting to note the appreciative statement that Simionato made about Maria Callas, which was published in the magazine *Rotosei*, April 19th, 1957, five days after the performance of *Anna Bolena*. "Callas will make Anna Bolena one of her most admirable interpretations. Listening to her in rehearsal was a true pleasure, and clear evidence of the maturity this singer has achieved. In the final aria, '*Al dolce guidami castel natio*,' in which Anna Bolena, before going to the scaffold, evokes the long-past years of her happy childhood, no one could have sung better than she."

In November 1954 Giulietta rushed from Monterrey to Chicago to be with Callas in *Norma*. She just made it on time to dress rehearsal, during a blizzard. She threw on a fur coat (it had been very hot in Mexico) and ran to the theater, where Maria welcomed her affectionately and jokingly told her: "You're a monster! You get here at the last minute and yet manage to give a stupendous performance!" Nor was Simionato's opinion of her colleague much different. "She was a good person if you knew how to take her; serious and very painstaking in her work: she strove for perfection and gave her all during rehearsals, which she never missed, even when she wasn't feeling well. Nor did she ever arrive late."

In 1965 Giulietta sang for the first and last time at the Paris

Opera, thanks to the insistent demands of Callas, who wanted her beside her in what would turn out to be her last *Norma*. Maria had become very upset by the contact she had had with certain other colleagues and wanted to have a friend near. It was she who asked Mr. Bing to permit Simionato, who was under contract to the Met at the time, to take part in the Paris production, and when Giulietta had been replaced in the operas she was to have sung at the Met, permission was granted for her to come.

When Onassis came into Callas's life their ties of friendship loosened, as they lived in different worlds. They saw each other again when Callas sang *Tosca* in London; they wrote each other and telephoned at times. Then, after the marriage to Onassis, Callas no longer got in touch. They saw each other only when Callas was on her way to the Orient to shoot the filmed version of *Medea* with Pasolini, at which time she met Giulietta at the Grand Hotel in Rome. Callas talked for three hours straight: about Meneghini, about Onassis — whom she considered crazy — and about her regret about having left the stage for him.

When the shooting of the movie was over — Callas was convinced at the time that it would be very successful — she stopped in Rome again and went to see Giulietta. She was dressed in a pale blue suit with pale blue sandals and was very chic, in great form. She showed her friend an album of photographs that had been made from the movie version of *Medea*. (Contrary to her expectations, however, the movie was coldly received by the public.)

The period with Di Stefano followed. Simionato kept receiving postcards signed by Callas and by Pippo Di Stefano, and felt that the two of them were clinging to each other in the hope of bringing their times of triumph back to life.

Then Callas called Giulietta and asked her to join her in Paris, saying that she had an urgent need to talk to her. This was the last time Giulietta would hear her voice on the telephone. Giulietta could not make the trip to see her old friend, and was never to see her again. A little while afterward Giulietta received the sad and unexpected news of her death. Giambattista Meneghini, who loved Giulietta dearly, never failed to invite her to the commemorations of the singer and her anniversary celebrations.

Giulietta had never felt as close to any other colleague as she had to Callas. After her death she continued to remain in close contact with Meneghini who had been severely tried by the loss of the woman with whom he had never stopped being hopelessly in love. Two months after Maria's passing he wrote to Simionato: "Dear Giulietta, I am grateful for the generous thought you expressed when this terrible tragedy befell me. You know better than anybody what Maria was (Maria!!) and how I felt about her. Your words made me feel better. I would like to see you. I will come to Rome. My best to your illustrious spouse and don't forget Battista."

In January of 1978 Giulietta, who in the meantime had lost her second husband, received more news from Meneghini. "Giulietta, my dear, I cannot tell you how grateful I am for your affectionate friendship, how much I think about you with Maria and how close I have felt to you since the departure of your beloved husband, the great scientist, remembering his distinguished presence during those various times he came with you to my house. As for me, Giulietta, I cannot describe how lonely and despondent I feel. You know better than anyone else how much I loved Maria and how much she loved me, you know that I had forgiven her frivolity, which was instilled in her soul by others, and you also know how I was waiting for her to come back, as I had mentioned to a reporter — Peter Dragase — a few weeks before she died. And she died in a horrible way: alone, lost and abandoned. And what's more, cremated. I have been to Paris many times and will have to go there many more! I will let you know when there's an end of this ordeal. Love me, remember me as I remember you and accept a grateful and affectionate embrace from... Battista."

The correspondence between Meneghini and Simionato continued. In July of 1978 she received another letter. "Back from my interminable, sad travels, I find your letter of April 12 and reading it I felt an indescribable pain. You are right, for the two of us, the world has vanished *with them*. Let's keep them in our hearts, as we both do, in the hope that God will have mercy on us. Giulietta, don't forget me. I have you always in my heart."

6

— *The Sketch for a Portrait* —

The time Simionato spent coming up through the ranks was a maturing. At La Scala listening to the great operatic personalities, people she greatly admired like Caniglia, Stignani, Favero, Pederzini she went through a real personal crisis during which she felt she was adrift. Confronted with these illustrious names she doubted herself, she doubted her vocal means, she saw the difficulties that she would encounter, without feeling any certainty of being able to emulate such prestigious models.

Now she often remembers the disappointments and bitterness of those days long ago. She recalls one time when she was the understudy for Lola in *Cavalleria rusticana*. Maestro Marinuzzi was conducting, La Stignani was Santuzza and Beniamino Gigli, Turiddu. Maria Marcucci had been entrusted with the part of Lucia and Cloe Elmo with that of Lola. La Elmo, who was singing the *Jongleur de Notre-Dame* in the meantime, cancelled because she was getting too tired. It was then that the assistant conductor told her to rehearse *Cavalleria* and get it ready for the following day, without specifying the role she was to be given. When Simionato learned that the role of Lola was for Marcucci and she would have to sing Mamma Lucia, she suffered such a shock that she lost her voice. La Mannarini, who was a protégée of Mascagni, was then called in to sing the cover and Giulietta was obliged to send the theater a medical excuse. She attended one performance, keeping strict silence, as she had been told. The superintendent of La Scala at the time was Jenner Mattaloni, a fascist party official with a mediocre knowledge of problems encountered in theatrical production. This man, running into Giulietta in corridor, told her: "You see, Simionato, we want you to sing but you become ill!" This was like pouring oil on the fire.

Giulietta also suffered from complexes as a result of her small stature. To get around this drawback she did not hesitate to resort to remedies that could be considered heroic: in *Aida*, for instance, she wore shoes that had a 14-centimeter platform! To this day she remembers that a substitute conductor at La Scala, at the time she was doing comprimario roles, told her: "You will always look like an adolescent boy!", and she was so humiliated she cried.

She was never totally satisfied with herself. On the contrary, when she had to weather a series of less-than-laudatory reviews at the start of her career, she became afraid of reading reviews of her performances. She knew that she was always giving the best she had in her from the standpoint of commitment, sensibility and vocal services, and she was conscious of her limitations. For example, she knew she suffered from dryness of the mucous membranes, so it was out of necessity that she became a master of technique. This dryness, which was a constitutional factor, was a grave handicap for a singer. The throat walls, which ought to amplify and shape the sound, were instead like mirrors upon which the sound was torn apart. But the artist had a will of iron and the ability to sacrifice and lead an almost monastic life (she admits today that, during her career, physical love did not exist for her). She managed to give up to 96 performances in a year, with an average over twenty years of 80 performances a year. And she was never content with herself, always thinking she could have done more. Every performance was very stressful for Giulietta, who was obliged to stay on top of her technique, whose continual control in this manner was what led her to the heights of perfection.

Yet she was gifted with such dependable intuitive powers that she could instantly enter into her parts (which was the case with Santuzza, a role for which she had a great affinity), and she also knew how to balance the emotional charge. She absolutely refused to interpret those roles which she felt didn't suit the particular characteristics of her voice. Her range, which enabled her to reach high B-natural and high C, made it possible for her to take on soprano roles (which would serve to demonstrate, according to Giorgio Gualerzi, that Giulietta is in reality a "Falcon"). The part of Leonora in *Trovatore* was offered to her, for example, but Giulietta didn't accept it, taking Maestro Votto's advice, just as she refused to sing Minnie in *Fanciulla del West* as Tullio Serafin had wished her to do, or Lady Macbeth, when it was offered her and she felt that her personality didn't fit the role.[1]

Among her qualities was certainly that of stamina, resistance to fatigue, the capacity to pass from one role to another in performances that followed very closely one upon the other. From the beginning of her career she managed to sing three consecutive evening performances in different theaters. For example, in 1935 during the famous season in Malta, she performed on the 19th of February in *Madama Butterfly*, on the 20th in Refice's *Cecilia*, and on the 21st in *Adriana Lecouvreur.* In 1941, at the Sferisterio in Bologna, on the 31st of July and the 2nd of August she sang Beppe in *L'amico Fritz* and on the lst and 3rd of August, Suzuki in *Madama Butterfly.* In February of 1942 at La Scala she sang Lodoletta (February 18), Hänsel (February 19th, a matinee), Hänsel (February 21st, a matinee), Lodoletta (February 21st, an evening performance) and Emilia in *Otello* (February 22nd).

In 1944 at the Teatro Verdi in Trieste she was Cherubino on the 15th and the 16th of February, and Siebel in *Faust* on the 17th; three years later, Ottavio in *Der Rosenkavalier* on the 3rd and 4th of January and Hänsel on the 5th. In May of 1956 at Milan she sang *Mitridate Eupatore* on the 14th and the 16th at the Piccola Scala, and on the 15th was Dalila at the "big house." Six months later in Chicago she was Preziosilla in *Forza del destino* on the 8th of November, Rosina in *Barbiere di Siviglia* on the 9th, and on the 10th she took part in a concert. In Milan and in Rome as well it fell to her lot to sing two operas, *Cavalleria rusticana* and Mascagni's *Zanetto*, on the same evening: in this case, there was a question of portraying two very different characters, and to make her accept this assignment La Scala doubled her cachet.

Practically speaking there were no breaks in her activity. In the Concert of the Nations, organized by UNESCO in April of 1964, Giulietta performed in Paris on the 7th, Vienna on the 8th, at Amsterdam on the 11th, London on the 12th, Hamburg on the 14th, Oslo on the 15th, Stockholm on the 16th, Copenhagen on the 17th, Berlin on the 19th.

Except for two occasions early in her career — in Malta, January 6, 1935, when she stepped in at the last moment for her colleague, Maria Cherici, in a performance of *Sonnambula*, and again on February 16, 1935, when she replaced Edmea Pollini in *Butterfly* — only twice during the rest of her career did she agree to replace a colleague. In a performance of *Trovatore* on December 18th, 1947, in Barcelona, she sang the cover for none other than La Stignani, who was ill with bronchitis. To discourage the theater management she asked for the same cachet as Stignani, whom she greatly admired and whom she was afraid of insulting by going on in her stead. Evidently not even the large sum was enough to convince the management. The last occasion was on December 19, 1953, when she agreed to substitute for Inge Borkh in *Carmen*, when her colleague had been criticized by Maestro Rodzinski during the dress rehearsal. Giulietta was made to accept because of the insistent demands of the San Carlo superintendent, who had asked her to rescue the performance the day before its premiere. The Yugoslavian conductor had also begged Giulietta to take over the role. She did it against her will, however, alternating these performances with her appearances in *Cenerentola* (two very different operas).[2]

Modesty was a characteristic of this singer.[3] Even the compensation she requested was not exaggerated. In December of 1955, when Callas was getting 700,000 lire per performance, she was content to get 400,000, little more than half.

Giulietta liked to have her meals at the same time, always: lunch at one in the afternoon, dinner at eight in the evening. When this was not possible she would eat a sandwich or a brioche, drink a cappuccino or a cup of tea. She was very frugal. For years she lived on rice with oil, grilled veal cutlet, fruit and dessert. On performance nights she would leave the theater afterward without even removing her stage makeup: with a scarf over her head she would make it to her hotel, wash her face, eat an apple and two cookies and go to bed. The rare times that she was obliged to eat out she would limit herself to a little prosciutto with melon and a crème caramel.

She gave the best of herself to the audience and in return the audience reciprocated with a love she felt she didn't deserve. In fact, she would have liked to have given them even more.

Even so, she felt that there was a mutual understanding and love between herself and her audience. Giulietta, who doesn't remember ever being kissed by her mother, or having received an affectionate word, more than anything else wanted — without doing anything to draw attention to herself — to be desired, listened to, appreciated, in one word: loved.

Today Simionato feels fulfilled and admits that she has achieved a serenity she never enjoyed before, not even with Professor Frugoni, as she was always afraid of losing her valued companion.

She loves the audience's applause as much as ever, or more. When she is an honored guest at clubs that have been formed by impassioned operalovers or at numerous ceremonies it gives her great pleasure to know that she is remembered with affection and admiration.

Simionato has always been liked by audiences and critics, as Mario Pasi remembers: "Our wonderful singer is probably the artist who has been most written about, excepting the special case of Callas and Tebaldi. Not only that, but there never was the pretext of a scandal, of extravagant or wild behavior. Giulietta never seized an administrator by the scruff of the neck, she never interrupted a performance, she never had everyone talking about her because of sensational love affairs, and she was never involved in useless controversies. She sang. She sang everywhere, all over the world, traveling extensively, often taking heavy burdens upon herself, and always giving the best of herself... She doesn't miss rehearsals, she doesn't leave the stage, she is not demanding with the conductors. Even though she is a genuine 'star,' she is the true and inimitable example of an *anti*-star. It is not a small accomplishment. Among the many things that have endeared this singer to audiences all over the world, certainly it is her seriousness, her professional conscience, that has enabled her to keep intact, after so many rehearsals and infinite performances, that voice of hers with its unmistakable timbre, its wonderful fullness, its incredible agility. That voice which no other mezzo-soprano in the world can touch."[4]

This portrait is not so very different from the one outlined by Mario Morini in the *Corriere Lombardo* in 1958. It is obvious, says the critic, "that she can, with Renata Tebaldi, the ultimate anti-diva, represent the ideal type of Italian prima donna, modern, informed, without anachronistic attitudes and fancies, at last set apart from the traditional image of the singer once caricatured by Gavarni or the humorist Ghislanzoni in his *Artisti da teatro*, unkindly portraits of the opera personalities of his time which resemble indictments. For her quality of smiling kindness and solid friendship, good sense and good taste, everyone loves her and, while they respect her rank, all her colleagues, the critics and the public, consider her such a friend that their hearts swell each time they see her, and they feel at ease. If Giulietta Simionato is therefore the only operatic artist of international celebrity who has been spared the scourge of divismo, we owe it not so much to fortunate circumstances as to her desire to be and remain everyone's friend, to avoid gossip and keep herself out of the tabloids."

In their newly published memoirs two of her great colleagues, now deceased, remember her. We will quote Mario Del Monaco, who had this to say: "I remember Giulietta Simionato, the mezzo-soprano, with whom I sang a great many performances over almost twenty years. A small, energetic woman, with a great force of will. She was a singer of great stamina with an exceptional repertory that included at the same time Verdi, Rossini and Mozart. And yet she had a very sweet nature. I never heard a word from her mouth blaming or criticizing a colleague."[5]

Then there was Mirto Picchi, certainly one of the most outspoken singers of those days: "I sang with her in *Carmen* in Chicago and in the *Dannazione di Faust* in Florence. She was an exuberant Carmen and full of 'ginger,' as they say. I remember that one evening, at the end of the third act, she suddenly took a knife from one of the smuggler's belts, and though she tried to hold back her attack, she succeeded in butting my right cheek. During the curtain call, while bowing to the audience, I saw some drops of blood falling. These gave her a bit of a fright as well, naturally. I still have a small mark there that is enough to make me think about her often. I hope she won't mind. She called me her Piripicchio. I knew her and admired her since her debut at La Scala in *Mignon*, in 1947, with Giuseppe Di Stefano and Cesare Siepi. It was an unforgettable evening!"[6]

Simionato has received more than one hundred awards, plaques and medals,[7] the most recent being a prestigious and coveted recognition, an honorary degree from the University for Senior Citizens in Rome [literally, for the Third Age, which is the collective term in Italy. Tr.], which was awarded on the 10th of November, 1986, during the opening ceremony of their sixth academic year. In addition Simionato was given the honorary citizenship of Rovigo on October 3, 1987, on the occasion of the presentation of this book in the city of her youth. As yet another proof of the high place she still occupies in the opera world Simionato twice received the "Grand Prix du Disque de l'Académie Française": for the recording of *Aida*, which took place at the Grosser Musikvereinssaal in Vienna during May, 1959, under the baton of Maestro von Karajan, and for the recording of *Suor Angelica* performed in April 1962 at the Teatro La Pergola with Maestro Lamberto Gardelli conducting.

We want to end with some very recent opinions, which confirm the general respect and admiration of the critics as well. In the splendid book, *Guide de l'Opéra* by Roland Mancini and Jean-Jacques Rouveroux, published in Paris in November 1986, it is written of Giulietta: "She had one of the great careers of the 20th century because of her richness of timbre, her well-blended registers and the range of her tessitura, qualities which remained unchanged for thirty-five years." (p. 780)

Next, Stinchelli has written in his beautiful book:[8] "Simionato's soft and flexible voice, governed by a highly refined style and technique, was adaptable to many different operas... More than the power of her voice that she herself had refined, we admire in Simionato her sense of balance and her amazing adaptability to all sorts of vocalism, from bel canto to verismo. Rigor and technical security enabled her to sing at the highest levels for over three decades."

Then, in his book published recently in New York, *Sopranos, Mezzos, Tenors, Bassos and Other Friends*[9] (accompanied by the beautiful photographs of James Radiches), Schuyler Chapin quotes the late Gilda dalla Rizza: "There have been many great singers, but few will leave a permanent place for themselves in the history of opera. Of the group who came after me, I would put Simionato at the top of the list, not Callas. They talk about Callas singing everything; yes, but how? With three voices, and only the coloratura was, for a few years, impressive. But Simionato sang everything, and with only one wonderful voice. She became a luminous star not through publicity, but through exceptional merit."

Giulietta maintains ties of affection to her two biographers, first of all to Professor Naomi Takeya Uchida, who has known her since 1961, and was the author of the first biography, *The Prima Donna's Path* (Bijutsugendai), which appeared in 1977, and with the author of this volume, who has maintained ties of affection with her since 1983. Professor Takeya Uchida, for whom Giulietta is "her Italian mother," kept her fellow Japanese well informed[10] when Giulietta's 85th birthday was celebrated at La Scala (May 12th, 1995), at the Vienna Staatsoper, and at New York's Metropolitan Opera (where a bronze statue of Simionato has been placed in front of the portrait of Maria Callas). In the message which Takeya Uchida sent her Italian mother for the occasion she wrote, with good reason, that she was a "living national treasure."

We will conclude with the judgment of Fernando Battaglia, who made a precise analysis[11] of Simionato's voice and her contribution to the interpretation of opera roles: "The voice was exceptionally sweet and even, with a precious and exotic smalto, and it may have lacked the vibrant aggression, the fullness of the lower register and the volume that was to be found in certain mezzos of the preceding generation. On the other hand, she was certainly more at ease in the high register, much more flexible and agile and, at the same time, more generous with warm sentimental and emotional reflections, tending more to lyrical flights. The foregoing enabled her to take on certain cultural operations, first among them the restoration, or at least the partial restoration, of the belcanto virtuosity which was the legacy of mezzos from the preceding century. She also managed to restore formal dignity—often given short shrift or simply unrecognized by contemporary opera critics—to characters such as Mignon, Santuzza or the Princess of Bouillon. Her work was intelligent, aware, and sustained by the confident mastery of a perfect and highly controlled technique, and it certainly couldn't have come at a better time. Her contribution, so generous, and with surprising artistic results, went side by side with the action of deep renewal that she was sponsoring."

[1] On this topic, see Lanfranco Rasponi, *The Last Prima Donnas,* Knopf, New York, 1982, p. 382.
[2] Ibid, p. 383
[3] We can find a confirmation of this judgment in *More than a Diva*, by Renata Scotto and Octavio Roca, London, 1986, p. 157.
[4] "Giulietta Simionato non dice mai di no" ("Giulietta Simionato never says no") in "Il Corriere della Sera", 1975.
[5] *La mia vita ed i miei successi*, Milano, 1982, p. 76.
[6] *Un trono vicino al sol*, Ravenna, 1978, p. 101.
[7] We will cite the major ones: Orfeo d'oro in Mantua in 1956 (with Renata Tebaldi and Nicola Rossi Lemeni); Viotti d'oro in 1958 (with Del Monaco); Maschera d'argento in 1959 (from the Union of Roman Journalists) with Magda Olivero; Leopardo d'oro in 1960; Arena d'oro in 1960; Golden Order of Merit in 1961 (awarded by the Emperor of Japan); Premio nazionale Fabriano in 1962; Premio internazionale Luigi Illica in 1963; Anfora d'oro at Chianciano Terme in 1964; Maschera d'argento in 1965; Premio "le Muse" in 1968, with la Mangano, Chailly, Aldo Guareschi, Quasimodo and De Laurentiis; Rosa d'oro at Bergamo in 1969; 1° Bastianini d'oro in 1978; Minatore d'argento, Premio Quadrivio, Premio Toti Dal Monte in 1981, Premio Frescobaldi in 1985... The list can be completed with the twelfth Lauri-Volpi Memorial in Reggio Emilia (October 27, 1996) and with the Caruso Prize in Lastra a Signa (July 21, 1996).
[8] Enrico Stinchelli, *Le stelle della lirica*, Rome, 1986, p. 159.
[9] Crown Publishers, New York, 1995, p. 128. This judgment is also quoted in *The Last Prima Donnas*, op. cit., p. 395.
[10] In the "Giornale Mainichi," July 14th, 1995. Professor Takeya has received the first Pico della Mirandola Prize in 1992 for her book (reported in the "Tokyo Journal," July 12, 1992). The "singular rapport" between La Simionato and Takeya was also described in the "Giornale," May 12th, 1990.
[11] *L'arte del canto in Romagna*, Fernando Battaglia, Bologna, 1979, p. 176.

7

— Tributes —

We thought it appropriate to ask Simionato's colleagues, the conductors who worked with her, the managers of the various theaters and the music critics who have heard her to give us their recollections, or a comment on the woman and the interpreter. For editorial reasons we could not publish all of the pieces that were received, nevertheless Giulietta's portrait is vivid and complete. We are grateful to all the people who answered our questions. Their advice was very useful in helping us to complete our text.

Kurt Herbert ADLER, *former General Director of the San Francisco Opera*

It must be said that Giulietta Simionato sang only in the 1953 and 1962 seasons of the San Francisco Opera. In 1953 she had already been put under contract by my predecessor, Maestro Gaetano Merola, who died ten days before the opening of the season. Numerous parts had been confided to her: Charlotte in *Werther*, Marina in *Boris Godunov*, and Rosina in *Il barbiere di Siviglia*; all three of them with Maestro Tullio Serafin conducting.

It was characteristic of Signora Simionato to be capable of assuming so many roles in a short season, and of performing them all with great *bravura* and artistic feeling.

In the season of 1962 she sang Azucena in *Trovatore*, under the direction of Maestro Molinari Pradelli and with James MacCracken in the part of Manrico.

Her other part was Dame Quickly in Verdi's *Falstaff*, with Sir Geraint Evans in the principal part, and Maestro Ferencsik as conductor.

I had great personal admiration for Giulietta. I remember having invited her to dinner; we dined alone at Chicago's Blackstone Inn — she performed more often in Chicago than in San Francisco.

The last time I saw Giulietta Simionato was when she had done me the honor of coming to San Francisco for a good many days on the occasion of one of my birthdays. I remember not only a remarkable artist but a singularly intelligent person and a great lady.

Lina AIMARO BERTASI, *soprano*

Giulietta Simionato was the very best sort of colleague from the very first days of my artistic career. She had already been performing for some years, making her way with ease through the rather too-long period she spent singing comprimario parts. Surely, however, inside herself the desire was there, the force, the confidence that she would "make it." And sure enough, the great day came! And at La Scala! In October 1947 it was time for her great debut as the protagonist of *Mignon*, and destiny willed that I was to become, so to speak, the godmother of it — to be precise, I was her Filina. This performance was a turning point for La Simionato. She told me that I had brought her luck. But the truth is that on this occasion she was finally able to give proof of all her great talent. The fine essence of her sublime artistic quality emerged from her voice and from her seasoning as an actress. From that day the world of lyric theater could boast the addition of a precious pearl. And from that day La Simionato was asked to sing in all the great theaters of the world. Her singing continued to flit insolently from the fullest-bodied tones to the merest wisps of mezza voce, with agility and surprising high notes. This is how I remember Giulietta Simionato.

Licia ALBANESE, *soprano*

It is with great admiration that I remember the career of Giulietta Simionato. Together we turned in many performances of the following operas in Europe: *L'amico Fritz, Andrea Chénier,* and it goes without saying, *Madama Butterfly*.

The *tournée* to Malta and Tripoli in 1934 and in 1935 was a great success. Giulietta Simionato immediately showed herself to be a magnificent artist whose career would take her to all the principal theaters of the world.

The dramatic agility of her voice allowed her to obtain one success after another and gave her a position of honor in the international opera world.

Pierluigi ALVERÀ, *former Italian Ambassador to Libya*

I first heard of Giulietta Simionato in 1933 when I read in the *Corriere delle sera* that a young woman by that name, who was totally unknown to me, had won a singing competition in Florence. That name stuck in my mind, perhaps because like mine it had a clear Venetian origin.

In the following years I carefully looked, without luck, for Giulietta's name in the theater news. The great opera institutions were only offering her the role of Mamma Lucia, or at best Lola, in *Cavalleria rusticana*, and when all went well, the role of Maddalena in *Rigoletto*. The first unforgettable meeting took place at the Edinburgh Festival, in 1947. I was then the Italian Consul in that city and felt a grateful admiration towards all who brought to Great Britain the voice and appearance of our country, dimmed by long years of war.

I heard with joy that the cast of the *Nozze di Figaro* at the Scottish capital's first festival was almost entirely Italian. The intelligent bass Italo Tajo was in the leading role, Tatiana Menotti was Susanna, and with them, at last in a prominent role, was Giulietta Simionato as Cherubino. The opening night tension was dissolved by the cordial applause that was heard after the overture, soon followed by resonant ovations after Giulietta's arias "*Non so più cosa son, cosa faccio*," and "*Voi che sapete.*"

This was the first time that I heard her, and I was quickly convinced that the jury at the Florence competition had made the right choice, and that our opera institutions had inexcusably neglected her.

The first act finale was one of the happiest moments I have ever experienced in a theater. Italo Tajo intoned the famous "*Farfallone amoroso*" doing a march step, soon followed by Susanna and Cherubino. Towards the end of the aria the protagonist wanted to punish the adolescent for his advances toward Susanna, and hit the bearskin he was wearing on his head. The hat fell over Giulietta's eyes and covered half her face, and she burst into an uncontrollable *fou rire*, which soon affected the other singers and the entire audience. I think that Lorenzo da Ponte and Mozart himself would have been charmed.

After the discovery of Giulietta the singer came the discovery of her extraordinary personality. The fourteen years of misfortune had apparently not left a mark, even though she confided that she had at times contemplated leaving the stage. Glory was not yet hers at Edinburgh, but it was a step in the right direction. Giulietta accepted the British cooking in good part, though it was never to her liking, and said that she wanted to take to Italy, for her friends, some of the salted, dry fish that was being served early in the morning accompanied by a "porridge" which resembled the glue that was used to put up playbills. Every so often she would use a falsetto "second voice" in conversation, a ventriloquist's voice, which was silenced during the years of glory which were about to begin.

I was delighted a few months later when I came across an article in the theatrical review section of the paper whose headline was "Giulietta Graduates." It had finally happened — a triumph at La Scala in an opera rarely performed, *Mignon* by Ambroise Thomas. Mignon was soon followed by the roles of the great repertory: Adalgisa, Azucena, Eboli, Amneris, Dalila,

Santuzza and the Verdi *Requiem*. Giulietta was also one of the first to sing Rosina in the mezzo-soprano version, before Alberto Zedda's critical revision.

I was lucky to hear her at La Scala in almost all these operas. I saw her lying on her back, with her head towards the audience, in the great seduction aria of *Sansone e Dalila*; quite a contrast with the effervescent and ambiguous Cherubino. And yet the rendering of the role was in both instances perfect. Now there was a new and rare power added to the purity of her voice's inherent luster. After a few years I asked her, "In Edinburgh, did you know you had such a big voice?" "No," she replied with candor, "I only realized it as I went on." In fact, one of the secrets of Simionato's long-lasting vocal power was that she never forced her voice.

At La Scala I always heard her in the role of the Princess of Eboli, while she repeatedly "cursed" her beauty. In her charm there was something more, something indefinable. As the French say, she was *"pire que belle."*

A few years later I heard her sing the same aria in Tokyo, during a benefit concert attended by the Empress of Japan, and she confessed to having been very afraid. "But why?" I asked, surprised. "I have heard you sing this aria at least ten times in the theaters." "First of all, you are not the Emperor of Japan," she replied. "Also, in the theater it is a different thing. As soon as I step on the stage, I get so deeply into the role that I cannot think of anything else."

Again during the Tokyo season in 1961 I sat near her in the orchestra one evening when she was not performing. During intermission a member of the audience recognized her and asked her for her autograph. In short order the entire auditorium was following suit. It looked like an ants' nest, in fast and orderly motion. I acted as her secretary, passing the programs to her one by one during the intermission. I never found a signing so endless, not even the ones that I frequently had to do during my long diplomatic and less glamorous bureaucratic career. But Simionato seemed indefatigable while she signed those programs with her clear, elegant and slightly elongated handwriting.

I saw Giulietta come out unscathed after an *Aida* performance at La Scala in which a great Scandinavian soprano had made a sort of Brünnhilde out of the Ethiopian slave, a mistake that practically ruined the evening. But Giulietta reigned with great assurance despite her defeat as a lover, with a costume that accentuated her slender and sexy figure.

For that role she had been awarded a kind of "Oscar" at the Verona Arena for best interpretation of the year.

In the same Arena I heard Giulietta in 1962 in a triumphant *Carmen*. She was already approaching middle age but this did not prevent her from descending the stairs of the Roman amphitheater on the arms of two young dancers, with an elegance and self-assurance worthy of the ballerina Carla Fracci. Renato Rascel told me that Giulietta, when she recognized him among the spectators at this performance, had greeted him from the stage with "*Buonasera Capitano*." I leave him responsible for the veracity of the anecdote.

The fourth act marked a triumph for Simionato and her worthy fellow artist Franco Corelli. At the end of the tragic finale Giulietta let herself roll dangerously down the steps onto the stage. The press wrote that after one of those performances she had to be taken to the emergency room. I never asked her to confirm it. Giulietta had a less traumatizing recollection of the *Carmen* she did with another great interpreter, Mario Del Monaco — "The only one who never hurt me," she would jokingly say.

She left the stage in 1966. Her voice was intact. But her calling now was to perform with the same commitment the equally noble role of the spouse of a man with high intellectual and moral standards, Professor Cesare Frugoni. She courteously invited me and my wife on May 4th of the following year. It was our host's birthday, as well as the birthday of the great Venetian tycoon, Vittorio Cini (who was also present that evening), and what's more, mine as well. I felt a healthy sense of modesty.

One of my most recent encounters with Giulietta took place at the Marseille Opera, where I was presenting one of my audiovisual programs about the history of the Italian Opera, and where the great Giulietta and the just as great Renata Tebaldi were introducing the excellent students of the La Scala singing school. It would not have been easy for any of those young singers, nor for any of today's leading singers, to receive an ovation such as was accorded the two famous ladies, who kept a dignified silence that night.

The last and least happy encounter was in 1981 in Salzburg at a Mozart *Requiem* in memory of Karl Böhm, who had passed away a few days earlier. Three years earlier Giulietta had celebrated the great Austrian maestro's 85th birthday in Salzburg, singing a choral version of "*Caro mio ben*" that she had rewritten for the occasion as "*Caro mio Böhm.*"

With this memory of Giulietta's humor and humanity I will conclude this brief profile of a very great Italian singer.

Nanny ANNOVAZZI, *wife of Napoleone Annovazzi, Artistic Director of the Teatro Liceu of Barcelona*

My husband, Maestro Napoleone Annovazzi, marveled that an exceptional singer like Simionato wasn't at La Scala or being utilized elsewhere for principal roles, which was the case in 1947. As artistic director of the Liceu of Barcelona (Gran Teatro del Liceo) and musical director of the opera Anna Bolena, he confided to her the role of Seymour, which Simionato sang for the first time there, and which, as predicted, was a great popular and critical success. In 1950, in the role of Carmen, in which she was engaged as an emergency expedient, La Simionato was judged by critics to have been magnificent. These were two grand moments in the history of the Liceu.

John ARDOIN, *musicologist*

Giulietta Simionato. Just writing or speaking her name still causes a rush of excitement within me. She was, in our time, without parallel — a true, Verdian mezzo-soprano capable of dramatic soprano flights. It is a vocal type that has sadly disappeared. And with its disappearance has come a devaluation in opera.

But Simionato was more than a sound. She was drama itself. She was like a soldier, and words were the armaments with which she did battle. Through words and by virtue of her raging sound, she was capable of conveying in full measure the emotions of a text, the intricacies of a feeling. After her, all who sang such roles as Azucena, Amneris and Eboli were merely marking time as we waited and hoped for another like her. We continue waiting.

My memories of her go back to a night in Rome in 1958, when I heard her for the first time opposite Magda Olivero in *Adriana Lecouvreur*. The two of these authentic heroines together were like a body blow. It took weeks to assimilate the impact of that blow.

Luckily I was on hand for her initial season at the Metropolitan beginning with a Thanksgiving Day performance of *Cavalleria rusticana* with Jussi Björling. Then came an ideal Amneris opposite Leonie Rysanek's Aida and the perfect Azucena to Carlo Bergonzi's Manrico. But perhaps the most revelatory thing she did that first year in New York was her Rosina.

She had a command of coloratura to put most sopranos to shame (and how many must have also envied her brilliant, easy top voice with its solid high C). By simply opening a fan and peering across the top of it, she conveyed more of the character and mischievousness of Rosina than a legion of singers before and since had been able to do in an entire evening of gesturing and posing.

There are some singers who should possess the gift of eternal youth, for they have so much to give and so much to teach us all. Giulietta Simionato was one such singer.

Raffaele ARIE, *bass*

I have always felt and continue to feel admiration and sympathy for my great friend, Simionato.

I had the good fortune of singing with Giulietta during the golden years of our opera theater. There was a Beethoven's 9th at Genoa, and Monteverdi's *Il ballo delle ingrate* at La Scala under Maestro Carlo Maria Giulini's marvelous direction. There were many *Don Carlo*s at the Vienna Staatsoper when our good friend sent the audience into raptures after Eboli's aria, "*O don* *fatale.*" There were tours abroad, for example a splendid *Mignon* in Mexico, and an unforgettable *Forza del destino* at the Teatro Fenice of Venice, where the Leonora was Renata Tebaldi, etc., etc.

Giulietta and I stayed friends outside the theater. For example, in Israel, where she had come to make a gift to this martyred country of a forest of some thousand trees. Her generous spirit and sensibility would not be limited by this: she helped and skillfully guided many young people both with precious words of advice as well as concrete and costly acts of kindness.

Giulietta is one of the last exponents of the real Italian bel canto and she always has time and energy to spare in sharing her long experience with young people.

Carlo Maria BADINI, *Superintendent of the Teatro alla Scala*

What do I remember first, Giulietta Simionato as a woman or as an artist?

I can honor the great singer only as a member of the audience at some unforgettable evenings at La Scala: an unsurpassed Azucena in the 1964 *Trovatore* and before that as Carmen in a splendid production of Bizet's opera (for the first time in the original language), conducted by Karajan in 1955. I also remember that Eugenio Montale wrote about that important event in the *Corriere d'Informazione.* I did not have the fortune of seeing Madame Simionato on stage as superintendent of the Teatro Comunale of Bologna, or of the Teatro alla Scala later on. When she retired she wanted to sing Mozart's *La clemenza di Tito* at the Piccola Scala on February 1st, 1966. Exactly thirty years earlier, on February 1st, 1936, she had her first contract with the Milanese opera house (La Scala). As I said before, however, as a theater administrator I cannot remember Simionato as a singer.

For this reason I want to remember her as a woman and as a stubborn teacher of La Scala's singing school. I have met her many times, at the end of performances, backstage at La Scala, among her colleagues and her former pupils, ready to applaud their success, without any hidden grudges or useless regrets. If I should define Simionato as a woman, I would have to say that she was and still is a woman without animosity. An artist who never argued and was always in a pleasant mood. We cannot forget that she had her greatest successes during the rather stormy "lyric" years, and she managed (together with another great, Giuseppe Di Stefano) to be able to enjoy good relations with both Tebaldi's fans and Callas's.

To this day I am impressed by Giulietta's strict discipline. It has always been very difficult for us at La Scala to invite her to an official dinner after a performance. Her life was, and still is, set like a clock. When she was still singing it was said that she would often skip her evening meals or just eat an apple and some cookies.

It is a habit she has never lost. Because of this strict discipline she was never ill. She missed only two performances during her fifteen-year career at La Scala. She traveled constantly from one theater to another, and often to save time she slept in the sleeping car.

A woman full of life and energy. And now, when we see her arriving at La Scala to give one of her priceless singing lessons, wearing one of her fancy hats (she admits to having an incredible collection of them), she is always smiling and as likable as she ever was.

Gino BECHI, *baritone*

Yes, it's true that Giulietta debuted in the smallest parts with me and discographic publications bear witness to the truth of it: Madelon in *Chénier*, Maddalena in *Rigoletto* and so forth, constantly improving the quality of her voice and always being entrusted with more compelling roles.

I can't cite the progression chronologically. Because in general after she began to do the leading roles, we no longer had occasion to sing together. No, I never performed *Sansone e Dalila*. In *Carmen* I have had other great interpreters sing opposite me, but never Giulietta. *Werther* wasn't in my repertory (though I performed many operas of the greatest French composers, including *Thaïs*, *Carmen*, *The Pearl Fishers*, *Hamlet*, etc.), therefore encounters with the by-now famous Simionato were limited to coincidences on the most famous opera stages, whether it be La Scala or the Rome Opera or other great theaters in the world. And clearly Giulietta as Rosina will be included in our onstage meetings.

But at the moment I'm required to give a testimonial that will bring to light the artistic and vocal gifts, is that right?

I have the clear impression that my eulogies upon her art as well as upon the joyous sympathy which she radiates will sound extremely obvious and rhetorical. I would only like to add, simply, that after Simionato my ears have been unable to discern an authentic mezzo-soprano who is any competition. We are not speaking of the epoch of Stignani, Elmo, Buades Aurora, Nicolai, and certainly not that of Minghini Cattaneo and Besanzoni.

I have had the good fortune to sing with her and my hardened arteries haven't yet dealt me such a blow that I have forgotten amplitude, timbre, color and temperament. But all this is another story.

Ugo BENELLI, *tenor*

My memory of Giulietta Simionato stems from 1963 when I was recording the opera *Cenerentola* at the Teatro della Pergola in Florence for Decca Records. We were having a problem in that no one wanted to cut a record at ten in the morning, which was the hour that Signora Simionato, having slept all night, preferred to begin, saying that it was the best time of all! At the time I believe she was commuting between Florence and Vienna, where she was engaged performing an opera that had nothing to do with Rossini (though I don't remember whether it was in the dramatic or verismo repertoire), but even so she could calmly and repeatedly pass from one style to the other, day after day, thinking nothing of it.

In those days I was a tenor just beginning an international career: I still hadn't sung *Cenerentola* in a theater. Thus my rendering of the part of Ramiro wasn't a completely mature characterization. Careful attention to my work on that record, though perhaps no one has listened that closely, would reveal the fact that I was throbbing with emotion. La Simionato was at the summit of a great career, was in other words a celebrity, and for the young Benelli to find himself in front of a microphone recording with her was stimulating, exalting, and also terrifying! She gave me a great bit of advice. I had a tendency to raise my head too much when I was taking high notes (I now understand that this practice can cause the highest notes to lose resonance) and she never stopped reminding me to lower my head, telling me: "Piccinella, get your head down!" I don't know why she called me "Piccinella," a name that stuck with me; perhaps it was because she had trouble at the time remembering who I was.

Adele BERGONZI

Giulietta Simionato was always a good colleague to my husband. She always considered the other castmembers important. For my part I always liked her and she was very pleasant to me. We became friends in spite of differences in age and standing. She was famous and I was a simple tenor's wife, always ready to fulfill my duties.

In New York, during the long period when both Carlo and Giulietta were performing at the Met, she was our guest and, as a very sensitive woman, she would be quite moved when I read my children's letters from Italy. She received big bouquets of red roses from an unforgettable medical luminary, who then became her husband. During our meetings sometimes we reminisced and commented on the expressions we used to use many years ago, and my expressions in dialect. Even though it doesn't happen too often because of our different schedules, it is always a great joy to see Giulietta.

Ernest BLANC, *baritone*

I met Giulietta Simionato on the occasion of my debut at La Scala, where I sang *Carmen* in 1959, beside her and Giuseppe Di Stefano. I was very happy and proud to work with such a famous artist and I have conserved the memory of a very great lady, with a great humanity and an unforgettable talent, who did honor to operatic art worldwide. I was very aware of the kindness she showed me during this performance and I remember it with great pleasure. Giulietta sang Carmen the way she felt it, taking her own personality into account: hers was a very distinctive Carmen, a little reserved.

Carmen was the only opera I did with her. I would have wished to have her close to me on other occasions but destiny didn't permit it.

Massimo BOGIANCKINO, *former Artistic Director of La Scala and Superintendent of the Paris Opera*

Trying to say something new about Giulietta's art is a very difficult task since she has interpreted all the great mezzo-soprano roles of the Italian and the French repertory — and I mean to include the Italian Mozart — and she sang them all sublimely, in ways that won't be surpassed.

We can once again stress her extraordinary adaptability, but that is where we become confused, as we cannot decide whether we prefer her in the great tragic roles or in the coloratura, belcanto roles. The emotions that we felt were different and yet extremely intense. The voice created the character but the character served the voice in a very rare exchange of functions that distinguishes the great interpreter.

And then, what a pleasure to meet her in person, to see her bright eyes, the harmony of her movements, to know her generosity, her vivacity and kindness.

I was fortunate to know other qualities of Simionato, also. I have seen with how much affection she supervises young singers and how she is ready to go to battle to defend her ideas about theater. Many still remember an evening at La Scala when she — at the time a mere spectator — stood up to the audience which was at the time loudly protesting a cast change in *Anna Bolena*. Which other goddess would descend from Olympus to take care of an argument here on earth?

I have also experienced her good heart when on a sad personal occasion her concern in helping me was that of an old friend, or better, of a sister.

I was also fortunate to spend several days during the staging of a *Cenerentola* which was being performed in Pesaro as a homage to Rossini. Here we were all influenced by Rossini's liveliness: in the evenings we had to spend together in a not-so-comfortable hotel, on rainy days in February, the vivacity of her character came sparkling to the fore, and it was straightforward, there was never anything artificial. Everyone tried to enjoy himself and to entertain the others, but in reality it was Simionato who was stirring the flames. She could very well have said, like Falstaff, "My wit makes the others witty."

I don't remember if it was 1952 or 1956, I know for sure it was a leap year. I will say why I remember it, and it will be for Giulietta, who might not know this anecdote about Rossini. At his death Rossini left a large legacy to the city of Pesaro on condition that a music conservatory should be established (I myself have taught there for many years), and also that his music should be performed regularly. Rossini perhaps did not have faith that his operas would survive, and this might also explain his long creative silences following periods of feverish and productive activity. However the money he left had diminished in value; the Italian government took over the conservatory and the city of Pesaro, lacking funds, decided to honor Rossini with some production at a high artistic level, but... on the day of Rossini's birthday, and he was born on the 29th of February!

Rossini was therefore sadly mistaken for a second time: first in fearing for the future of his operas, and second in the conditions of his will!

We must say, however, that the city and the Italian government have made up for lost time by creating a festival which is a true Rossini festival every year instead of every four years. I have been talking at length about Rossini but it is not out of place, as we are also talking about Giulietta Simionato, and she has been an admirable interpreter of her roles in *Cenerentola*, *L'Italiana in Algeri*, *Barbiere di Siviglia*, *Tancredi*, *Semiramide*, *Mosè*.

During those long-ago evenings, listening to Simionato sing Cenerentola, we did not know if we were on earth, in a fairy tale world, or in heaven. Maybe we were in a place which as the combination of the three thanks to Giulietta Simionato.

Nicola BENOIS, *set designer*

I am an old admirer of our magnificent artist, Giulietta Simionato, and my admiration is unconditional. I am also proud of having had many times the pleasure of designing the stage costumes for her roles, which, if I am not mistaken, are at least twenty.

I remember it being a great joy, always, to see her wear the costumes that I had created, because there were few artists that could really "embody" a character the way the author had wanted, making it real, convincing, and above all bringing it to life as Simionato did with her temperament, which could really ignite the enthusiasm of an audience.

Two of the characters interpreted by Simionato wearing my costumes are particularly present in my mind: the seductive and cruel Dalila and the heartless rival of Anna Bolena, the wicked and treacherous Lady Jane Seymour, who appears in a flaming red velvet dress which immediately gives intensity to the tragic events to follow.

Great artist that she was, Simionato knew how to make the greatest use of the costume she was wearing with exquisite self-assurance and absolute self-control.

I also cannot forget her facial expressions which were always "on duty," always meaningful, even in moments when the technical demands of her singing were greatest. It was as if she were talking with great simplicity.

Ruggero BONDINO, *tenor*

In regard to Signora Simionato, I regret that I only sang once — *La dannazione di Faust* in Naples, 1964 — with this great colleague. She was an exquisite and *simpatico* woman and a great singer.

Umberto BORSO, *tenor*

It was a great pleasure and honor for me to have been a partner of the great artist (G.S.) in such important operas as *Aida*, *Carmen*, *Trovatore* and *Cavalleria rusticana*. A perfectly beautiful voice with a sublime technique and the possession of fascinating stage presence made Giulietta Simionato one of the greatest opera artists in history.

I think I was her last Manrico when we sang *Trovatore* in the Great Hall of the Kremlin in Moscow with the La Scala company. With her I had a great success in *Cavalleria* at La Scala and I will never forget her great art in the famous duet. I remember that at a certain point she threw herself imploringly at my feet (while I was trying to get away) in a manner so desperate... no other Santuzza could have produced that effect. I was always in perfect harmony with her with the exception of one time when I made her angry involuntarily while we were singing the last scene in *Carmen*. Before beginning the last act she had begged me to be careful not to pull on her mantilla, but even so, carried away by the part and throwing myself imploringly at her feet, I grasped at precisely this accessory of her costume, which made her start back. She continued to sing, her manner more nervous than usual, which made her appear grander than ever.

I wish her a long, happy life...

Jacques BOURGEOIS, *music critic*

I hope I don't sadden those who would follow in her footsteps when I say that Giulietta Simionato was the last of the great Italian mezzo-sopranos. As great in her vocal means as she was in the variety of her talents, belonging to a generation that contained names as famous as Gianna Pederzini, Ebe Stignani and Fedora Barbieri, she was the one to bring together the large-voiced, explosive quality of the Verdian mezzo-drammatico with the agile virtuosity of the Rossinian *contraltino*. Interpreting a vast repertoire she distinguished herself particularly in Amneris and Eboli, Leonora of *La favorita*, Carmen, Cenerentola and Rosina, finally showing stupendous prowess as Valentina in *Gli Ugonotti*, one of her last roles at La Scala (1962). I had the joy of applauding her as all of the above characters during my career as a critic. None of the singers who have taken her place since then has brought to the task such a complex of vocal, musical and dramatic qualities, because in Giulietta Simionato beautiful singing was enriched by her admirably cultivated gifts as an actress, which gave to the characters she brought to life, in comedy as well as tragedy, complete believability.

Cesy BROGGINI, *soprano*

To talk about Giulietta Simionato is easy and simple.

A great artist, a great actress, a stupendous, even voice of dark color, a continuous phrase as soft as a caress... She was a great mezzo, a voice which won't be easily forgotten.

In addition to all her beautiful talents her pretty face radiated an exceptional sympathy and cordiality.

We happened to be together often, and it was a joy to be in her company.

I always remember her with affection and I wish her more happiness, as much as she gave her affectionate audiences.

Letizia CAIRONE BUITONI

The first thing I got to know about her was her voice, a mezzo-soprano voice, stupendous, soft, perfectly modulated like an instrument being played by very expert hands. I have heard her sing many times in the major European theaters and in the United States, and her voice always struck me as being a very exceptional thing. A voice that cannot be easily forgotten complemented by uncommon acting gifts which made her the perfect interpreter of all the operas she has sung, and won her a wider critical and public consensus.

Later I had the opportunity to know her personally and as I had at first, I admired in her the perfect artist, but then I got to appreciate her exquisite womanly gifts: her sweetness, her nobility, her goodness of heart, which never lets her hold back when there is a good deed to do, her exquisite sensibility, her kind and gentle manner. These are the things that make her a true lady in the deepest sense of the word. And that is how her husband referred to her: "The lady..." Never "Giulietta" or "my wife." I personally experienced this a few years after I met Giulietta when I had the good fortune to meet Professor Frugoni.

There was a profound respect to be heard in his manner of speech as well as a great affection. And it was also clear, listening to him talk about her, that for the great scientist Giulietta was like the dream that one could not believe had come true; there was a sense of amazement in the professor's words, and yes, the fear that the dream would vanish as suddenly as it had come.

I still sometimes see Giulietta Simionato, always beautiful, her hair now white and her profoundly human personality rich in noble gifts, such as goodness of heart and generosity, which are an important part of her being as a woman and an artist. I keep some of her recordings with great care, and every time I listen to them I experience the same great emotion, always finding in them the splendid artist and the exquisite lady.

Ettore CAMPOGALLIANI, *singing teacher*

For my part I can only add a word of admiration for the singer La Simionato has been; exceptional because of her vocal gifts, her musicality and intelligent interpretation. A model which should be looked up to by present and future generations that are involved in (but not worried about!) professional singing.

Piero CAMPOLONGHI, *baritone*

I sang many times with Giulietta Simionato. I remember in particular a *Carmen* with her and Corelli at Castello di San Giusto in Trieste, a *Sansone* in Catania, a *Carmen* with her and Annaloro at Coccia, a *Werther* at La Scala with her and Prandelli. She was a great artist, very conscientious in everything. She had a sense of responsibility and showed herself capable of great professionalism. As Carmen she was vivacious and I had the impression that she was interpreting the part the way Bizet would have wished. With her colleagues she was cordial, a friend, and I remember her with so much affection.

Anna Maria CANALI, mezzo-soprano

I was great friends with Giulietta Simionato, and we got on well together. She was a great artist whom I remember with strong affection. My husband was very fond of Professor Frugoni's company.

We sang *Falstaff* the world over: Salzburg, Vienna, Chicago; *Cenerentola* at Como and Lisbon, *Barbiere* in Rome, *Carmen* in Verona, *Mignon* in Venice, *Rosenkavalier* in Naples.

I remember that we were returning from Austria where we had sung together in *Falstaff* and we had to take a sleeping car to get home, but Giulietta wanted to take me in her car and we went as far as Venice together. What a wonderful trip we had!

I am always pleased to see her again. The last time ewas when she came to Lucca for a competition...

Francesco CANESSA, *music critic and Superintendent of the Teatro San Carlos, Naples*

If specialization is necessary to be successful in life and in today's society, in science and in art it has become indispensable. For instance, in the medical profession, the era of the great clinician is over, a physician cannot win the Nobel Prize if he does not excel in the specific medical field in which he is a specialist. The same thing happens in the art of singing, the critic and the audience both expect specialization in order to decree glory for an artist.

Appreciation and fame adhere to an artist by playing one, at best, of the cards that music history has to offer — baroque or romantic, classic or modern — rarely by playing them all together. Rare indeed are the artists who can obtain equal results in all these musical byways while staying on one artistic path illumined by one ideal, and also possess the professional capacity to find the right synthesis for each different expressive necessity.

Thinking of Giulietta Simionato, remembering all that I saw and heard, these are the qualities that most stand out, that seem most extraordinary: not only because of the modern point of view they express, but because I cannot find another singer of her generation who presented them so clearly and consistently. To pay tribute to the exceptional character of a voice, as I had set out to do, now seems to me to be too limited; my homage must include the personality of an artist of historical importance in the development of the art of interpretation. I remember her Octavian in *Die Rosenkavalier* at the San Carlo in 1951. The ambiguity of the disguise was rendered by Simionato with such poise that it fascinated and disturbed both myself and my companion, who is today my wife: she was upset when Octavian was a man, I when he was a woman.

In 1959, on the occasion of an *Adriana Lecouvreur* in Naples, one of her great interpretations, Simionato gave a recital at the Circolo della Stampa in the course of which she sang the two Cherubino arias with such a purity of phrasing that at a stroke her voice, portamento and musicality had taken us back 150 years to the most sublime classical model. I also recall the grueling schedule which in ten days saw her in both *Cenerentola* and *Carmen*. If the excellence of her interpretation in the last opera is a given, it must be emphasized that the Rossinian bel canto, whose resurgence in popularity some would love to think a recent conquest, was already being produced by Simionato in 1953.

The emotions which are still the most intact in my memory are related to an *Orfeo* and a *Dannazione di Faust* which were given at the San Carlo in January and in December of 1964, respectively. The *Orfeo* benefited from a fantastic staging by Margherita Wallmann, but after the general rehearsal the corps de ballet of the San Carlo went on strike and the performance for the audience was given in concert form. La Simionato was stupendous, and it seemed to me, after attending the dress rehearsal, that Simionato had freed herself from something which had been limiting the character in the theatrical fiction and liberated its real nature as a musical miracle. She had real ovations from the audience, which had been disappointed at first by the sudden exclusion of the dance sequences. As for *Dannazione*, her Margherita is still vivid in my mind, the wonders of her great aria have been with me in memory for a long time as a model of vocal majesty which continues to remain a reference point.

I think I heard Simionato at the San Carlo for the last time in *Aida*, I can't remember in what year, but I remember her furious Amneris in the judgment scene, her elegant and lively figure hugged by her splendid costume of gold lamé, and the black depths of her voice, which was so perfectly Verdian. I went to see her in her dressing room after the performance and was surprised by the redness of her cheeks which was showing through her makeup. "I have a 39-degree fever," she told me. Nobody onstage or in the hall could have guessed it.

Rosanna CARTERI, *soprano*

The Simionato that I have known in the theater was always an excellent colleague, always smiling and in good spirits. To talk about her vocal and interpretive gifts is superfluous because everybody has sung their praises. I have often sung with her at La Scala and other theaters. In one La Scala production I was Micaela to her Carmen. Then we performed in other operas together, among which it gives me pleasure to remember a *Zanetto* by Mascagni and *I Capuleti ed i Montecchi* by Bellini, because of this amusing anecdote. Giulietta, thanks to her deep voice, could perform trouser roles which many composers had written in the right key for a mezzo. So it happened that Simionato was my cavalier, both in *Zanetto* (one of Mascagni's slighter operas, but with much beautiful music) and in *Capuleti*. The funny thing was that in this last opera she... Giulietta... was Romeo and I was Juliet. During rehearsals this was a reason for laughter and even during the performance while I was singing "Romeo, where are you?" Giulietta was backstage whispering her address and telephone number. You can imagine how difficult it was not to laugh! This is how Giulietta was, always ready for a joke!

Renzo CASELLATO, *tenor*

I had the chance to know Signora Simionato personally in March of 1964 when I was singing the *Cenerentola* of Rossini at La Scala (with Maestro Gavazzeni conducting and Di Lullo directing). Giulietta showed me great kindness and friendliness — I was making my first appearances on the stage. Again I had the good fortune to sing with her in September of the same year in Moscow, in a concert at the Hall of State in the Kremlin: the concert was live on television. Again I was with her when she was giving her farewell in 1966, in *Clemenza di Tito*. She stopped with me many times during the breaks and we spoke in the friendliest way. The part of Servilia didn't permit her to stand out, but perhaps she wanted to say her goodbye to the theater, she who had been accustomed to the greatest roles, with a modest part, the way she had begun her career.

As a colleague she was always extremely kind to me, a true lady, and there aren't that many, of whom I can only speak well. Afterwards we had other occasions to meet each other: at the Rome Opera when I sang the *Tancredi* of Rossini with La Horne, and at Treviso in the *Traviata* with La Ricciarelli; when she came to hear a concert at Carpi and afterward we went to dinner together; several months ago in Adria, where she came at the behest of a *concorso*, and where we saw each other again with the greatest pleasure. I have always had the highest regard for Giulietta, as an artist, as a woman, and as the dearest of colleagues.

Carla CASTELLANI, *soprano*

I have dear memories of Giulietta Simionato for her beautiful voice, sweet and expressive, and also as a colleague who was always kind and compassionate.

I remember particularly an *Aida* we did together. And as a spectator I heard Giulietta in *Carmen* at the Arena di Verona in 1955. She was really a stupendous Carmen beside Corelli. I also heard her in *L'amico Fritz*: she was a marvelous Beppe.

Giulietta had a tremendous range: we did our *vocalises* together, a soprano and a mezzo-soprano!

Nini CASTIGLIONI, *public relations*

It seems a contradiction, but I find it very difficult to talk about a person that I know deeply. And I have known Giulietta Simionato for many years and was close to her for fifteen. I was her secretary, press agent, lady's companion, factotum.

I met her at the most important time of her career (the year of the *Carmen* with Karajan at La Scala). That is to say, I met her when her career was becoming international.

Naturally, I *knew* La Simionato before; I was practically born in the theater, and I have always been around singers and artists. From the time I was a young girl I had seen and heard Giulietta Simionato in theaters. Better still, I was one of the few people who heard her in the very small roles she was doing at the beginning of her career. In *Manon*, beside La Favero and Gigli, I heard her sing "*E la cena, Signor....*"

The curious fact is that I did not particularly like her. She seemed too aloof.

I remember that once in Verona (she was singing *Aida*) we met on the street by a traffic light and almost bumped into each other, literally. She made a gesture of annoyance and I felt even more sure that I was right not to like her.

Then I left for Bilbao with Rosetta Noli, for whom I was taking care of public relations, and in Bilbao I found Simionato also. She was at a difficult moment of her private life and, in the course of conversation, she took me into her confidence. Suddenly I discovered a different person. Far from the cantankerous person she had seemed I discovered her to be amiable and very cordial, with a great need for affection, which she probably only allowed to surface in special circumstances. I felt the need to protect her. We took such a liking to one another that I offered to follow her in her career. She left for Mexico and when she came back the "deal" was concluded.

I followed her everywhere, Europe, the United States, Japan.

Fifteen years of a great career which was perhaps never equaled in operatic history: fifteen years during which Simionato only missed two performances.

Once was when we went to see Antonietta Stella when she was hospitalized.

Stella suggested a certain snuff as a way to stop a cold in the early stages. But Simionato always had strange reactions to medications. Often they produced the opposite effect, and this is one characteristic we have in common. After hesitating for a while Giulietta inhaled the powder and became very ill. Convulsions, dizziness... She had to cancel the next day's performance, a *Don Carlo*.

The other time was *La favorita* at La Scala. They had produced this opera especially for her, in fact this was the only time that Simionato ever asked to sing a particular character.

The premiere was scheduled for January 4th, 1962. After dress rehearsal Giulietta had a migraine attack. She thought it was a common headache and did not take the medication right away. As a result she had to cancel a few hours before the performance. La Scala decided to go on with the performance and cast another singer. Personally, I think this decision was discourteous to Simionato, who was an irreproachable artist who had never missed a performance, and in light of the fact that this *Favorita* had been staged for her. They should have canceled the performance of that evening as a gesture of respect for an indisposed artist. It had been done before for Del Monaco in *Otello*, for Raimondi in *William Tell* and for Scotto in *Capuleti e Montecchi*!

As for Simionato's career: it was a lesson in professionalism. Her singing engagements were her first priority. She had a spartan lifestyle. She never accepted any social engagements after the performance. She would go back to her home or to her hotel and her evening meal was a package of cookies and an apple.

She managed her voice in a formidable way. I remember that once I had arranged a concert in Venice, a recital with Maestro Favaretto at the piano. Giulietta was still in Vienna and I had gone ahead to Venice to organize the evening. I received a phone call announcing that La Simionato had no voice! Both Maestro Favaretto and I were dismayed. Giulietta arrived and in fact she had no voice! That is, she didn't have any speaking voice. But when she sang, the voice was there! I will never know where it came from, but she sang perfectly well and the concert was a great success!

Her technique couldn't be surpassed. As for her punctuality, she and Del Monaco competed to see who would be at the theater first when there was a performance. She never created any problem for artistic management. She was the first in her dressing room. She was also very proud, a characteristic which came from her Sardinian mother. When she was a comprimario at La Scala and she was being paid by the week, often at the end of the month she had to decide whether to take a bus or buy a sandwich, but she never asked for an advance. She preferred to go without dinner.

Giulietta Simionato has been one of the opera singers who sang the most and was the most successful. It reached the point that the taxi drivers in Japan wanted an autographed photo instead of their fare. At the Wiesbaden Festival, in *Cenerentola*, she had 37 curtain calls! Seven was her lucky number and we often left for her most important engagements on Friday the 17th... In Wiesbaden it was her highest seven!

Then came the farewell. The last performance at the Piccola Scala, in February, 1966. During the 1965-66 season Simionato had sung *La forza del destino* on December 7, 1965. She asked management what was on the program at the Piccola Scala in February and they told her: Mozart's *Clemenza di Tito*. She asked for the role of Servilia, a small role, not in the great repertory and also new to her. This way, without anybody's knowledge, she had decided to leave the stage, singing on the same day she had made her debut thirty years earlier.

This decision, however, became known and the audience did not want to let her go. There was real turmoil for almost one hour. Mafalda Favero was in the theater, sobbing and yelling, "Giulietta, don't leave us!"

I still get goosebumps when I think about it. It was one of the most emotional moments of my life.

Giulietta Simionato reserved another great emotion for me: getting me to know Professor Cesare Frugoni (whom she had secretly married a week before her farewell to the stage). This was the most illuminating encounter of my life, the man had an immense intellectual capacity. I was also near Giulietta at her latest wedding; I was the witness for Dr. De Angeli, her husband. Tatiana Menotti was Giulietta's.

Anita CERQUETTI, *soprano*

It isn't hard for me to speak of Giulietta Simionato with enthusiasm because Giulietta is an artist that everyone knows: skillful, musical, versatile, sensitive, lively, sincere and friendly. That is how I remember her.

Each one of the operas I performed with her was a beautiful and significant experience, almost entirely devoid of the jitters and anxieties that are a recurring problem for an artist. Her presence as an artist made the atmosphere serene because she succeeded in infusing the performance with the necessary confidence.

She was there for me in private moments — for example, with a telegram on the occasion of my daughter's birth. From a distance of a twenty years I want to express all my gratitude once again.

Giulietta Simionato made a mark in the world of opera theater which will never be effaced and will be difficult to match. I'm glad for this opportunity to show my admiration and affection for her. Perhaps I haven't said everything that she deserves to have said about her but my words are sincere, heartfelt and full of affection.

Boris CHRISTOFF, *bass*

I have had La Simionato at my side onstage, a serious artist, well-prepared, and in lots of memorable performances I have a most agreeable recollection of her artistry.

In her I always found a colleague with whom one was inspired to make good music.

Irma COLASANTI, *mezzo-soprano*

When I arrived at La Scala Giulietta Simionato was a few years into her career. At that time she was very timid, but serious, conscientious, very intelligent and musical. In my opinion she could have made her debut in leading roles and it hurt me a lot to see her sacrificed in the beginning. We found ourselves together in Honegger's *Anfione* in 1938, and we didn't have another occasion to sing together until Giulietta had the good fortune to do *Mignon*...

Anselmo COLZANI, *baritone*

I remember with immense pleasure having often sung in the major theaters of the world with the great Simionato.

I have both pride and joy to have collaborated artistically with so grand a diva of bel canto and master of interpretation.

Truly it is a pity that this, as with other rare joys in this life, had to end.

Franco CORELLI, *tenor*

Giulietta Simionato: what a formidable singer, and what a personality! It was such a blend that one could not be separated from the other. I had her as an incomparable partner in almost all my *Carmen*s, from my debut in Turin and in all the greatest theaters of the world.

She was complete: her persuasive and forceful singing was reinforced by an overwhelming acting sense, enhanced by a glamorous physique (Carmen!).

Who could forget her Azucena in *Trovatore*? Her second act, so intense, real, and so dramatic and credible that during the unforgettable evenings in Salzburg she was defined as the "unsurpassable Azucena"?

Still, of the many operas we sang together many times over, my fondest memories are of *Gli Ugonotti* (The Huguenots), of the exciting moments we spent together during those La Scala performances, where Simionato, singing a soprano role for the first time, showed her great technique and her exceptional range.

Viorica CORTEZ, *mezzo-soprano*

For me Simionato was one of the stars that I had the desire to match, because of her vast repertoire, because of her talent and her magnificent personality. (The colleagues who sang with her told me that she was beautiful in every respect.) I don't think that there's a single recording of hers that I don't have, because her round, powerful voice always gave me the desire to become more and more like her...

Régine CRESPIN, *soprano*

I have a great respect for Giulietta Simionato, who conducted her career in exemplary fashion, knowing how to choose her repertory. She sang the right operas at the right time with a particularly intelligent technique, with patience and with wisdom. I sang *Ballo in maschera* with her at the Vienna Staatsoper on February 8, 1962, with Maestro Serafin conducting, who had a triumph. It was an extraordinary performance. Giulietta Simionato is an example to young singers.

Fedora DEL MONACO

My husband and Giulietta worked together in the greatest theaters of the world, and collaborated on many recordings as well. More than colleagues, they were also friends all their lives. Giulietta adored Mario and would often send him humorous telegrams when she knew that he was going to sing a difficult role, either at La Scala or the Met. "Take heart, Mario, you are the only one."

My husband and I had greatly admired Giulietta, who was truly the great singer and the leading mezzo-soprano of the La Scala Golden Age.

More I can't say. Only that Giulietta attends every event and commemoration in remembrance of Mario.

Giuseppe Di STEFANO, *tenor*

Every time I have the joy of meeting Giulietta Simionato — and luckily, it happens often — my dear colleague never fails to remind me of 1949, and reprimand me for that time long ago when we sang together in four operas at the Teatro Bellas Artes in Mexico City: *Mignon*, *Favorita*, *Barbiere* and *Werther*.

"What you put me through that time in Mexico!" she tells me as soon as she sees me. And of course she has all the reason in the world. Giulietta suffered the torments of hell on that occasion because as a conscientious and well-prepared artist she found herself always singing with the undersigned, who of the four operas was "improvising" in three of them. In fact I had to sing them, studying them on spot, because of an iron-fisted impresario, Dr. Carazza Campos, a great man of the operatic theater. (In 1952 he engaged me to sing with Maria Callas in five operas: *Puritani*, *Lucia* — her first *Lucia* — *Traviata*, *Rigoletto* and *Tosca* — my first *Tosca*).

"You are irresponsible," Giulietta kept saying during the performances. "It is not possible to sing with someone who changes the text constantly and makes up the notes, and the music as well!"

"Giulietta," I would reply, "it is beyond my control, you know it is not entirely my fault! The manager has taken my passport and has literally forced me to sing these operas under penalty of prolonged stay in Mexico! And I am also on my honeymoon..." (I had just been married.)

Giulietta was right, of course, and Donizetti, Rossini and Massenet were suffering right along with her. During intermissions she would lock herself in her dressing room crying and laughing, breaking anything she could get her hands on.

The audience, however, was delirious and all those performances were recorded "live" and issued by bootleg recording companies. Every opera lover in the world has them.

Dear colleague, it is very true that in spite of the terrible moments during those unforgettable evenings we became part of the history of one of the most prestigious Latin American opera theaters, and the audiences there have not forgotten us: you with your mastery and knowledge, and me improvising, but always united in our way of singing, full of passion and sweetness, which is, after all is said and done, what pleases audiences everywhere.

Jean DUPOUY, *tenor*

I am happy to attest that, on two occasions, I have had the pleasure of hearing and seeing this most beautiful of artists, La Simionato.

The first time was when I was a student at the Conservatory of Paris, the year of my first prize in singing. I was present at the Paris Opera on 17 May, 1965, for a most beautiful performance of *Norma*, in which, with Maria Callas at her side, Giulietta Simionato took the part of Adalgisa. I remember it very well to this day.

The second time, much later, in April of 1980, I was in Turin where I was singing *Werther* at the Teatro Reggio. As a spectator at another performance I found myself in the room at the moment in which, just before the raising of the curtain, I saw all the spectators standing and continuing to cheer for a lady, who, after she was seated, had to realize that the cheering was for her and acknowledge all the congratulations. I knew in a moment that the lady at issue was La Simionato. This demonstration of affection was very moving and I had a moment's regret then as I thought to myself that in France no such reaction could have greeted one of my older colleagues.

Martine DUPUY, *mezzo-soprano*

Giulietta Simionato brings back to my mind an important voice, with a very wide range, an incomparable timbre and a perfect blending of the registers. At ease in all repertoires she had a rather late but decisive career: she was the first to sing Rossini in a manner which is called today "Rossini's vocal style." In Maria Callas's footsteps she announced the "Rossini Revival."

Nelly FAILONI KLIER, *impresario*

It's possible for me to say of La Simionato that there is no other artist as great, and you see, I've known a lot of artists!

When she was on the stage she was always the character she had to impersonate: Eboli, Carmen, Amneris, and she never left the impression that she was only a singer. She always made the effort to understand the feelings of her characters and to feel them, transforming herself into Eboli, or some other. Her method of singing was unique. The voice was a marvel, and Giulietta sang as naturally as one speaks, taking no account of the difficulty of the score. The public lived with her and right along with her it was transformed. Many times it came into my head to ask myself what Giulietta might do if I were to go onstage and bother her with a question that would have nothing to do with her character: I believe she would not have understood anything of it because she was in another world, a world far from this earth...!

Antonio José FARO, *coordinator of the opera theater of Rio di Janeiro*

As a member of the ballet of the theater in the fifties I have many excellent memories of the great singer, Giulietta Simionato. I remember her affability with everyone. Along with the supernumeraries I remember that good humor of hers that was permanently tied to her musicality and professionalism. The way in which she rehearsed was the best sort of lesson for all of us. One never saw a performance that left one indifferent, even if she sang very little in it.

Whether as Maddalena or Preziosilla, when she was taking what were clearly supporting roles, she was magnificent because of her dedication, her grace onstage and the conscientiousness of her musicianship, which imbued every one of her appearances.

In 1983, la Signora Simionato came to judge the biannual song competition in Rio di Janeiro. She had scarcely come onstage when the entire hall stood to applaud her.

Giorgio FELICIOTTI, *musicologist*

The idea of telling a story in a few pages has always fascinated me, and the occasion has finally come thanks to Jean-Jacques Hanine Roussel, who has invited me to write my personal recollections of that great artist, Giulietta Simionato.

A most beautiful woman, a most skillful singer, an exceptional interpreter, Giulietta Simionato holds an important place in the history of the lyric theater in this century, and offers a model standard of comparison.

Personally, every time I listen to one of her records or remember one of her performances it is as if I were hearing a marvelous messenger from celestial regions, the voice of an angel transmitting its messages on earth.

She began by interpreting small parts, and after several years, with tenacity and deep study and an admirable will power, she plucked the fruits of a dazzling career, full of triumphs. And this was so thanks to the elegance of her phrasing, to her velvet timbre, to her musical intelligence, which was quite out of the ordinary, and to her strong communicative urgency which imbued her interpretations with a warmth and sensuality which were the essence of her charm.

I would like to add that La Simionato was provided with a voice that never needed to be forced in the upper register, so that she was permitted the luxury of taking on roles like Carmen and Dalila with exceptional results.

Many were the occasions that I heard her and applauded her all over Italy; here for reasons of space I will remember only some performances at the theater of my home town, the Teatro dell'Opera and the Terme di Caracalla.

If I remember rightly I believe I have seen her altogether in at least ten roles and in numerous performances: Amneris, Annetta, Cherubino, Cenerentola, Carmen, Preziosilla, Zanetto, Principessa di Bouillon, Dalila, Santuzza.

The first time I heard her was on the 10th of January, 1952, when I went to the Teatro dell'Opera with my parents and my brothers to see *Aida* with the singer who was considered the greatest-ever interpreter of Verdi opera: Giacomo Lauri-Volpi. All of musical Rome was speaking of the event; in fact the tenor from Lenuvio hadn't sung this opera since 1928 and his appearance was eagerly anticipated. It was an unforgettable evening which revealed, as well as the tenor, a great Amneris. A few years later, in the second autobiographical book that Lauri-Volpi had written, *A viso aperto*, I read the following in his description of this performance where he comments on Amneris: "This was when La Simionato, all elegance, seriousness and interior discipline, gave us an Amneris that no one expected of her, being accustomed to parts that were vocally less weighty." So in spite of my youth I had seen things aright. She truly was one of the greats!

A few days later I saw her in *Le nozze di Figaro* and I remember again with pleasure the success she obtained as Cherubino. On account of this it pleased me to read over and over what Il Lunghi wrote about her in Il Giornale d'Italia on February 15, 1952: "Giulietta Simionato (Cherubino), with vocal and dramatic spirit, full of musicality..."

I also have an excellent recollection of her Carmen, her

Preziosilla, her Principessa di Bouillon, her Dalila, but where Simionato succeeded more than in any other opera to leave an indelible record in my memory was in *Cenerentola* and in *Cavalleria rusticana*: two operas that seem to have been written expressly for her.

In the first, the elegance of her expression, her voice warm and most musical, rich in tenderness, her dramatic expression refined and yet spontaneous, brought her to the attention of the public immediately, and it was immediately captivated by her charming and feelingful singing.

As for Santuzza, penetrating quickly to the heart of the character by means of incisive phrasemaking, expressive variation, dramatic energy and temperament that was quite extraordinary, she succeeded in standing out from the others quite literally, as in the score. Her miraculous vocal line set her apart as well. Never once did she reach for any low effects. In my opinion it was the most finished Santuzza of the last forty years.

Eugenio FERNANDI, *tenor*

I sang with that great lady, Giulietta Simionato, at the Vienna State Opera, at Salzburg and at the Metropolitan Opera. For me it was always pleasant to work with her! I also had the pleasure and privilege of attending several receptions with her. (In person she was simply herself in spite of her name; and she was an excellent artist, very devoted and conscientious about her work, who gave advice to her colleagues and to promising young singers.)

One fact comes to mind: we were at the Met where we were singing together in *Aida*, and on that day I wasn't doing very well... It was a matinee. I explained my situation to her and she immediately gave me some advice and encouraged me in such a way that the performance went ahead without problems... In 1984 I sang at Milano in the Casa Verdi, where the great genius was buried. La Simionato honored me with her presence, congratulating me, speaking to the public and consigning me the prize. ("*Orfeo lirico del successo ai grandi della lirica.*") Last year I found her again together with La Tebaldi and La Olivero at the Auditorio di Torino for an interview. I was invited as a spectator. For me, that was an unforgettable reunion!

Agostino FERRIN, *bass*

I sang with Giulietta Simionato very often, and all over the world, also during the first period of my career at La Scala, where I made my debut when very young, in 1961. Memorable premieres with the lady were *I troiani* [Les Troyens], *Aida*, *Don Carlos*, *Semiramide*, *Favorita*, *Trovatore*, always at La Scala. Above all I remember our first La Scala tour to Moscow in September of 1964. There I could admire the lady even more, not only as a great and unsurpassed artist, but also as an exquisite colleague whose refinement has always been a part of her *modus vivendi*, inside and outside the theater. I also remember a personal anecdote.

We were singing in the Kremlin auditorium in front of an audience of six thousand people — Madame Simionato, myself and other famous colleagues. During the second part of the concert, after my colleagues had sung and given encores, it was my turn to sing the aria "*Ella giammai m'amò*" (from *Don Carlo*) as an encore. The audience did not stop applauding and asking for one more encore. I was very embarrassed by so much enthusiasm and wanted to leave the stage, also knowing that Giulietta Simonato was waiting to sing after me and bring the evening to a close. But Madame Simionato, with words that I will never forget, said to me: "Dear Ferrin, where are you going? In the land of basses this is a double success. This is your evening, too. Go and sing all you want to. I will wait." So I sang "*La calunnia*" from *Barbiere* in front of a Simionato who was applauding me in her enthusiasm, and in front of a public that accorded me an unforgettable triumph!

Wladimiro GANZAROLLI, *bass*

I met Giulietta Simionato personally during the season 1960-61 at the Arena in Verona. I was there in the first years of my career, while Giulietta was already very famous. Her great humanity, her delicacy, her affability smoothed away the great difference between us as if by magic, permitting me an artistic collaboration without a single complication. We were then in a time of great *divismo* among operatic artists, yet Giulietta's nobility of character was so great that it canceled any trace of *divismo*. That which struck me most in her personality was the perfect dominion over the state of her soul before going onstage. Her eyes expressed enormous concentration, but at the same time, calm and serenity.

The Arena in Verona puts the vocal gift of the operatic artist in high relief. The immense theater disperses nearly the entire visible part of one's interpretation. It was at La Scala in Milano that I had been able to appreciate this great artist on the expressive level (in *Gli Ugonotti*, in the 1961-61 season; in *Semiramide*, in the 1962-63 season, and in *Cenerentola*, in the 1963-64 season, which I believe coincided with Giulietta's farewell performance at La Scala).

I believe that the three characters interpreted by Giulietta in the three La Scala seasons cited above represent the maximum of vocal and technical difficulty for the mezzo-soprano. However she overcame them all, receiving ovations every evening. In *Cenerentola* I recall that, because of exigencies involving the set, she had to make a quick onstage costume change.

Dear Giulietta, nothing about the twenty-year-olds could have given you reason for envy.

Gianandrea GAVAZZENI, *conductor*

I met Giulietta Simionato for the first time in 1940 at the Donizetti Theater in Bergamo, my native town, where I was conducting Puccini's *Suor Angelica*; Giulietta was singing the small part of the Mistress of Novices. These were the years when she was still being limited to so-called "secondary" roles. (Which were wrongly considered secondary, when singers like Simionato, whose musical abilities were already taking shape, were interpreting them.) Later on these roles were truly "secondary" or worse because of the quality of singers available to perform them.

Later, when her glorious career was under way, and she had developed those great vocal and musical gifts which we had all got to know over time, I always thought that the years during which she was sacrificed in the second roles were the foundation of her future development. Since then her professionalism, her love for music and the theater, her natural musical sensitivity and the quality of her vocal sound were already evident. Still, no one could have foretold such a brilliant future as the one that transpired. This happened thanks to her natural gifts, her will to study and to succeed, her intelligence and the development of her artistic feelings.

Thus, though her voice was not of great volume to begin with, through a rigorous technique she was able to develop it, along with a remarkable variety of tone colors and timbres, and master the great mezzo-soprano parts. She was capable of wide range, from chest voice to head voice. She could go from the dramatic roles to the coloratura roles for mezzo, from Mozart to Verdi, from Rossini to Saint-Saëns and Mascagni, and at the same time, thanks to the control of her vocal and musical means, she could take an intense schedule and adhere to it for such a long period of time. For almost three decades Giulietta Simionato was untouched by the wear and tear of passing time.

So it is that for decades she has been among the major operatic mezzo-sopranos of this century, in all the major theaters of Europe and of the Americas. Her main characteristic has been the ability to sing Azucena, Amneris, Eboli and Adalgisa with an exemplary interpretative outline and to be during the same years Mozart's Cherubino, Cimarosa's Fidalma, Thomas's tenderly French Mignon, the fascinating Dalila, and so forth. This is an example we cannot forget. It remains a truly special artistic benchmark because of the range of prerogatives she had secured for herself, being able to pass without discomfort or imbalance from Mascagni's Santuzza, rendered with passionate intimacy and amorous accents, to the baroque arias of Händel's *Giulio Cesare* in the performance I conducted at La Scala (one of the arias was sung from behind a gate that was part of the set, where the imprisoned character liberates baroque song with memorable emotion), and being able always to shift from one style to another staying in tune with the various musical languages, without giving up her own individuality. All of this derived from a background of musical and theoretical experience and a complete control of her intelligence. Nor could I forget the Seymour of Donizetti's *Anna Bolena*, a character as fiery as the costume Lucchino Visconti wanted: an event which, in the interpretive and visual context of the show, culminated in the famous duet with Maria Callas, and became a historic moment in the annals of La Scala during the fifties.

Some of the happiest moments of my long theatrical career are linked to these characters, themselves linked by the sovereign art of Giulietta Simionato.

Leyla GENCER, *soprano*

My first clear memory of Giulietta Simionato is a kind of gesture of solidarity. When I began singing at La Scala in 1958 I had been engaged to sing the world premiere of Poulenc's *Dialoghi delle Carmelitane*, and Giulietta Simionato had already achieved an important place in the operatic world — she was the leading mezzo-soprano at the time. We were living at the same hotel, the Hotel Duomo, where many famous artists had resided for years. I had a room at the end of the corridor on the fourth floor which was opposite Giulietta's suite. Every time I passed by I could see lots of flowers through the opened doors — the true image of the prima donna submerged by flowers.

Before singing the *Dialoghi*, at the beginning of January 1958, I was engaged to sing one of the famous "Martini & Rossi" radio concerts. The program went from Costanza's aria from the *Ratto dal Seraglio* (Die Entführung aus dem Serail) to "*Pace mio Dio*," to Lucia's mad scene. The evening was a success. As soon as I got back to the hotel the telephone rang; it was the warm voice of Giulietta Simionato, who had heard me on the radio and was expressing her enthusiasm with flattering words. A rare gesture of solidarity and sincere sympathy which greatly encouraged me at the time of my La Scala debut.

From my first encounter I was struck with Giulietta's appearance. Always very soignée, her hairstyle impeccable, her voice calm and harmonious.

In those days we were all frequenting the Biffi Scala. Giulietta had her table in a corner in the first room; at the opposite corner was Callas with her entourage: her husband, Ghiringhelli, and some admiring friends. I was alone in my corner facing them. So during the time spent at La Scala we saw each other every day. She was very moderate and frugal and did not drink; she had an enviable figure which she has kept to this day as the reward of a discipline and a civility in her life that I have always admired.

I remember Giulietta in a moment of sadness for her, in 1964, when La Scala had its Russian tour. I have kept an affectionate letter from her in which she expressed her gratitude for my solidarity during her Russian engagements.

Of course I remember Giulietta on stage, the many performances together. *Norma* at La Scala, *Aida* in Verona, *Don Carlo*... The *Don Carlo* at La Scala in 1961 stands out in my memory. It was an extraordinary cast: Giulietta Simionato, Boris Christoff, Ettore Bastianini, Nicolai Ghiaurov. She was inimitable in her "*O don fatale*" (as were Christoff and Ghiaurov in their duet).

The *Aida* in Verona... Her imperturbable calm before the performance... I can still see her, seraphic in her dressing room, putting a net over her hair before wearing the strange stylized Egyptian wig, while all around her the agitation was intensifying in anticipation of the performance. All of a sudden strange vocalises, muttered with the mouth closed, were proceeding from her dressing room. It was the way she tested her voice. I, on the other hand, was trying to sing entire phrases, to sing the first act at the piano, the last act, the most difficult phrases. Not her: she went over a couple of lines and went to sing. And she sang beautifully.

Our *Norma* at La Scala... It was so exciting because it was the first time a singer had interpreted the character after Callas. And there were doubters among the Callas fans, and the usual divided factions.

The evening was very tense at the beginning and ended in triumph, with Giulietta and I embracing, moved, amid the audience's ovations. In *Norma* Giulietta was unsurpassable. I sang with other Adalgisas during my career, but Giulietta gave a different emotion, because of the way her voice was veiled with melancholy—that particular, fascinating sound. There was contrast and pain in her phrasing, and you could hear the character's emotions and remorse; her voice could give such depth and complexity to her intentions. It was the same when she sang the Princess of Eboli, the stormy duet of lights and shadows with the Queen.

I would also like to remember *Anna Bolena*... Giulietta had sung in the famous La Scala production with La Callas, and had a personal triumph; radiant in her red costume she sang "*Di quella fiamma indomita*" with verve and virtuosity. When I was chosen to sing the opera on the RAI in the summer of 1958, Giulietta was again Jane Seymour. It was a memorable evening, especially for me, because I was beginning to understand how I was going to sing "my" Donizetti. I realized then that this was a modern composer who should be explored.

Giulietta for me is inseparable from all my theatrical and personal memories taken together. She was an unforgettable artist and a sweet and human colleague.

Carlo Maria GIULINI, *conductor*

I think that Giulietta Simionato is an accomplished artist who possesses the three essential qualities: diction, musicality, and an ability to act on stage. To this I can personally add a feeling of friendship.

Tilde GOBBI

Tito called her Mulieta from the beginning of their career at La Scala, and Mulieta she has always remained for us.

Sometimes circumstances and engagements kept us apart for long periods of time, but seeing each other again was so natural that we might have just parted the day before.

We have experienced the excitement of performance and the elation of success all over the world, and I dare to say *we have* because I have also intensely lived the performers' life, almost breathing with them.

We have shared the pain that life mercilessly imposes, but when I think about Mulieta I can only remember her radiant smile and her sharp humor. We often organized trips to the United States together, the first trips after the war, taking our Cecilia, a devilish ten-year-old. Tito was of course at the head of the expedition, with passports and tickets, and I was at his side. Mulieta and Cecilia would follow behind, hand in hand — they got along so well.

"Dad, can you buy us candy?" "Dad, can you buy us ice cream?"

We were laughing but the airlines personnel were very worried about taking good care of *Commendatore* Gobbi's little girls.

In those days the Atlantic crossing was still a little bit of an adventure and was also very long. Some airplanes had berths for the passengers who wanted to sleep. One time the steward told Tito that there was a sleeping berth available and it would have been perfect for the "little girls." The two devils climbed up happily, but the unwary Mulieta had bought a rubber ostrich at the airport that could say "cro-cro" and my dear little girl made it sing all night, kicking Mulieta with one foot and dangling the other from her berth. In the morning poor Mulieta's face was as worn out as Azucena's, and she must have bitterly regretted buying that noisy toy.

In Chicago after the performances we often went all together to eat: there was a long table that the Italian Village kept for us in a private room. There we would tell jokes and imitate the other singers that were present, laughing loudly to get rid of the excitement of the performance. Mulieta would make Maria Callas laugh loudly when she would imitate the diva in *Traviata*, waving an improvised fan in front of her face and trilling: "*Gioir, gioir...*"

In Salzburg also, after the premiere of a very successful

Falstaff, conducted by Karajan, we found the time to enjoy ourselves under the constant drizzle. There were attempts to play tennis that were suddenly frustrated, card games, dangerous auto excursions under torrential rains, but everything was fine, we were happy in each other's company.

A few years ago Giulietta Simionato, the president of AMAL in Milan, wanted to offer Tito the prize "A Life for Opera." On the stage they both were talking and joking with such ease that one could picture them in the brilliant duet between Rosina and Figaro in *Barbiere*, in which they had been incomparable for wit and elegance of style.

Madame President's opening line was "Ladies and gentlemen, this time I am going to introduce a really 'big' character." The double meaning had the audience laughing there in the hall of the Teatro S. Babila, for indeed Tito was very tall and big next to her petite figure.

I do not want to talk about the sad things we shared like sisters. We both had the comfort of a sincere friendship, which is so rare in the competitive world of the performing arts.

Now that I am alone and destiny has taken away my beloved companion, Mulieta writes and telephones me with great tenderness. Thank you, Mulieta.

Rita GORR, *mezzo-soprano*

I heard Giulietta Simionato for the first time at La Scala, in *Aida* with Birgit Nilsson in 1963 (I was in the theater to sing *Tristan und Isolde*).

She seemed to be a stupendous Amneris. I heard her again in *I Capuleti e I Montecchi* in New York. She was then about 54 years old. And she was formidable. The agility and softness in her voice had remained intact. I was very impressed. It will be difficult to come up with another artist to equal her.

Giorgio GUALERZI, *music critic and historian of vocal style and opera theater*

The ten years during which Simionato sang in major theaters but in secondary roles enabled her vocal instrument to mature day by day so that she could make the time of fullest vocal maturity coincide with the time her career began to take off, which is to say, when she had the vocal means to put behind it. She had a great career thanks to her technique, but also because she had been "resting," so to speak, singing the odd Beppe, Maddalena, Dorabella, etc.

She took up the great Verdi roles when she was almost forty, and very carefully. The role she sang the most was Amneris, whose high tessitura is particularly suited to her, because Giulietta is in reality a "falcon." This is demonstrated by the fact that in 1962, when she was fifty-two, she had the courage to sing the role of Valentina in *The Huguenots*, a role that reaches as high as a C.

This also explains how she could sing the C in unison with Callas in the famous second act duet of *Anna Bolena*.

Giulietta was a great professional, a woman with a splendid physique, very resistant to fatigue. I think she averaged 80 to 100 performances a year, from the mid-fifties until the beginning of the sixties. We must remember that in Italy, in her repertoire, Simionato was confronting the declining Ebe Stignani at a very high level; then there was the authentic mezzo-soprano voice of Barbieri, though inferior from the standpoint of technique.

I saw Simionato's Carmen: she was too much of a convent girl. Giulietta was afraid of going beyond certain limits. She certainly cannot be accused of lacking good taste, however Carmen needs some fire, which Pederzini possessed, the last great Italian Carmen. Italy has never had another Carmen to rival Pederzini's.

Simionato considers herself a great Rossini singer. There can be no doubt that she has made great progress in respect to what went before, and no doubt that she will have her place in history. However, today, from the historical viewpoint, in respect to La Horne and La Berganza, she has been left behind. Today Rossini is sung with more attention to the operas' philological, and therefore also their stylistic, aspects.

The fact remains that La Simionato is the bridge between the pioneers (Supervia, Pederzini, Anitua) and the rebirth at the absolute level, with *tempo pieno,* exemplified by Horne and Berganza. Everyone seems to consider her Verdi and Rossini roles among the best she performed. I appreciate more her *Cavalleria*, precisely because of her sense of sorrow, where she expressed the best of herself. (In *Carmen* the best things she did were in the third and fourth acts and not the first and second.) She also had the right voice for Santuzza, which is an ambiguous role, neither for soprano or mezzo. Simionato was a mezzo-soprano who had built her voice, but she was less artificial than Cossotto.

We must put special emphasis on Simionato's professionalism. She left her career at the right moment, having the good sense, something very rare, to understand she should retire; in fact she didn't even announce her intention.

From a historical point of view Simionato switched the personal and historical dates; compared with Cloe Elmo (who was also born in 1910) Giulietta began practically where Elmo ended.

Giangiacomo GUELFI, *baritone*

It gives me joy to talk about Giulietta Simionato. So many indelible memories! As a singer she was exceptional. Her technique was impeccable and she could keep the smalto and tone of her voice unchanged throughout her range. It was a wide-ranging voice, large in theatrical terms, with a dazzling high register. She could afford to sing everything and sing it well. I sang with her for the first time at La Scala in *Proserpina e lo straniero* by Castro, and then in *Carmen*, *Aida*, *Mosè*, *Trovatore*, *Forza*, *Sansone e Dalila*, *Cavalleria rusticana*. So many performances and such emotions!

A great professional, she lived for her art and I always heard her in good voice. And her *Werther*? And her *Cenerentola*? And her *Il conte Ory* and *Tancredi* at the Maggio Fiorentino? Great shows and Giulietta was superb in all of them. That was the artist. As woman and colleague she was likable, friendly, witty and always ready with a clever remark or trick, but always under control. She knew she was a diva, but had the good taste never to let it influence her. Great! Great!

Frederick GUTHRIE, *bass*

The first time I met Giulietta Simionato was in 1954 when she came to Vienna to sing in a concert performance of *Carmen* at the Musikverein. This concert was conducted by Herbert von Karajan, who wanted to present his conception of *Carmen*. This opera was one of his favorites and he conducted it over his entire career. In 1954 he had not been able to present it at the Vienna Opera, but was determined to do a *Carmen* in Vienna, if only in a concert version. He brought together a brilliant cast and Signora Simionato was his glorious Carmen. I remember being stupefied by her magnificent voice, but even more so by her technique, which was without defects, making it possible for her to begin where other artists, unfortunately, would have given up. For her technique was a way of reaching for perfection rather than an end in itself. Besides her marvelous voice and a noteworthy technical facility she had great personal warmth, without a single trace of that condescending attitude that one cannot help but notice in so many of our great artists.

I had the honor and the pleasure of singing *Carmen, Le nozze di Figaro, Aida, La forza del destino* and *Un ballo in maschera* with her. These were the turning points in my personal career. I was always impressed with her humility and with her warm, friendly personality. Certainly she was an ideal colleague and artist and I greatly admired her.

Dame Gwyneth JONES, *soprano*

My only meeting with Giulietta Simionato was during a *Trovatore* at the Royal Opera House in London. The conductor was Giulini.

This was just the beginning of my career and it was the first time that I had sung with famous singers who had attained the highest level of artistic achievement.

Giulietta was very maternal with me. She was a great lady, always kind, sincere, generous. She showed me a great deal of interest and affection, and her help and friendship contributed a great deal to my success in that unforgettable performance.

Herbert von KARAJAN, *conductor*

Signora Simionato first appeared in the circle of my relations at the beginning of the fifties. Her first role was Carmen. Since then she has honored us with her voice and presence in numerous operas in Vienna, in Berlin and especially at the Salzburg Festival.

Her great nature and her deep expressivity have caused us to feel the greatest respect and admiration for this extraordinary artist, who lives only for art, which she shares with her pupils, who will all be able to bear witness to how much can be achieved through devotion and sacrifice.

She will always be an example to us.

Ilva LIGABUE, *soprano*

The first time I approached her she complimented me for arriving at the theater before her. Giulietta arrived at her "work" at least two hours before the performance. She loved to walk on the empty stage before she went to her dressing room to get ready. It was from Giulietta, who was an example for me, that I had one of the nicest compliments. This happened at La Scala, at the opening of the 1965-66 season, during which we sang together in *La forza del destino*. The year before she had been my godmother at my debut in *Don Carlo* at the Teatro Massimo in Palermo. These were the only opportunities I had to sing with her. Shortly after the *Forza* at La Scala she bid farewell to the stage... In that theater where she had suffered and struggled to succeed, and where she had established her prodigious vocal art, which still marks a magic moment in the life of the theater.

Alberto LITTA MODIGNANI, *Secretary and founding member of the Milanese Association of Friends of Opera (AMAL or the Associazione Milanese Amici della Lirica)*

Giulietta Simionato was made president of the AMAL in January, 1982.

It was a happy choice. No other artist, at that time, was better qualified to hold the office.

Her fame and the fame of her curriculum vitae, which speaks for itself, would have been enough to give luster to our association, but the famous singer has been able to add to her great personal experience from a didactic point of view, having assumed the responsibility of teaching at the school for the improvement of opera singers at La Scala in addition to being the artistic advisor in numerous singing seminars in Japan.

La Simionato is able thus to remain in the lively circles of theater people and voices, evaluating their potential and "market," to know the new methods and studies and to remain in direct contact with young singing students.

This is what the AMAL wants above all, since one of its goals is to introduce new belcanto talent to the public, as well as to recognize, by awards, the great lives that have been consecrated to international lyric art.

Giulietta Simionato also possesses a social spirit that is indispensable to her position. She represents us where it is good for us to be. She is an attentive, tireless, lavish and skilled President. Her splendid home in Milan is a meeting place for friends and artists so that thanks to her, friendship and art get together in a perfect atmosphere.

Angelo LO FORESE, *tenor*

I knew Giulietta Simionato while I was debuting in *Carmen* at Lugano in 1953 and 1954. Afterward I sang *Aida* and *Cavalleria rusticana* in Japan, and *Carmen* and *Cavalleria* at La Scala, where I was covering for Giuseppe Di Stefano. In my judgment, Giulietta succeeded in being a great Carmen and a great Santuzza, two very different characters. It was said that as Carmen she was cold. However, her portrayal communicated a great deal to me through her attitudes, especially in the last act where she showed fear in confronting Don José and was looking for a chance to flee. As I see it, Giulietta was certainly one of the best Carmens I ever sang with, if not the best.

I always found La Simionato to be willing to help make a given evening a success. I think of her as a woman who is very human and distinguished. I remember in particular when she and La Tebaldi were friendly and considerate to me in Tokyo, in 1961, when I was suffering from lumbago at the beginning of the Italian opera season and still had to make the rehearsals for the show — with the difficulty which you can imagine!

James MacCRACKEN, *tenor*

I have great admiration for Giulietta: she was a marvelous colleague and the best mezzo-soprano in the whole world during the epoch I knew her and sang with her. I was always surprised that such a little woman could emit such marvelous, powerful tones. I remember that she had a singular way of vocalizing and imagine that she must have been a very good teacher, for the correctness of her technique was obvious.

Luisa MARAGLIANO, *soprano*

The greatest gift of Giulietta Simionato — the great artist, great singer, great lady — after the aforesaid qualities — was to shine by her modesty, and by her knowledge of how to live by living. I did not have a chance to be onstage with her a great many times — all the same, the few times that I was able to interpret my favorite opera, *Aida* (at La Scala, at the Arena di Verona, at the San Carlo di Napoli) she was a great rival/colleague who was helping rather than trying to hinder me, supporting me with an inventive, enlightened spirit.

Yes, because another of her great qualities was that of knowing how to submit herself immediately (in her singing and stage movement) to the exigencies of the moment. Stupendous!

My first meeting with her took place in Geneva when I was very young, little more than a debut artist, and we were recording *Trovatore* for Decca. She was the only one recording her arias cold without any precautionary run-throughs with the orchestra. Later between La Scala and the San Carlo di Napoli we gave some of our best performances artistically and my admiration for her was increasing in a constant crescendo.

I only met her once outside the theater — when she was at Sulmona in 1985, in the course of the Maria Caniglia competition in which we were members of a jury. Giulietta Simionato remained the same dear and gentle woman she had been at the first, always ready to smile...

One could write volumes and volumes about her, and without doubt Giulietta deserves them!

Galliano MASINI, *tenor*

I remember Giulietta with so much admiration and affection for having sung so many times with her. She was one of my favorite Carmens.

Ferruccio MAZZOLI, *bass*

I had little to do with Signora Simionato directly, but I remember the immense humanity and the sustained friendship that she always had for her colleagues and her complete and exemplary dedication to the moral and scientific figure of Professor Frugoni.

Tatiana MENOTTI, *soprano*

In a few words I would say that I have known La Simionato and had affection for her for fifty years now, therefore how can I relate *episodes*? It would be necessary to talk about them, describe, comment on them.

In a few words I can synthesize all of it by saying that hers really *was* the fable of Cinderella: from being a humble but very skillful singer she became a star of the greatest brilliance which is shining still many years after the end of her career.

Angelo MERCURIALI, *tenor*

When I came to La Scala in 1939 Giulietta was doing small parts. She was a sprightly little thing, very engaging and disposed to playing tricks. We sang together in so many cities (Bologna, Ferrara, etc.).

In 1947 I saw La Simionato at La Scala in *Mignon* and it was a revelation: I remember her as tense during the rehearsal. I also remember a *Matrimonio segreto* we did together in Lausanne in 1950 (she was very entertaining and made everyone laugh during the duet with the tenor) and also a *Werther* that was prepared for Rovigo in 1955 (these performances, organized in her honor, were a noteworthy success).

At Bilbao, for a *Cenerentola*, the stage was filled with rose petals, an amazing thing!

Giulietta Simionato succeeded with lots of seriousness and hard work; the gravity of her professional stature should be taken as an example to all. She was great in all her roles and could easily pass from dramatic roles to those of the coloratura.

Robert MERRILL, *baritone*

Signora Simionato was a truly marvelous artist and colleague. I always found her tremendously dedicated to her art. We had quite a few performances together at the Metropolitan Opera and we recorded a *Trovatore* together in Rome. I can only say that I appreciated all my performances with her. She had a magnificent voice and was a great lady. All our artistic collaborations were a joy and it was a great privilege for me to work with such a magnificent artist.

Alvinio MISCIANO, *tenor*

I can say the following about that great artist, Giulietta Simionato, with whom I had the pleasure to sing many times in so many theaters in Italy and abroad: in the first place, aside from her tremendous artistic versatility, she was always set off from the rest by an exquisite gentleness which was allied in her case with a rare sense of comraderie with all colleagues, who cherish the memory of it. In my case, besides a splendid recording of *Il barbiere di Siviglia* by Rossini for the Italian Decca, I sang with her in the United States and Brazil. In the U.S.A. and in Portogallo I had her as a superb leading lady in the *Mignon* of Ambroise Thomas and in the *Cenerentola* of Rossini.

In many concerts together she was always responsible for the lion's share of the enthusiastic successes which we enjoyed everywhere.

Giuchi MIYAZAWA, *music critic*

Signora Simionato came to Japan four times (1956, 1959, 1961 and 1963) as a member of the Italian Opera Tour organized by the NHK [Japanese National Broadcasting Corporation] and took the parts of Amneris, Cherubino, Carmen, Azucena, Santuzza and Rosina at Tokyo and Osaka. She obtained the admiration of the Japanese public for her inimitable voice and her attractive stage personality. Newspaper reviewers exclaimed over the perfection of her vocalism, her solid technique, the virtuosity of her musicianship, but above all, our critics appreciated the artistic gift which enabled her to enter into so many characters and succeed in living through their feelings. It was well-known that her repertory was quite large: when she did a comic part from an opera buffa, she sang the difficult aria with great facility and lightness, and when she did a serious part like Amneris or Azucena, she knew how to give a strong personality to each of these characters with delicate and refined expression. She was a true prima donna, a precious one, rare in this world. But Signora Simionato as a person also won great popularity among the Japanese for her sincere gentleness and warm solicitude for others. I well remember the great respect in which she was held by her colleagues: Del Monaco and Tucci, for example, were frequently calling "Giulietta!" and entering her dressing room as if she were their advisor.

Paolo MONTARSOLO, Bass

Giulietta had an extraordinary versatility. She could easily go from dramatic roles to the buffo sort. I was made aware of this when we were doing *Italiana in Algeri* in Dallas. She was having so much fun that she had to ask me *sotto voce* during rehearsal not to make her laugh.

I was present at a marvelous, exceptional *Mignon* at La Scala a year later and went to her dressingroom afterward to congratulate her.

In the *Carmen* we sang together in Tokyo she invented the dance with the pearls.

The Cinderella she recorded in 1963 is extraordinary and confirmed the vocal resources which enabled her to have a vast repertory, unlike other mezzo-sopranos who had to stick to dramatic parts.

Marisa MOREL, *soprano, stage director and producer*

In 1933 I took part in the national singing competition in Florence. The preliminaries were in March, the finals in May. I got to know Giulietta superficially in May, but I do not recall speaking to her before the final evening at the Florentine Politeama and during the awarding of prizes in the Sala dei Cinquecento at the Palazzo Vecchio. However, I remember her perfectly. Her huge eyes in a small alabaster face and a lot of black hair. She was not unfriendly, but not very talkative. I, on the contrary, liked to talk. I clearly remember that she did not feel comfortable in the midst of the vociferous crowd of participants in the rehearsal halls of the Politeama, and it showed, but as soon as she was on stage she was transformed. She was almost unrecognizable. Because of the great impression she made on me I did not forget her for many years, even though we were not friends.

During the competition she had sung "*O mio Fernando*" from *Favorita*, but I heard her during the awards concert in "*Non conosci il bel suol*" from *Mignon*. That voice remained with me and I could never forget it; the very particular tone, the perfect diction and also the intelligent phrasing. Also, physically she was a little doll. There was even an incredible rayon dress (that stuff of imitation silk, shiny to the point of being incredible, remember?), thick with material and with a big black velvet rose on the waist. Really a horror! I come from Torino, the Italian Paris, and I remember this attire because later, when I saw her dressed as a Spanish girl, I was a little disconcerted. But what importance did it have? When she started singing, many of us thought about leaving the competition, so who gave the dress another thought? Rosina Storchio (the creator of Puccini's Mimì), the tenor Bonci, La Krusceniski (who was, I think, the first interpreter in Italy of *Salomé*) had good ears and their judgment was very generous to me, if only fair to Giulietta, as they put me at her level together with the great bass Giulio Neri and tenor Aldo Sinnone.

In 1944, while I was working steadily at the Bern Stadttheater, the Grand Théâtre of Geneva gave me the production of *Così fan tutte*. For the female roles I chose Suzanne Danco, making her debut, and Luise Helletsgruber from Vienna, a singer I had heard at Glyndebourne. She was vocally excellent but I wasn't satisfied with her appearance in the part.

I went to Milan to look for Simionato. I remember we met at the Caffè della Scala, it was either in April or May. Giulietta wore a light gray dress with a small tie at the neck. She did not seem happy, I recall. Perhaps deep inside she had given up the dreams that we all have at the beginning of our careers. She was shy and reserved and I believe the theater world always scared her. She was also married and therefore not independent. For these reasons she suffered for nine years. However, La Scala had been a useful experience; she understudied so many roles and this became very useful later on.

I gave her all the work that I could put together, but it was not a lot. I remember I let her have a tour of concerts in the Ticino, which were coupled with some lectures. In Geneva her debut as Dorabella was a triumph. Her talent was a great help to her colleagues as well. Danco was an excellent singer, almost perfect, but on stage she was a disaster. With Giulietta on stage night after night it was always a new pleasure for me. I could see how much intelligence she brought to bear in approaching her characters (though it is an innate intelligence that doesn't call attention to itself). Her Dorabella, and then Fidalma, had become finely chiseled works of art — never exaggerated, but no matter how many times I saw them, not just excellent, perfect. It was a joy to work with her; you only had to suggest an expression or a gesture and immediately she would make it her own.

Albert MOSER, *President of the Salzburg Festival*

The saying of Goethe that would define art as the mediator of the unknown seems exact in a special way when one contemplates saying a few words about the phenomenon which, famed as La Simionato, has for a long time now been clothed in the nobility conceded her by her public.

What more can be said of a singer who brilliantly distinguished herself 50 years ago and rose ever higher thereafter, installing herself at the top for decades, at the absolute vertex for a singer of her repertory, and about whom one could read something every day in the world press? The problem becomes even more complicated if the request is: what can one say of her in the context of the Salzburg Festival? The Festival of Salzburg which by this time also is carrying the burden of 65 years of age, and which no artist of world fame can afford to leave out of account. And certainly at such a festival Simionato is one of the hundred all-time greats. Yet it was impossible not to hear and feel that she was a singular personality at Salzburg.

The 85th birthday of Karl Böhm was another occasion for her to make an appearance, nearly seventy years old, on the Palace stage at the festival. In honor of the maestro she sang Cherubino's aria "*abbassata di un'ottava*," as the program noted.

Then we read: "Giulietta Simionato sang with the voice she has today, that is to say, of a bass, the aria of Cherubino, '*non so piú cosa son, cosa faccio.*' Probably the most beautiful gift accepted by Karl Böhm, and with great emotion." This happened in 1979? It was her 25th performance at the Salzburg Festival, whether she knew it or not.

This happy relationship had begun in 1957 when Herbert von Karajan, who had a keen sense of her exalted artistic qualities, brought her to Salzburg for his dramatic and musical production of Verdi's *Falstaff*. Simionato's debut, when it came about, could not have been an easy thing: it was a question of showing her stuff next to Schwarzkopf and Anna Moffo, with Tito Gobbi singing opposite. Besides, it is widely known by now that von Karajan didn't make it easy on his singers.

That overwhelming success was taken for granted, and Giulietta Simionato had to establish further links to Salzburg. She had her chance when a very interesting project offered itself: the *Don Carlo* of the famous *Felsenreitschule* with Herbert von Karajan as conductor and Gustav Gründgens as director, which was planned for 1958. Once again there was a splendid cast: Sena Jurinac, Anneliese Rothenberger, Cesare Siepi, Ettore Bastianini. She sang the part of Princess Eboli. "The splendor and timbre of her voice were captivating, and she fascinated us all the more with her incredible ability to breathe life into her character, to give her a shape and a soul," said the newspapers. And from that moment on the Salzburg Festival spoke with pride now of "its" Simionato. Now nothing seemed in the way of a continual collaboration. On the contrary, she was able to be a better Orfeo. This time too the *Felsenreitschule* was chosen for the scene of the crime, with Oscar-Fritz Schuh as stage director and once again with Herbert von Karajan conducting. "A Splendid *Orfeo* in the Felsenreitschule," said the newspapers, and of Simionato: "her magnificent contralto voice filled the enormous room with crackling tensions, and her *piannissimi* were as if suspended in air. The greatest melodic masterpiece of Gluck, '*Che faró senza Euridice,*' became an indescribably noble and interiorized lament." (This quote was picked up by the German daily the *Düsseldorfer Nachrichten* on 14 August 1959 and was signed Alfons Neukirchen.)

Naturally the Verdi *Requiem* wasn't forgotten, with Simionato, of course, and Leontyne Price, Giuseppe Zampieri and Nicolai Ghiaurov singing opposite her. Herbert von Karajan conducted the Berlin Philharmonic Orchestra and the "*Singverein der Gesellschaft der Musikfreunde*" of Vienna (chorus). This event in 1962 wasn't her only engagement at Salzburg that year. In the great hall of the Festival Palace von Karajan staged and conducted Verdi's *Il trovatore* and Giulietta Simionato sang one of her most splendid roles, Azucena. Among other names the cast included Leontyne Price, Franco Corelli and Ettore Bastianini. At the end of the spectacle "as bunches of flowers cascaded onto the stage and beyond the orchestra pit they formed a bridge among all unknown Salzburg citizens and their noble artist-guests, amidst roaring applause from the international opera public," as Friedrich Hommel wrote in the daily *Stuttgarter Zeitung* on 2 August, 1962.

In 1963 *Il trovatore* was repeated four times with James MacCracken in the part of Manrico. For the last performance on August 30, 1963, Giulietta Simionato met with "unparalleled jubilation."

Robert Schumann said: "To transmit light into the depths of the human heart: this is the artist's mission." Giulietta Simionato, a star from the musical heavens, was truly the possessor of such a luminosity.

Let us return one last time to her last trip to Salzburg on the occasion of Karl Böhm's 85th birthday. The influential critic Franz Endler of *Die Presse* wrote: "Notwithstanding the ranks of stars who were offering their congratulations, the matinee's most touching moment was supplied by Giulietta Simionato. She had left the stage of her own free will and returned there to sing a homage to Böhm one last time — an aria of Cherubino, which had been lowered in pitch, of course. For everyone in the Festival Palace the magic of her personality was there again, the grace, the force of conviction that no one since had been able to bestow upon us..." We want to appropriate these words because it seems that the gratitude and veneration that we of the Salzburg Festival have always nourished for Giulietta Simionato could not be expressed in a more convincing fashion.

Petre MUNTEANU, *tenor*

In the course of my career I came up against Giulietta Simionato many times, as we sang many important operas together.

In particular it gives me great pleasure to recall my debut at La Scala, way back in April of 1947, in *Cosí fan tutte.* If I am not mistaken this was also Giulietta's debut in a major role. It was our first collaboration, she was my first Dorabella. From the very first rehearsal I was struck with her warm timbre, full of harmonies, with her expressiveness, her way of expressing herself, her style and musicality. Everything went marvelously well at the evening performance. Our voices fit very well together in the duets and trios, and all of the rest in the company were of the first rank. The conductor was Jonel Perlea, who was in my opinion the greatest Mozart conductor of his time. La Danco was Fiordiligi, Cortis was Guglielmo. It was a success: a crossroads in my career and in Giulietta's, careers that would take us ever higher. Many other times we had the good fortune to sing together at La Scala in the *Arlecchino* of Busoni, conducted by Mitropoulos, at the Teatro Comunale of Trieste in *L'italiana in Algeri*, conducted by Antonino Votto, at the Mórlacchi of Perugia in the *Gionata* of Puccini for the "Sagra Umbra" and again at the Comunale of Bologna, in Händel's *Messiah*, conducted by Gui... and there were many other times. All sorts of musical works, of all styles and historical epochs. Giulietta managed everything very skillfully: she gave enjoyment and she enjoyed herself, moved the public and conquered them, seeming to be completely involved with the other performers onstage.

As a person she was charming: full of enthusiasm, good humor and gifted with an enviable talent for mimicry. The leading lady of *Traviata* was one of her specialties, but she could also do a parody of an auditioning singer that was no less fine, and the performance of a young girl at a recital. These were the *shticks* that all of us wanted to hear her do, wherever, whenever.

With her exceptionally harmonious qualities of voice and her solid professionalism she was destined to make a great career. And she did!, entirely on her own. My sincere congratulations, my dear, great colleague!

Alicia NOTI, *soprano*

The memory I have of Giulietta's performances in Mexico is of a marvelous and unforgettable experience, not only for her Mexican public but for all the artists who had the honor of singing with her. She was not only an exceptional artist, but a great lady in every sense of the word.

Luigi OLDANI, *former Secretary General of La Scala*

In the fall of 1947, after the inauguration of La Scala, in order to give work to the artistic staff which hadn't by then been formally stabilized, there was a popular season, and Thomas's *Mignon* was programmed, among others, for an important, illustrious singer. Because of *force majeure*, however, the singer couldn't make the performance and had to cancel.

The conductor, Antonio Guarnieri, was understandably anxious, but he was swayed by the fact that this was a popular season, and that La Simionato had just sung the same opera in Geneva, and by the presence of Giuseppe Di Stefano in the cast, who was coming from a clamorous success in *Manon* at La Scala the previous year, and of Cesare Siepi, another young man who had also debuted at La Scala with success.

On the 10th of June, 1948, at La Scala, Toscanini conducted the second part of *Nerone* to celebrate the thirtieth anniversary of Arrigo Boito's death, and he chose Simionato to sing the role of Rubria.

On the 14th of April, 1957, on the occasion of the presentation of *Anna Bolena* by Donizetti, under the baton of Gavazzeni, the stage direction of Lucchino Visconti and the set design of Nicola Benois, La Simionato had as great a success as her colleague Maria Callas, particularly in the great duet in the second part of the opera.

La Simionato has always been here, every season, and she was von Karajan's favorite singer. She was chosen to sing in many operas in the Italian repertory which were directed by him in Vienna and Salzburg, and in *Carmen* at La Scala.

Magda OLIVERO, *soprano*

Giulietta Simionato is an artist that I have always very much admired, especially in Rossini's repertoire. She has a great personality and great organization. I sang *Adriana Lecouvreur* with her and she was a formidable princess!

This is all I can say about this artist who has given so much to the theater and has left the world so many unforgettable moments.

Luigi OTTOLINI, *tenor*

My contact with Giulietta Simionato were numerous: with her I did so many performances of *Aida*, *Forza del destino*, *Trovatore* at La Scala and at the Vienna Staatsoper, in Chicago, etc. She was the very best colleague and she sang like an angel.

Paolo PADOAN, *musicologist*

Giulietta Simionato stands for the force of tenacity, and for professionalism.

Today, looking back, it seems incredible that an artist of her class could put up with years and years singing in the ranks before emerging as a star, and it is equally surprising that she quit the stage after a very intense career, while she was in perfect vocal form.

Fortunately, all her triumphs at the great theaters of the world were ample compensation for the difficulties and humiliations at the beginning of her career. Her retirement from the stage was regretted by all.

She was a complete singer, of great musical breadth, such that she was able to confront the most varied repertoire with purity and roundness of tone, with an authoritative accent, stylistic coherence, perfect musicality, clear diction; she was able to master her roles, which were chosen with her eyes open so that she was always able to invest them with the necessary cunning, or sensitivity, or rigor, or agility, or elegance.

Many characterizations benefited from her art and her sunny voice by means of a sort of cultural operation by which she knew how to replace them in the proper social context, removing them from the oblivion to which they had been consigned by colleagues whose vision had been exclusively veristic.

With characters that had been widely known and loved by a mass public, and had been for a long time now ensnared in a degrading routine, she knew how to give them back their dignity, or how to renew or restore others which had been long forgotten for lack of interpreters or the ignorance of producers — all thanks to her perfect control of a perfect technique.

She has therefore left us something besides a lesson in how to sing: a lesson in style and sensibility, as well as a highly cultured musicality of great prestige.

Nicoletta PANNI, *soprano*

I always admired the art and the voice of Giulietta Simionato, and when I was given the chance to sing with her in the role of Euridice in Gluck's *Orfeo* I considered it a special privilege and a great honor.

Our performances at La Scala, La Fenice and at the San Carlo from 1962 to 1964 were artistic successes of the highest order, and naturally this was the case thanks to Simionato, who was singing Orfeo in such a miraculous way, with her marvelous legato, elegiac beginnings which gradually reached an intense emotional involvement that made her character unique and, in my opinion, unreproducible. In my small way I lived a little bit in the reflection of her success and in the artistic light which she generated with her singing, that showed me the true path I had been seeking to follow with my own voice. Before knowing La Giulietta I had thought of her as a species of *monstre sacrée*, or at least thought that she would assume the manner of a diva, but there was none of that. Right away I saw how unpretentious she was, how sympathetic, how communicative, and what an outstanding sense of humor she had. She was very serious about her work and always arrived early, even when the rehearsals were 10 in the morning, even when there had been a performance the night before in Vienna! In that case she would arrive half asleep and then surprisingly, without a single *vocalise*, her voice came out miraculously with all its beauty of tone. A miracle? Or the fruit of a rare intelligence?

I learned that even she was vulnerable in spite of all the confidence she had acquired. Indeed, one evening before a performance I saw her in the wings where she was eating an apple (her supper), seeming absorbed and maybe a little tense. I asked if she was afraid and she, resolute and abrupt, as if she didn't want to talk about it, said: "Yes, but it will pass." Therefore even she suffered from legitimate fears, just as I did in my insignificance (insignificant by comparison to her), even she suffered from fear for fleeting moments. Then her extraordinary power got the upper hand and made her a lioness who was facing down "her" public to defend yet again what she had worked so hard for and conquered. I know, having known her, that every time the curtain was raised her power, her art and her splendid voice were a reason for victory.

My artistic meetings with Giulietta Simionato are among those most dear to me that I will conserve among my very best memories.

Mario PASI, *music critic*

I don't want to add my voice to the chorus of admirers of Giulietta Simionato, the singer. She was great, a true artist, but there is no need for repetition. I would like instead to pay homage to this great singer on a human level. I met her at the beginning of my journalistic career, when I did the "color" pieces and when the *Corriere della Sera* hadn't given me space for a critical column. She used to say hello to me by saying "*Pasi e bene*," a paraphrase of "*Pace e bene*" and tried to help me understand her world, conscious of the fact that I didn't have experience and I was surrounded by so many "wolves."

That "*Pasi e bene*" is still a part of our friendship after so many years, with an added Venetian flavor.

Another of Giulietta Simionato's characteristics was and still is her personal and artistic courtesy: as a singer she never asked for anything, never demanded interviews, press conferences or photographs. She always put work first and respected other people's opinions. Of course, she could afford to: she was an infallible interpreter with an inimitable professionalism. All her life, she told me, she had only canceled two performances, and that was only when she was too weak to stand.

She played down everything, and was happy with the world. She could sing one night in Verona and the following night in Salzburg without any effort. She had been a long time in the ranks, and that had made her stronger and wiser. Today so much "waiting" seems incredible. If a new Simionato were to be born today she would immediately be singing in all the major theaters of the world. Giulietta left her art with simplicity; she can teach everything to everybody, including how it is possible to be happy and smiling in spite of the passing of time. For this reason she remains a friend and a source of good luck.

Gianna PEDERZINI, *mezzo-soprano*

Giulietta was a most appealing sort of woman, very vivacious in company and entertaining in her own right: she could whistle in her lips in a way that was truly very funny.

As an artist she is a singer who knew how to manage her vocal inheritance and to gain great satisfaction from it.

I think she could be an excellent voice teacher.

Clara PETRELLA, *soprano*

I often had the chance to sing with Giulietta Simionato, whom I consider my dear friend, whose voice I have always appreciated — I remember it as one of the most beautiful mezzo-soprano voices which has not been equalled for its sweet timbre, color, and facility of emission.

I particularly remember the pleasure of singing with her several times in *Adriana Lecouvreur*, an opera which permitted her to express not only her vocal gifts but also to perform, giving her the chance to show the public her personality.

Rigorous and precise in her preparation of the opera, she never allowed herself to improvise, for she was always conscious of the responsibility she had to the public for which she had a great respect. I remember also the wonderful laughs we had together, because theater was for her, as it was for me, our very life.

Gianni POGGI, *tenor*

I had many chances to sing with Giulietta Simionato. I remember particularly a *Marta* we sang together in 1947 at the Liceo of Barcelona. Afterward we were again together in *Ballo in maschera* and in *Favorita*. I recorded this last opera for Decca with Giulietta and the late lamented Ettore Bastianini who was also a member of the cast at the Arena di Verona, under the baton of Alberto Erede.

Giulietta was always a very appealing woman with an engaging personality. She was a perfectionist, too, who had a sense of responsibility and worked with commitment and seriousness.

Giulietta Simionato: a great artist and a most beautiful voice.

Georges PRÊTRE, *conductor*

Giulietta Simionato is an artist I loved and still love very much; she is a complete artist. In addition to having a beautiful voice, she is a magnificent interpreter and lives her roles. The last time I performed with Giulietta Simionato was at the Opera in Paris with Maria Callas in *Norma*. I could not have dreamed of having a better cast for this opera, as these two artists, in spite of their different personalities, could sing with the same style, which produced splendid duets, as their stupendous voices were attuned.

Signora Simionato has often defended French music (*Mignon*, *Werther* and *Carmen*). The only regret I have is that I did not conduct these operas when she sang them, because when I came to La Scala, Signora Simionato had already decided not to sing anymore. At that time, and I think I should stress this, I had demanded that French operas be sung in French, which was not done in Italy, so I would have liked to do this repertory with her.

In addition to the high esteem I have for Giulietta Simionato as an artist, I also consider her a friend, and I am always happy to see her in Milan, together with her husband.

Bruno PREVEDI, *tenor*

I sang with Giulietta Simionato at the Vienna State Opera in *Don Carlo*, in *Trovatore* in London and Moscow, 1964, and in *Norma* at La Scala in 1965. Simionato was always a very polite lady. She always followed the conductor's suggestions without ever making an issue of the artist she was. I never heard her saying anything unpleasant about anybody. I liked her best in *Don Carlo*, because her acting was especially good in that opera. It was a great honor to have sung with her.

Aldo PROTTI, *baritone*

I knew Signora Simionato way back in 1949: I was debuting in *Pagliacci* and she was singing a *Cavalleria* at the Teatro Augustus in Genoa. We ran into each other ever more often after that and I sang *Carmen* with her, *Rigoletto*, *Aida*, *Don Carlo*, *Forza del destino*, *Barbiere*, *Cavalleria*, *Trovatore*, *Ballo in Maschera*, *Gioconda*. She has a surprising personality, even sad, and she found her real personality on the stage where she was an outstanding artist with a flexible voice of the first rank. I remember her as being completely dedicated to the theater, and for me she is a perfect example for young performers.

Gianni RAIMONDI, *tenor*

To speak of Giulietta Simionato as a singer and as a colleague is very easy for me. Because Giulietta, an exquisite and intelligent lady, was born to sing and had on her side the beauty of her voice, a great musical knowledge, and a great gift for dramatic portrayal combined with an enviable vocal technique (this last an indication of long and profound study). It was therefore inevitable that she become one of the greatest singers of this century.

Eugenia RATTI, *soprano*

I came to La Scala in 1955. By what door? The one young girls go through to make their debuts. The chance to be able to take part in a *Mignon*, in the part of Filina, with the great and gentle protagonist, the Mignon of Giulietta Simionato, was a great honor for me. (Gavazzeni was the conductor, Zeffirelli the stage director). We were together again in *L'italiana in Algeri* (Giulini conducted, Zeffirelli directed) and again in *Nozze di Figaro* at La Scala. Then we performed together once more at the Piccola Scala in *Matrimonio segreto* (Sanzogno conducting, Strehler directing).

I remember that Giulietta amused herself by calling me "Circassa" because of my long, black tresses. Giulietta was a lady of great intelligence who was always ready with a smile or a witty remark. As a singer I can only say one thing: she was "tops."

Then came more *Mignons,* Adalgisa, and Jane Seymour in *Anna Bolena* with La Callas. All the others could be replaced, but not her with her magical personality.

The last time we met was in a magic castle on a hill in Piacenza where we were being awarded a prize, a beautiful plaque from UNICEF for our cultural and artistic activities.

Regina RESNIK, *mezzo-soprano*

I never had the good fortune to know Giulietta Simionato personally, in private life, but I had the honor and privilege of hearing her as a spectator on some great occasions. We were catching a glimpse of each other at all the great opera theaters of the world, particularly in the sixties; quite often we sang the same roles on alternate nights, night after night, in the repertory which both of us often sang. One thing was sure: on the nights when Simionato sang, I was there listening to her. Santuzza, Eboli, Amneris — also Cherubino at Vienna — are particularly fresh in my mind. Certainly one of the most memorable evenings of my life was the great opening night of the *Ugonotti* at La Scala, at the beginning of the sixties, with a cast which included Corelli, La Sutherland, Ghiaurov, Tozzi, and naturally, La Simionato, at the very height of her career as Valentina. That was the day I signed my contract to sing at La Scala, and I know that that performance brought me luck. Brava, Simionato!

Nicola ROSSI LEMENI, *bass*, and VIRGINIA ZEANI, *soprano*

I have many memories which are scattered over many years and many events. I remember her during the years when she was unwell, sad and very lonely — and then during the years of success and luck surrounded by admirers and friends who kept her away from her colleagues. Her life was her precious private property and depended in great part upon sentimental vicissitudes.

She was always a lively colleague when we were together, and above all an admirable artist because she was always prepared and ready to give her best even on a mediocre evening. My wife agrees with what I have just said and joins me in admiring the artist and the woman who has dealt wonderfully with the passing of time and has remained beautiful, attractive and elegant.

Michel ROUX, *baritone*

A few words on the great Simionato... I will give you them with pleasure. Before everything else, the woman — simple, gracious, kind, the very best sort of colleague to work with.

The artist: please let me tell you that if Signora Simionato would still sing Carmen she would eclipse *all* of her rivals, including the most famous, about whom so much publicity has been made. (I'm not naming a single one of them!)

Thanks to Giulietta Simionato the workplace was a wonderful place for me to be.

Here's to Giulietta Simionato, a great lady!

Daniele RUBBOLI, *writer*

It was an evening in 1985.

At the Teatro San Babila in Milan the stylish concert given by the Italian and Parisian pupils of Rosetta Noli, a successful soprano of the not-so-distant past, who was at the same time a teacher at the Paris Opera, was coming to an end.

Giulietta Simionato, who was the hostess, paid her public tribute while thanking her, comparing her among all colleagues to a violet: a flower which loves to hide, representing shyness and discretion in the world of flowers, but not less beautiful than others and also the most sweet-smelling of them all.

Thus, graciously, Her Majesty the Rose, was welcoming a colleague in art in whom she had faith.

Giulietta Simionato is in fact the ultimate rose of post-war Italian female singers, and of the world.

She carries herself with the same nobility we see in the flower, but as with the flower, there may also be thorns, a certain elegant distance brought about by her aristocratic vision and intellectualism born of many years experience singing.

With humility, persistence and self-determination, after severe studies to perfect her vocal instrument, Simionato brought her sovereign intelligence onto the scene, where it blossomed like a flower after long and careful cultivation.

Whether in the spontaneous sensuality and warmth that animate her Amneris or in the vocal illuminations that bring to life her *Favorita*, and the elegiac abandon of her *Mignon*, Simionato brings the lyric sensibility we expect from her to her entire repertoire, as well as an acute stylistic differentiation.

She also imposes the noble instincts of a great artist on all the characters she interprets.

Going beyond the dime-a-dozen feminine wiles of Rosina in *Barbiere* she shades the character of the young girl with a maturity that has the authoritarian overtones of a wilful personality.

Her displays of agility yield sparkling high notes which resemble nothing less than jewels in a royal collection.

The impeccable technique and breath control she brings to Cenerentola makes us aware of the princess behind the rags.

Santuzza not only looks like a peasant, she is a peasant by definition, but her soul tears itself apart because of the offense to her honor and loyalty as much as her heart is torn apart by passion.

Simionato seems to be painting her own portrait in Domenico Cimarosa's *Matrimonio segreto* when she sings: "*E vero che in casa io son la padrona...*"

As elegant in real life as in her presence on the stage, this mezzo-soprano, who was born in Romagna of a Venetian father and Sardinian mother, brought a historic presence to the stage.

And in the 1950s she, together with Callas (but with the greater professional responsibility and a more accurate technique, which helped her to avoid blurring the fullness of her timbre and keep from developing a hard, shiny *smalto*), offered readings of scores which respected the composer's wishes at the time of their writing, reviving interpretive styles that had gone by the wayside for some decades.

She was born in 1910, only hours after Guido Gozzano had written paragraph five of "La signorina Felicita."

> "*...già tutta luminosa nel sorriso*
> *ti sollevasti vinta d'improvviso,*
> *trillando un trillo gaio di fringuello.*
> *Donna: mistero senza fine bello!*"

With regal dignity, without ado, she left the stage in the mid-sixties.

I have heard that many roses bloomed in the theater since then. I have gone to admire them. From a distance they appear to be beautiful, full and fragrant. But as I reach out to pick them my hand is disappointed to find paper flowers pierced by a stem with an iron core.

Ornella ROVERO, *soprano*

I was right at Simionato's side on many occasions.

Of course she was a great singer with a flexibility quite out of the ordinary in the upper register which not all mezzo-sopranos possess — as well as an innate agility which permitted her to do a rondo in *Cenerentola* almost without vocalizing first, or warming up very little. It was a gift of nature, her voice, which she had improved with study.

I did a lot of *Cenerentolas* with her and about ten *Matrimonio segreto*'s — and with great amusement because she played Fidalma to great comic effect. We did *Il combattimento di Tancredi e Clorinda*, a *Marta* of von Flotow at Barcelona, where she deserved the applause of the orchestra because her voice was truly an instrument. She was Carlotta in *Werther*, and she did a Cherubino in *Nozze di Figaro* that was delicious and malicious; there was *Così fan tutte* of Mozart, and others...

She was always a dear and lively companion and further in her career I remember her in the most pleasing possible way.

Vladimir RUZDJAK, *baritone*

I sang with Giulietta Simionato quite a few times: the first time was at the Stadtsoper of Hamburg (in Verdi's *Don Carlo*, in which she was Eboli and I was Rodrigo Posa, I think in 1960). Afterward I sang with her several times at the Metropolitan Opera in New York in Verdi's *Aida*, she as Amneris, I as Amonasro.

I remember Giulietta Simionato as being someone who was always in good spirits, with a lively character, taking everything in a good humor. As a colleague she was very nice, and naturally very much the professional in everything regarding her work.

Suzanne SARROCA, *soprano*

Even though I didn't know Giulietta Simionato personally I sang *Aida* with her at Covent Garden. Like everyone else, I admired the beauty of her voice, her technique, and the conviction of her dramatic interpretations, which I was able to appreciate especially well as a spectator the night of the *Norma* she did with Maria Callas at the Paris Opera, a performance in which the innate aggressiveness of the two artists seemed superb and at the same time painful. It's a memory that has had a profound effect on me through so many evenings of opera.

Egon SEEFEHLNER, *former Director of the Vienna State Opera*

What things come to mind at the sound of her name!

One of the most splendid periods in the annals of the Wiener Staatsoper that comes vividly to mind is that of Herbert von Karajan. And belonging to this epoch was one of the greatest stars, La Simionato, as the Viennese fondly called her. In the Theater of the Ring she sang eleven different parts, enthralling the public to the point of hurricanes of enthusiasm and ovations, whether as Eboli or as Carmen, whether as Amneris or Santuzza, Azucena, Ulrica or Preziosilla, but also as Quickly and Maddalena, shining not only in the Italian repertoire. Her incomparable, unsurpassable art also manifested itself in interpretations of Orfeo and Cherubino. At the zenith of her career she retired from the stage, leaving her portrait in all our hearts, intact. The portrait of an artist of unforgettable grandeur.

Carlo Florindo SEMINI, *composer*

It was the war years, a time when many Italians took refuge in Switzerland, bringing with them their pain, either suffered in silence or displayed as a sign of defiance. Giulietta Simionato had also landed in Lugano after leaving Milan with her first husband, who was a violinist and became the *prima viola* of the Swiss-Italian Radio Orchestra. At that same time, back from Napoli where I had completed my studies and started a career as a musician, I was active both as a teacher and a music critic.

Among the many lines written, struck out and rewritten in

the difficult Ticino province, which frowned on critical activity understood as the history of a civilization, some of my discourses weren't entirely useless, as I sometimes was able to predict brilliant careers. It will suffice to mention the names of Dinu Lipatti, who had just come from Geneva to Lugano for a concert, and, of course, Giulietta Simionato.

In fact when the poet Francesco Chiesa, then the president of the Circolo della Cultura, invited me to give various lecture-concerts in the main cities of the province devoted to vocal and instrumental Italian chamber music of all eras, Simionato immediately agreed to collaborate.

This was a stimulating experience for both of us. At piano rehearsals we saw La Simionato involved, outside of the province of opera, in analyzing in detail, always with grace and good humor, a literature that was quite new to her. Rather than limit her, these studies gave her incentive.

Giulietta also showed her surprising quickness, the intuition that later enabled her to perform on stage roles from Mozart, Rossini and particularly the Verdi repertory, all roles of complex and contrasting psychology.

Perhaps without realizing it at the time, La Simionato discovered ways of resolving problems of taste characteristic of a certain late nineteenth century literature, and some technical links between "archaic" vocal technique and current practice (she also performed some lyrics of mine from the period 1940-45 — the first performance of them anywhere), thanks to her command of the various registers, of light soprano and dramatic soprano, as if she might want to establish — and this was also the case with certain excellent singers of the nineteenth century — the historical end of certain traditional academic values.

Audiences of the time immediately grasped the rich expressive range of our artist, who, if she seemed reserved in private, yet knew how to manifest her true nature, which was passionate and overpowering, on the stage. For the same reason, as far as I am concerned, Giulietta Simionato became a prima donna without ever having been a "diva," if one accepts the latter term to connote negative associations and a gratuitously eccentric temperament.

Only once did she appear to be different, if only in the usual respect of having given a performance where she seemed subdued or even crushed. This was at a concert at the Lugano Penitentiary in a series organized by the attorney Sergio Jacomella, who was the prison director, and was already internationally known at the time for his studies and meritorious initiatives on behalf of the moral and civic rehabilitation of prisoners.

Timid, ingenuous, irresistible, at the end of the concert, at the end of that memorable and humanly intense afternoon, she stood surrounded by her somewhat extraordinary audience, upon whose faces one could no longer read the melancholy acceptance of their various destinies; even the initial almost mocking indifference had given way to a light of conscience and hope.

I will end paraphrasing something of Borges, who lived in memory: books about famous people, not less than those about today's arrogant and shabby television personalities, are read so that we can forget them. But when we read about prima donnas, who are the opposite of superficial dissipators of artistic values, they remain in our memory.

Francesco SICILIANI, *Director of the National Academy of Santa Cecilia*

The years of Giulietta Simionato's musical activity coincide with the flowering of an entire generation of vocal and musical talent of which Italy can be proud.

Flexible and agile, sensitive and tender, cunning and lively, incisively dramatic, Giulietta knew how to bring together in harmony the various aspects of a very dramatic personality.

Cesare SIEPI, *bass*

The memory of Giulietta Simionato is vivid, wide and deep; it reaches far back in time, and yet it seems only yesterday. In 1947 in Barcelona there was a revival of *Anna Bolena* in which Giulietta was already preparing for a Seymour that in a later production was going to put her in the small cluster of La Scala's stars. But it was at La Scala in 1947-48 that the opera *Mignon* established her as a great diva, always welcomed and loved by the audience, as well as by all the theater people. All this affection was generated by her human qualities, and the magic she let out as easily as the notes she sang. Her behavior was always carefree and yet positive. She was always ready to have fun and a good laugh. An *antidiva*, if you like, because she was confident in her discipline. And she was completely lacking in arrogance.

Paolo SILVERI, *baritone*

I had the chance to sing with Giulietta Simionato in many operas: her ability to identify with the characters she was singing was such that one could believe each role had been written especially for her.

She had the gift of a voice which could easily cover two octaves and she could use it as she pleased, with excellent results, especially in Rossini's operas, where agility is predominant and in which she could be described as a *mezzo-soprano coloratura*.

Also, off the stage, everywhere, her behavior was "high class."

Enzo SORDELLO, *baritone*

Regarding the *Carmen* which was performed at Vienna on the 8th and 10th of October 1954 at the Grosser Musikvereinssaal, under the direction of Maestro von Karajan, my memories are somewhat faded by time. Just a little before that I had my official debut at the Teatro alla Scala in *Vestale* (the 7th of December, 1954). I still remember the anxieties of my illustrious colleague, Giulietta Simionato, whose temperament was particularly sensitive (I remember having seen her weep prior to the Rome recording of *Forza del destino*, in June, 1956!). The anxiety was caused in part by the fact that Dr. Ghiringhelli and Dr. Oldani were present at the performance, who had come to hear her in particular because on 18th of January in 1955 they were going to present *Carmen* at La Scala. The warmth and sensuality of the Simionato voice was exactly what was required for the character of Carmen. I was very excited and enthusiastic about her vocalism and was moved to go to her after the performance, at which time there was a crowd present in the room to pay her tribute, among whom were Ghiringhelli and Oldani, who in spite of their reserve were unable to contain their enthusiasm... In fact, La Simionato was Carmen at the Teatro alla Scala in January, 1955.

There was a big celebration afterwards and many toasts were drunk to La Simionato, who was being celebrated all over again by her colleagues, all of whom were overjoyed by her enormous success.

I remember that we all went together to a big restaurant every day for breakfast. It was there that I met La Simionato for the first time, and she was always most kind to me. Thanks to her exuberant temperament she kept everybody in good spirits.

Antonietta STELLA, *soprano*

Giulietta, besides being a great singer, is also a very dear friend of mine. From the beginning there was mutual sympathy and esteem.

We sang together very often: I was surprised when Giulietta was not in the cast. All my performances of *Trovatore*, *Aida*, *Forza del destino*, *Ballo in maschera* were always with Giulietta.

She was a colleague who radiated confidence. She hid her emotions because she was a sensitive woman. Among all my colleagues, Giulietta has the highest place, because she gained my affection. Today she is still a model for everybody: her professionalism and the precision she achieved in her interpretations were her trademark.

Joan SUTHERLAND, *soprano*

The performances with Giulietta were a true pleasure, both from a vocal standpoint and because of the friendly conversations we had about our work.

We shared the same preoccupations and anxieties and the same panic typical of performers: is the hairstyle all right or is it too heavy? Is the makeup all right? Isn't the train too long or too cumbersome, and is the wig of the right color? Can we see the conductor, and still follow the stage director's orders? That is to say, aren't we going to trip on this barely lit staircase?

All this was not too important, but the condition of the voice was. I had heard Giulietta sing at Covent Garden and in Verona at the Arena and listened to her recordings, but I was not prepared for the splendid voice I heard during the performances of *Semiramide* and *Ugonotti*.

It was a great joy to hear this elegant singer and I remember her with great affection.

Ferruccio TAGLIAVINI, *tenor*

All I can say of this dear colleague is about her professional responsibility, her exceptional artistic training and the fact that she never made anybody aware of her place in the pantheon of great artists. One of her distinguishing qualities was her "good humor" and her wit, which she knew how to apply at just the right moment.

Italo TAJO, *bass*

I think I am one of the few remaining artists who had the pleasure and the privilege to share the stage with Giulietta Simionato during both periods of her career. During the "first period" as a "luxury comprimario" at La Scala in 1942: I was making my debut in the great theater as Don Basilio in *Barbiere*; the conductor was Marinuzzi, and the other singers were Bechi, Pederzini, Ferruccio Tagliavini. Giulietta was Berta, and Valdengo, a beginner, was Fiorello. In 1941 at the Milan Conservatory we recorded for His Master's Voice what I would call a historic 78 rpm performance of *Andrea Chénier*. Olivero Fabritiis was conducting andGigli, Caniglia and Bechi were the main characters. In the secondary roles were Simionato (the countess), Taddei (Fléville) and myself (the poet Roucher).

After 1942 it took five long years, the war years, before I met Simionato again. The Simionato of the "second period," the new Giulietta, liberated from the joke of doing comprimario roles at La Scala, and ready to take off in the leading roles at the highest level, and already reaching out for her postwar international career.

I don't only remember her because of her exceptional artistic and vocal qualities, but also for her extraordinary humanity. Giulietta was a perfect colleague; even after she became famous, she was never jealous, she was always ready to smile, always cordial and ready with an encouraging word for everyone. On the stage she gave a pleasant sense of tranquility. Her voice was easy and sustained by a perfect technique, without problems: a pure spring which flowed serenely, without effort. The scales were like purest pearls.

I think about her with great emotion and joy, not only because of the experiences we shared and suffered on stage, but especially because of her extraordinary and open "human" quality.

Naomi TAKEYA UCHIDA, *professor of Italian literature at the University of Osaka*

There are two reasons I call Giulietta Simionato my Italian mother. In the first place, through her singing I discovered my interest in Italian culture, the study of which ultimately became my profession. The second reason is that during a certain period of my youth I lived near her for four years, during which time she told me about many of the joys and sufferings she had undergone in her life.

Our first meeting took place in her dressing room in a theater in Osaka after I had got past tight security. I was only 15 years old. My infantile questions, in broken English, gained the interest of the great prima donna, who was living a very exhausting life. Afterwards she wrote me often, comparing my letters to "fresh peach blossoms." In 1972, when I went to Italy on a scholarship funded by the Italian government, Giulietta helped me and protected me with a affection that I hadn't expected: she found me an apartment, she helped me deal with the bureaucracy, and brought covers and sheets and showed me how beds were made in Italy.

She helped with my studies and was a good tutor. When she realized I was preparing a thesis on Vittorini, she also read his book. "I did not like it at all. Why do you always read left-wing writers? My generation does not approve of this orientation," she commented. But whenever Giulietta found articles by this writer in various magazines and newspapers, she brought them to me immediately. With this attentiveness she encouraged me to study.

My stay in Rome coincided with a period in Giulietta's life when she had already retired and was completely cut off from the world of music. At the Frugoni's there was no piano; there was not even a photograph in the living room to attest to the lifelong activity of the mistress of the house.

"Is it true that you have no nostalgia for the stage? Why don't you teach, so that you can transmit your art to others?" I often asked her. Her answer was: "Now I live for someone more important than I am. One cannot do two things at once."

Her husband, Professor Frugoni, was losing his eyesight: she read newspapers and letters to him; he had difficulty moving about on his own: she helped him walk day and night, sustaining him on her arm. At the table she filled his glass and helped debone his fish. The professor, for his part, said to me often: "Do you know the simple element that distinguishes Giulietta from other singers?" Before I could answer he said: "Her great strength lies not only in her voice, she is wonderful because she is intelligent." Once, winking at me, he said "Have you noticed that when she gets angry she becomes like an SS officer?"

It was pleasant to see this couple joined by mutual respect. Although they were two retired people they never questioned the value of their lives. I will never forget the conversation between them that took place ten days before the professor's death. Seated in an armchair in his hospital room, Frugoni insisted upon reading. In reality he could no longer see. Giulietta said to him: "My dear, I understand you. But at a certain point it is important to accept things as they are and to resign yourself to them. Before I decided to stop singing, I too suffered terribly. But you know I was determined. You, up to now, have read many books, and you have already studied and learned enough. Now the time has come to rest."

"You are always right, my dear." The professor, smiling wearily, extended his hand to his wife, who squeezed it with a gentleness full of understanding. We will speak another time of the terrible trials Giulietta underwent after her husband's death. It is still too early to make an objective comment. I can only say that my real Italian mother, Giulietta, has returned and she is once again a prima donna in the wings, waving as if intermission had just ended. With her iron will she has reinvented her life and refuses to look back. But before making this decision, I witnessed her terrible suffering.

In her recent letters to me I find this sentence: "Strange to say, nowadays, but I feel fulfilled and serene. But you must understand, this does not take away at all the pain I feel when I remember the Professor. But... that is something else!!!"

Renata TEBALDI, *soprano*

Giulietta and I knew each other for a long time. Unfortunately I was unable to follow her many career turns, and we did not appear together very often.

We first met abroad, both in North America and South America. We first sang together in *Adriana Lecouvreur* in Chicago and in the dress rehearsals for the same opera at the San Carlo before I became ill and had to be replaced. We did *Falstaff* and *Forza del destino* together in Chicago. And of course we made many recordings together. Every so often we would meet each other at a restaurant when we were singing in the same city, and now and then at galas. I remember Giulietta well in a special performance of *Mignon* and I was also in the audience for her

Cenerentola and for her *Nozze di Figaro*. Her Cherubino was brilliant and full of life.

I never saw her worried. She was always playful. She never did vocalises before a performance, but rather seemed to warm up by imitating the sound of a trumpet. She traveled constantly. I envied her because I could never sleep on a plane; she, on the other hand, could go to her spot wherever it might be and fall asleep easily. I also remember that after performances she drank lots of water, ate an apple and went on her way...

Emma TEGANI, *soprano*

Giulietta was and is a dear friend. We were together on many occasions in many different theaters, beginning at La Scala with *Gianni Schicchi* and Monteverdi's *Il combattimento di Tancredi e Clorinda*. With the last we went to Prague together in 1942, while all of Europe was going through that unhappy period, and our theater had a great success. We sang *Così fan tutte* together, and a number of times, *Carmen*.

Today still, at a distance of... alas, of so many years, we see each other with great pleasure, sometimes in our houses, sometimes at concerts or musical events. I should add that I have always had a great admiration for Giulietta the artist, and today I have the same admiration for the woman who has been active on behalf of so many enterprises which benefit art and artists.

Wally TOSCANINI, *daughter of The Maestro*

A voice born for singing with a stupendous musical quality.

Gabriella TUCCI, *soprano*

I had some memorable performances with Giulietta Simionato. I remember a *Trovatore* in Moscow, an *Aida* in Verona, and so many others!

On stage we were often rivals (Aida/Amneris, Adriana Lecouvreur/Principessa di Bouillon, and others, many others still) but we sang with the intensity of high professionalism and reciprocal esteem, and for my part, with admiration for the great Giulietta!

Giuseppe VALDENGO, *baritone*

If I am to speak from the heart about my dear colleagues, Giulietta Simionato gets first place.

Her name is dear to me because I remember our youth when we sang together. After many years I can open my heart and say what she meant to me then: she represented the love that young artists can bear for each other, the honesty and understanding.

I remember that in 1938 we were singing together at the Teatro Donizetti in Bergamo in *Boris Godunov*. Giulietta was singing the part of Theodore, the Tsar's son while I was Tchelkalov, the secretary of the Duma. Boris was Tancredi Pasero. The conductor was the great Dobrowen. Giulietta and I became friends instantly. I remember that during the rehearsals Giulietta amused herself by pelting me with chestnuts from the top of the stage. So many laughs.

In Siena I remember that we rehearsed on the piano that part of an opera which was to be broadcast on the Radio di Roma.

For a number of years we trod the stage of La Scala in Milan and I had the unconditional affection of a great friend: I remember the hospitality at her house. In those days at La Scala it was customary to have a long apprenticeship: that's how it was for us.

Only in 1942 did we have leading roles. We sang together in *Hänsel und Gretel* by Humperdinck, with Nino Sanzogno conducting, as well as in second roles in lots of operas. The last time I sang with her in 1945 was at the Teatro Excelsior in Milan, a concert for the allied troops. To play a trick on me Giulietta had put in the program Pierracini's song "*Peppino rubacuori.*"

In 1946 we left for the United States. Giulietta became the uncontested queen of operatic art in those years.

Upon my return from America I sang various performances

of *Barbiere di Siviglia* in 1956 during the season of the Teatro Regio in Turin.

When on the 5th of March, 1984, I had the joy to receive the prize "*Una vita per la lirica*" presented by AMAL in Milan, it was at the hands of Giulietta Simionato, which for me was an experience that went beyond the usual sort of recognition — to have the prize from such a great friend and colleague.

Lucia VALENTINI TERRANI, *mezzo-soprano*

Two words only for Signora Simionato even though my heart and my admiration suggest whole pages!

Giulietta Simionato! I was still a child in conservatory and she was already a mythical figure. Later I had the joy of meeting her and of loving her in real life, too.

Robert WEISS

Giulietta Simionato's art left an unforgettable impression on all of us who had the good fortune to see her and hear her. Wherever she sang she quickly conquered the public. She was adored by the Chicago public where she sang a great variety of roles, demonstrating total mastery of her art. For example, during one season she was playing Cherubino in *Nozze di Figaro* and *Santuzza*, while during another she was at the same time Quickly in *Falstaff* and a dazzling Rosina in *Barbiere di Siviglia*.

New Yorkers quickly embraced her, first on the occasion of her concert performance with the American Opera Society and then in the opening night performance of the 1959 season at the Metropolitan Opera: comments on her Azucena filled the first pages of the newspapers. Her Amneris and her Santuzza, which she interpreted in the historic *Cavalleria* with Jussi Björling, are considered the standard of comparison. Critics and audiences in this city who heard her make respectful reference even to this day.

Her voice was warm and glorious, with a unique high register, and her personality exploded across the footlights in a way that has never been equalled. To be in the theater when she sang was truly a privilege.

John WUSTMAN, *pianist*

At the end of the fifties a "volcanic voice" in the person of Giulietta Simionato made her debut in New York. She sang the part of Jane Seymour in Donizetti's *Anna Bolena* prepared by the American Opera Society. The first performance took place at Town Hall, but as a result of its immense success a second performance was immediately scheduled for Carnegie Hall, a much larger and more suitable venue. As always her voice and personality filled the hall with beauty, passion and grace. I was the rehearsal pianist, and my long friendship with this great artist began then and there.

For her concerts in America she asked me to be the accompanist. For a young man that was a great honor and a great joy. Our first concerts took place in Havana, Cuba, in March 1960. The success was incredible. The program began with Rosina's beautiful aria "*Una voce poco fa.*" I sensed the public's amazement at the marvelous succession of notes, ornaments and trills. Then there came arias by Bellini, Donizetti and Verdi, followed by numerous songs from various regions in Italy and finally other opera arias. In every recital "*O don fatale*" from *Don Carlo* was last on the program, but when Giulietta wasn't feeling up to it right away, we had the habit of substituting Azucena's first aria. After two or three encores Simionato was ready for Eboli and then the volcano really let loose its boiling lava. She was splendid.

This extraordinary singer's entire personality is expressed in music and in her way of singing. Offstage she is reflective, kind, simple, and truly grand in the fullest sense of the word. I am truly grateful for her interest in me as a young musician.

Franco ZEFFIRELLI, *stage director*

When I arrived at La Scala in 1953 I understood at once that I had entered a world of passionate creativity. To my surprise I discovered that opera's situation had changed. With the reconstruction of the theater and the successes of new directors and singers a new listener had emerged: younger and more attuned to livelier and better-put-together productions. It was clear that singers were more involved in the drama. Emotions were provoked by highly publicized rivalries like the supposed rivalry between Renata Tebaldi, the leading exponent of pure bel canto, and Maria Callas, whose performances were variable but always highly dramatic. Their fans were as avid and partisan as soccer fans. The dying art form of opera was newly invigorated. Notwithstanding the attention lavished on these two *dive* and a list of names that included Di Stefano, Del Monaco, Corelli, Gobbi, etc., one name emerged from all the others: Giulietta Simionato. She was the greatest mezzo-soprano of her time, and was scheduled to sing in *L'italiana in Algeri*, designed by the director Corrado Pavolini. Even though I tried to hide as best I could, I was terrified at being in the midst of so many lions. Up to then I had been known as someone who worked for Lucchino Visconti — one of a team, with no special status. Pavolini had seen my stage designs for Visconti's production of *A Streetcar Named Desire* and had promised to invite me to Milan. I felt very isolated as I worked in my little room at the hotel, a stranger who knew almost no one.

It was Giulietta Simionato who showed me the greatest kindness and helped me overcome my first experience of "going cold." Our production was considered by La Scala management to be the key production of the season. It was to be the first in a planned series of Rossini revivals and was conceived specifically as a vehicle for Giulietta's artistry.

Thank God she was a mezzo-soprano! At least we would avoid the rivalries, the pitched battles we found ourselves involved in when we had to deal with sopranos.

Both Tebaldi and Callas adored Simionato who was then as she is today one of the sweetest people to have ever trod an opera stage. More important was the part she played in convincing me I had the ability to succeed. Often she would extend little compliments as I worked on *L'italiana* and she could feel when I was having a nervous crisis or a crisis of indecision and she would go out of her way to show me her friendly support. We remain great friends today.

It was thanks to her that we were able to take another step forward, an even bolder step considering the times. As a result of the success thus far of this "Rossini Revival," Ghiringhelli decided to mount *Cenerentola* with the same cast. Giulini, Simionato and the rest of us. However, Pavolini was not well. He had become ill during much of the rehearsal for *L'italiana* and I had to become a sort of assistant director in charge of production. Ghiringhelli was aware of this and when it became clear that Pavolini would not be able to do *Cenerentola*, I, encouraged and supported by Giulietta, summoned the courage to ask if I could be both director and designer. Ghiringhelli was not so surprised by my request as I had feared. I was the one who was surprised when I realized he had agreed. He was immensely grateful for the devoted support of my "leading lady." Fortunately the audience and critics supported the freshness of my conception as well and could not stop applauding Giulietta on opening night.

Debuts

1932 CAVALLERIA RUSTICANA (Pietro Mascagni): Lola, 1932; Mamma Lucia, 15 March 1938; Santuzza, 15 May 1948.

RIGOLETTO (Giuseppe Verdi): Maddalena, 1932; Giovanna, 1 October 1938.

1934 IL TROVATORE (Giuseppe Verdi): Azucena, 17 October 1934.

UN BALLO IN MASCHERA (Giuseppe Verdi): Ulrica, 10 November 1934.

MIGNON (Ambroise Thomas): Federico, 27 November 1934; Mignon, 18 January 1947.

MANON LESCAUT (Giacomo Puccini): Musico, 1 December 1934.

BORIS GODUNOV (Modest Mussorgsky): Hostess and Nurse, 13 December 1934; Feodor, 15 January 1941; Marina, 19 November 1948.

FRANCESCA DA RIMINI (Riccardo Zandonai): Slave, 20 December 1934; Donella, 6 March 1942.

1935 LA SONNAMBULA (Vicenzo Bellini): Teresa, 6 January 1935.

NORMA (Vicenzo Bellini): Adalgisa, 13 January 1935.

ANDREA CHENIER (Umberto Giordano): Contessa di Coigny, 15 January 1935; Bersi, 11 October 1941.

LE PREZIOSE RIDICOLE [LES PRECIEUSES RIDICULES](Felice Lattuada): (Cathos) 17 January 1935.

CECILIA (Licinio Refice): Blind woman, 2 February 1935.

MADAMA BUTTERFLY (Giacomo Puccini): Suzuki, 16 February 1935; Mother of Cio-Cio-San, 12 January 1938.

ADRIANA LECOUVREUR (Francesco Cilea): Princess of Bouillon, 21 February 1935.

LA GIOCONDA (Amilcare Ponchielli) Laura, 11 March 1935.

ORSEOLO (Ildebrando Pizzetti): Young and old ladies, 4 May 1935.

MEFISTOFELE (Arrigo Boito): Marta and Pantalis, 24 September 1935.

1936 SUOR ANGELICA (Giacomo Puccini): Mistress of novices, 29 January 1936.

PARSIFAL (Richard Wagner): Flower Maiden, 25 March 1936.

1937 HÄNSEL E GRETEL [HÄNSEL UND GRETEL] (Engelbert Humperdinck): The Sandman (Nano Sabbiolino), 11 February 1937; Hänsel, 30 August 1941.

MARIA EGIZIACA (Ottorinio Respighi): Povero, 24 February 1937.

LUCREZIA (Ottorino Respighi): Servia, 27 February 1937.

LA MORTE DI FRINE (Lodovico Rocca): Antide, 24 April 1937; Aglaia, 1 November 1941.

LA TRAVIATA (Giuseppe Verdi): Flora, 12 October 1937.

FAUST (Charles Gounod): Siebel, 27 October 1937.

1938 SADKO (Nikolai Rimsky-Korsakov): First sorceress, 2 February 1938.

LE JONGLEUR DE NOTRE DAME (Jules Massenet): Angelo, 9 March 1938.

I QUATTRO RUSTEGHI (Ermanno Wolf-Ferrari): Marini's servant, 26 March 1938.

MARCELLA (Umberto Giordano): Lea, 23 April 1938.

LA LEGGENDA DELLE SETTE TORRI (Alberrto Gasco): Dorabella, 25 July 1938.

LA FORZA DEL DESTINO (Giuseppe Verdi): Preziosilla, 9 November 1938.

IL GOBBO DEL CALIFFO (Franco Casavola): Ciabattina, 15 November 1938.

L'AMICO FRITZ (Pietro Mascagni): Beppe, 3 December 1938.

1939 LA DAMA BOBA: 1 February 1939.

FEDRA (Ildebrando Pizzetti): The fourth supplicant, the fourth infantryman, 1 March 1939.

MARIA D'ALESSANDRIA (Giorgio Federico Ghedini): The second shepherd, 1 April 1939; The blind woman, 30 September 1941.

LA FIAMMA (Ottorino Respighi): 2 July 1939; Sabina, 8 August 1942.

FEDORA (Umberto Giordano): Dimitri, the little Savoyard, 11 October 1939; Fedora, 20 July 1950.

1940 LE NOZZE DI FIGARO (Wolfgang Amadeus Mozart): Cherubino, 16 January 1940.

OBERON (Carl Maria von Weber): Puck, 26 March 1940.

MANON (Jules Massenet): A soldier, 18 April 1940.

I PURITANI (Vincenzo Bellini): Enrichetta, 1 September 1940.

OTELLO (Giuseppe Verdi): Emilia, 4 November 1940.

PALLA DE' MOZZI (Gino Marinuzzi): Suora, 4 November 1940.

1941 SALOME (Richard Strauss): Page of Herodiade, 15 May 1941.

VILLON (Alberto Bruni Tedeschi): Margot, 24 September 1941.

FRA GHERARDO (Ildebrando Pizzetti): An angry voice, a mother, 27 December 1941.

1942 IL COMBATTIMENTO DE TANCREDI E CLORINDA (Claudio Monteverdi): Clorinda, 15 January 1942.

IL BARBIERE DI SIVIGLIA (Gioacchino Rossini): Berta, 29 January 1942; Rosina, 3 March 1948.

GIANNI SCHICCHI (Giacomo Puccini): La Ciesca, 31 January 1942.

LODOLETTA (Pietro Mascagni): The madwoman, 18 February 1942.

THAÏS (Jules Massenet): Mirtale, 28 February 1942.

95

95. In the title role of *Zanetto*. La Scala, Milan, 1955.

96. *Zanetto* with Rosanna Carteri and Maestro Votto. La Scala, Milan, 1955.

96

97. *Nabucco* with Poggi, Cerquetti, Bastianini, Maestro Votto, and Zaccaria. La Scala, Milan, 1958.

98. In *Nabucco* with Ettore Bastianini. La Scala, Milan, 1958.

99. *Ifigenia in Aulide*. La Scala, Milan, 1959.

100. As Orpheus at the Salzburg Festival in *Orfeo e Euridice*. Felsenreitschule, 1959.

101. *Orfeo e Euridice*. Felsenreitschule, Salzburg, 1959.

102. *Orfeo e Euridice* with Jurinac. Felsenreitschule, Salzburg, 1959.

103. *Orfeo e Euridice* with Lipp and Adami. La Scala, Milan, 1962.

104. As Neris in *Medea* with Maria Callas. La Scala, Milan, 1961.

105

106

105. In *Medea* with Ghiaurov and Callas. La Scala, Milan, 1961.

106. In *Medea*. La Scala, Milan, 1961.

107. Rehearsing *Medea* with Callas. La Scala, Milan, 1961.

108. In *Medea* with Callas. La Scala, Milan, 1961.

109. As Valentine in *Gli Ugonotti* with Maestro Gavazzeni. La Scala, Milan, 1962.

110. As Pirene in *Atlantida*. La Scala, Milan, 1962.

111. As Arsace in *Semiramide* with Ganzarolli. La Scala, Milan, 1962.

112. In *Semiramide* with Joan Sutherland. La Scala, Milan, 1962.

113. *Semiramide* with Sutherland. La Scala, Milan, 1962. (Photo courtesy of Dame Joan Sutherland.)

112

113

114. As Servilia in *La clemenza di Tito*, Simionato's last operatic performance. Piccola Scala, Milan, 1966.

115. *La clemenza di Tito*. Piccola Scala, Milan, 1966.

116. Taking the last curtain call of her operatic career after *La clemenza di Tito*. Piccola Scala, Milan, 1966.

117

117. Simionato (standing) with her sister, Regina, and nieces. Rovigo, 1931.

118. At age 23, after the contest in Florence. 1933.

118

119. Giulietta in 1947.

120. In Mexico City, 1950.

121 and 122. Giulietta in the 1950s.

121

122

123

123 and 124. In Rome during the 1950s.

124

125. Relaxing in Capri.

126. In Milan with Gianni Poggi and Renata Tebaldi.

127. With Güden, Gedda, and Roux in Vienna for a concert performance of *Carmen* with von Karajan in the Grosser Musikvereinsaal. 1954.

128. All of the *Carmen* principals: Sordello, Del Signore, Roux, Güden, Gedda, Carlin, Sciutti, Guthrie, Ribacchi. Vienna, 1954.

129. A concert in Japan, 1956.

130. With Prandelli, Zeani, and Rossi Lemeni. Paris, 1957.

131. With King Umberto and Magda Olivero, Lisbon. About 1954.

132. At La Scala in the 1950s with colleagues, among whom are Elmo, Carteri, Picchi, Guelfi, and Barbato.

133. Rehearsal for *Werther* with Tagliavini. La Scala, Milan, 1951.

134. Rehearsal for *Norma* with Zaccaria, Callas, Del Monaco. La Scala, Milan, 1955.

135. With Rossi Lemeni and Zeani. 1958.

136. La Scala, Milan, 1959.

137. La Scala, Milan, 1959.

138. Dvořák's *Stabat Mater* with Poggi, Scotto, and Modesti. La Scala, Milan, 1959.

139

140

139. Going by plane to Moscow for *Il trovatore*. 1964.

140. On tour with Bastianini.

141. Simionato at home in Milan. 1980.

142. With husband Prof. Cesare Frugoni.

143. Attending the last concert of Renata Tebaldi with her husband, Prof. Frugoni.

144

145

144. With Prof. Naomi Takeya Uchida in Japan. 1981.

145. In Vienna, with her last husband, industrialist, Flores De Angeli.

146

146. In Vienna for her 80th birthday. 1990.

147. Being honored at the Vienna State Opera on her 80th birthday.

147

148. Being honored at La Scala on her 85th birthday. 1995.

149. Happy 86th birthday! Milan, May, 1996.

150. Choosing photographs with author, Jean-Jacques Hanine Roussel, for the Italian edition of her biography.

Repertory

Bartók	*Il castello del principe Barbablú* [*Bluebeard's Castle*] (Giuditta - Judith)
Beethoven	*Ninth Symphony*
Bellini	*Capuleti e Montecchi* (Romeo) *Norma* (Adalgisa) *I Puritani* (Enrichetta) *La sonnambula* (Teresa)
Berlioz	*La dannazione di Faust* (Margherita) *I Troiani* [*Les Troyens*] (Didone - Dido)
Bizet	*Carmen* (Carmen, Mercedes)
Boito	*Mefistofele* (Marta, Pantalis) *Nerone* (Rubria)
Bruni Tedeschi	*Villon* (Margot)
Busoni	*Arlecchino* (Colombina)
Casavola	*Il gobbo del califfo* (Ciabattina)
Casella	*La donna serpente* (Canzade)
Castro	*Proserpina e lo straniero* (Demetria)
Cherubini	*Medea* (Neris)
Cilea	*Adriana Lecouvreur* (Principessa di Bouillon) *L'Arlesiana* (Rosa Mamai)
Cimarosa	*Il matrimonio segreto* (Fidalma)
	Gli Orazi e i Curiazi (Orazia)
De Falla	*Atlantida* (Pirene)
Donizetti	*Anna Bolena* (Jane Seymour) *La Favorita* (Leonora)

Dvorák	*Stabat Mater*
Flotow	*Marta* (Nancy)
Gasco	*La leggenda delle sette torri* (Dorabella)
Ghedini	*Maria d'Alessandria* (2° Pastore, la Cieca - 2nd Shepherd, Blind woman)
Giordano	*Andrea Chénier* (Bersi, Contessa di Coigny) *Fedora* (Fedora, Dimitri, Piccolo Savoiardo [the Savoyard boy]) *Marcella* (Lea) *Il re* (Astrologa)
Gounod	*Faust* (Siebel)
Gluck	*Ifigenia in Aulide* (Ifigenia) *Orfeo ed Euridice* (Orfeo)
Händel	*Giulio Cesare* (Cornelia) *Il Messia* [The Messiah]
Honegger	*Anfione* (3ª Musa - Third muse) *Giuditta* [Judith] *Il re David* [King David]
Humperdinck	*Hänsel e Gretel* (Hänsel, Nano Sabbiolino [The Sandman])
Lattuada	*Le preziose ridicole* [*Les Précieuses Ridicules*] (Cathos)
Marinuzzzi	*Palla de' Mozzi* (Suora)
Mascagni	*L'amico Fritz* (Beppe) *Cavalleria rusticana* (Santuzza, Lola, Mamma Lucia) *Lodoletta* (La pazza - The madwoman) *Zanetto* (Zanetto)
Massenet	*Don Chisciotte* [Don Quichotte](Dulcinea) *Le jongleur de Notre Dame* [*The Hunchback of Notre-Dame]* (Angelo) *Manon* (Una fante) *Thaïs* (Mirtale) *Werther* (Carlotta)
Menotti	*Amahl e gli ospiti notturni* [*Amahl and the Night Visitors*] (La madre - The mother)
Meyerbeer	*Gli Ugonotti* [*Les Huguenots*](Valentina)
Monteverdi	*Il ballo delle ingrate* (Venere) *Il combattimento di Tancredi e Clorinda* (Clorinda) *Il ritorno d'Ulisse in patria* (Melanto)

Mozart	*La clemenza di Tito* (Servilia) *Cosí fan tutte* (Dorabella) *Don Giovanni* (Donna Elvira) *Le nozze di Figaro* (Cherubino) *Requiem*
Mussorgsky	*Kovancina* [*Khovanshchina*] (Marfa) *Boris Godunov* (Marina, Ostessa [Hostess], Nutrice [Nurse], Teodoro [Feodor])
Pizzetti	*Fedra* (4ª supplice, 4ª fante - 4th supplicant, 4th soldier) *Fra Gherardo* (Una madre, una voce rabbiosa - A mother, An angry voice) *Orseolo* (Vecchia e giovane dama - An old woman, a young woman)
Ponchielli	*La Gioconda* (Laura)
Puccini	*Gianni Schicchi* (La Ciesca) *Madama Butterfly* (Suzuki, the mother of Cio-Cio-San) *Manon Lescaut* (Musico) *Suor Angelica* (Maestra delle Novizie - Mistress of the novices)
Purcell	*Didone e Enea* [*Dido and Aeneas*] (Didone)
Refice	*Cecilia* (La vecchia cieca - The blind old woman)
Respighi	*La fiamma* (Sabina) *Lucrezia* (Servia) *Maria Egiziaca* (Povero)
Rimsky-Korsakov	*Sadko* (1° Stregone - First sorcerer)
Rocca	*La morte di Frine* (Antide, Aglaia)
Rossini	*Il barbiere di Siviglia* (Rosina, Berta) *La Cenerentola* (Cenerentola - Cinderella) *Il conte Ory* (Isolier) *L'Italiana in Algeri* (Isabella) *Mosé* (Sinaide) *La pietra del paragone* [The Touchstone](Clarice) *Semiramide* (Arsace) *Stabat Mater* *Tancredi*
Saint-Saëns	*Sansone e Dalila* (Dalila)
Scarlatti	*Mitridate Eupatore* (Stratonice)
Strauss	*Il cavaliere della rosa* [*Der Rosenkavalier*] (Octavian) *Elettra* [*Elektra*] (Ancella) *Salomé* (Paggio d'Erodiade - Herodiade's page)

Thomas	*Mignon* (Mignon, Federico)
Verdi	*Aida* (Amneris) *Un ballo in maschera* (Ulrica) *Don Carlo* (Eboli) *Falstaff* (Mrs. Quickly, Meg Page) *La forza del destino* (Preziosilla) *Messa da Requiem* *Nabucco* (Fenena) *Otello* (Emilia) *Rigoletto* (Maddalena, Giovanna) *La traviata* (Flora) *Il trovatore* (Azucena)
Vivaldi	*Stabat Mater*
Wagner	*Il crepuscolo degli dei* [*Die Götterdämmerung*] (Prima Norna - First Norn) *L'oro del Reno* [*Das Rheingold*] (Flosshilde) *Parsifal* (Fiore - Flower maiden) *La Walkiria* [*Die Walkyrie*] (Rossweise)
Weber	*Il franco cacciatore* [*Der Freischütz*] (Annetta) *Oberon* (Puck) *La Dama* Boba
Wolf Ferrari	*I quattro rusteghi* (Serva di Marini - Marini's servant)
Zandonai	*Francesca da Rimini* (Donella, Schiava [Slave])

Chronology

1927

14 May	Rovigo Teatro Sociale	NINA, NO FAR LA STUPIDA (2) Giuseppe Padoan, Carla Padoan, Mazzetto, Valente, Ollari, Benatti, Pace, Suriani. Conductor: Padoan
end of May	Montagnana	NINA, NO FAR LA STUPIDA (1) Giuseppe Padoan, Carla Padoan, Mazzetto, Valente, Ollari, Benatti, Pace, Suriani. Conductor: Padoan
end of May	Piove di Sacco	NINA, NO FAR LA STUPIDA (1) Giuseppe Padoan, Carla Padoan, Mazzetto, Valente, Ollari, Benatti, Pace, Suriani. Conductor: Padoan
end of May	Monselice	NINA, NO FAR LA STUPIDA (1) Giuseppe Padoan, Carla Padoan, Mazzetto, Valente, Ollari, Benatti, Pace, Suriani. Conductor: Padoan
5 Oct	Rovigo T. Sociale	OSTREGO, CHE SBREGO! (2) Mazzetto, Palmieri. Conductor: Padoan
22 Oct	Rovigo T. Sociale	NINA, NO FAR LA STUPIDA (2) Giuseppe Padoan, Carla Padoan, Mazzetto, Valente, Ollari, Benatti, Pace, Suriani. Conductor: Padoan

1932

*	Montagnana	CAVALLERIA RUSTICANA Sasso.
*	Padova Teatro Verdi	RIGOLETTO

1933

*	Mestre Circolo Sociale	Concerto (1) Music of Lucatello, Tirindelli, Respighi. Ticani, piano.

1934

*	Mestre T. dei Figli del Popolo	CONCERT (1) F. Zezzi-Giacomazzi, piano Lucatello: Lettera Pinsutti: Libero santo Donizetti: O mio Fernando Thomas: Non conosci il bel suol Verdi: Stride la vampa
5 Jan	Florence T. della Pergola	RIGOLETTO (1)
9 Feb	Rovigo Liceo Musicale F. Venezze	CONCERT L. Ruggero, piano.
19 May	Treviso T. Comunale	CAVALLERIA RUSTICANA (4) Scuderi, Bagnariol, Lulli. Conductor: Lualdi
17 Oct	Trieste Politeama Rossetti	IL TROVATORE (2) Lois, Visciola, DeFranceschi, Sciacqui, Calegari, Colli, Curiel. Conductor: Sigismondo
10 Nov	Malta Royal Opera House	UN BALLO IN MASCHERA (4) Gaio, Trevisani, Garuti/Gallo, Basiola, Sciacqui. Conductor: Cordone
12 Nov	Malta Royal Opera House	RIGOLETTO (1) Archi, Gallo, Basiola, Sciacqui. Conductor: Cordone
27 Nov	Malta Royal Opera House	MIGNON (4) Archi, Falliani, Perulli, Sciacqui, Soley, Friggi. Conductor: Santarelli
1 Dec	Malta Royal Opera House	MANON LESCAUT (4) Tassinari, Garuti, Satariano, Soley, Benatti, Friggi. Conductor: Cordone
13 Dec	Malta Royal Opera House	BORIS GODUNOV (4) Cirino, Falliani, Villa, Pollini, Galli, Sciacqui, Soley, Benatti. Conductor: Cordone
20 Dec	Malta Royal Opera House	FRANCESCA DA RIMINI (4) Gaio, Garuti, Trevisani, Villa. Conductor: Cordone

1935

6 Jan	Malta Royal Opera House	LA SONNAMBULA (1) Archi, Villa, Perulli, Sciacqui, Nicoletti, Benatti. Conductor: Santarelli
13 Jan	Malta Royal Opera House	NORMA (1) Monti, Gallo, Sciacqui, Benatti, Cherici. Conductor: Cordone

15 Jan	Malta Royal Opera House	ANDREA CHENIER (3) Raineri, Garuti, Poli, Friggi. Conductor: Santarelli
17 Jan	Malta Royal Opera House	LE PREZIOSE RIDICOLE (3) Raineri, Perulli, Poli, Soley, Villa, Benatti, Friggi. Conductor: Santarelli
2 Feb	Malta Royal Opera House	CECILIA (8) Licia Albanese, Garuti, Satariano, Sciacqui, Poli, Benatti, Friggi. Conductor: Cordone
16 Feb	Malta Royal Opera House	MADAMA BUTTERFLY (2) Licia Albanese, Gallo, Satariano, Cherici, Benatti, Soley, Friggi, Nicoletti. Conductor: Cordone
21 Feb	Malta Royal Opera House	ADRIANA LECOUVREUR (2) Campigna, Garuti, Soley, Satariano, Benatti, Nicoletti, Friggi, Cherici, Pollini. Conductor: Cordone
2 Mar	Tunis Théâtre Municipal	CONCERT (1)* Archi, Perulli. Conductor: Santarelli
3 Mar	Tunis Théâtre Municipal	ADRIANA LECOUVREUR (1) Campigna, Poli, Garuti, Satariano. Conductor: Cordone
6 Mar	Tunis Théâtre Municipal	CAVALLERIA RUSTICANA (1) Campigna, Satariano, De Gaviria, Cherici. Conductor: Santarelli
11 Mar	Tunis Théâtre Municipal	LA GIOCONDA (1) Campigna, Garuti, Poli, Sciacqui. Conductor: Santarelli
Mar	Tripoli Real Teatro Miramare	UN BALLO IN MASCHERA (1) Campigna, Viviani, Garuti. Conductor: Cordone
28 Mar	Tripoli Real Teatro Miramare	LA GIOCONDA (1) Campigna, Poli, Garuti. Conductor: Santarelli
4 May	Florence T. Comunale	L'ORSEOLO (3) Pasero, Somigli, Rubino, G. Tomei, Fort, Cilla, Bergamini. Conductor: Serafin
24 Sept	Adria T. Comunale	MEFISTOFELE (4) Pampanini, Malipiero, Scuderi / Serafina di Leo, Pasero, Bergamini. Conductors: Serafin / Mecenati
16 Oct	Turin T. Vittorio Emanuele	IL TROVATORE (3) Lois, Benni, Manacchini, Sciacqui. Conductor: *

1936

29 Jan	Milan La Scala	SUOR ANGELICA (5) Oltrabella, Casazza. Conductor: Marinuzzi
22 Feb	Milan La Scala	RIGOLETTO (4) Sinnone, Borgioli, Archi, Baronti / Zaccarini, Palombini. Conductors: Antonicelli / Polzinetti

25 Mar	Milan La Scala	PARSIFAL (4) Rossi Morelli, Zaccarini, Pasero, Parmeggiani, Cobelli, Giampieri, Menotti, Del Signore, Marcucci. Conductor: Marinuzzi
28 Mar	Milan La Scala	RIGOLETTO (1) Sinnone, Borgioli, Archi, Zaccarini, Palombini, Tito Gobbi (usher). Conductor: Polzinetti
1 Oct	Trieste Politeama Rossetti	RIGOLETTO (3) De Bernardi, Paggi, Borgonovo, Roberto Silva. Conductor: Moresco

1937

6 Jan	Milan La Scala	MIGNON (4) Pederzini, Schipa, Carosio, Pasero, Baracchi. Conductor: Ghione
11 Feb	Milan La Scala	HANSEL E GRETEL (6) Pederzini / Elmo, Carosio / Menotti, Casazza, Biasini, Camilla Rota. Conductor: Ghione
24 Feb	Milan La Scala	MARIA EGIZIACA (4) Carbone, Tagliabue, Del Signore. Conductor: Marinuzzi
27 Feb	Milan La Scala	LUCREZIA (3) Caniglia / Carbone, Civil, Parmeggiani, Baracchi. Conductor: Marinuzzi
24 Apr	Milan La Scala	LA MORTE DI FRINE (3) Oltrabella, Tagliabue, Del Signore, Marcucci, Civil. Conductor: Antonicelli
4 May	Florence T. Comunale	MARIA EGIZIACA (1) Caniglia, Tagliabue, Palai, Villani. Conductor: Marinuzzi
		LUCREZIA (1) Caniglia, Civil, Parmeggiani, Viviani, Paci, Coda,Villani, Baracchi. Conductor: Marinuzzi
12 Oct	Carpi T. Comunale	LA TRAVIATA (1) Pagliughi, Voyer, Valentino, Gubbiani. Conductor: Martini
27 Oct	Turin E.I.A.R.	FAUST (2) Olivero, Malipiero, Valentino, Pasero. Conductor: Tansini

1938

12 Jan	Milan La Scala	MADAMA BUTTERFLY (8) Iris Adami Corradetti, Marcucci, Lugo / Costa Lo Giudice / Gallo, De Franceschi / Biasini, Nessi, Luise. Conductors: De Sabata / Polzinetti

2 Feb	Milan La Scala	SADKO (4) Giampieri, Parmeggiani, Nini Giani, Elmo, Nessi, Del Signore, De Franceschi, Carosio. Conductor: Marinuzzi
9 Mar	Milan La Scala	LE JONGLEUR DE NOTRE DAME (7) Malipiero / Elmo, Maugeri, Bettoni, Del Signore. Conductors: Marinuzzi / Negrelli.
15 Mar	Milan La Scala	CAVALLERIA RUSTICANA (1) Gigli, Nava, Stignani, Marcucci. Conductor: Marinuzzi
26 Mar	Milan La Scala	I QUATTRO RUSTEGHI (5) Dragoni / Menotti, Baccaloni, Elmo, Fort, Adami Corradetti, Luise, Favero, Del Signore. Conductor: Capuana
23 Apr	Milan La Scala	MARCELLA (2) Olivero, Marcucci, Villani, Schipa, Manacchini. Conductor: Capuana
June	Chiusi T. Mascagni	L'AMICO FRITZ (2) Perris, Solari, Gubiani. Conductor: Ferrari
25 July	Turin E.I.A.R.	LA LEGGENDA DELLE SETTE TORRI (2) Brunazzi, Parmeggiani, Zangheri, Natali. Conductor: La Rosa Parodi
25 July	Turin E.I.A.R.	LA MORTE DI FRINE (2) Carbone, Pauli, Lombardi, Zangheri, Natali, Queirolo, E. Benedetti, Caselli, Miglietta. Conductor: La Rosa Parodi
29 Sept	Merano T. Puccini	FRANCESCA DA RIMINI (2) Adami Corradetti, Ferrari, E. Montanari, Chiorboli, Marcucci, Avogadro, Granda, Maugeri, Baracchi, Toffanetti. Conductor: Zandonai
1 Oct	Carpi T. Comunale	RIGOLETTO (1) Aimaro, Filippeschi, Bechi. Conductor: Martini
8 Oct	Bergamo T. Donizetti	BORIS GODUNOV (4) Pasero, Elmo, Cravcenko, Civil, Camillo Rota, Wesselowski, Valdengo, Romani, Sdanovski, Iekeli. Conductor: Dobrowen
5 Nov	Palermo Politeama Garibaldi	RIGOLETTO (1) Merlini, De Falchi, Tumminia, Sciacqui. Conductor: Ziino
9 Nov	Palermo Politeama Garibaldi	LA FORZA DEL DESTINO (1) Di Leo, Bechi, Sciacqui, Botti, Roggio. Conductor: Cordone
15 Nov	Palermo Politeama Garibaldi	CAVALLERIA RUSTICANA (3) Piera Roberti / Di Leo, Botti, Laffi / De Falchi. Conductor: Ziino

		IL GOBBO DEL CALIFFO (3) Sciacqui, Roggio, Gero, Laffi. Conductor: Ziino
18 Nov	Palermo Circolo della Stampa	CONCERT (1) Bechi, Gero. Conductor: Ziino Thomas: Non conosci il bel suol * : Povero amico
1 Dec	Bologna T. Comunale	FAUST (4) Malipiero, Pasero, Valentino, Olivero, Baracchi, Marcucci. Conductor: Calusio
3 Dec	Bologna T. Comunale	L'AMICO FRITZ (3) Tassinari, Galbiati, Vanelli, Baracchi, Mercuriali. Conductors: Mascagni / Marini.
Dec	Fiuggi	L'AMICO FRITZ (*) Conductor: Mascagni
*	Fiume	RIGOLETTO (*) Menotti, De Franceschi. Conductor: *

1939

1 Feb	Milan La Scala	LA DAMA BOBA (4) Favero, Di Leo, Baccaloni, Landi, Beuf, Baronti, Perris, Micelli, Poli, Girardi, Nessi, Scattola, Zecca, Baracchi, Meletti, Sciacqui, Coda, Arbuffo, Dalbo, Minazzi, De Crescenzi. Conductor: Berrettoni
23 Feb	Milan La Scala	HANSEL E GRETEL (3) Elmo, Menotti, Poli, Marcucci, Palombini. Conductor: Negrelli
1 Mar	Milan La Scala	FEDRA (1) Pacetti, Parmeggiani, Reali, Nicolai, Rossi Morelli, Palombini. Conductor: Capuana
1 Apr	Milan La Scala	MARIA D'ALESSANDRIA (3) Reali, Ziliani, De Franceschi, Mongelli, Meletti, Del Signore, Baracchi. Conductor: Rossi
31 May	Turin T. della Moda	ANDREA CHENIER (3) Masini, Reali, Oltrabella, Zanti, Avogadro, Tajo, Serpo, Gelli, Nessi, Villa, Rakovski. Conductor: Berrettoni
11 June	Turin T. della Moda	LA TRAVIATA (4) Caniglia, Tagliabue, Malipiero. Conductor: Marinuzzi
2 July	Turin T. della Moda	LA FIAMMA (3) Ziliani, Reali, Tajo, Walter, Negrelli Noe, Elmo, De Franco. Conductor: Berrettoni
29 July	Riccione Open-air theater	ANDREA CHENIER* Pampanini, Masini, Bechi, Flamini, Pallai. Conductor: Questa

11 Oct	Florence T. Comunale	FEDORA (3) Pederzini, Dori / Martucci, Masini, Mascherini / Meletti, Colella, Azzimonti. Conductor: Rossi
12 Oct	Florence T. Comunale	RIGOLETTO (5) Tagliavini, Bechi, Aimaro / Mannucci Contini, Colella / Sbalchiero, Nannini. Conductor: Rossi
24 Oct	Florence T. Comunale	L'AMICO FRITZ (2) Tagliavini, Meletti, Antonacci. Conductor: Colonna
20 Dec	Milan La Scala	L'AMICO FRITZ (4) Licia Albanese / Cirillo / Favero, Malipiero / Landi, Mercuriali, Vannelli. Conductors: Guarnieri / Berrettoni

1940

16 Jan	Trieste T. Comunale G. Verdi	LE NOZZE DI FIGARO (3) Stabile, Di Lelio, Scuderi, Giri, Gubiani, Tedesco. Conductor: Gui
17 Mar	Milan La Scala	RIGOLETTO (4) Pagliughi, Basiola / Galeffi, Malipiero, Baronti, Neroni. Conductor: Capuana
21 Mar	Milan La Scala	PARSIFAL (4) De Sved, Robanti, Pasero, Tasso, Umberto di Lelio, Menotti, Marcucci. Conductor: Serafin
26 Mar	Milan La Scala	OBERON (2) Gilda Alfano, Gatti, Elmo, Biasini, De Pataky. Conductor: Serafin
18 Apr	Milan La Scala	MANON (2) Favero, Gigli, Poli, Nessi, Baronti, Luise. Conductors: Berrettoni / Marinuzzi
17 May	Rome E.I.A.R.	CAVALLERIA RUSTICANA (2) Bruna Rasa, Mannarini, Bertelli, Tagliabue. Conductor: Mascagni
9 June	Turin E.I.A.R.	MADAMA BUTTERFLY (2) Adami Corradetti, Salvarezza, Vanelli, Zagonara. Conductor: Tansini
1 Sept	Roma E.I.A.R.	I PURITANI (1) Carosio, Gentilini, Basiola, Tajo, Conti, Mercuriali. Conductor: Serafin
3 Oct	Bergamo T. Donizetti	SUOR ANGELICA (2) Olivero, Sani, Mannarini, Marcucci, Villani, Lerch, Rettore. Conductor: Molinari Pradelli
4 Nov	Bologna T. Comunale	OTELLO (4) Merli, Bechi, Caniglia, Zambelli, Del Signore, Mercuriali, Baracchi. Conductors: Serafin / Marini

5 Nov	Bologna T. Comunale	PALLA DE' MOZZI (3) Tagliabue, Adami Corradetti, Ziliani, Zambelli, Togliani, Nessi, Mercuriali, Baracchi, Badioli. Conductor: Marinuzzi
1 Dec	Milan La Scala	CONCERT (2) Antonelli, Palombini, Fort / Alio, Marchio, Neroni, Ardelli. Conductor: Marinuzzi L'ORO DEL RENO (DAS RHEINGOLD): The entrance of the Gods to Valhalla

1941

15 Jan	Milan La Scala	BORIS GODUNOV (4) Pasero, Sdanovski, Righetti, Modesti, Magnoni / Corsi, Cravcenko, Rota / Palombini, Mercuriali, Nessi, Pigni, Soracco, Wesselowski. Conductor: Guarnieri
8 Mar	Milan La Scala	MANON LESCAUT (4) Caniglia, Poli, Gigli, Molinari / Umberto di Lelio, Del Signore, Luise, Nessi. Conductor: Marinuzzi.
15 Mar	Milan La Scala	SALOME (2) Tasso, Somigli, Bechi, Palombini / Falliani, Del Signore, Mercuriali, Nessi, Luise. Conductors: Marinuzzi / Sanzogno
2 Apr	Milan La Scala	L'AMICO FRITZ (3) Favero, Malipiero, Poli, Mercuriali. Conductor: Mascagni
13 May	Prague Deutsches Theater	IL COMBATTIMENTO DI TANCREDI E CLORINDA (2) Tegani, Del Signore. Conductor: Sanzogno
14 June	Turin E.I.A.R.	BORIS GODUNOV (2) Pasero, Corsi, Wesselowski, Pigni, Neroni, Di Lelio, Valdengo, Nessi, Giannotti, Palombini. Conductor: La Rosa Parodi
26 July	Bologna Salone del Giornale	CONCERT (1)* Antonelli, Granda, Poli, Archi. Baroni and Sabino, piano. Donizetti: O mio Fernando
31 July	Bologna Sferisterio	L'AMICO FRITZ (2) Ottani, Malipiero, Togliani, Luise, Giunta, Antonelli. Conductor: Sabino
1 Aug	Bologna Sferisterio	MADAMA BUTTERFLY (4) Adami Corradetti, Ferrauto, Gobbi, Antonelli, Giunta, Luise Badioli, Busacchi, Grandi. Conductor: Sabino
5 Aug	Bologna Sferisterio	RIGOLETTO (2) Filippeschi, Pellegrini / Marinelli, Tagliabue, Zambelli, Grandi, Antonelli, De Vita, Luise, Giunta, Adancora. Conductor: Zamboni

30 Aug	Pesaro T. Rossini	HANSEL E GRETEL (2) Montanari, Vanelli, Marcucci, Casazza, Lindi, Garani. Conductor: Marini
8 Sept	Prato T. Metastasio	MADAMA BUTTERFLY (2) Carbone, Filippeschi, Vanelli, Luise. Conductor: Clepace
24 Sept	Bergamo T. Donizetti	VILLON (2) Voyer, Baracchi, Giunta, Carlo Badioli, Serpo, Cecchetelli, Maggi, Cilla, Antonelli, Righini, Cassinelli, Mercuriali, Sigalla. Conductor: Gavazzeni
30 Sept	Turin E.I.A.R.	MARIA D'ALESSANDRIA (1) Di Lelio, Civil, Reali, Mongelli, Zangheri, Mercuriali, Unnia, Coda, Giannotti. Conductor: La Rosa Parodi
2 Oct	Ferrara T. Verdi	LA FORZA DEL DESTINO (2) Castellani, Momo, Tagliabue, Neroni, Ghirardini. Conductor: Parenti
11 Oct	Ferrara T. Verdi	ANDREA CHENIER (2) Masini, Scuderi, Reali, Friggi, Chiorboli, Checchi, Novelli. Conductor: Parenti
25 Oct	Reggio Emilia T. Municipale	MADAMA BUTTERFLY (3) Hasegawa, Alfieri, Colombo. Conductor: Gavazzeni
1 Nov	Reggio Emilia T. Municipale	LA MORTE DI FRINE (2) Oltrabella, Pauli, Luffi, Bignozzi. Conductor: Podestà
4 Nov	Ferrara T. Verdi	MADAMA BUTTERFLY (2) Favero, Del Monaco, Poli, Mercuriali. Conductor: Giampietro.
27 Dec	Milan La Scala	FRA GHERARDO (3) Tasso, Salsedo, Carbone, Nessi, Nini Giani, Palombini, Luise, Valdengo. Conductor: Votto
31 Dec	Milan La Scala	MEFISTOFELE (4) Pasero, Malipiero, Tassinari / Fioroni, Palombini, Magnoni, Mercuriali. Conductor: Ghione

1942

29 Jan	Milan La Scala	IL BARBIERE DI SIVIGLIA (2) Tagliavini, Bechi, Pederzini, Pasero, Valdengo, De Taranto. Conductor: Marinuzzi
31 Jan	Milan La Scala	GIANNI SCHICCHI (3) Montesanto / Stabile, Aimaro / Tegani, Malipiero, Coda, Mercuriali, Scattola, Ticozzi / Rota, Villani, Zecca. Conductor: Ghione
5 Feb	Como T. Sociale	L'AMICO FRITZ (2) Ottani, Malipiero, Vanelli, Colajacovo, Lombardo, Villa. Conductor: Sabino

14 Feb	Milan La Scala	OTELLO (4) Lauri Volpi, Stabile, Del Signore / Casavecchi, Caniglia, Mercuriali / Zoffanetti, Valdengo. Conductor: Marinuzzi
18 Feb	Milan La Scala	LODOLETTA (3) Favero, Villani, Marcucci, Malipiero, Poli, Valdengo. Conductor: Ghione
19 Feb	Milan La Scala	HANSEL E GRETEL (5) Menotti / Cortini, Poli / Valdengo, Casazza / Palombini / Cravcenko, Salagaray / Marcucci / Ticozzi. Conductor: Sanzogno
28 Feb	Milan La Scala	THAIS (4) Bechi, Del Signore, Favero, Caselli, Marcucci / Fornari. Conductor: Marinuzzi
6 Mar	Milan La Scala	FRANCESCA DA RIMINI (4) Cigna, Margherita Bordoni, Valdengo, Ziliani, Maugeri, Nessi, Marcucci, Palombini, Luise. Conductor: Guarnieri
17 Mar	Milan La Scala	MADAMA BUTTERFLY (3) Adami Corradetti, Ziliani / Salvarezza, Vanelli / Valdengo, Luise, Nessi, Coda. Conductor: Sanzogno
25 Mar	Milan La Scala	IL RE (4) Carosio, Salvarezza, Bettoni, Cravcenko, Maugeri. Conductor: Marinuzzi
6 Apr	Milan La Scala	IL COMBATTIMENTO DI TANCREDI E CLORINDA (2) Tegani, Bechi / Gobbi, Parmeggiani. Conductor: Sanzogno
7 May	Forlì T. Comunale	CAVALLERIA RUSTICANA (2) Del Monaco, Bruna Rasa, Marchi. Conductor: Zeetti
17 May	Ravenna T. Alighieri	L'AMICO FRITZ (2) Tagliavini, Tassinari, Vanelli, Baracchi, Cilla. Conductor: Del Campo
21 May	Rovigo T. Sociale	L'AMICO FRITZ (2) Tagliavini, Tassinari, Poli, Scattola. Conductor: Podestà
18 June	Trieste Politeama Rossetti	IL BARBIERE DI SIVIGLIA (2) Aimaro, Borgonovo Sinnone / Casavecchi, Luise, Bettoni. Conductor: Podestà
8 Aug	Turin E.I.A.R.	LA FIAMMA (2) Cigna, Stignani, De Stefani, Tagliabue, Pauli, Ticozzi, Tumiati, Cassinelli, Avogadro. Conductor: Failoni
15 Aug	Turin E.I.A.R.	LA WALKIRIA [DIE WALKYRIE] (2) De Nemethy, Carbone, Benedetti, Tasso, Neroni, Marone, Ferrari, Ticozzi, Pogliani, Milani, Avogadro, Marcucci. Conductor: La Rosa Parodi

29 Aug	Turin E.I.A.R.	IL BALLO DELLE INGRATE (2) Tegani, Neroni. Conductor: Simonetto
12 Oct	Milan La Scala	ANFIONE (3) Brunazzi, Colasanti, Huder, Cova. Conductor: Erede
31 Oct	Milan La Scala	LA DONNA SERPENTE (3) Adami Corradetti, Salsedo, Huder, Luise, Maugeri, Ferrauto, Garbaccio, Nessi, Vanelli, Villano. Conductor: Previtali

1943

1 Jan	Milan La Scala	ELETTRA [ELEKTRA] (3) Höngen, Runger, Ursuleac, Witt-Russ. Conductors: Von Hoesslin / Moralt
13 Jan	Milan La Scala	IL RITORNO DI ULISSE IN PATRIA (2) Venturini, Pasero, Tasso, Elmo, Barbieri, Magnoni, Del Signore, Canali, Nessi. Conductor: Rossi
30 Jan	Milan La Scala	CARMEN (5) Gigli / Masini, Reali / Pasero, Luise, Nessi, Valdengo, Pederzini, Minazzi. Conductors: Guarnieri / Sanzogno
20 Feb	Milan La Scala	L'ORO DEL RENO [DAS RHEINGOLD] (2) Pasero, Zambelli, Casavecchi, Tasso, Neri, Poli, Nicolai, Falliani. Conductor: Von Hoesslin
6 Mar	Milan La Scala	IL CREPUSCOLO DEGLI DEI [GÖTTERDÄMMERUNG] (2) Hartmann, Dadò, Pasero, Poli, Nicolai, Ticozzi. Conductor: Von Hoesslin
24 Mar	Rome T. della Opera	OBERON (2) G. Alfano, Sinnone, Ghirardini, Gatti, Huder, Vitali Marini. Conductor: La Rosa Parodi
7 May	Rovigo Liceo Musicale F. Venezze	CONCERT (1) Margherita Furlanetto, piano. Giordani: Caro mio ben Monteverdi: Lasciatemi morire Scarlatti: Se Florindo è fedele Gluck: Oh del mio dolce ardor Vivaldi: Un certo non so che Mozart: Voi che sapete Schubert: Barcarola Schumann: Sei bella mia dolcezza Brahms: Ninna nanna Respighi: Nebbie Respighi: Nevicata Malipiero: Cancheri e Beccafichi Calliera: La lavanderia di San Giovanni Pieraccini: Beppino Rubacuori Lucatello: La mamma no vol

11 June	Valdagno T. Impero	MADAMA BUTTERFLY (2) Coda, Perris, Mari, Filippeschi, Vanelli, Nessi, Azzimonti. Conductor: Sabino
14 July	RAI	CONCERT Il Piccolo Castore (1). Conductor: Simonetto

1944

6 Jan	Trieste T. Comunale G. Verdi	HANSEL E GRETEL (6) Menotti, Piccioli, Anelli, Cravcenko, Monego, Nerina Ferrari. Conductor: Cordone
21 Jan	Como T. Sociale	IL BARBIERE DI SIVIGLIA (2) Bechi, Carosio, Francesco Albanese, Pasero, Mercuriali, Baldo, Tagliani. Conductor: Del Campo
26 Jan	Como T. Sociale (Scala)	IL BARBIERE DI SIVIGLIA (2) Bechi, Carosio, Francesco Albanese, Pasero, Mercuriali, Baldo. Conductor: Del Campo
12 Feb	Trieste T. Comunale G. Verdi	LE NOZZE DI FIGARO (4) Stabile, Cassinelli, Scuderi, Menotti, Palombini, Gubiani, Lozzi. Conductor: Gavazzeni
17 Feb	Trieste T. Comunale G. Verdi	FAUST (4) Malipiero, Mongelli, Fortunati, Mascherini, Serpo, Curiel. Conductor: Lucon
27 Feb	Bergamo T. Donizetti (Scala)	FALSTAFF (3) Stabile, Poli, Francesco Albanese, Mercuriali, Somigli, Minazzi, Elmo. Conductor: Del Campo
11 Mar	Milan T. Lirico (Scala)	FALSTAFF (2) Stabile, Poli, Francesco Albanese, Elmo, Oltrabella, Bettoni, Mercuriali, Minazzi, Somigli, Nessi. Conductor: Del Campo
16 Mar	Milan T. Lirico (Scala)	IL BARBIERE DI SIVIGLIA (3) Francesco Albanese, Baldo, Carosio, Bechi, Pasero, Mercuriali. Conductor: Del Campo
19 Mar	Milan T. Lirico (Scala)	BORIS GODUNOV (3) Pasero, Bettoni, Elmo, Wesselowsky, Baronti, Cravcenko, Mercuriali, Nessi, Pigni, Villani. Conductor: Del Campo
Mar	Como *	CONCERT (1)* Carenzio, violin; Mulazzi, piano. Mussorgsky: Canti della morte Arias of Pergolesi, Mozart, Monteverdi, Galliera
1 Apr	Milano T. Lirico (Scala)	LE NOZZE DI FIGARO (3) Pasero, Favero, Stabile, Baronti, Carbone, Del Signore, Sani, Nessi. Conductor: Marinuzzi

10 Apr	Milan T. Lirico (Scala)	PARSIFAL (3) Inghilleri, Zini, Pasero, Tasso, Poli. Conductor: Marinuzzi
14 Apr	Milan T. Lirico (Scala)	GIANNI SCHICCHI (2) Prandelli, Biasini, Modesti, Menotti, Coda, Nessi / Mercuriali, Villani, Zecca, Ticozzi. Conductor: Marinuzzi
25 Apr	Genoa T. Augustus	LE NOZZE DI FIGARO (2) Scuderi, Menotti, Sani, Giunta, Biasini, Zini, Gelli. Conductor: Gavazzeni
3 June	Milan T. del Popolo	IL COMBATTIMENTO DI TANCREDI E CLORINDA (1) Mercuriali, Poli. Conductor: Rapp
24 Oct	Turin T. Carignano	CONCERT (1) Mercuriali, Poli, Sciacqui. Conductor: Rapp Orlando di Lasso: Madrigals for four voices Filippo da Monte: Madrigals for six voices B. Troboncino: Frottola (Nonsense song) Anonymous: Vilotta (Earthy story) G. Caccini: Amarilli Anonymous: Invito al ballo G. G. Gastoldi: A lieta vita Monteverdi: Il combattimento di Tancredi e Clorinda
Nov	Verona*	CONCERT (1)*
Dec	Milan T. Nuovo	CONCERT (1)* Nino Rota, piano; Camillo Olbach, cello; Riccardo Brengola, violin.
31 Dec	Como Società Musicale M. E. Bossi	CONCERT (1)* Nino Rota, piano; Camillo Olbach, cello; Riccardo Brengola, violin.

1945

14 Apr	Milan T. Carcano	LA FORZA DEL DESTINO (3) Di Giulio, Beval, Borgonovo, Lombardo, Donaggio. Conductor: Podestà
23 May	Bellinzona T. Touring	CONCERT (1) C. F. Semini, piano. Arias (songs) of Verdi, Gordigiani, Tosti, Martucci, Pizzetti, Respighi, Tocchi, Semini, Persico, Nussio.
11 Aug	Campo Isonzo Gradisca Open-air theater	LA TRAVIATA (3) Coda, Adami Corradetti / Piccarolo, Prandelli, Reali, Buratti, Del Signore, Baracchi, Paiola, Taliani. Conductor: Simonetto
15 Aug	Gradisca d'Isonzo T. dei Tremila	RIGOLETTO (3) Piccarolo, Tagliabue, Poiesi, Stefanoni, Nessi, Coda, Bellon, Buratti, Baracchi, Paiola, Ricci. Conductor: Simonetto

18 Aug	Gradisca d'Isonzo T. dei Tremila	CAVALLERIA RUSTICANA (2) Elmo, Del Monaco, Piccioli. Conductor: Simonetto
5 Oct	Geneva Grand Théâtre	COSÌ FAN TUTTE (2) Morel, Rehfuss, Danco, Chabay, Rothmuller, Privez. Conductor: Von Hoesslin
18 Nov	Milan T. Excelsior	CONCERT (1) with Valdengo, Renzi, Danese Pedrazzoli, piano; Vidusso, piano; Turri, violin.

1946

3 Jan	Turin T. Lirico	HANSEL E GRETEL (4) Piccioli, Bossi, Bertola, Marcucci. Conductor: Gedda
22 Jan	Turin T. Lirico	COSÌ FAN TUTTE (3) Renzi, Montorri, Tegani, Molinari, Morel. Conductor: Ackermann
end of Jan	Aix-les-Bains Théâtre du Casino	COSÌ FAN TUTTE (2) Renzi, Montorri, Tegani, Molinari, Morel. Conductor: Ackermann
2 Feb	Turin T. Lirico	IL MATRIMONIO SEGRETO (1) Renzi, Poli, Rovero, Ollendorf, Morel. Conductor: Ackermann
8 Feb	Geneva Grand Théâtre	IL MATRIMONIO SEGRETO (2) Morel, Rovero, Renzi, Ollendorf, Poli. Conductor: Galliera
8 Mar	Milan T. Lirico (Scala)	CONCERT Ave Maria (Verdi) (1) Rovero, Del Signore, Siepi. Conductor: Scherchen
29 Mar	Lyon T. de L'Opéra	COSÌ FAN TUTTE (2) Danco, Morel, Papazian, Cortis, Badioli. Conductor: Ackermann
Apr	Toulouse T. du Capitole	COSÌ FAN TUTTE (2) Danco, Morel, Cortis, Badioli, Papazian. Conductor: Ackermann
6 Apr	Turin T. Lirico	LA FORZA DEL DESTINO (3) Beval, Pierotti, Ghirardini, Pasero, Castellani / Corridori. Conductors: Questa / Gedda.
17 Apr	Paris Théâtre de la Gaîté Lyrique	COSÌ FAN TUTTE (3) Danco, Morel, Papazian, Cortis, Badioli. Conductor: Ackermann
2 May	Geneva Grand Théâtre	FALSTAFF (2) Scuderi, Morel, Palombini, Biasini, Piccioli, Moraro, Stefanoni, Giunta, Nardi. Conductor: Sanzogno

8 May	Geneva Grand Théâtre	UN BALLO IN MASCHERA (2) Castellani, Morel, Del Monaco, Biasini, Stefanoni, Giunta, Belloni, Nardi. Conductor: Sanzogno
21 May	Lugano Liceo, Aula Magna	CONCERT (1) Semini, piano Verdi: Ad una stella Verdi: Stornello Tosti: Vorrei morire Tosti: Non t'amo più *: A che serve trascinar la vita *: Quando l'amor è morto *: Giovanottin che passí per la via Tosti: Marecchiare Pizzetti: I pastori Respighi: Nebbie Persico: Una rota si fa in cielo
end of May	Lugano Penitenziario	CONCERT (1) C. F. Semini, piano. same program as 21 May, 1946
June	Chiasso*	CONCERT (1) C. F. Semini, piano. same program as 21 May, 1946
June	Mendrisio*	CONCERT (1) C. F. Semini, piano. same program as 21 May, 1946
30 July	Trieste Castello di San Giusto	LA FORZA DEL DESTINO (5) Fortunati, Momo, Savarese, Mongelli, Noto, Majonica. Conductor: Votto
10 Sept	Lugano (Radio)	CONCERT (1) C. F. Semini, piano. same program as 21 May, 1946
9 Nov	Bologna T. Comunle	COSÌ FAN TUTTE (2) Menotti, Morel, Cortis, Badioli, Papazian. Conductor: Ackermann
29 Dec	Trieste T. Comunale G. Verdi	IL CAVALIERE DELLA ROSA [ROSENKAVALIER] (4) Oltrabella, Bettoni, Piccioli, Menotti, Majonica, Wladimiro Badioli, Lozzi. Conductor: Ackermann

1947

5 Jan	Trieste T. Comunale G. Verdi	HANSEL E GRETEL (4) Menotti, Piccioli, Sani, Casazza, Slodini, Marta Lantieri. Conductor: Terni
18 Jan	Genoa T. Grattacielo	MIGNON (3) Basile, Madonna, Lazzari, Sartori, Modesti. Conductor: Gavazzeni

8 Feb	Barcelona T. del Liceo	COSÌ FAN TUTTE (4) Bossy, Morel, Papazian, Cortis, Badioli. Conductor: Ackermann
6 Apr	Turin T. Lirico	LA FORZA DEL DESTINO (3) Beval, Pierotti, Ghirardini, Pasero, Castellani. Conductor: Questa
17 Apr	Milan La Scala	COSÌ FAN TUTTE (4) Danco, Menotti, Cortis, Schuh, Munteanu, Ollendorf. Conductor: Perlea
13 May	Bologna T. Comunale	CONCERT - Beethoven 9th Symphony (2) Voyer, Siepi, Vivante. Conductor: Van Kempen
16 May	Paris Théâtre de la Gaîté Lyrique	FALSTAFF (6) Palombini, Morel, M. L. Cioni, Cortis, Boriello, Badioli, Moraro. Conductor: Ackermann
26 Aug	Edinburgh King's Theatre (Glyndebourne Festival)	LE NOZZE DI FIGARO (9) Tajo, Brownlee, Menotti / Alnar, Brannigan, Steber, Lawson, Flegg. Conductors: Susskind / Cellini.
2 Oct	Milan La Scala	MIGNON (3) Di Stefano, Siepi, Aimaro Bertasi, Ticozzi, Paci. Conductor: Guarnieri
11 Oct	Geneva Grand Théâtre	LE NOZZE DI FIGARO (2) Cassinelli, Piccioli, Paci, Fortunati, Morel, Sani, Thommes, Giunta, Guerra. Conductor: Böhm
28 Oct	Turin T. Carignano	MIGNON (2) Di Stefano / Moraro, Grani, Mariano Caruso, Roan, Beuf, Marone. Conductor: Simonetto
11 Nov	Barcelona T. del Liceo	FALSTAFF (3) Biasini, Caniglia, Rovero, Salagaray, Borgonovo, Moraro, Linares, Giunta, Modesti. Conductor: Annovazzi
15 Nov	Barcelona T. del Liceo	LA FORZA DEL DESTINO (2) Sanzio, Beval, Siepi, Borgonovo, Anglada, Riaza. Conductor: Sabater
22 Nov	Barcelona T. del Liceo	MARTA (3) Poggi, Rovero, Modesti, Ghirardini, Riaza. Conductor: Annovazzi
18 Dec	Barcelona T. del Liceo	IL TROVATORE (3) Gamazo, Soler, Borgonovo, Corbella. Conductor: Sabater
30 Dec	Barcelona T. del Liceo	ANNA BOLENA (3) Scuderi, Siepi, Soler, Ausensi, Antic, Giunta. Conductor: Annovazzi

1948

15 Jan	Venice T. La Fenice	MIGNON (4) Moraro, Siepi, Grani, Canali, Ghirardini. Conductor: Guarnieri
3 Feb	Trieste T. Comunale G. Verdi	MIGNON (4) Moraro, Dora Gatta, Cassinelli, Serpo, Majonica, Canali. Conductor: Berrettoni
3 Mar	Milan La Scala	IL BARBIERE DI SIVIGLIA (4) Infantino / Moraro, Mascherini / Cesari, Pasero, Badioli / Molinari, Ticozzi. Conductors: Guarnieri / Quadri.
19 Mar	Milan La Scala	CONCERT - Verdi, Requiem Mass (2) Infantino, Pasero, Fornarina Vieri. Conductor: De Sabata
22 Mar	RAI	MARTINI AND ROSSI CONCERT (1) with Infantino. Conductor: Questa Donizetti: O mio Fernando Bizet: Habañera Thomas: Io conosco un garzoncel Verdi: O don fatale
26 Mar	Bologna T. Comunale	CONCERT - Händel, The Messiah (2) Gatti, Munteanu, Christoff. Conductor: Gui
8 Apr	Bergamo T. Donizetti	CONCERT - Donizetti, Requiem Mass (1) Arié, Magnoni, Pola, Tagliabue. Conductor: Gavazzeni
15 May	Turin T. Lirico	CAVALLERIA RUSTICANA (3) Voltolini, Pierotti, Montorfano. Conductor: Braggio
10 June	Milan La Scala	NERONE (Act III & Act IV, part 2) (1) Nelli, Siepi, Guarrera, Nessi, Ticozzi. Conductor: Toscanini
23 June	Milan La Scala	IL RE DAVID (1) Prandelli, Vivante. Conductor: Previtali
8 July	Rome R.A.I.	CARMEN Lauri Volpi, Montanari, Nava, Marcangeli, Limberti, Valentini, Mariano Caruso, Tomei. Conductor: Serafin
8 Aug	Verona Arena	IL BARBIERE DI SIVIGLIA (3) Bechi, Infantino, Corena, Rossi Lemeni. Conductor: Perlea
21 Aug	Verona Arena	LA FAVORITA (Act IV) (1) Gentilini, Pasero. Conductor: Gavazzeni
8 Sept	Milan La Scala	ADRIANA LECOUVREUR (3) Favero, Filippeschi, Modesti, Boriello, Mariano Caruso. Conductor: Berrettoni

19 Sept	Perugia T. Comunale F. Morlacchi (Sagra Musicale Umbra)	GIUDITTA [JUDITH] (2) Carosio, Pederzini, Ariè, Christoff, Munteanu. Conductor: Santini
30 Sept	Bergamo T. Donizetti (Scala)	LA FAVORITA (2) Poggi, Bechi, Siepi, De Cecco. Conductor: Capuana
7 Oct	Milano La Scala	WERTHER (3) Prandelli, Gatta, Compolonghi, Coda. Conductor: Perlea
16 Oct	Bologna T. Comunale	WERTHER (4) Prandelli, Poli, Erato, Majonica, Salvarini, Zana. Conductor: Sanzogno
19 Nov	Bologna T. Comunale	BORIS GODUNOV (3) Rossi Lemeni, Cadoni, Birolo, Fiorio, Wesselowski, Modesti, Voyer, Zambelli, Malaguti. Conductor: Ackermann
30 Dec	Venice T. la Fenice	CARMEN (3) Del Monaco, De Falchi, Calaresu, Vajani, Masini, Baracchi, Franchi, Majonica. Conductor: Serafin

1949

14 Jan	Geneva Grand Théâtre	COSÌ FAN TUTTE (2) Danco, De Luca, Cortis, Stabile, Morel. Conductor: Böhm
27 Jan	Rome T. dell'Opera	DIDONE ED ENEA (DIDO AND AENEAS) (4) Boriello, Leonelli. Conductor: Santini
15 Feb	Brescia T. Grande	MIGNON (3) Vilsoni, Landi, Feliciati, Carlo Bergonzi. Conductor: Del Cupolo
5 Mar	Milan La Scala	HANSEL E GRETEL (3) Menotti, Boriello / Campi, Cravcenko, Ticozzi. Conductor: Sanzogno
30 Mar	Milan La Scala	LA FORZA DEL DESTINO (5) Filippeschi, Barbato / Kelston, Silveri, Christoff / Siepi, Meletti, Ticozzi, Caselli / Piero Bassi. Conductors: De Sabata / Sanzogno
23 Apr	Turin T. Nuovo	L'ITALIANA IN ALGERI (2) Oncina, Vannelli, Latinucci, Bettoni, Avogadro. Conductor: Berrettoni
28 May	Milan La Scala	CONCERT - Beethoven, 9th Symphony (1) Prandelli, Siepi, Winifried Cecil. Conductor: Furtwängler
31 May	Genoa T. Carlo Felice	LA FORZA DEL DESTINO (3) Castellani, Campagnano, Tagliabue, Neroni, Meletti, Majonica. Conductor: Questa

2 June	Genoa T. Carlo Felice	ADRIANA LECOUVREUR (3) Favero, Prandelli, Boriello, Majonica. Conductor: Gavazzeni
24 June	Mexico City Italian Embassy	CONCERT (1) Fineschi, Albanese, Poggi, Di Stefano, Mascherini, Siepi. Conductor: Picco
28 June	Mexico City Palacio de Bellas Artes	MIGNON (3) Di Stefano, Siepi, Guajardo, Milera. Conductor: Picco
7 July	Mexico City Palacio de Bellas Artes	IL BARBIERE DI SIVIGLIA (3) Di Stefano, Mascherini, Pechner, Siepi, De Los Santos. Conductor: Cellini
12 July	Mexico City Palacio de Bellas Artes	LA FAVORITA (2) Di Stefano, Mascherini, Siepi, Tortolero, Rodriguez. Conductor: Picco
23 July	Mexico City Palacio de Bellas Artes	WERTHER (3) Di Stefano, Rocabruna, Del Prado, Ruffino, Tortolero, Cerda. Conductor: Cellini
8 Sept	Genoa T. Augustus	CAVALLERIA RUSTICANA (3) Cavallari, Marchiandi, Vinci. Conductor: Savini
18 Sept	Turin R.A.I.	LA CENERENTOLA (1) Rovero, Truccato Pace, Valletti, Meletti, Dalamangas, Susca. Conductor: Rossi
1 Nov	Genoa T. Carlo Felice	CONCERT - Beethoven 9th Symphony (2) Laszlo, Spruzzola, Ariè. Conductor: Erede
3 Dec	Catania Teatro Bellini	MIGNON (3) Vilsoni, Oncina / Lazzari, Petri. Conductor: Berrettoni
26 Dec	Venice T. La Fenice	IL MATRIMONIO SEGRETO (3) Menotti, Ottani, Valletti, Stefanoni, De Taranto. Conductor: Votto

1950

3 Jan	Novara T. Coccia	CARMEN (2) Annaloro, Compolonghi. Conductor: Podestà
12 Jan	Piacenza T. Municipale	WERTHER (2) Valletti, Borgonovo, Bulgaron, Righini, Ciulli, Giorgio Giorgetti. Conductor: Parenti
16 Jan	RAI	MARTINI AND ROSSI CONCERT (1) with Christoff. Conductor: Rossi Saint-Saëns: Amor i miei fini proteggi Mascagni: Voi lo sapete Giordano: O grandi occhi lucenti Weber: Ah, che non giunge il sonno

19 Jan	Modena T. Comunale	CARMEN (2) Del Monaco, Taddei, Tegani. Conductor: Tieri
28 Jan	Brescia T. Grande	CARMEN (3) Noli, Del Monaco, Torres, Baronti, Villani, Marcucci, Pancari, De Palma, Albertini. Conductor: Narducci
3 Feb	RAI	CONCERT (1) – DONIZETTI REQUIEM with Fleri, Berdini, Panerai, Petri. Conductor: Gavazzeni
19 Feb	Brescia T. Grande	CAVALLERIA RUSTICANA (2) Ferrando Ferrari, Zangheri. Conductor: Del Cupolo
19 Mar	Cagliari T. Massimo	IL MATRIMONIO SEGRETO (1) Rovero, Arizmendi, De Taranto, Christoff, Valletti. Conductor: Serafin
8 Apr	Milan La Scala	KHOVANSHCHINA (3) Francesco Albanese, Christoff, Piero Guelfi, Majonica, Nessi, Penno, Zanolli. Conductor: Dobrowen
16 Apr	Milan La Scala	MOSÈ (4) Pasero, Pedrini, Piero Guelfi, Gallo, Francesco Albanese, Modesti, Amadini. Conductor: Capuana
28 Apr	Brussels T. de la Monnaie	IL MATRIMONIO SEGRETO (1) Bruscantini, Rovero, Noni, Stefanoni, Valletti. Conductor: Rossi
23 May	Mexico City Palacio de Bellas Artes	NORMA (2) Callas, Baum, Moscona, De los Santos, Sagarminaga. Conductor: Picco
30 May	Mexico City Palacio de Bellas Artes	AIDA (3) Callas, Baum / Filippeschi, Weede, Moscona, Ruffino, Sagarminaga, Rodriguez. Conductor: Picco
13 June	Mexico City Palacio de Bellas Artes	CAVALLERIA RUSTICANA (2) Filippeschi, Morelli, De Los Santos, Farfan. Conductor: Mugnai
20 June	Mexico City Palacio de Bellas Artes	IL TROVATORE (3) Callas, Baum, Warren / Petroff, Moscona, Sagarminaga, Feuss. Conductor: Picco
6 July	Mexico City Palacio de Bellas Artes	FALSTAFF (2) Warren, Petroff, Noti, Rocabruna, Ibanez, Silva, De Paolis. Conductor: Cellini
11 July	Mexico City Palacio de Bellas Artes	CARMEN (3) Filippeschi, Morelli, Salinas / Noti, Ruffino. Conductor: Limantour
20 July	Mexico City Palacio de Bellas Artes	FEDORA (2) Filippeschi, Rocabruna, Morelli, Ruffino. Conductor: Cellini

6 Aug	Milan R.A.I.	L'ITALIANA IN ALGERI (1) Gatta, Farolfi, Barollo, Taddei, Dalamangas, Latinucci. Conductor: Giulini
8 Sept	Cesena T. Comunale A. Bonci	CARMEN (2) Masini, Rizzieri, Pierotti. Conductor: De Fabritiis
23 Sept	Bergamo T. Donizetti	LE NOZZE DI FIGARO (2) Petri, De Cavalieri, Taddei, Rizzieri, Coda, Baracchi, Del Signore. Conductor: Gavazzeni
10 Oct	Milan R.A.I.	IL BARBIERE DI SIVIGLIA (1) Infantino, Taddei, Cassinelli, Badioli, Broilo. Conductor: Previtali
17 Oct	Genoa T. Carlo Felice	IL BARBIERE DI SIVIGLIA (3) Ticozzi, Moraro, Taddei, Cassinelli, De Taranto. Conductor: Tieri
8 Nov	Lausanne Théâtre Municipal	IL MATRIMONIO SEGRETO (2) Rovero, Morel, Petri, Coda, Mercuriali. Conductor: Gavazzeni
16 Nov	Lausanne Radio Lausanne	IL MATRIMONIO SEGRETO (1) Rovero, Morel, Petri, Coda, Mercuriali. Conductor: Gavazzeni
7 Dec	Barcelona T. del Liceo	CARMEN (3) Annaloro, Ezquerra, Maria del Carmen Tarancon, Elias, Torres, Cabanes, Bardagi. Conductor: Annovazzi
26 Dec	Milan R.A.I.	CARMEN (1) Pagliughi, Berdini, Boriello, Broilo, Marcucci, Latinucci, Carlin, Clabassi. Conductor: Previtali
28 Dec	Modena T. Comunale	MIGNON (2) Moraro, Dora Gatta, Algorta, Togliani. Conductor: Molinari Pradelli

1951

4 Jan	Piacenza T. Municipale	CARMEN (2) Pelizzoni, Girotti / Marchio, Cataldo, Villani, Piccini, Guerra. Conductor: Wolf Ferrari
19 Jan	Trieste T. Comunale G. Verdi	LA CENERENTOLA (4) Valletti, Corena, Menotti, Cattelani, Gianpietro Malaspina, Susca. Conductor: Berrettoni
3 Feb	Venice T. La Fenice	LA DANNAZIONE DI FAUST (3) Voyer, Mascherini, Lopatto. Conductor: Gui
24 Feb	Rome T. dell'Opera	L'ARLESIANA (3) Valletti, Carol, Panerai, Tita / Maiorana, Di Lelio. Conductor: De Fabritiis

14 Mar	Palermo T. Massimo	LA FORZA DEL DESTINO (3) Barbato, Turrini, Mascherini, Neri, Meletti. Conductor: Questa
18 Apr	Milan La Scala	WERTHER (6) Tagliavini / Prandelli, Dora Gatta, Orlandini, Bruscantini. Conductor: Capuana
15 May	Turin T. Alfieri	L'ARLESIANA (3) Lazzari, Piero Guelfi, Carol / Droghetti. Conductor: Questa
12 June	Rome R.A.I.	AIDA (1) Mancini, Filippeschi, Panerai, Neri, Massaria. Conductor: Gui
21 June	Strasbourg International Festival (San Carlo de Napoli)	IL MATRIMONIO SEGRETO (3), Carosio, Valletti, Rovero, Poli, Tajo. Conductor: Markevitch. IL COMBATTIMENTO DI TANCREDI E CLORINDA (3) Valletti, Rovero. Conductor: Markevitch
28 June	Genoa T. Augustus	CAVALLERIA RUSTICANA (3) Cavallari, Lucchiari, Pierotti. Conductor: Moresco
28 July	Trieste Castello di San Giusto	LA FORZA DEL DESTINO (3) Martorel, Turrini, Savarese, Siepi, Corena, Susca. Conductor: Berrettoni
25 Sept	Perugia Basilica di San Pietro	LA BETULIA LIBERATA (1) Kelston, Berdini, Tajo. Conductor: Capuana
5 Oct	RAI	CONCERT (1) - VERDI REQUIEM Kelston, Campora, Siepi. Conductor: Rossi
30 Oct	Brussels T. de la Monnaie	LA CENERENTOLA (2) Menotti, Montorfano, Monti, Meletti, Corena, Coda. Conductor: Gavazzeni
3 Nov	Catania T. Bellini	NORMA (4) Callas, Penno, Christoff / Wolowsky, Cannizzaro, Valori. Conductor: Ghione
15 Nov	Catania T. Bellini	SANSONE E DALILA (3) De Santis, Campolonghi, Wolowsky. Conductor: Albert
26 Dec	Naples T. San Carlo	IL CAVALIERE DELLA ROSA [ROSENKAVALIER] (3) Stella Roman, Tajo, Poli, Dora Gatta, Canali, De Palma. Conductor: Swarowsky

1952

10 Jan	Rome T. dell'Opera	AIDA (4) Stella, Lauri Volpi / Turrini, Bechi, Neri, Clabassi, Caroli, Di Giove. Conductor: Capuana

17 Jan	Rome T. dell'Opera	IL FRANCO CACCIATORE [DER FREISCHÜTZ] (4) Mancini, Francesco Albanese, Christoff. Conductor: Capuana
4 Feb	RAI	MARTINI AND ROSSI CONCERT (1) with Petri. Conductor: Fighera Purcell: Morte di Didone Rossini: Nacqui all'affano Berlioz: Perduta ho la mia pace Verdi: O don fatale
14 Feb	Rome T. dell'Opera	LE NOZZE DI FIGARO (4) Tebaldi, Taddei, Rizzieri, Bruna Rizoli, Dubbini, De Taranto, Sininberghi. Conductor: Gui
17 Mar	Milan La Scala	PROSERPINA E LO STRANIERO (4) Barbato, Carteri / Castro, Demetz, Elmo, Gardino, Giangiacomo Guelfi, Picchi, Prandelli. Conductor: Castro
12 Apr	Naples T. San Carlo	IL COMBATTIMENTO DI TANCREDI E CLORINDA (3) Valletti, Rovero. Conductor: Sanzogno IL MATRIMONIOI SEGRETO (3) Tajo, Rovero, Noni, Poli, Valletti. Conductor: Sanzogno
13 Apr	Milan R.A.I.	GLI ORAZIE I CURIAZI (1) Vercelli, Spataro, Del Signore, Broilo, Artioli, Caselli, Wolowsky. Conductor: Giulini
24 Apr	Milan La Scala	IL BARBIERE DI SIVIGLIA (3) Tagliavini, Bechi, Rossi Lemeni, Luise, Canali. Conductor: De Sabata
10 May	Florence T. La Pergola	IL CONTE ORY (2) Barabas, Pini, Capecchi, Petri, Mercuriali, Gardino, Londi. Conductor: Gui
17 May	Florence T. La Pergola	TANCREDI (2) Francesco Albanese, Stich-Randall, Petri, Mafalda Masini, Gardino. Conductor: Serafin
29 May	Florence T. La Pergola	LA PIETRA DEL PARAGONE [The Touchstone] (2) R. Corsi, Carmen Forti, Petri, Taddei, Gianni Raimondi, Luise, Calabrese. Conductor: Santini
9 June	Florence T. Comunale	CONCERT (1) Conductor: Stokowski De Falla: El amor brujo
31 July	Trieste Castello di San Giusto	CARMEN (3) Corelli, Campolonghi, Zanolli, Hussu, Ronchini, Susca, Cappuccilli (Morales). Conductor: Bamboschek
29 Aug	Rio de Janeiro T. Municipal	LA GIOCONDA (3) Prandelli, Savarese, Petri, Martinis, Borelli / Henriques, La Porta. Conductor: De Fabritiis

9 Sep	Rio de Janeiro T. Municipal	RIGOLETTO (1) Prandelli, Carmen Forti, Savarese, Petri, Audisio Masini Conductor: De Fabriitiis
17 Sep	Rio de Janeiro T. Municipal	CONCERT (1) with Savarese, Carmen Forti, Petri, Prandelli, Sà Earp, Tebaldi, Fortes, Coelho Netto de Freitas, De Los Angeles, Poggi, Caniglia. Conductor: Spedini Cinderella's aria (Nacqui all'affanno?) Duet from *Werther* with Prandelli
25 Sep	Rio de Janeiro T. Municipal	DON GIOVANNI (2) De Los Angeles, Carmen Forti, Prandelli, Petri, Damiano, Clabassi, Gonçalves. Conductor: De Fabritiis
29 Sep	Rio de Janeiro T. Municipal	CONCERT (1) with Carmen Forti, Misciano, Sà Earp, Petri, Leozzi. Conductor: De Fabritiis Aria from *Trovatore* (Stride la vampa?)
18 Oct	Turin T. Nuovo	CARMEN (2) Corelli, Mongelli, Tegani. Conductor: Antonicelli
14 Nov	Trieste T. Comunale G. Verdi	L'ITALIANA IN ALGERI (4) Mongelli, Munteanu, Corena, Erato, Gardino, Dallamangas. Conductor: Votto
26 Nov	Milano R.A.I.	LA FAVORITA (1) Poggi, Silveri, Bruscantini. Conductor: Gavazzeni
13 Dec	Bologna T. Comunale	DON CHISCIOTTE [DON QUICHOTTE] (2) Tajo, Monachesi, Cadoni, Cavalieri, Blaffard, Mariano Caruso, Fogli, Zana. Conductor: Questa
15 Dec	RAI	MARTINI AND ROSSI CONCERT (1) with Taddei. Conductor: Antonicelli Gluck: Che faro' senza Euridice Bizet: Card song Verdi: Condotta ell'era al ceppi Rossini: Ai capricci della sorte (with Taddei)

1953

9 Jan	Venice T. La Fenice	LE NOZZE DI FIGARO (3) Petri, Jurinac, Bruscantini, Corena, Badioli, Rizzieri, Pini. Conductor: Gui
18 Jan	Milan	IL CASTELLO DEL PRINCIPE BARBABLÚ [BLUEBEARD'S CASTLE] (1) with Petri. Conductor: Giulini
4 Mar	Milan La Scala	L'ITALIANA IN ALGERI (5) Valletti, Petri / Dallamangas, Bruscantini, Dobbs, Campi. Conductor: Giulini

25 Mar	Palermo T. Massimo	IL BARBIERE DI SIVIGLIA (4) Bechi, Tajo, Oncina / Monti, Luise. Conductor: Molinari Pradelli
10 Apr	Lisbon T. São Carlos	DON CHISCIOTTE [DON QUICHOTTE] (2) Tajo, Poli, Viana, Cadoni, Guerreiro, Mariano Caruso. Conductor: De Freitas Branco
24 Apr	Lisbon T. São Carlos	SANSONE E DALILA (1) Vinay, Duarte d'Almeida, Susca, Corena, Mariano Caruso. Conductor: Molinari Pradelli
9 May	Florence T. Comunale	AMAHL E GLI OSPITI NOTTURNI (3) Cordova, Lazzari, Capecchi, Corena, Giorgio Giorgetti. Conductor: Stokowski
4 June	London Covent Garden	AIDA (3) Callas, Baum, Walters, Neri / Nowakowski, Langdon, Thomas, Sutherland. Conductor: Barbirolli
15 June	London Covent Garden	NORMA (4) Callas, Sutherland, Picchi, Neri, Asciak. Conductor: Pritchard
26 June	London Covent Garden	IL TROVATORE (3) Callas, Johnston, Walters, Modesti / Langdon, Mills, MacAlpine, Emlyn Jones, Littlewood. Conductor: Erede
9 July	Bolzano Open-air theater	CARMEN (2) with Corelli, Colzani, Carol. Conductor: Ziino
29 July	Milan R.A.I.	I CAPULETI E I MONTECCHI (1) Gavarini, Rizzoli, Massaria, Caselli. Conductor: Giulini
21 Aug	Naples Arena Flegrea (San Carlo)	CARMEN (4) Corelli, Protti, Rizzieri, Vercelli, Cattelani, Della Pergola, De Palma. Conductor: Reiner
19 Sept	San Francisco War Memorial Opera House	WERTHER (1) Valletti, Warenskjold, Lombardi. Conductor: Serafin
29 Sept	San Francisco War Memorial Opera House	BORIS GODUNOV (2) Rossi Lemeni, Sullivan, Alvary, Bardelli, Baccaloni, De Paolis, Moudry, Chauveau. Conductor: Serafin
9 Oct	San Francisco War Memorial Opera House	IL BARBIERE DI SIVIGLIA (2) Valletti, Guarrera, Rossi Lemeni, Baccaloni. Conductor: Serafin
10 Oct	Sacramento Memorial Auditorium (S. F. Opera)	IL BARBIERE DI SIVIGLIA (1) Valletti, Guarrera, Rossi Lemeni, Baccaloni Conductor: Serafin
18 Oct	San Francisco Radio	CONCERT (1) with Valletti. Conductor: Cleva Mozart: Non so più Saint-Saëns: S'apre per te il mio cor Final duet from *Favorita* with Valletti

21 Oct	Los Angeles Shrine Auditorium (S. F. Opera)	BORIS GODUNOV (1) Rossi Lemeni, Sullivan, Alvary, Bardelli, Baccaloni, De Paolis, Moudry, Chauveau. Conductor: Serafin
26 Oct	Los Angeles Shrine Auditorium (S. F. Opera)	WERTHER (1) Valletti, Warenskjold, Lombardi. Conductor: Serafin
29 Oct	San Diego Russ Auditorium (S. F. Opera)	IL BARBIERE DI SIVIGLIA (1) Valletti, Guarrera, Tajo, Baccaloni. Conductor: Serafin
31 Oct	Los Angeles Shrine Auditorium (S. F. Opera)	IL BARBIERE DI SIVIGLIA (1) Valletti, Guarrera, Baccaloni, Tajo. Conductor: Serafin
26 Nov	Florence T. Comunale	LA DANNAZIONE DI FAUST (3) Picchi, Petri, Stefanoni. Conductor: Gui
12 Dec	Naples T. San Carlo	LA CENERENTOLA (3) Oncina, Taddei, Tajo, Dora Gatta, Cadoni, Caselli. Conductor: Serafin
19 Dec	Naples T. San Carlo	CARMEN (6) Corelli, Savarese, Jurinac, Herze, West, Herent, De Palma. Conductor: Rodzinski
28 Dec	RAI	MARTINI AND ROSSI CONCERT (1) with Tagliabue. Conductor: Bogo Monteverdi: Addio a Roma Mozart: Non so più Verdi: Condotta ell'era al ceppi Verdi: O don fatale

1954

20 Jan	Rome T. dell'Opera	LA CENERENTOLA (4) Arnaldi, Cadoni, Oncina, Bruscantini, Tajo, La Porta. Conductor: Gui
10 Feb	Palermo T. Massimo	I CAPULETI E I MONTECCHI (3) Carteri, Gavarini, Taddeo / Borghi. Conductor: Gui
24 Feb	Naples T. San Carlo	LE NOZZE DI FIGARO (3) Colombo, Tebaldi, Tajo, Noni, De Palma, Dallamangas, Giuliana Raimondi. Conductor: Perlea
14 Mar	Milan La Scala	LA CENERENTOLA (5) Monti, Petri, Bruscantini, Badioli, Dora Gatta, Cadoni. Conductor: Giulini
20 Mar	Genoa T. Carlo Felice	LA FORZA DEL DESTINO (3) Mancini, Turrini, Bastianini, Tozzi, Luise. Conductor: Ghione

8 Apr	Lisbon T. São Carlos	LE NOZZE DI FIGARO (2) Lidonni, Tajo, Susca, Dow, Carteri, Filacuridi, Betner, Giorgio Giorgetti, Micheluzzi, Mariano Caruso. Conductor: De Fabritiis
12 Apr	Lisbon T. São Carlos	DON CHISCIOTTE [DON QUICHOTTE] (2) Tajo, Monachesi, Viana, Betner, Guerreiro, Mariano Caruso. Conductor: De Freitas Branco
22 Apr	Lisbon T. São Carlos	DON CARLO (2) Barbato, Gobbi, Picchi, Tajo, Sbalchiero, Susca, Mariano Caruso. Conductor: De Fabritiis
23 Apr	Lisbon T. Monumental	CONCERT (1) Erato, Picchi, Barbato, Gobbi, Tajo. Conductor: * NORMA: duet from the 1st Act with Picchi CAVALLERIA RUSTICANA: Voi lo sapete
29 Apr	Lisbon T. São Carlos	MIGNON (2) Erato, Misciano, Tajo, Betner, Susca, Mariano Caruso. Conductor: De Freitas Branco
26 May	Milan La Scala	ARLECCHINO (4) Baroni, Corena, Munteanu, Panerai, Petri, Cazzato, Moretti. Conductor: Mitropoulos
30 June	The Hague Holland Festival (La Scala)	LA CENERENTOLA (2) Cadoni, Dora Gatta, Badioli, Bruscantini, Petri, Valletti. Conductor: Giulini
3 July	Amsterdam Holland Festival (La Scala)	LA CENERENTOLA (2) Cadoni, Dora Gatta, Badioli, Bruscantini, Petri, Valletti. Conductor: Giulini
14 July	Turin R.A.I.	CAVALLERIA RUSTICANA (1) Cadoni, Braschi, Tagliabue, Pellegrino. Conductor: Basile
18 July	Rome Terme di Caracalla	CARMEN (4) Di Marco / Tegani, Turrini / Corelli, Silveri / Ariè, Marcangeli, Huder, La Porta, Zagonara, Tomei, Sacchetti. Conductor: Bellezza
29 July	Rome Terme di Caracalla	AIDA (4) Aimaro, Del Monaco / Vertecchi, Gobbi / Silveri / De Falchi, Mongelli / Sbalchiero / Majonica. Conductor: Questa
7 Aug	Verona Arena	AIDA (2) De Cavalieri, Del Monaco, Protti, Neri / Rossi Lemeni, Majonica. Conductor: Cleva
22 Aug	Bilbao T. Coliseo Albia	NORMA (1) Pedrini, Turrini, Petri, Mercuriali, Pellegrino. Conductor: Parenti
25 Aug	Bilbao T. Coliseo Albia	AIDA (1) Pedrini, Borso, Protti, Ferrin, Catania, Mercuriali, Pellegrino. Conductor: Parenti

28 Aug	Bilbao T. Coliseo Albia	CARMEN (1) Turrini, Protti, Noli, Ester, Pellegrino, Mercuriali, Barbesi, Catania, Erauzquin. Conductor: Parenti
2 Sept	Rio de Janeiro T. Municipal	LA FORZA DEL DESTINO (3) Tebaldi, Penno / Soler, Silveri, Neri, Damiano, Pimentel, Walter, Crimi, Lembo. Conductor: De Fabritiis
17 Sept	Rio de Janeiro T. Municipal	CECILIA (2) Tebaldi, Soler, Fortes, Modesti, Braga, Jaray, Lembo. Conductor: De Fabritiis
30 Sept	Rio de Janeiro T. Municipal	CAVALLERIA RUSTICANA (1) Pacheco, Salsedo, De Pennafort, Pimentel. Conductor: De Guarnieri
8 Oct	Vienna Grosser Musikvereinssaal	CARMEN (2) Gedda, Güden, Roux, Sciutti, Ribacchi, Sordello, Del Signore, Guthrie, Carlin. Conductor: Karajan
23 Oct	Monterrey T. Florida	MIGNON (2) Gianni Raimondi, Ariè, Garfias,Woodrow. Conductor: Picco
27 Oct	Monterrey T. Florida	WERTHER (1) Di Stefano, Morelli, Fabila, Pazos. Conductor: Picco
1 Nov	Chicago Lyric Opera	NORMA (2) Callas, Picchi, Rossi Lemeni, Lind, White. Conductor: Rescigno
6 Nov	Chicago Lyric Opera	IL BARBIERE DI SIVIGLIA (2) Simoneau, Badioli, Gobbi, Rossi Lemeni, Brazio, Kreste. Conductor: Rescigno
16 Nov	Chicago Lyric Opera	CARMEN (2) Picchi, Giangiacomo Guelfi, Badioli, Jordan, Lind, Kreste, Brazio, Foldi, Assandri. Conductor: Perlea
6 Dec	Rome T. dell'Opera	LA FORZA DEL DESTINO (6) Tebaldi, Penno / Turrini, Protti / Mancaserra, Capecchi, Neri. Conductor: Santini
20 Dec	R.A.I.	MARTINI AND ROSSI CONCERT (1) with Tagliavini. Conductor: Argento Rossini: Di tanti palpiti Bellini: O tu, bell, anima Massenet: Gridar sento i bambini (Letter Aria) Thomas: Io conosco un garzoncel

1955

18 Jan	Milan La Scala	CARMEN (6) Di Stefano, Roux, Carteri / Angelici, Modesti, Sciutti, Carlin, Del Signore, Sordello, Ribacchi. Conductor: Karajan

3 Mar	RAI	CONCERT (1) Conductor: Fragna
12 Mar	Rome T. dell'Opera	ZANETTO (4) Carteri / Magnoni. Conductor: De Fabritiis L'AMICO FRITZ (2) Carteri, Tagliavini, Poli, Marcangeli, Enzo Titta, Russo. Conductor: De Fabritiis
31 Mar	Rome T. dell'Opera	LA CENERENTOLA (4) Sciutti, Cadoni, Colasanti / Parravicini, Oncina, Bruscantini, Wallace. Conductor: Gui
24 Apr	Lisbon T. São Carlos	LA CENERENTOLA (3) Bruscantini, Misciano, Tajo, D'Angelo, Canali, Susca. Conductor: De Freitas Branco
29 Apr	Lisbon T. São Carlos	CARMEN (2) Corelli, Colzani, Pobbe, Castro, Canali, De Palma, Campi, Susca, Giorgio Giorgetti. Conductor: De Fabritiis
10 May	Milan La Scala	ZANETTO (4) with Carteri. Conductor: Votto CAVALLERIA RUSTICANA (4) Di Stefano, Giangiacomo Guelfi, Carturan / Perez, Beggiato. Conductor: Votto
21 May	Wiesbaden Staatstheater (La Fenice)	LA CENERENTOLA (1) Lazzari, Capecchi, De Taranto, Betner, Dora Gatta, Maddalena. Conductor: De Fabritiis
27 May	Saarbrucken Theaterblatter	LA CENERENTOLA (1) Lazzari, Capecchi, De Taranto, Betner, Dora Gatta, Maddalena. Conductor: De Fabritiis.
24 June	The Hague Holland Festival (La Scala)	L'ITALIANA IN ALGERI (3) Mafalda Masini, Ratti, Campi, Cortis, Petri, Valletti. Conductor: Giulini
26 June	Amsterdam Holland Festival (La Scala)	L'ITALIANA IN ALGERI (3) Mafalda Masini, Ratti, Campi, Cortis, Petri, Valletti. Conductor: Giulini
24 July	Verona Arena	CARMEN (4) Raffaella Ferrari / Fabrini / Pobbe, Corelli / Del Monaco, Colzani / Protti / Giangiacomo Guelfi, Nerina Ferrari / Di Lelio, Canali. Conductor: Votto
6 Aug	Verona Arena	AIDA (1) Stella, Zambruno, Gobbi, Vinco, Majonica. Conductor: Molinari Pradelli
22 Aug	Bilbao T. Coliseo Albia	NORMA (1) Pedrini, Vertecchi, Neri, Mercuriali, Brandolin. Conductor: Quadri

24 Aug	Bilbao T. Coliseo Albia	CAVALLERIA RUSTICANA (1) Vertecchi, Giangiacomo Guelfi, Brandolin, Torres. Conductor: Parenti
29 Aug	Bilbao T. Coliseo Albia	AIDA (1) Miranda Ferraro, Giangiacomo Guelfi, Neri, Stella, Washington, Mercuriali, Brandolin. Conductor: Quadri
20 Sept	Bologna T. Duse	CARMEN (2) Del Monaco, Valtriani, Ferrara, Vaiani, Mastropaolo, Barbesi, Mariano Caruso, Maprocchi, Righi. Conductor: Marini
24 Sept	Livorno T. La Gran Guardia	CARMEN (3) Del Monaco / Masini, Mascherini, Micheluzzi. Conductor: Bellezza
16 Oct	Fermo Teatro dell'Aquila	WERTHER (1) Zampighi, Mantovani, Valtriani, Caselli, Castagnoli, Fogli, Celani, Tomesani. Conductor: Verchi
29 Oct	Rovigo T. Sociale	WERTHER (2) Zampighi, Valtriani, Fabbri, Coda, Pasella, Mercuriali. Conductor: Parenti
9 Nov	Turin T. Carignano	CAVALLERIA RUSTICANA (3) Planinsek, Piero Guelfi, Gerbino. Conductor: De Fabritiis
18 Nov	Bologna T. Communale	LA FORZA DEL DESTINO (3) Stella, Turrini, Christoff, Giangiacomo Guelfi, Susca, Capecchi, Mercuriali, Giorgio Giorgetti. Conductor: De Fabritiis
25 Nov	Bologna T. Comunale	LE NOZZE DI FIGARO (2) Noni, Pobbe, Tajo, Bruscantini, Panni, Susca, Betner, Pirino, Ercolani. Conductor: De Fabritiis
7 Dec	Milan La Scala	NORMA (7) Callas, Del Monaco, Zaccaria, Carturan, Zampieri. Conductor: Votto
12 Dec	RAI	MARTINI AND ROSSI CONCERT (1) with Galiè. Conductor: Scaglia Gluck: Che faro' senza Euridice Bellini: Casta Diva Verdi: O don fatale Cilea: Esser madre
26 Dec	Milan Piccola Scala	IL MATRIMONIO SEGRETO (9) Alva / Monti, Badioli, Calabrese, Ratti, Sciutti / Ribetti. Conductor: Sanzogno
30 Dec	Rome T. dell'Opera	IL BARBIERE DI SIVIGLIA (6) Tagliavini / Lazzari, De Taranto, Gobbi / Capecchi, De Tommaso, La Porta / Sacchetti, Neri, Canali. Conductor: Questa

1956

2 Feb	Venice T. La Fenice	CARMEN (4) Corelli, Giangiacomo Guelfi, Scotto. Conductor: De Fabritiis
15 Feb	Como T. Sociale	CAVALLERIA RUSTICANA (2) Annaloro, Mazzoni, Carta, Brandolin. Conductor: La Rosa Parodi ZANETTO (2) Fabbrini. Conductor: Basile
29 Feb	Pesaro T. Rossini	LA CENERENTOLA (2) De Taranto, Oncina, Panerai, D'Angelo, Cadoni, Meucci. Conductor: Bartoletti
8 Mar	Genoa T. Carlo Felice	CARMEN (3) Rizzieri, Polleri, Colzani, Maddalena. Conductor: Dervaux
23 Mar	Lisbon T. São Carlos	DON CARLO (2) Cerquetti, Bergonzi, Taddei, Christoff, Stefanoni, Susca, De Palma, Castro. Conductor: Capuana
27 Mar	Lisbon T. São Carlos	CAVALLERIA RUSTICANA (2) Ortica, Azzolini / Casais, Cattelani, Barros. Conductor: De Freitas Branco
8 May	Milan La Scala	SANSONE E DALILA (4) Vinay, Colzani, Rossi Lemeni / Majonica, Zaccaria. Conductor: Gavazzeni
11 May	Milan Piccola Scala	MITRIDATE EUPATORE (3) Bertocci, De Los Angeles, Ferrando Ferrari, Gardino, Roma, Zampieri. Conductor: Sanzogno
24 May	Wiesbaden Hessische Stadttheater	IL BARBIERE DI SIVIGLIA (2) Misciano, Gobbi, Neri, Badioli. Conductor: Questa
7 June	Milan La Scala (Hall)	CONCERT (W. A. Mozart - Requiem) (2) Sciutti, Alva, Siepi. Conductor: Walter
13 June	Vienna Akademitheater (Scala)	IL MATRIMONIO SEGRETO (2) Alva, F. Calabrese, Ratti, Sciutti. Conductor: Sanzogno
31 July	Rio de Janeiro T. Municipal	IL BARBIERE DI SIVIGLIA (2) Tagliavini, Taddei / Fortes, Henriques, Paiva, Damiano. Conductor: Stinco
16 Aug	Rio de Janeiro T. Municipal	CARMEN (2) Salgado, Del Monaco, Giangiacomo Guelfi, Clabassi. Conductor: Ghione
25 Aug	Bilbao T. Coliseo Albia	AIDA (1) Mancini, Filippeschi, Ausensi, Vinco, Ferrin, Mercuriali, Cavallari. Conductor: Quadri

27 Aug	Bilbao T. Coliseo Albia	LA CENERENTOLA (1) Monti, Luise, Vinco, Ausensi, Octaviani, Cavallari. Conductor: Quadri
30 Aug	Bilbao T. Coliseo Albia	IL TROVATORE (1) Mancini, Filippeschi, Bastianini, Vinco, Cavallari, Mercuriali. Conductor: Quadri
29 Sept	Tokyo Takarazuka Theatre	AIDA (2) Stella / Bertolli, Borsò / Puma, Giangiacomo Guelfi, Cava, Cassinelli, Carlin. Conductors: Gui / Verchi.
3 Oct	Tokyo Sankei Hall	LE NOZZE DI FIGARO (4) Taddei, Cassinelli, Boyer, Moscucci, Noni, Cava, Corsi, Carlin, Scarlini, Ito. Conductor: Gui
23 Oct	Osaka Takarazuka Theatre	AIDA (2) Bertolli, Borsò, Giangiacomo Guelfi, Cava, Cassinelli, Carlin. Conductor: Gui
27 Oct	Osaka Takarazuka Theatre	LE NOZZE DI FIGARO (1) Taddei, Cassinelli, Boyer, Moscucci, Noni, Cava, Corsi, Carlin, Scarlini, Ito. Conductor: Gui
8 Nov	Chicago Lyric Opera	LA FORZA DEL DESTINO (2) Tebaldi, Tucker, Bastianini, Rossi Lemeni, Badioli, Harris, Krainik, Mariano Caruso, Izzo. Conductor: Solti
9 Nov	Chicago Lyric Opera	IL BARBIERE DI SIVIGLIA (3) Simoneau, Badioli, Gobbi, Rossi Lemeni, Harris, Nekolny, Alberts. Conductor: Buckley
10 Nov	Chicago Lyric Opera	CONCERT (1) Bastianini, Tucker, Tebaldi. Conductors: Solti / Buckley Mascagni: Voi lo sapete Ponchielli: L'amo come il fulgor (with Tebaldi) Mozart: Voi che sapete Saint-Saëns: Mon coeur s'ouvre à ta voix
26 Nov		MARTINI AND ROSSI CONCERT (1) with Di Stefano. Conductor: Sanzogno Rossini: Pensa alla patria Di tanti palpiti Una voce poco fa Nacqui all'affanno
7 Dec	Milan La Scala	AIDA (10) Stella, Di Stefano / Corelli, Giangiacomo Guelfi / Dondi, Zaccaria, Majonica. Conductor: Votto
10 Dec	Milan La Scala	GIULIO CESARE (4) Corelli, Zeani, Rossi Lemeni, Petri, Cassinelli. Conductor: Gavazzeni

1957

18 Jan	Milan Piccola Scala	IL MATRIMONIO SEGRETO (1) Alva, Badioli, Calabrese, Ratti, Sciutti. Conductor: Sanzogno
26 Jan	Rome Teatro dell'Opera	AIDA (6) Cerquetti, Marcangeli, Corelli / Vertecchi, Giangiacomo Guelfi / De Falchi, Neri, Dari, Sacchetti. Conductor: Santini
25 Feb	Rome T. dell'Opera	CARMEN (4) Grandi / Di Stefano, Mascherini, Beltrami, La Porta, Cassinelli, Sacchetti, Oliva, Cattelani, Zagonara. Conductor: Questa
16 Mar	Catania T. Bellini	CARMEN (3) Beltrami, Borsò, Zanasi. Conductors: Sebastian / Massa
14 Apr	Milan La Scala	ANNA BOLENA (7) Callas, Rossi Lemeni, Gianni Raimondi, Clabassi, Carturan, Rumbo. Conductor: Gavazzeni
23 Apr	Milan La Scala	LA FORZA DEL DESTINO (7) Stella / Parada, Di Stefano, Protti, Zaccaria, Majonica / Calabrese, Capecchi. Conductor: Votto
15 May	Vienna State Opera (Scala)	AIDA (4) Stella, Corelli, Protti, Majonica, Zaccaria. Conductor: Votto
29 May	Forlì T. Esperia	CONCERT (1)* with Poggi. Conductor: Savini Thomas: Non concosci il bel suol Massenet: Letter aria from *Werther* Mascagni: Voi lo sapete Donizetti: final duet from *Favorita* with Poggi
14 June	Paris T. Sarah Bernhardt (T. des Nations)	LA CENERENTOLA (3) Monti, Bruscantini, De Taranto, Ribetti, Gardino, Mariotti. Conductor: De Fabritiis
18 July	Verona Arena	NORMA (4) Cerquetti, Corelli / Puma, Neri, Zanini, Mariano Caruso. Conductor: Molinari Pradelli
28 July	Venice Piazza San Marco	CAVALLERIA RUSTICANA (2) Bergonzi, Piero Guelfi, Masini, Villani. Conductor: Wolf Ferrari
10 Aug	Salzburg Festspielhaus	FALSTAFF (4) Gobbi, Panerai, Alva / Zampieri, Schwarzkopf, Moffo, Canali, Petri, Spatafora, Ercolani. Conductor: Karajan
15 Sept	Vienna State Opera	FALSTAFF (4) Gobbi, Panerai, Zampieri / Alva, Spataro, Ercolani, Petri, Schwarzkopf, Moffo, Canali. Conductor: Karajan

28 Sept	Rome RAI	LA FORZA DEL DESTINO (1) Cerquetti, Miranda Ferraro, Protti, Capecchi, Christoff. Conductor: Sanzogno
1 Oct	Lugano T. Kursaal	CARMEN (1) Lo Forese, Perotti, Oppicelli, Caselli, Vayani, Giordano. Conductor: Del Cupolo
6 Oct	New York Town Hall	ANNA BOLENA (1) Davy, Cassily, David Smith, Kenneth Smith. Conductor: Gamson
Oct	New York Carnegie Hall	ANNA BOLENA (1) Davy, Cassily, David Smith, Kenneth Smith. Conductor: Gamson
19 Oct	Chicago Lyric Opera	MIGNON (2) Moffo, Nadell, Misciano, Wildermann, Mariano Caruso, Foldi. Conductor: Gavazzeni
23 Oct	Chicago Lyric Opera	CAVALLERIA RUSTICANA (2) Sullivan, MacNeil, Nadell, Kramarich / Fraher. Conductor: Kopp
1 Nov	Chicago Lyric Opera	LA GIOCONDA (2) Farrell, Kramarich, Tucker / Di Stefano, Wildermann, Protti, Harris, Mariano Caruso, Kenneth Smith, Vaznelis. Conductor: Serafin
8 Nov	Chicago Lyric Opera	LE NOZZE DI FIGARO (2) Gobbi, Berry, Badioli, Steber, Moffo, Nadell, Mariano Caruso, Foldi, Velis, Diamond. Conductor: Solti
13 Nov	Chicago Lyric Opera	ADRIANA LECOUVREUR (2) Tebaldi, Di Stefano, Badioli, Gobbi, Mariano Caruso, Kenneth Smith, Velis, Diamond, Krainik. Conductor: Solti
22 Nov	Dallas Civic Opera	L'ITALIANA IN ALGERI (2) Monti, Montarsolo, Taddei, Borghi, Carroll, Hilgenberg. Conductor: Rescigno
7 Dec	Milan La Scala	UN BALLO IN MASCHERA (5) Callas, Di Stefano, Bastianini / Romano Roma, Cassinelli, Stefanoni, Ratti / Tavolaccini, Mercuriali, Ricci. Conductor: Gavazzeni
30 Dec	RAI	MARTINI AND ROSSI CONCERT (1) with Lazzari. Conductor: La Rosa Parodi Mozart: Non so più; Voi che sapete Thomas: Non conosci il bel suol Cilea: Acerba voluttà Thomas: Io conosco un garzoncel

1958

4 Jan	Milan La Scala	ADRIANA LECOUVREUR (6) Petrella, Di Stefano / Filacuridi, Franco Calabrese / Badioli, Bastianini / Fioravanti, Mercuriali. Conductor: Votto
22 Jan	Milan La Scala	MIGNON (6) Gianni Raimondi / Misciano, Modesti / Zaccaria, Ratti / Pastori, Ricciardi. Conductor: Gavazzeni
12 Feb	Como T. Sociale	LA CENERENTOLA (2) Monti, Bruscantini, Luise, Ribetti, Canali, Mariotti. Conductor: Quadri
21 Feb	Palermo T. Massimo	NORMA (4) Cerquetti, Corelli, Modesti. Conductor: Serafin
14 Mar	Palermo T. Massimo	AIDA (4) Curtis Verna, Miranda Ferraro / Vertecchi, Colzani / Spatafora, Modesti, Ferrin. Conductor: Ziino
21 Mar	Lisbon T. São Carlos	L'ITALIANA IN ALGERI (2) Alva, Bruscantini, Petri, Baruffi, Cesari, Canali. Conductor: Ghione
9 Apr	Milan La Scala	ANNA BOLENA (5) Callas, Siepi, Gianni Raimondi, Majonica, Carturan, Rumbo. Conductor: Gavazzeni
26 Apr	Venice T. La Fenice	LA CENERENTOLA (3) Monti, Bruscantini, Dora Gatta, Betner, Badioli, Monreale. Conductor: Cillario
8 May	Rome T. dell'Opera	ADRIANA LECOUVREUR (2) Olivero, Huder, Palmieri, Tagliavini, Zagonara, Cesari, Tomei, Sacchetti, Caroli, Ticozzi. Conductor: La Rosa Parodi
18 May	Turin T. Nuovo	IL BARBIERE DI SIVIGLIA (2) Pontiggia, Valdengo, Rossi Lemeni, Badioli, Betner. Conductor: De Fabritiis
24 May	Vienna State Opera	AIDA (2) Leontyne Price, Guichandut, Weber, Protti, Guthrie. Conductor: Karajan
1 June	Milan La Scala	NABUCCO (2) Bastianini, Zaccaria, Cerquetti, Poggi. Conductor: Votto
8 June	Vienna State Opera	FALSTAFF (2) Gobbi, Panerai, Zampieri, Mariano Caruso, Ercolani, Petri, Schwarzkopf, Moffo, Canali. Conductor: Karajan
12 June	Venice T. La Fenice	LA FORZA DEL DESTINO (2) Tebaldi, Savio, Giangiacomo Guelfi, Ariè, Mazzini, Zagonara. Conductor: De Fabritiis

19 June	Venice T. Verdi all'Isola di San Giorgio Maggiore	CARMEN (3) Borsò, Giangiacomo Guelfi, Scotto, Maddalena. Conductor: Questa
9 July	Milan La Scala	ADRIANA LECOUVREUR (2) Campora, Cassinelli, Olivero, Fioravanti. Conductor: Gavazzeni
11 July	Milan RAI	ANNA BOLENA (1) Gencer, Bertocci, Clabassi, Rota, Carlin. Conductor: Gavazzeni
16 July	Lyon T. de Fourvière	NORMA (3) Curtis-Verna, Del Monaco, Clabassi, Cesarini, Thevenon. Conductor: Bogo
26 July	Salzburg Felsenreitschule	DON CARLO (4) Fernandi, Siepi, Zaccaria, Bastianini, Schmidt, Stefanoni, Jurinac, Ruess, Sjoestedt, Balatsch, Rothenberger. Conductor: Karajan
30 July	Verona Arena	LA FAVORITA (4) Bastianini, Poggi, Vinco, Romanato, Di Lelio / Zanolli. Conductor: Quadri
9 Sept	Vienna State Opera	AIDA (1) Nilsson, Di Stefano, Zaccaria, London, Koreh. Conductor: Karajan
14 Sept	Vienna State Opera	FALSTAFF (2) Gobbi, Wachter, Alva, Spataro, Ercolani, Petri, Schwarzkopf, Beltrami, Canali. Conductor: Karajan
19 Sept	Vienna State Opera	DON CARLO (1) Jurinac, Zampieri, Zaccaria, Bastianini, Edelmann, Foster. Conductor: Erede
23 Sept	Vienna State Opera	UN BALLO IN MASCHERA (1) Nilsson, Di Stefano, Bastianini, Koth. Conductor: Mitropoulos
3 Oct	Monterrey T. Florida	MIGNON (1) Lazzari, Zaccaria, Garfias, Solorzano. Conductor: Picco
10 Oct	Chicago Lyric Opera	FALSTAFF (2) Gobbi, Misciano, MacNeil, Tebaldi, Moffo, Canali, Mariano Caruso, Vellucci, Kenneth Smith. Conductor: Serafin
14 Oct	New York Carnegie Hall American Opera Society	I CAPULETI E I MONTECCHI (1) Hurley, Cassily, Flagello. Conductor: Gamson
20 Oct	Chicago Lyric Opera	IL TROVATORE (3) Björling, Ross, Wildermann, Bastianini, Vellucci, Vaznelis, Canali, Wolfe. Conductor: Schaenen

12 Nov	Chicago Lyric Opera	IL BARBIERE DI SIVIGLIA (2) Misciano, Corena, Gobbi, Montarsolo, Noel, Canali, Harris. Conductor: Schaenen
24 Nov	Chicago Lyric Opera	AIDA (3) Rysanek, Björling, Gobbi, Wildermann, Kenneth Smith, Vellucci, Steffan. Conductor: Sebastian
4 Dec	Turin T. Carignano	LA CENERENTOLA (2) Lazzari, Bruscantini, Badioli, Mariotti, Dora Gatta, Canali. Conductor: Cillario
18 Dec	Milan La Scala	MOSÈ (5) Christoff, Roberti, Zaccaria, Giangiacomo Guelfi, Gianni Raimondi, Lazzarini, Bertocci, De Palma. Conductor: Gavazzeni

1959

10 Jan	Rome T. dell'Opera	CARMEN (7) Limarilli / Vertecchi, Tucci / Micheluzzi / Di Marco / Panni, Piero Guelfi / Verlinghieri / Giangiacomo Guelfi / De Falchi, Marimpietri / Oliva, Cadoni / Sunara / Canali / Di Stasio. Conductor: Santini
3 Feb	Palermo T. Massimo	CARMEN (4) Corelli, Giangiacomo Guelfi, Freni / Tavolaccini, Di Lelio, Palmieri, Ercolani, Malfatti, Viaro, Rossetti. Conductor: Dervaux
19 Feb	Tokyo Takarazuka Theatre	CARMEN (4) Rina Gigli / Vercelli, Del Monaco, Colombo / Protti, Chissari, Di Stasio, La Porta, Montarsolo, Mariano Caruso, Miyamoto. Conductor: Verchi
25 Feb	Tokyo Takarazuka Theatre	CONCERT (1) Tagliavini, Montarsolo, Protti, Tucci, Clabassi, Noni. Conductors: Erede / Verchi Donizetti: O mio Fernando
4 Mar	Osaka Festival Hall	CARMEN (1) Del Monaco, Chissari, Di Stasio, La Porta, Montarsolo, Mariano Caruso. Conductor: Verchi
9 Apr	Milan La Scala	CARMEN (7) Corelli / Del Monaco, Beltrami / Scotto, Giangiacomo Guelfi, Cassinelli, De Palma. Conductor: Sanzogno
29 Apr	Vienna State Opera	AIDA (2) Leontyne Price, Usunov / Puma, Protti / Paskalis, Kreppel, Welter. Conductors: Von Matacic / Erede
1 May	Vienna State Opera	CAVALLERIA RUSTICANA (1) Zampieri, Anday, Berry, Lotte Rysanek. Conductor: Klobucar

11 May	Milan La Scala	IL TROVATORE (4) Bastianini, Corelli, Roberti / Nache, Zaccaria / Cassinelli. Conductor: Votto
5 June	Milan La Scala	IFIGENIA IN AULIDE (4) Christoff, Miranda Ferraro, Lazzarini, Zaccaria / Cassinelli. Conductor: Conz
12 June	Milan La Scala	CONCERT - Dvorák, Stabat Mater (2) Scotto, Poggi, Modesti. Conductor: Kubelik
16 June	Vienna State Opera	DON CARLO (1) Fernandi, Bastianini, Goltz, Uhde, Schöffler, Foster. Conductor: Votto
22 June	Vienna State Opera	AIDA (2) Tebaldi, Fernandi, Gobbi, Frick, Welter. Conductor: Karajan / Votto
24 June	Vienna State Opera	CAVALLERIA RUSTICANA (1) Zampieri, Anday, Berry, Lotte Rysanek. Conductor: Klobucar
21 July	Milan La Scala	CARMEN (2) Bastianini, Lo Forese / Di Stefano,Tucci / Vercelli, Cassinelli. Conductor: Von Matacic
26 July	Verona Arena	IL TROVATORE (3) Tucci / Leontyne Price, Bastianini / Protti, Corelli, Mongelli. Conductor: De Fabritiis
5 Aug	Salzburg Felsenreitschule	ORFEO E EURIDICE (5) Sciutti, Jurinac. Conductor: Karajan
2 Sept	Vienna State Opera	CAVALLERIA RUSTICANA (2) Terkal / Sergi, Anday, Berry, Lotte Rysanek. Conductor: Klobucar
13 Sept	Vienna State Opera	AIDA (1) Davy, Bergonzi, Gobbi, Kreppel, Ferrin. Conductor: Karajan
15 Sept	Vienna State Opera	DON CARLO (1) Fernendi, Zaccaria, Zadek, Bierbach, Uhde. Conductor: Erede
26 Oct	New York Metropolitan Opera	IL TROVATORE (4) Stella, Bergonzi, Warren / Sereni, Wildermann, Vanni, Anthony, Reitan, Nagy. Conductor: Cleva
31 Oct	New York Metropolitan Opera	CAVALLERIA RUSTICANA (3) Elias, Peerce / Björling, Cassel, Votipka. Conductor: Verchi
8 Nov	New York Carnegie Hall	CONCERT (1) with Bergonzi. Schick, piano. Gluck: Che farò senza Euridice

		Cimarosa: È vero che in casa Mozart: Non so più; Voi che sapete Donizetti: Duet from *Favorita* Pizzetti: Rossignol Respighi: Nebbie; Pioggia Rossini: Una voce poco fa Donizetti: O mio Fernando Verdi: Duet from *Aida*
Nov	Naples Circolo della Stampa [Press Club]	CONCERT (1) * Mozart: *No so più; Voi che sapete*
28 Nov	Naples T. San Carlo	ADRIANA LECOUVREUR (4) Olivero / Frazzoni, Corelli, Bastianini, Cassinelli, Mariano Caruso, Ercolani, Rosanna Zerbini, Di Stasio. Conductor: Basile
11 Dec	Vienna State Opera	LE NOZZE DI FIGARO (1) Stich-Randall, Güden, Berry, Hongen, Wachter. Conductor: Karajan
13 Dec	Vienna State Opera	DON CARLO (2) Zampieri, Goltz / Jurinac, Hotter / Hurshel, Wachter, Bierbach / Foster, Schöffler / Van Mill. Conductors: Erede / Swarowsky
15 Dec	Vienna State Opera	ORFEO E EURIDICE (3) Lipp, Rothenberger. Conductor: Karajan

1960

8 Jan	Vienna State Opera	CARMEN (3) Zampieri, Zeani, Berry / Heater. Conductor: Cluytens
12 Jan	Vienna State Opera	LE NOZZE DI FIGARO (1) Jurinac, Streich, Kunz, Wächter. Conductor: Hollreiser
1 Feb	Milan La Scala	CARMEN (5) Blanc, Di Stefano / Usunov, Tucci, De Palma, Cassinelli. Conductor: Sanzogno
18 Feb	New York Metropolitan Opera	AIDA (2) Amara / Stella, Bergonzi / Baum, Sgarro / Flagello, Guarrera / Lisitsian, Scott / Moscona, Nagy, Vanni. Conductor: Cleva
24 Feb	New York Metropolitan Opera	CAVALLERIA RUSTICANA (1) Barioni, Valentino, Vanni, Votipka. Conductor: Mitropoulos
27 Feb	New York Metropolitan Opera	IL TROVATORE (1) Stella, Bergonzi, Bastianini, Wildermann, Vanni, Anthony, Reitan, Nagy. Conductor: Cleva

7 Mar	Havana	CONCERT (1) J. Wustman, piano. Rossini: Una voce poco fa Händel: Lascia ch'io pianga Spontini: Les riens d'amour Bellini: Dolente immagine Verdi: Stornello Donizetti: O mio Fernando Favara: A la Barcillunisa Tomasi: O Ciucciarella Bellini: Fenesta che lucive Donizetti: Te voglio bene assaje Granados: El majo discreto Verdi: O don fatale
8 Mar	Havana	CONCERT (1) J. Wustman, piano. Same program as 7 Mar except for: Rossini: "Nacqui all'affanno" instead of "Una voce poca fa" Bellini: "Casta Diva" instead of Donizetti: "O mio Fernando"
13 Mar	Ann Arbor, Michigan Hill Auditorium	CONCERT (1) J. Wustman, piano. Same program as 7 mar
15 Mar	River Forest, Illinois Rosary College Auditorium	CONCERT (1) J. Wustman, piano. Same program as 7 Mar
20 Mar	Vienna State Opera	CAVALLERIA RUSTICANA (2) Zampieri, Milinkovic, Hurshel, Janowitz / Lotte Rysanek. Conductor: Santi
26 Mar	Vienna	CONCERT (1) Favaretto, piano. Gluck: Che farò senza Euridice Pergolesi: Ogni pena più spietata Händel: Lascia che io pianga Mozart: Voi che sapete; Non so più Cimarosa: E vero che in casa Spontini: Les riens d'amour Bellini: Dolente immagine Verdi: Stornello Pizzetti: I pastori Respighi: Nebbie De Falla: El paño moreno De Falla: Jota Granados: El majo discreto Favara: A la Barcillunisa Bellini: Fenesta che lucive Donizetti: Te voglio bene assaje
29 Mar	Vienna State Opera	CARMEN (1) Vickers, Protti, Güden. Conductor: Loibner

14 Apr	Milan La Scala	AIDA (7) Ferrin, Ghiaurov / Vinco / Zaccaria, MacNeil / Meliciani, Miranda, Ferraro / Puma, Nilsson / Leontyne Price. Conductors: Sanzogno / Tonini
11 May	Milan La Scala	UN BALLO IN MASCHERA (2) Stella, Poggi, Bastianini, Tavolaccini, Cassinelli, Zaccaria. Conductor: Gavazzeni
27 May	Milan La Scala	I TROIANI [Les Troyens] (4) Del Monaco, Cossotto, Rankin, Zaccaria, Cassinelli, Ferrin, Lazzarini, Puglisi, De Palma, Romani, Novelli / Forti. Conductor: Kubelik
10 June	Vienna State Opera	AIDA (2) Leonie Rysanek / Leontyne Price, Ottolini / Miranda Ferraro, Bastianini, Frick, Guthrie / Weber. Conductors: Karajan / Molinari Pradelli
22 June	Vienna State Opera	DON CARLO (1) Goltz, Hurshel, Zampieri, Paskalis, Welter, Ariè. Conductor: Molinari Pradelli
25 June	Vienna State Opera	LE NOZZE DI FIGARO (1) Schreier, Adani, Kunz, Schöffler. Conductor: Hollreiser
29 June	Milano La Scala	CONCERT - Rossini, Stabat Mater (2) Cerquetti, Gianni Raimondi, Ghiaurov. Conductor: Molinari Pradelli
21 July	Verona Arena	AIDA (5) Stella / Maragliano, Bergonzi, Giangiacomo Guelfi, Vinco, Ganzarolli. Conductor: Gavazzeni
24 July	Verona Arena	CAVALLERIA RUSTICANA (6) Cossotto, Barioni, Colzani / Bastianini, Bonato. Conductor: De Fabritiis
2 Sept	Stuttgart ZDF-TV	TELEVISED CONCERT (1) Selections from *Don Carlo* Conductor: *
6 Sept	Hamburg	CONCERT (1) Favaretto, piano. Gluck: Che farò senza Euridice Pergolesi: Ogni pena più spietata Händel: Lamento d'Almirena Mozart: Voi che sapete; Non so più cosa son Cimarosa: E vero che in casa Spontini: Les riens d'amour Bellini: Dolente immagine Verdi: Stornello Pizzetti: I pastori Respighi: Nebbie De Falla: El paño moreno De Falla: Jota Granados: El majo discreto

		Favara: A la Barcillunisa Tomasi: O Ciucciarella Bellini: Fenesta che lucive Donizetti: Te voglio bene assaje
9 Sept	Vienna State Opera	AIDA (3) Leontyne Price, Bergonzi, Bastianini, Frick / Zaccaria / Kreppel / Guthrie / Welter. Conductors: Von Matacic / Karajan / Erede
12 Sept	Vienna State Opera	UN BALLO IN MASCHERA (2) Stella, Di Stefano, Bastianini, Streich. Conductor: Klobucar
23 Sept	Vienna State Opera	LA FORZA DEL DESTINO (3) Stella, Di Stefano, Bastianini, Kreppel, Dönch. Conductor: Mitropoulos
14 Oct	Chicago Lyric Opera	DON CARLO (3) Roberti, Tucker, Gobbi, Christoff, Mazzoli, Ventriglia, Diamond, Mariano Caruso, Johnson. Conductor: Votto
17 Oct	Chicago Lyric Opera	AIDA (4) Roberti / Leontyne Price, Bergonzi / Ottolini, Merrill, Mazzoli, Ventriglia, Mariano Caruso, Yarick. Conductor: Votto
1 Nov	New York Town Hall (American Opera Society)	ORFEO E EURIDICE (1) Irma Gonzales, Allen. Conductor: De Almeida
5 Nov	New York Metropolitan Opera	AIDA (4) with Sgarro, Rysanek / Curtis-Verna, Bergonzi / Fernandi, Colzani, Tozzi / Wildermann / Giaiotti / Siepi, Nagy, Dunn / Ordassy. Conductor: Verchi
12 Nov	Kalamazoo, Michigan*	CONCERT (1)*
14 Nov	New Orleans, Louisiana*	CONCERT (1) Leo Taubman, piano. same program as 26 March, 1960
16 Nov	Macon, Georgia*	CONCERT (1)*
22 Nov	Northhampton, Massachusetts*	CONCERT (1)*
25 Nov	New York Waldorf-Astoria Hotel (Harlem Philharmonic Society)	CONCERT (1) Ballin, piano. Mozart: Non so più cosa son Mozart: Voi che sapete Cimarosa: E vero che in casa Rossini: Una voce poco fa Donizetti: O mio Fernando Mascagni: Voi lo sapete
13 Dec	Milan La Scala	DON CARLO (5) Labò, Christoff, Ghiaurov, Stella / Gencer, Bastianini / Gobbi, Ferrin. Conductor: Santini

1961

10 Jan	Milan La Scala	LA FORZA DEL DESTINO (7) Labò, Majonica, Cavalli / De Osma, Bastianini / Meliciani, Ghiaurov, Capecchi. Conductor: Votto
8 Feb	Palermo T. Massimo	LA CENERENTOLA (3) Oncina, Taddei, Tajo, Ratti, Cadoni, Campi. Conductor: Gui
5 Apr	Milan La Scala	SANSONE E DALILA (6) Del Monaco, Giangiacomo Guelfi / Gualtieri, Ferrin / Cassinelli, Zaccaria / Riggiri. Conductor: Gavazzeni
7 May	Venice T. La Fenice	ORFEO E EURIDICE (3) Panni, Fusco. Conductor: Caracciolo.
21 May	Vienna State Opera	DON CARLO (1) Goltz, Vickers, Hotter, Welter, Wächter, Kreppel. Conductor: Molinari Pradelli
22 May	Vienna State Opera	LA FORZA DEL DESTINO (1) Paruto, Bergonzi, Bastianini, Kreppel, Dönch. Conductor: Molinari Pradelli
26 May	Budapest Magyar Allami Opera House	AIDA (1) Takács, Simándy, Jámbor, Mészáros, Antalfly. Conductor: Gardelli
29 May	Budapest Magyar Allami Opera House	DON CARLO (1) Warga, Simándy, Fodor, Melis. Conductor: Lukacs
31 May	Budapest Magyar Allami Opera House	CONCERT (1)* Conductor: Gardelli
2 June	Vienna State Opera	DON CARLO (1) Jurinac, Vickers, Hotter, Welter, Bastianini, Kreppel. Conductor: Molinari Pradelli
5 June	Vienna State Opera	AIDA (2) Leontyne Price, Vickers, Bastianini, Kreppel / Zaccaria, Guthrie. Conductor: Cluytens / Karajan
12 June	Vienna State Opera	LE NOZZE DI FIGARO (3) Stich-Randall / Della Casa / Jurinac, Rothenberger, Kunz / Berry, Schöffler / Wächter. Conductor: Böhm
27 June	Vienna State Opera	DON CARLO (1) Jurinac, Vickers, Zaccaria, Guthrie, Bastianini, Kreppel. Conductor: Molinari Pradelli
1 July	Reggio Calabria	CONCERT (1) with Tucci, Borrelli, Lazzari. Conductor: Ziino Cilea: Esser madre è un inferno

		Cilea: Tu pur sei figlio (with W. Borrelli) Cilea: Acerba voluttà
27 July	Verona Arena	CARMEN (7) Scotto, Corelli, Bastianini, Cattelani, Grigolato. Conductor: Molinari Pradelli
3 Sept	Vienna State Opera	AIDA (3) Davy / Nilsson / Arroyo, Vickers / Bergonzi, Bastianini / Hotter, Kreppel / Frick / Zaccaria, Welter / Pernerstorfer / Guthrie. Conductors: Von Matacic / Klobucar / Karajan
5 Sept	Vienna State Opera	LA FORZA DEL DESTINO (2) Stella, Bergonzi, Bastianini, Kreppel / Zaccaria, Dönch. Conductors: Cleva / Loibner
18 Sept	Vienna State Opera	UN BALLO IN MASCHERA (1) Stella, Bergonzi, Bastianini, Martino. Conductor: Cleva
21 Sept	Vienna State Opera	DON CARLO (2) Stella, Givin / Labò, Zaccaria, Guthrie, Bastianini / Wächter, Kreppel. Conductors: Cleva / Santi
23 Sept	Hamburg State Opera	AIDA (1) Lang, Tobin, Winters, Van Mill, Roth-Erhan. Conductor: Kulka
26 Sept	Vienna State Opera	LE NOZZE DI FIGARO (1) Schwarzkopf, Seefriend, Kunz, Wächter. Conductor: Karajan
6 Oct	Berlin Hochschule für Musik	CONCERT - Verdi, Requiem Mass (2) Stella, Bergonzi, Zaccaria. Conductor: Karajan
13 Oct	Tokyo Metropolitan Hall	AIDA (3) Tucci / Heredia, Del Monaco / Lo Forese, Protti / Giangiacomo Guelfi, Washington, Pagliucca, Kawauchi, Cesarini. Conductors: Capuana / Morelli
21 Oct	Tokyo Metropolitan Hall	CAVALLERIA RUSTICANA (3) Di Stasio, Lo Forese, D'Orazi, Pini. Conductor: Morelli
24 Oct	Tokyo Bunka Kaikan	CONCERT (1) Tebaldi, Poggi, Protti, Tucci, D'Orazi, Del Monaco, Washington. Conductors: Basile / Morelli Verdi: O don fatale
31 Oct	Osaka Festival Hall	CAVALLERIA RUSTICANA (1) Lo Forese, Di Stasio, D'Orazi, Pini. Conductor: Morelli
2 Nov	Osaka Festival Hall	AIDA (1) Tucci, Del Monaco, Protti, Washington, Pagliucca, Cesarini. Conductor: Morelli
15 Nov	Chicago Lyric Opera	IL BARBIERE DI SIVIGLIA (4) Alva, Corena, Christoff, Bruscantini, Izzo, Magrini, Harris. Conductor: Cillario

11 Dec	Milan La Scala	MEDEA (5) Callas, Vickers, Ghiaurov, Tosini / Rizzoli. Conductor: Schippers

1962

8 Jan	Milan La Scala	LA FAVORITA (12) Bastianini / Meliciani, Gianni Raimondi / Jaia, Ghiaurov / Ferrin / Vinco, De Palma. Conductor: Gavazzeni
3 Feb	Vienna State Opera	RIGOLETTO (4) Zampieri, Protti, Pütz / Güden, Mazzoli / Guthrie. Conductor: Serafin
8 Feb	Vienna State Opera	UN BALLO IN MASCHERA (1) Crespin, Zampieri, Protti, Maikl. Conductor: Serafin
12 Feb	Vienna State Opera	CAVALLERIA RUSTICANA (1) Höngen, Zampieri, Protti, Maikl. Conductor: Serafin
25 Feb	Berlin Deutsche Opera	CONCERT (1) with Bastianini
6 Mar	Vienna State Opera	UN BALLO IN MASCHERA (2) Zampieri, Paruto, Protti, Maikl. Conductor: De Fabritiis
9 Mar	Vienna State Opera	LE NOZZE DI FIGARO (2) Jurinac / Scheyrer, Loose/ Sciutti, Kunz, Braun / Poell. Conductor: Klobucar
13 Mar	Vienna State Opera	RIGOLETTO (1) Zampieri, Moffo, Protti, Kreppel. Conductor: De Fabritiis
18 Mar	Vienna State Opera	DON CARLO (1) Christoff, Jurinac, Labò, Wächter, Hotter, Franc. Conductor: De Fabritiis
20 Mar	Vienna State Opera	AIDA (1) Bernard, Limarilli, Christoff, Protti, Welter. Conductor: Karajan
Mar	Rome*	CONCERT (1)*
11 Apr	Budapest Magyar Allami Opera House	CARMEN (1) Orosz, Udvardy, Jámbor, Pavlánszky, Elek, Kishegyi, Katona. Conductor: Ferencsik
14 Apr	Budapest Magyar Allami Opera House	IL TROVATORE (1) Sved, Takács, Simándy, Bódy. Conductor: Lukacs
14 May	Milan La Scala	ORFEO E EURIDICE (4) Lipp / Panni, Adani. Conductor: Sanzogno

28 May	Milan La Scala	GLI UGONOTTI (5) Corelli, Sutherland, Ganzarolli, Ghiaurov, Tozzi, Cossotto, Majonica, Bertinazzo, Spatafora, De Palma, Giacomotti, Cassinelli, Gullino, Mercuriali, Foti, Carbonari, Morresi, Antonini, Guagni. Conductor: Gavazzeni
18 June	Milan La Scala	ATLANTIDA (5) Bertinazzo, Browne, Cassoni / Del Fante, Cucchio, Di Minno, Didier, Fiorentini, Galli, Greco, Halley, Heyns, Nardi, Puglisi, Stratas, Zerbini, P.F. Poli, De Palma, Pezzettti. Conductor: Schippers
2 July	Rome Terme di Caracalla	AIDA (4) Stella / Mancini, Bergonzi / Limarilli, Protti, Vinco / Ariè, Marcangeli, Cassinelli, Pandano. Conductors: Gavazzeni / Annovazzi
31 July	Salzburg Neues Festspielhaus	IL TROVATORE (6) Leontyne Price, Corelli, Bastianini, Zaccaria, Dutoit, Frese, Zimmer / Caslavsky. Conductor: Karajan
9 Aug	Salzburg Neues Festspielhaus	CONCERT - Verdi, Requiem Mass (1) Leontyne Price, Zampieri, Ghiaurov. Conductor: Karajan
1 Sept	Vienna State Opera	LE NOZZE DI FIGARO (2) Sheyrer, Kunz, Loose, Wächter. Conductor: Hollreiser
4 Sept	Vienna State Opera	UN BALLO IN MASCHERA (1) Fernandi, Bastianini, Stella, Streich. Conductor: Verchi
11 Sept	Vienna State Opera	DON CARLO (2) Stella, Fernandi, Kreppel, Welter, Franc, Bastianini / Wächter. Conductor: Verchi
23 Sept	Vienna State Opera	AIDA (1) Leontyne Price, Usunov, Frick, Bastianini, Welter. Conductor: Karajan
2 Oct	San Francisco War Memorial Opera House	IL TROVATORE (2) MacCracken, Ross, Hecht, Bastianini. Conductor: Molinari Pradelli
23 Oct	San Francisco War Memorial Opera House	FALSTAFF (2) Evans, Lipp, Meyer, Meneguzzer, Peterson, Stewart, Langdon. Conductor: Ferencsik
13 Nov	New York Metropolitan Opera	CAVALLERIA RUSTICANA (1) Olvis, Cassel, Roggero, Chookasian. Conductor: Cleva
20 Nov	New York Metropolitan Opera	AIDA (2) Amara / Tucci, Corelli / Konya, Ruzdak / Merrill, Tozzi / Siepi, Sgarro, Nagy, Vanni / Pracht. Conductor: Santi
25 Nov	New York Metropolitan Opera	IL BARBIERE DI SIVIGLIA (2) Merrill, Formichini, Corena, Siepi, Vanni, Cehanovsky, Paolis, Mayreder. Conductor: Schippers

17 Dec	Milan La Scala	SEMIRAMIDE (7) Sutherland, Ganzarolli, Gianni Raimondi / Jaia, Mazzoli / Ferrin, Bianchi Porro, Zerbini. Conductor: Santini

1963

12 Jan	Rome Teatro dell'Opera	SANSONE E DALILA (5) Del Monaco, Giangiacomo Guelfi, Clabassi, Amodeo. Conductor: Capuana
7 Feb	Rome Teatro dell'Opera	LA CENERENTOLA (4) Micheluzzi, Cadoni, Sinimberghi, Poli, Montarsolo, Mariotti. Conductor: Capuana
20 Feb	Rome Circolo Dante Alighieri	CONCERT (1) Favaretto, piano. Cimarosa: E vero che in casa Bellini: Dolente immagine Spontini: Les riens d'amour Rossini: Nacqui all'affanno Pizzetti: Pastori Respighi: Nebbie Verdi: Stornello
14 Mar	Milan La Scala	CARMEN (9) Del Monaco / Limarilli, Freni / Marimpietri, Puglisi, Zerbini. Conductor: Sanzogno
13 Apr	Vienna State Opera	DON CARLO (2) Leonie Rysanek, Zampieri, Hotter / Welter, Franc, Bastianini. Conductor: Erede
28 Apr	Hamburg State Opera	DON CARLO (1) Leonie Rysanek, Vickers, Christoff, Ruzdak, Fliether, Roth-Ehrang, Steiner. Conductor: Ludwig
2 May	Rome*	CONCERT (1)*
3 May	Hamburg State Opera	UN BALLO IN MASCHERA (1) Leonie Rysanek, Vickers, Ruzdjak, Rothenberger, Roth-Ehrang, Pfendt. Conductor: Stein
12 May	Naples T. San Carlo	LA FAVORITA (3) Zanasi, Gianni Raimondi, Zaccaria, P.F. Poli, Zanolli. Conductor: Previtali
25 May	Rome T. dell'Opera	CAVALLERIA RUSTICANA (3) Fozzer, Barioni, Giangiacomo Guelfi / Verlinghieri, Vozza. Conductor: De Fabritiis
28 May	Vienna State Opera	DON CARLO (1) Leonie Rysanek, Zampieri, Hotter, Guthrie, Protti, Kreppel. Conductor: Molinari Pradelli

Date	Venue	Performance
3 June	Vienna State Opera	AIDA (2) Leontyne Price / Leonie Rysanek, Usunov / MacCracken, Kreppel, Bastianini / London, Franc / Welter. Conductors: Von Matacic / Molinari Pradelli
5 June	Vienna State Opera	UN BALLO IN MASCHERA (1) Bergonzi, Paskalis, Leonie Rysanek, Sciutti. Conductor: Molinari Pradelli
10 June	Vienna State Opera	DON CARLO (1) Christoff, Stella, Zampieri, Zaccaria, Bastianini, Guthrie. Conductor: Molinari Pradelli
17 June	Vienna State Opera	LE NOZZE DI FIGARO (1) Prey, Scheyrer, Rothenberger, Kunz. Conductor: Krips
28 June	Vienna State Opera	LA FORZA DEL DESTINO (1) Scheyrer, Paskalis, MacCracken, Dönch. Conductor: Molinari Pradelli
30 June	Vienna State Opera	CAVALLERIA RUSTICANA (1) Zampieri, Milinkovic, Berry, Lotte Rysanek Conductor: Patanè
24 July	Verona Arena	AIDA (5) Tucci / Gencer, Limarilli, Giangiacomo Guelfi, Giaiotti, Zerbini. Conductor: Serafin
13 Aug	Salzburg Festival	IL TROVATORE (4) MacCracken, Leontyne Price, Bastianini, Zaccaria, Dutoit, Frese, Zimmer. Conductor: Karajan
28 Aug	Munich	TELEVISED CONCERT (1) Songs of Lucatello. Conductor: *
6 Sept	Munich Hercules Saal	CONCERT (1)*
10 Sept	Vienna State Opera	AIDA (1) Stella, Bergonzi, Taddei, Welter. Conductor: De Fabritiis
14 Sept	Vienna State Opera	LA FORZA DEL DESTINO (2) Stella, Paskalis, Bergonzi, Siepi, Dönch / Corena. Conductor: De Fabritiis
21 Sept	Milan La Scala (Hall)	CONCERT - Verdi, Requiem Mass (2) Ligabue, Bergonzi, Petrov. Conductor: Karajan
26 Sept	Vienna State Opera	CAVALLERIA RUSTICANA (1) Corelli, Milinkovic, Paskalis, Lotte Rysanek. Conductor: De Fabritiis
29 Sept	Vienna State Opera	UN BALLO IN MASCHERA (2) Gianni Raimondi, Bastianini, Stella, Martino / Sciutti. Conductor: Krips

6 Oct	Vienna State Opera	AIDA (2) Tucci, Welter, Usunov / Guichandut, Vinco, Protti / Taddei. Conductors: Karajan / Santi
15 Oct	Osaka Festival Hall	IL TROVATORE (1) Parada, Limarilli, Protti, Marangoni, Di Stasio, Guggia, Onesti, Pedroni. Conductor: De Fabritiis
16 Oct	Tokyo Metropolitan Hall	IL TROVATORE (4) Bastianini / Protti, Stella / Parada, Limarilli / Annaloro, Marangoni, Di Stasio, Guggia, Onesti, Pedroni. Conductor: De Fabritiis
17 Oct	Osaka Festival Hall	IL BARBIERE DI SIVIGLIA (2) Protti, Sabatucci, Rossi Lemeni, La Porta, Di Stasio, Onesti, Guggia, Kume / Arima, Kuwayama / Kobayashi. Conductor: Verchi
23 Oct	Tokyo Metropolitan Hall	IL BARBIERE DI SIVIGLIA (5) Protti, Sabatucci, Rossi Lemeni, La Porta, Di Stasio, Onesti, Guggia, Kume / Arima, Kuwayama / Kobayashi. Conductor: Verchi
7 Dec	Milan La Scala	CAVALLERIA RUSTICANA (8) Corelli / Borsò / Lo Forese, Giangiacomo Guelfi / Dondi, Carturan, Allegri. Conductor: Gavazzeni

1964

11 Jan	Palermo T. Massimo	DON CARLO (3) Ligabue, Gibin, Quilico, Hines, Marangoni. Conductor: Votto
25 Jan	Naples T. San Carlo	ORFEO E EURIDICE (3) Panni, Meneguzzer. Conductor: Maag
4 Feb	London Covent Garden	AIDA (6) Vishnevskaya, Vickers, Shaw / Glossop, Robinson, Rouleau, Godfrey. Conductor: Balkwill
18 Mar	Milan La Scala	LA CENERENTOLA (7) Casellato, Panerai / Monachesi, Ganzarolli, Tavolaccini, Zanini, Tadeo. Conductor: Gavazzeni
6 Apr	Zürich Hall of Congress	CONCERT OF THE NATIONS (1)* Koth, Bergonzi, Bream (guitar), Von Karolyi (piano), Ashkenazy (violin). Conductor: Caridis
7 Apr	Paris Salle Pleyel	CONCERT OF THE NATIONS (1)* Conductor: Caridis
8 Apr	Vienna Konzerthaus	CONCERT OF THE NATIONS (1)* Conductor: Caridis
11 Apr	Amsterdam Concertgebouw	CONCERT OF THE NATIONS (1)* Della Casa, Bergonzi, Bream (guitar), Von Karolyi (piano), Ashkenazy (violin). Conductor: Caridis

12 Apr	London Albert Hall	CONCERT OF THE NATIONS (1)* Della Casa, Venturi, Bream (guitar), Von Karolyi (piano), Ashkenazy (violin). Conductor: Caridis
14 Apr	Hamburg Auditorium Max.	CONCERT OF THE NATIONS (1)* Varnay, Bergonzi, Bream (guitar), Von Karolyi (piano), Ashkenazy (violin). Conductor: Caridis
15 Apr	Oslo Royal Opera	CONCERT OF THE NATIONS (1)* Varnay, Bergonzi, Bream (guitar), Von Karolyi (piano), Ashkenazy (violin). Conductor: Caridis
16 Apr	Stockholm Konzerthaus	CONCERT OF THE NATIONS (1)* Conductor: Caridis
17 Apr	Copenhagen Falkoner Center	CONCERT OF THE NATIONS (1)* Varnay, Venturi, Bream (guitar), Von Karolyi (piano), Ashkenazy (violin). Conductor: Caridis
19 Apr	Berlin Hall of Congress	CONCERT OF THE NATIONS (1)*
28 Apr	New York Carnegie Hall	I CAPULETI E I MONTECCHI (2) Costa, Montal, Michalski, Bottcher. Conductor: Gardelli
3 May	New York	TELEVISED CONCERT (1) Selections from the last act of *Aida* with Jon Vickers Conductor: *
9 May	Vienna State Opera	LA FORZA DEL DESTINO (1) Ottolini, Protti, Scheyrer, Ghiaurov, Dönch. Conductor: Ferencsik
16 May	Vienna State Opera	LE NOZZE DI FIGARO (1) Scheyrer, Streich, Kunz, Kerns. Conductor: Loibner
18 May	Vienna State Opera	AIDA (1) Bernard, MacCracken, Kreppel, Protti, Welter. Conductor: Santi
23 May	Vienna State Opera	CAVALLERIA RUSTICANA (2) Zampieri, Milinkovic / Höngen, Protti, Lotte Rysanek. Conductor: Klobucar
26 May	Vienna State Opera	UN BALLO IN MASCHERA (1) Leonie Rysanek, Ottolini, Bastianini, Sciutti. Conductor: Krips
7 June	Vienna State Opera	IL TROVATORE (1) Leontyne Price, Protti, MacCracken, Zaccaria. Conductor: Karajan
14 June	Vienna State Opera	AIDA (2) Welter, Leontyne Price / Shuard, Labó / Usunov, Zaccaria, Bastianini. Conductors: Karajan / Santi
28 June	Vienna State Opera	LA FORZA DEL DESTINO (1) Stella, Protti, MacCracken, Kreppel, Dönch. Conductor: Santi

29 June	RAI-TV	CONCERT (1) Favaretto, piano; Conductor: Rosada Donizetti: Te voglio bene assaje Bellini: Fenesta che lucive Cherubini: Solo un pianto Mascagni: Voi lo sapete Rossini: Una voce poco fa
10 Sept	Moscow Boshoi Theater	IL TROVATORE (2) Cappuccilli, Tucci, Bergonzi, Vinco. Conductor: Gavazzeni
14 Sept	Moscow Bolshoi Theater	CONCERT (1)* Scotto, Borsò, Cappuccilli. Conductor: Salerno
18 Sept	Moscow T. of the Palace of Congresses, The Kremlin	IL TROVATORE (4) Cappuccilli, Tucci / Vajna, Bergonzi / Prevedi / Borsò, Vinco / Ferrin. Conductor: Gavazzeni
20 Sept	T. of the Kremlin	CONCERT (1)* Tucci, Casellato, Ferrin. Conductor: Salerno
1 Oct	Vienna State Opera	RIGOLETTO (1) Nikolov, Protti, Moffo, Zaccaria. Conductor: Erede
3 Oct	Vienna State Opera	IL TROVATORE (2) Bastianini, Stella, Nikolov, Zaccaria. Conductor: Erede
8 Oct	Budapest Magyar Allami Opera House	IL TROVATORE (1) Sved, Dunszt, Simándy, Bódy. Conductor: Toth
10 Oct	Vienna State Opera	DON CARLO (1) Siepi, Stella, Zampieri, Zaccaria, Franc, Bastianini. Conductor: Erede
11 Oct	Budapest Magyar Allami Opera House	SANSONE E DALILA (1) Palós, Pálocz, Varga, Bódy. Conductor: Varga
14 Oct	Vienna State Opera	CAVALLERIA RUSTICANA (1) Zampieri, Höngen, Protti, Lotte Rysanek. Conductor: Wallberg
2 Nov	London Covent Garden	AIDA (2) Tynes, Craig, Shaw, Robinson, Godfrey. Conductor: Loughran
19 Nov	London Covent Garden	IL TROVATORE (8) Jones, Prevedi, Glossop, Rouleau, Bainbridge, Dobson, Owen, Clothier. Conductor: Giulini
26 Dec	Naples T. San Carlo	LA DANNAZIONE DI FAUST (3) Bondino, Bastianini, Clabassi. Conductor: Maag

1965

9 Jan	Milan La Scala	NORMA (9) Gencer, Prevedi / Cecchele, Zaccaria, De Palma, Piccolo. Conductor: Gavazzeni
20 Feb	Naples T. San Carlo	AIDA (3) Maragliano, Bergonzi, Colzani, Ferrin, Campi. Conductor: Previtali
23 Apr	Boston Hynes Auditorium Met Opera Tour	AIDA (1) Curtis-Verna, Corelli, Guarrera, Macurdy. Conductor: Adler
27 Apr	Cleveland Public Auditorium Met Opera Tour	SANSONE E DALILA (1) Vickers, Macurdy, Mittelmann, Diaz. Conductor: Cleva
1 May	Cleveland Public Auditorium Met Opera Tour	AIDA (1) Curtis-Verna, Corelli, Guarrera, Macurdy. Conductor: Adler
4 May	Atlanta Civic Auditorium Met Opera Tour	SANSONE E DALILA (1) Usunov, Macurdy, Mittelmann, Diaz. Conductor: Cleva
14 May	Paris T. National de l'Opéra	NORMA (2) Callas, Cecchele, Vinco, Calès, Bellary. Conductor: Prêtre
22 May	Minneapolis Northrop Auditorium Met Opera Tour	AIDA (1) Amara, Corelli, Mittelmann, Flagello. Conductor: Adler
25 May	Detroit Masonic Temple Auditorium Met Opera Tour	AIDA (1) Curtis-Verna, Corelli, Bardelli, Flagello. Conductor: Adler
28 May	Detroit Masonic Temple Auditorium Met Opera Tour	SANSONE E DALILA (1) Vickers, Macurdy, Mittelmann, Diaz. Conductor: Cleva
15 June	Vienna State Opera	DON CARLO (1) Ghiaurov, Jurinac, Prevedi, Hotter, Franc, Paskalis. Conductor: Swarowsky
19 June	Vienna State Opera	LA FORZA DEL DESTINO (1) Scheyrer, Sereni, MacCracken, Siepi, Dönch. Conductor: Basile
22 June	Vienna State Opera	CAVALLERIA RUSTICANA (1) Zampieri, Milinkovic, Berry, Lotte Rysanek. Conductor: Wallberg

21 July	Munich	CARMEN(*) Del Monaco. Conductor: *
25 July	Verona Arena	CARMEN (5) Freni / Pobbe, Limarilli, Giangiacomo Guelfi, Rezzadore, Grigolato. Conductor: Sanzogno
7 Sept	Venice Sala del Gran Consiglio	CONCERT - Verdi, Requiem Mass (1) Scotto, Bergonzi, Modesti. Conductor: Karajan
30 Sept	Vienna State Opera	CAVALLERIA RUSTICANA (1) Zampieri, Milinkovic, Paskalis, Bösch. Conductor: Wallberg
3 Oct	Vienna State Opera	UN BALLO IN MASCHERA (3) Di Stefano, Paskalis / Protti, Leonie Rysanek / Stella, Guglielmi / Miljakovic. Conductors: Krips / Wallberg / Quadri
10 Oct	Vienna State Opera	RIGOLETTO (1) Oncina, Paskalis, Coertse, Franc. Conductor: Klobucar
17 Oct	Vienna State Opera	LA FORZA DEL DESTINO (2) Scheyrer, Paskalis, Di Stefano, Dönch, Kreppel. Conductor: Quadri
7 Dec	Milan La Scala	LA FORZA DEL DESTINO (8) Bergonzi, Cappuccilli / Meliciani, Ligabue / Genger, Ghiaurov / Zaccaria, Capecchi, De Palma, Clabassi. Conductor: Gavazzeni

1966

24 Jan	Milan Piccola Scala	LA CLEMENZA DI TITO (4) Alva, Casellato, Gordoni. Conductor: Sanzogno

1979

27 Aug	Salzburg Kleines Festspielhaus	CONCERT in honor of Karl Böhm with Cappuccilli, Carreras, Cotrubas, Freni, Gruberova, James King, Ludwig, Prey, Talvela, Behrens, Boesch, Goertz, Lohner, Prawy, Taussig, Weigel, Otti. Conductors: Karajan / Bernstein / Levine. Mozart: Non so più

Discography

Official Discography (Studio Recordings)

Cilea — ADRIANA LECOUVREUR
1961 — Decca — Met/Set — 221/3
With: Tebaldi, Del Monaco, Fioravanti. Cond. Capuana.

Cimarosa — IL MATRIMONIO SEGRETO
1950 — Cetra Lpc 1214 — Reprinted Cetra Lps 3214 (1968)
With: Noni, Valletti, Bruscantini, Rovero, Cassinelli. Cond. Wolf Ferrari.

Donizetti — LA FAVORITA
1955 — Decca Lxt — 5146/48 — Reprinted by Decca Gos 525/27 (1968) —
Reprinted by Richmond Srs (1969)
With: Poggi, Bastianini, Hines. Cond. Erede.

Giordano — ANDREA CHÉNIER
1941 — HMV Qalp 10069 — Reprinted by Seraphim IB 60 (1967) —
World Record Club H 105/6 (1968) — Emi Qso 41/42 (1968)
(as Contessa di Coigny) With: Caniglia, Gigli, Bechi, Huder, Tajo, Taddei, Palombini.
Cond. De Fabritiis.

Mascagni— CAVALLERIA RUSTICANA
1940 — Victor Lct 6000 — Reprinted by Seraphim IB 6008 (1958) — HMV Alp 1610/12
and Qalp 108/9 (1958)
(as Lucia) With: Bruna Rasa, Gigli, Bechi, Marcucci. Cond. Mascagni.
1952 — Cetra Lpc 1238 — Reprinted by Cetra Lps 3238 (1968)
With: Braschi, Tagliabue, Cadoni. Cond. Basile.
1960 — Decca Lxt 5643/4 and Sxl 2281/2 — Reprinted by Decca Gos 588/9 (1970)
With: Del Monaco, MacNeil, Satre. Cond. Serafin; with *Casta Diva* conducted by Previtali.

Mascagni — LA GIOCONDA
1957 — Decca Lxt 5400/02 and Sxl 2225/7 — Reprinted by Decca Gos 609/11 (1972)
With: Cerquetti, Del Monaco, Bastianini, Siepi, Sacchi. Cond. Gavazzeni.

Puccini — SUOR ANGELICA
1962 — Decca Lxt 6123
With: Tebaldi. Cond. Gardelli.

Rossini — IL BARBIERE DI SIVIGLIA
1950 — Cetra Lpc 1211 — Reprinted by Cetra Lps 3211 (1967)
With: Infantino, Taddei, Badioli, Cassinelli, Broilo. Cond. Previtali.
1956 — Decca Lxt 5283/85 — Reprinted by Richmond RS 63011 (1969) —

Decca Eclipse 211/13 (1975)
With: Misciano, Bastianini, Corena, Siepi, Cavallari. Cond. Erede.

Rossini — CENERENTOLA
1950 — Cetra Lpc 1218 — Reprinted by Cetra Lps 3208
With: Valletti, Rovero, Meletti, Dalamangas, Susca, Truccato-Pace. Cond. Rossi.
1963 — Decca — Met/Set — 265/7 — Reprinted by Decca Gos 631/33 (1973)
With: Benelli, Bruscantini, Montarsolo, Foiani, Carral, Truccato-Pace. Cond. De Fabritiis.

Rossini — L'ITALIANA IN ALGERI
1954 — Columbia Qcx 10111/12 — Reprinted by Emi C 163-00981/2
With: Valletti, Petri, Cortis, Sciutti, Campi. Cond. Giulini.

Verdi — AIDA
1951 — Cetra Lps 1228
With: Mancini, Filippeschi, Panerai, Neri, Massaria. Cond. Gui.
1958 — Decca Sxl 2167/9 and Lxt 5539/41
With: Tebaldi, Bergonzi, MacNeil, Van Mill, Corena. Cond. Karajan.

Verdi — UN BALLO IN MASCHERA
1961 — Decca — Met/Set — 215/17
With: Bergonzi, MacNeil, Nilsson, Stahlman, Corena, Arbace. Cond. Solti.

Verdi — FALSTAFF
1964 — RCA Ser 5509/11 — Reprinted by Decca 2BB 104/6 (1971)
With: Evans, Ligabue, Freni, Kraus, Elias, Merrill. Cond. Solti.

Verdi — LA FORZA DEL DESTINO
1955 — Decca Lxt 5131/34 — Reprinted by Decca Sxl 2069/72 (1959) —
Decca Gos 597/9 (1970)
With: Tebaldi, Del Monaco, Bastianini, Siepi, Corena. Cond. Molinari Pradelli.

Verdi — RIGOLETTO
1954 — Decca Lxt 5006/8 — Reprinted by Decca Acl 203/5 (1964) — Decca Acln 295/7
and Ecsi 215/7 (1970)
With: Protti, Del Monaco, Güden, Siepi. Cond. Erede.

Verdi — IL TROVATORE
1956 — Decca Lxt 5260/2 and Sxl 2129 — Reprinted by Decca Gos 614/6 — (1971)
With: Savarese, Tebaldi, Del Monaco, Tozzi. Cond. Erede.
1964 — Emi Angel An/San 151/3
With: Merrill, Tucci, Corelli, Mazzoli. Cond. Schippers.

Recitals (Commercial Recordings)

OPERATIC RECITAL (in Italian)
1954 — Decca Lw 5139. Cond. Ghione

OPERATIC RECITAL (in French)
1956 — Decca Lxt 5458. Cond. Previtali

LYRIC OPERA AT CHICAGO
1956 — Decca Lxt 5326. Cond. Solti

GALA PERFORMANCE (in the Pipistrello)
Anything you can do with Ettore Bastianini
1960 — Decca Met/Set 201. Cond. Karajan

DISCOGRAPHY

Various Compilations of Studio Recordings

FAMOUS SINGERS — FAMOUS ARIAS
Decca CEP 505

FAMOUS LOVE SCENES
Decca CEP 671/ SEC 5070
Decca 672

SIMIONATO RECITAL
Decca CEP 659

RIGOLETTO QUARTET
with Mario Del Monaco
Decca 45.71081

DON CARLOS
Decca 45.71094

WORLD OF ITALIAN OPERA
Decca SPA 105

FAVOURITE OPERA
Decca DPA 507

FAVOURITE OPERATIC DUETS
Decca DPA 517

FAVOURITE COMPOSERS — VERDI
Decca DPA 555

GRANDI VOCI — SIMIONATO
GRV 16

NB: Most of Simionato's 78 RPM recordings appear on the record dedicated to her in the EMI anthology "HISTORICAL ARCHIVES" — Classic Library (3 C 053- 18031 m)
Thomas: *Non conosci il bel suol* (March 14, 1949)
Thomas: *Io conosco un garzoncel* (March 14, 1949)
Bizet: *Habañera* (May 4, 1951)
Saint-Saëns: *O aprile foriero* (May 8, 1951)
Saint-Saëns: *Amor, i miei fini proteggi* (May 8, 1951)
Massenet: *Aria delle lettere del Werther* (April 20, 1951)
Massenet: *Va, non è mal se piango* (May 4, 1951)
Cond. A Quadri
On the first side of the record there are selections from the complete I'TALIANA IN ALGERI (1955) and from IL TROVATORE (1964) listed in the official discography above.

Discography of Live Recordings and Tapography

Line 1: opera
Line 2: place and date of the performance
Line 3: cast
Line 4: tapography and live discography
E: Selection
Ital: opera sung in Italian
Fr: opera sung in French

Abbreviations: Live performances on disc
ARPL: Replica
ARK: Arkadia
BJR: BJR
Cetra Doc: Cetra Documenti
Cetra LO: Cetra Opera Live
E/A: Estro Armonico
EJS: The Golden Age of Opera
EL: Edizione Lirica
ERR: ERR
FO: Foyer
FWR: FWR
GDS: Giuseppe Di Stefano
GFC: Gean Franco Caravaggio
GOP: Great Opera Performances
HOPE: HOPE
HRE: Historical Recording Enterprises
IE: Impresario Editions
LVOP: Live Opera
LR: Legendary Recordings
Mel: Melodram
MM: Movimento Musica
MOR: Morgan
MRF: MRF
NHK: Japanese National Broadcasting Corporation—Lirica Italiana
OD: Opera Dubbs
PAR: Paragon
Raritas: Raritas OPR
RHR: Robin Hood Records
RPCL: Replica
RPP: Rodolphe Productions
RR: Recital Records
Seven Seas: Seven Seas
STR: Stradivarius
UORC: Unique Opera Record Corporation

Tapes: the indication MT refers to the catalog of Mr. Tape, which is no longer in business. We have been informed that owner Ralph Ferradina is deceased. (For owners of the Italian edition of this book, the address, P.O. Box 138, 6 Murray Hill Station, New York, N.Y. 10016, is no longer valid.) Disposition of the inventory is not known.

Live Opera (Charles Handelman, principal) may be reached by mail at:
P.O. Box 3141, Steinway Station, Long Island City, N.Y., 11103.

Bellini — CAPULETI E MONTECCHI
Carnegie Hall — 14 Oct. 1958
With: Hurley, Cassily, Flagello. Cond. Gamson.
LVOP 02477, MT 611 — MRF 19
Carnegie Hall — 28 April 1964
With: Costa, Montal, Michalski, Botcher. Cond. Gardelli.
LVOP 02474, MT 5533

Bellini — NORMA
Mexico City — 23 May 1950
With: Callas, Baum, Moscona. Cond. Picco.
MT 1036 — HRE 252
Bellini — NORMA
Mexico City — 27 May 1950

With: Callas, Baum, Moscona. Cond. Picco.
LVOP 01947
Scala — 7 Dec. 1955
With: Callas, Del Monaco, Zaccaria. Cond. Votto.
LVOP 01777, MT 915 — Cetra LO 31, IE 3005
Scala — 9 Jan. 1965
With: Gencer, Prevedi, Zaccaria. Cond. Gavazzeni.
LVOP 01935 (date given as 1/13/65), MT 1413 — HRE 320, Mel 468, GFC 033
Opéra de Paris — 14 May 1965 (E)
With: Callas, Cecchele, Vinco. Cond. Prêtre.
MT 3066
Opéra de Paris — 17 May 1965 (E)
With: Callas, Cecchele, Vinco. Cond. Prêtre.
MT 3066 — HRE 373

Berlioz — LA DANNAZIONE DI FAUST
Naples — 26 Dec. 1964 (Ital)
With: Bondino, Bastianini, Clabassi. Cond. Maag.
LVOP 03625, MT 3678 — E/A 037

Berlioz —I TROIANI
Scala — 27 May 1960
With: Del Monaco, Rankin, Cossotto. Cond. Kubelik.
LVOP 03805 (date given as 3/30/62), MT 458 — HRE 291, PAR 52011

Bizet — CARMEN
RAI — 26 Dec. 1950 (Ital)
With: Berdini, Pagliughi, Boriello. Cond. Previtali.
(Acts I, II)
Naples — 30 Dec. 1953 (Ital)
With: Corelli, Jurinac, Savarese (The recording mistakenly lists Carlo Tagliabue).
Cond. Rodzinski.
LVOP 00245, MT 5547 — EL 001
Naples — * Dec. 1953 (Ital)
With: Corelli, Jurinac, Savarese. Cond. Rodzinski.
LVOP 02572
Vienna — 8 Oct. 1954 (Fr)
With: Gedda, Güden, Roux. Cond. Karajan.
LVOP 00197, MT 2135 — GFC 026
Scala — 18 Jan. 1955 (Fr)
With: Di Stefano, Carteri, Roux. Cond. Karajan.
LVOP 00207, MOR 5502, Cetra LO 22, RR 470
Rio de Janeiro — 17 Aug. 1956 (Ital)
With: Del Monaco, Salgado, Guelfi. Cond. Ghione.
LVOP 02566, MT 4109
Rome — 25 Feb. 1957 (Ital)
With: Di Stefano, Beltrami, Mascherini. Cond. Questa.
MT 481 — UORC 303
Palermo — 8 Feb. 1959 (Ital)
With: Corelli, Freni, Guelfi. Cond. Dervaux.
LVOP 00254, MT 4110 — STR 1003, GOP 30
Tokyo — 19 Feb. 1959 (Ital)
With: Del Monaco, Tucci, Colombo. Cond. Verchi.
MT 8263 — LR 190, Mel 416, Seven Seas K 25 C 307
Rio — 2 Aug. 1961 (Ital)
With: Scotto, Corelli, Bastianini, Maddalena. Cond. Molinari Pradelli
LVOP 06666

Boito — NERONE
Scala — 10 June 1948
With: Siepi, Nelli, Guarrera. Cond. Toscanini.
MT 1560 — MOR 4801, HOPE 222, HRE 257

Cherubini — MEDEA
Scala — 11 Dec. 1961
With: Callas, Vickers, Ghiaurov. Cond. Schippers.
LVOP 04639 (date given as 12/14/61), MT 1023 — MRF 102, Cetra Doc 21

Cilea — ADRIANA LECOUVREUR
Naples — 28 Nov. 1959
With: Olivero, Corelli, Bastianini. Cond. Rossi.
LVOP 00285, MT 793 — MOR 5901, EJS 497, MRF 47, HOPE 246, Mel 043, Cetra Doc 19, RR 294

De Falla — ATLANTIDA
Scala — 18 June 1962 (Ital)
With: Stratas, Ganzarolli, Browne, Holley. Cond. Schippers.
LVOP 02327, MT 781

Donizetti — ANNA BOLENA
Scala — 17 Apr. 1957
With: Callas, Raimondi, Rossi Lemeni. Cond. Gavazzeni.
LVOP 00421, MT 314 — MOR 5703, Cetra LO 53, BJR 109, MRF 42, HOPE 226, Cetra Doc 22, ARPL 32493, RPCL 32029, FWR 646, FO 1014
RAI — 11 July 1958
With: Gencer, Bertocci, Clabassi, Cond. Gavazzeni
LVOP 00421, MT 550 — EJS 167, ARPL 32407

Donizetti — LA FAVORITA
Mexico City — 12 July 1949
With: Di Stefano, Mascherini, Siepi. Cond. Picco.
LVOP 01338, MT 333 — Cetra LO 2, EJS 319, Raritas 406
Naples — 11 May 1963
With: Raimondi, Zanasi, Zaccaria. Cond. Previtali.
LVOP 01339, MT 4144

Gluck — ORFEO ED EURIDICE
Salzburg — 5 Aug. 1959
With: Jurinac, Sciutti. Cond. Karajan.
LVOP 02287, MT 3159 — LR 132, ARPL 22436
Salzburg — * Aug. 1959
With: Jurinac. Cond. Karajan.
LVOP 03234

Mascagni — CAVALLERIA RUSTICANA
Mexico City — 13 or 18 June 1950
With: Filippeschi, Morelli. Cond. Mugnai.
LVOP 02579, MT 6030
Scala — 10 May 1955
With: Di Stefano, Guelfi. Cond. Votto.
LVOP 00504, MT 1250 b — UORC 259, Cetra LO 15, MRF 142 (E), GDS 1001
Met — 16 Nov. 1959
With: Björling, Elias, Cassel. Cond. Verchi.
LVOP, MT 363 — HRE 301

Tokyo — 21 Oct. 1961
With: Lo Forese, D'Orazi. Cond. Morelli.
LVOP, Seven Seas K 25 c-310
Scala — 7 Dec. 1963
With: Corelli, Guelfi. Cond. Gavazzeni.
MT 1408 a, MOR 6301, HRE 413, Cetra Doc 58
Scala — 9 Dec. 1963 (E)
With: Corelli, Guelfi. Cond. Gavazzeni.
LVOP 00257, Cetra Doc 58

Mascagni — ZANETTO
Scala — 10 May 1955
With: Carteri. Cond. Votto.
LVOP, MT 789 — MRF 81

Massenet — WERTHER
Mexico City — 26 July 1949 (Ital)
With: Di Stefano, Rocabruna, Del Prado. Cond. Cellini.
LVOP 01713 (date given as 7/30/49), MT 1012 — Cetra LO 30, EJS 303 (E), EJS 547, ERR 111
Scala — 21 Apr. 1951 (Ital)
With: Gatta, Tagliavini, Orlandini. Cond. Capuana.

Menotti — AMAHL E GLI OSPITI NOTTURNI
Florence — 9 May 1953 (E)
With: Corena, Cordova, Lazzari. Cond. Stokowski.
LVOP 02828

Meyerbeer — GLI UGONOTTI
Scala — 28 May 1962 (Ital)
With: Sutherland, Corelli, Cossotto, Ghiaurov, Ganzarolli, Tozzi. Cond. Gavazzeni.
LVOP 02920 (date given as 6/7/62), MT 1406 — MOR 6202, EJS 246, MRF 18, HOPE 248, Cetra Doc 34, GOP 2

Monteverdi — IL COMBATTIMENTO DI TANCREDI E CLORINDA
Naples — 12 Apr. 1952
With: Valletti, Rovero. Cond. Sanzogno.
LVOP 03616, EJS 453, HRE 301

Mozart — COSÌ FAN TUTTE
Geneva — 14 Jan. 1949
With: Danco, Morel, Stabile, Cortis, De Luca. Cond. Böhm.
LVOP 05217, RPP 12456

Mozart — LA CLEMENZA DI TITO
Piccola Scala — 24 Jan. 1966
With: Casellato, Alva, Gordoni, Morelli. Cond. Sanzogno.
MT 4213
Piccola Scala — 1 Feb. 1966
Farewell as Servilia
LVOP 05875

Mozart — LE NOZZE DI FIGARO
Naples — 24 Feb. 1954 (E)
With: Tebaldi, Noni, Tajo, Colombo, Raimondi. Cond. Perlea.
Excerpts: Acts I and II
LVOP 03328, MT 8428

Salzburg Festival — 27 Aug. 1979 ("*Non so più*")
85th Birthday of Karl Böhm
MT 4857

Rossini — IL BARBIERE DI SIVIGLIA
Mexico City — 7 July 1949
With: Di Stefano, Mascherini, Siepi, Pechner. Cond. Cellini.
LVOP 00320, MT 5724 — EJS 302 (E)
Tokyo — 23 Oct. 1963
With: Protti, Sabatucci, Rossi Lemeni. Cond. De Fabritiis.
LVOP 00324, MT 1251

Rossini — LA CENERENTOLA, Naples — 12 Dec. 1953
With: Gatta, Oncina, Taddei, Tajo. Cond. Serafin.
LVOP 03045

Rossini — SEMIRAMIDE
Scala — 19 Dec. 1962
With: Sutherland, Raimondi, Ganzarolli. Cond. Santini.
LVOP 03828, MT 412 — EJS 259, Cetra Doc 40

Saint-Saëns — SANSONE E DALILA
Met (in Atlanta) — 4 May 1965
With: Usunov, Mittelmann, Diaz. Cond. Cleva.
Met (in Detroit) — 28 May 1965
With: Vickers, Macurdy, Diaz. Cond. Cleva.
MT 1047

Thomas — MIGNON
Mexico City — 28 June 1949 (Ital)
With: Di Stefano, Siepi, Ruffino. Cond. Mugnai.
LVOP 03373, MT 1085 — EJS 302 (E), ERR 112

Verdi — AIDA
Mexico City — 30 May 1950
With: Callas, Baum, Weede, Moscona. Cond. Picco.
LVOP 00061, MT 1088 — UORC 200, HRE 310
Mexico City — 3 June 1950 (E)
With: Callas, Baum, Moscona. Cond. Picco.
OD 2
Covent Garden — 4 June 1953 (Act III)
With: Callas, Baum, Walters. Cond. Barbirolli.
LVOP 00097, MT 153 — RHR 500, FWR 646
Scala — 7 Dec. 1956
With: Di Stefano, Stella, Guelfi. Cond. Votto.
LVOP 00040, MT 1172 — UORC 317, GDS 1003, PAR 52026, ARPL 32448
Scala — 21 Apr. 1960
With: Nilsson, Miranda Ferraro, MacNeil, Ghiaurov. Cond. Sanzogno.
LVOP 00070, MT 2146
Tokyo — 16 Oct. 1961
With: Tucci, Del Monaco, Protti. Cond. Capuana.
LVOP, MT 5074 — Seven Seas K 25 C 317
Met — 1 Dec. 1962
With: Tucci, Konya, Merrill, Siepi. Cond. Santi.
LVOP
Vienna — 3 June 1963
With: Price, Usunov, Bastianini, Kreppel. Cond. Von Matacic.
LVOP 00116, MT 2683 — Mel 410, FO 1036

Covent Garden — 4 Feb. 1964
With: Vishnevskaya, Vickers, Glossop, Rouleau. Cond. Balkwill.
MT 4335
Met (in Cleveland) — 1 May 1965 (E)
With: Curtis Verna, Corelli, Guarrera, Cond. Adler.
LVOP

Verdi — UN BALLO IN MASCHERA
Scala — 7 Dec. 1957
With: Callas, Di Stefano, Bastianini, Ratti. Cond. Gavazzeni.
LVOP 00338, MT 329 — MOR 5709, MRF 83, Cetra LO 55, BJR 127 — ARPL 32445, GOP 13

Verdi — DON CARLO
Salzburg — 26 July 1958
With: Fernandi, Jurinac, Bastianini, Siepi. Cond. Karajan.
LVOP 00447 (Date given as 9/7/58), MT 1187 — ERR 119, Cetra LO 72, FO 1029
Chicago — 14 Oct. 1960
With: Tucker, Roberti, Gobbi, Christoff. Cond. Votto.
LVOP 00449, MT 1426 — EL 014, STR 1026, GOP 38
Vienna — 23 Sep. 1961
With: Stella, Labo, Waechter, Kreppel. Cond. Cleva.
LVOP 01881

Verdi — FALSTAFF
Salzburg — 10 Aug. 1957
With: Gobbi, Schwarzkopf, Panerai, Moffo, Canali, Alva. Cond. Karajan.
LVOP 06673, MT 5090
Chicago — 10 Oct. 1958
With: Gobbi, Tebaldi, Moffo, Misciano, MacNeil. Cond. Serafin.
LVOP 01003, MT 546 — HRE 282

Verdi —LA FORZA DEL DESTINO
RAI Rome — 28 Sep. 1957
With: Cerquetti, Miranda Ferraro, Protti, Christoff, Capecchi. Cond. Sanzogno.
LVOP 06763, MT 1210 — UORC 332, ARPL 32499
Vienna — 23 Sep. 1960
With: Di Stefano, Stella, Bastianini, Kreppel, Dönch. Cond. Mitropoulos.
LVOP 01920, MT 1207 — Mel 023, MOR 6002
Scala — 7 Dec. 1965
With: Ligabue, Bergonzi, Cappuccilli (Act I) and Meliciani, Christoff, Capecchi. Cond. Gavazzeni.
MT 2150

Verdi — REQUIEM
Salzburg — 9 Aug. 1962
With: Price, Zampieri, Ghiaurov. Cond. Karajan.
LVOP 02812, MT 2749

Verdi — IL TROVATORE
Mexico City — 20 June 1950
With: Callas, Baum, Warren, Moscona. Cond. Picco.
LVOP 03017, MT 318 — HRE 207
Mexico City — 27 June 1950
With: Callas, Baum, Petroff, Moscona. Cond. Picco.
LVOP 03018
Met — 27 Feb. 1960
With: Stella, Bergonzi, Bastianini, Wildermann. Cond. Cleva.
MT 472 — GFC 005

Salzburg — 31 July 1962
With: Price, Corelli, Bastianini. Cond. Karajan.
LVOP 03011, MT 106 — MOR 6201, HRE 287, HOPE 247, Mel 710, ARK 7, MM 03018
Salzburg — 13 Aug. 1963
With: Price, MacCracken, Bastianini, Zaccaria. Cond. Karajan.
MT 5428
Tokyo — 16 Oct. 1963
With: Stella, Limarilli, Bastianini, Cond. De Fabritiis.
LVOP 03801, MT 1252 — Seven Seas K 25 C 351
Moscow — 10 Sep. 1964
With: Tucci, Bergonzi, Cappuccilli. Cond. Gavazzeni.
HRE 340 (E)
Covent Garden — 26 Nov. 1964
With: Jones, Prevedi, Glossop, Rouleau. Cond. Giulini.
MT 3968 — LR 175

Various Compilations of Live Recordings

GIULIETTA SIMIONATO (Mel. 7):
Gluck— ORFEO E EURIDICE (Salzburg, 1959)
Restar voglio da sol... Chiamo il mio ben così
Che puro ciel ...
Ove trascorsi... Che farò senza Euridice
Donizetti — ANNA BOLENA (Milan 1957, with Gencer and Clabassi)
Act I, scena and duet with Giovanno - Enrico
Act II, scena and duet with Anna - Giovanna
Bellini — NORMA (Scala 1955, with Callas and Del Monaco)
Act I, scene VIII, duet with Norma - Adalgisa, and trio with Norma - Adalgisa - Pollione
Act II, scene III, duet with Adalgisa, Norma
Verdi — DON CARLO (Salzburg, 1958 with Fernandi, Bastianini and Jurinac)
Act II, scene II, *Tra queste mura pie... Nel giardino*
Act II, scene I
Act IV, *Pietà, pietà, perdon...*, *...Ah, non più non vedrò la Regina*

GREAT MEZZO-SOPRANOS — previously unissued selections (Voce 111)
Giulietta Simionato sings:
Mozart: *Non so più*
Saint-Saëns: *S'apre per te il mio cor*
Donizetti: Final duet from LA FAVORITA, *Pietoso al par del nume...*
With Cesare Valletti. Cond. Fausto Cleva
Radio concert in San Francisco, 18 Oct. 1953

THE LEGENDARY GIULIETTA SIMIONATO "LIVE" (LR 1470)
Arias from L'ITALIANA IN ALGERI, TANCREDI, IL BARBIERE DI SIVIGLIA, LA CENERENTOLA, DON CARLO, AIDA, LA FAVORITA

GIULIETTA SIMIONATO (Tima 77/78)
Neglia: *Il saluto di Beatrice*
Neglia: *Come quel fior*
Piano: Renzo Bossi — Dec. 1946

Thomas: *Non conosci il bel suol*
Cond. A. Quadri — 14 Mar. 1949

Thomas: *Eccomi sola ... Io conosco un garzoncel*
Mozart: *Non so più cosa son*
Mozart: Voi che sapete
Cond. La Rosa Parodi — 30 Dec. 1957

Massenet: Dividecri dobbiam (with F. Tagliavini)
Massenet: Letter scene (with D. Gatta)
Massenet: final duet from WERTHER (with F. Tagliavini)
Cond. F. Capuana — 21 Apr. 1951

Cilea: *Esser madre è un inferno*
Cilea: *Tu pur sei figlio* (with W. Borrelli)
Cond. O. Ziino — 1 July 1961

Gordigiani: *L'addio del pastore*
Paer: *Il bacio della partenza*
Campana: *M'hai tradito*
Piano: Luciano Bettarini — 18 Dec. 1956

Berlioz: *Ci fu una volta in Thule un rè*
Berlioz: *Perduta è la mia pace*
Cond. F. Capuana — 26 Dec. 1964

Cilea: *Acerba voluttà*
Cond. O. Ziino — 1 July 1961

Bizet: *Habañera*
Cond. A. Quadri — 1951

Brahms: *Ninna nanna* (probably 1983)

VOCI CELEBRI DELLA LIRICA (MPV 5)
Giulietta Simionato:
Thomas: *Io conosco un garzoncel*
Rossini: *Di tanti palpiti*
Massenet: *Letter aria*
Bellini: *Ecco la tomba ... Deh, tu, bell'anima*
Cond. Argento — 20 Dec. 1954 — Martini and Rossi Concert
The 20 Dec. 1954 Martini and Rossi Concert is also on Fonit Cetra LMR 5006 (record)

MARTINI AND ROSSI CONCERT of 26 Nov. 1956
Cond. Sanzogno — Fonit Cetra LMR 5015
Rossini: *Pensa alla patria*
Rossini: *Di tanti palpiti*
Rossini: *Una voce poco fa*
Rossini: *Nacqui all' affano*

MARIO DEL MONACO "LIVE" (LR 185)
There are excerpts from the AIDA sung in Tokyo in 1961 with Simionato, Tucci, Protti.

OPERA CONCERT IN 1959/1961 (NHK K25C-315/6)
Excerpts from DON CARLO and FAVORITA sung in Tokyo

DONIZETTI MEZZO ARIAS (LVOP 04804)
Excerpts from FAVORITA, LA ZINGARA, BOLENA, DON SEBASTIANO with Berganza, Rota, Barbieri, Stignani, Cossotto, Verrett, Simionato.

GOLDEN DUETS (LVOP 04792)
Simionato, Callas, Gencer, Horne, Caballé, Rysanek, Milanov, Warren, Kullman, Weede in duets from live performances.

GREAT ARTIST POT-POURRI - VOL. 3 (LVOP 05303)
Della Casa, Tucker, Varnay, Vinay, Ponselle, Pinza, Stignani, Simionato, Valletti, Schwarzkopf. Live material from TV, Radio, live perf.

GREAT HIGHLIGHTS FROM ENTIRE COLLECTION (LVOP 04855)
Suliotis, Callas, Simionato, Ludwig, Gencer, Resnik, Caballé, Cigna, Vartenissian, Kraus. Live and from disc.

MEZZO-SOPRANOS OF ITALY (LVOP 04730)
Elmo, Stignani, Barbieri, Simionato, Cossotto.

O DON FATALE (LVOP 04728)
18 famous mezzos sing the aria from DON CARLO.

RARE DONIZETTI DUETS (LVOP 04803)
Rota, Cappuccilli, Aragall, Gencer, Alberti, Simionato, Bottion, Adami, Gimenez, Taddei sing Donizetti arias.

ROSSINI MEZZOS (LVOP 04825)
Cossotto, Reynolds, Horne, Rota, Simionato, Companez sing arias from TANCREDI, ITALIANA, ZELMINA, SEMIRAMIDE, CORINTO, etc.

SOPRANO POT-POURRI 1941-1968 (LVOP 06299)
Giannini, Tebaldi, Carteri, Welitsch, Roman, Simionato, Traubel, Farrell, others.

UNPUBLISHED MATERIAL COMPILATION (LVOP 06331)
Kirsten, Giannini, Caballé, Tebaldi, Cobelli, Stignani, Favero, Pacetti, Pagliughi, Simionato.

WHO CAN DO IT BETTER? (LVOP 04729)
Cigna, Simionato, Soviero, Callas, Milanov, Olivero, Ludwig, Kraus, Nilsson, Warren. Live opera scenes.

Videos — Live Performances

Bizet — CARMEN
Tokyo, Feb. 1959.
With: Del Monaco. Cond. Verchi. (Excerpts) Habañera, Seguidilla. (B/W)
LVOP 04299

Mascagni — CAVALLERIA RUSTICANA
Tokyo, Oct. 1961.
With: Lo Forese, D'orazi. Cond. Morelli. (B/W)
LVOP 04372

Verdi — AIDA
Verona — Aug. 1963.
With: Gencer, Limareilli. Cond. Serafin. (E) Act 1, Act II sc. I. (B/W)
LVOP 07076

Videos — Compilations of Live Performances

GREAT OPERA STARS 1953-1981
With: Simionato, Corelli, Tebaldi, Scotto, Bergonzi, Gobbi, Del Monaco, Di Stefano, Tucker, Nilsson.
LVOP 06603

LIRICA ITALIANA IN TOKYO 1957-1961
AIDA,CARMEN, FIGARO, ELISIR, CAVALLERIA, FALSTAFF, TRAVIATA (Excerpts) with Del Monaco, Borso, Stella, Simionato, Tucci, Iaia, Taddei, Guelfi, Noni, Protti. (B/W)
LVOP 05905

DISCOGRAPHY

Compact Discs — Made from Commercial Recordings

Cilea — ADRIANA LECOUVREUR — 1961: Decca 430-256-2

Cimarosa — IL MATRIMONIO SEGRETO — 1950: Nuova Fonit Cetra CDO 32

Donizetti — LA FAVORITA — 1955: Gruppo Editoriale Bramante M CBCD 8029/30

Giordano — ANDREA CHÉNIER — 1941: Emi CHS 769996 2;

Mascagni — CAVALLERIA RUSTICANA — 1952: Fonit Cetra CDO 27;
1960: Decca 421 807 2

Ponchielli — LA GIOCONDA — 1957: Decca 433 770 2

Rossini — CENERENTOLA — 1954: Nuova Fonit Cetra CDON 34

Rossini — IL BARBIERE DI SIVIGLIA — 1950: Nuova Fonit Cetra CDO 6

Rossini — L'ITALIANA IN ALGERI — 195*: Emi 764041 2

Verdi — AIDA —1960: Decca 414 087 2

Verdi — IL TROVATORE — 1956: Decca 411 874 2

Verdi — LA FORZA DEL DESTINO — 19**: Decca 421 598; 1964: Emi 763640 2

In the Decca Anthology "GRANDI VOCI" (440 406 2) the CD dedicated to Giulietta Simionato contains extracts of studio takes of FAVORITA, TROVATORE (1956), BALLO IN MASCHERA, FORZA DEL DESTINO, two recitals recorded with the Orchestra of the Academy of Santa Cecilia in 1954 (conducted by Franco Ghione) and in 1956 (conducted by Fernando Previtali), and finally the *Casta Diva* recorded in 1961 with the same orchestra conducted by Alberto Paoletti, very difficult to find on LP.

Compact Discs — Made from Live Recordings

Bellini — CAPULETI E MONTECHI — 14 Oct. 1958 — Melodram CDM 27509

Bellini — NORMA — 23 May 1950 — Melodram 26018
8 Oct. 1954 — Gala GL 100.511
7 Dec. 1955 — Melodram 26036; HRE 1007.2; Arkadia HP 517.2; Hunt Q 517;
9 Jan. 1965 — CURCIO OPI 17

Berlioz — LES TROYENS (I TROIANI) — 27 May 1960 — VAIA 1026

Berlioz — LA DANNAZIONE DI FAUST — 26 Dec. 1964 — Great Opera Performances GOP 776

Bizet — CARMEN — 8 Oct. 1954 — Melodram 27012; Gala GL 100.603
18 Jan. 1955 — Giuseppe Di Stefano GDS 102
25 Feb. 1957
8 Feb. 1959 — Great Opera Performances GOP 727
19 Feb. 1959
2 Aug. 1961— Golden Age of Opera GAO 118/9

Cherubini — MEDEA — 11 Dec. 1961 — Compagnia Generale des Disco
CGD CDLSMH 34028

Cilea — ADRIANA LECOUVREUR — 28 Nov. 1959 — Phoenix PX 502 2; Melodram CDM27009

Cimarosa — ORAZI E CURIAZI — 13 Apr. 1952 — Melodram CDM 29500

Donizetti — ANNA BOLENA
14 Apr. 1957 — Melodram 26010; Hunt Q 518; Emi 7649128; GOP 768
11 July 1958 — Memories HR 4517/18; Phoenix PX 503 2

Donizetti — LA FAVORITA — 12 July 1949 — Standing Room Only SRO 816.2
11 May 1963 — Golden Age of Opera GAO 105/6

Gluck — ORFEO E EURIDICE — 5 Aug. 1959 — Nuova Eera 2215/6; DG 439 101/2

Giordano — ANDREA CHÉNIER — 1960: Fonit Cetra CDE 1017

Mascagni — CAVALLERIA RUSTICANA — 21 Oct. 1961 — Gala GL 100 518; Rodolphe Productions RPC 32755 and RPV 32693/4 (together with PAGLIACCI)
7 Dec. 1963 — Arkadia CDHP 564.1

Meyerbeer — LES HUGUENOTS (Gli Ugonotti) — 28 May 1962 — Great Opera Performances GOP 701; Melodram 37026

Rossini — IL BARBIERE DI SIVIGLIA — 7 July 1949 — Giuseppe Di Stefano GDS 105.2

Rossini — SEMIRAMIDE — 19 Dec. 1962 CURCIO OPI 14

Thomas — MIGNON — 28 June 1949 (excerpts) — Golden Age of Opera GAO 128/9 (together with RIGOLETTO)

Verdi — AIDA 30 May 1950 — Melodram 26009
3 June 1950 (excerpts) — Eklipse EKP CD 44
10 June 1953 — Legato Classics LCD 187; Eklipse EKRCD 14 (excerpts)
7 Dec. 1956 — Legato Classics LCD 204-2
16 Oct 1961 — Gala GL 100 507
3 June 1963 — Foyer CF 2018/2

Verdi — IL BALLO IN MASCHERA — 7 Dec. 1957 — Hunt Q 517; Melodram

Verdi — DON CARLO — 26 July 1958 — CDKAR 220.2
14 Oct. 1960

Verdi — FALSTAFF — 10 Aug. 1957
10 Oct. 1958 — CDKAR 226.2; Legato Classics LCD 206 2

Verdi — LA FORZA DEL DESTINO — 28 Sep. 1957 — Golden Age of Opera GAO 174/176

Verdi — IL TROVATORE — 20 June 1950 — Melodram 26017
27 June 1950 (excerpts) — Eklipse EKRCD 14
27 Feb. 1960
31 July 1962 — Movimento Musica MM 051; Rodolphe Productions RPP 32482
16 Oct. 1963 — NHK (Japanese National Broadcasting Corporation)/ King Record Co., Ltd. K33Y 109/10; (excerpts) — Rodolphe Productions RPP 32752
10 Sep. 1964 — Phoenix PHE 6621; Melodram 27008; (excerpts) —Legato Classics LCD 147.2

With the compact disc GIANNI POGGI — Bongiovanni GB 1097.2 — excerpts of a concert at the Teatro Esperia of Forlì (29 May 1957) are reproduced, one of which is the last duet of FAVORITA sung by Gianni Poggi and Giulietta Simionato

With the compact disc HOMAGE TO RENATA TEBALDI — 5 GOP 721— excerpts of a concert in Chicago (10 Nov. 1956) are reproduced, one of which is the duet from GIOCONDA, *L'amo come il fulgor* sung by Renata Tebaldi and Giulietta Simionato

With the compact disc HOMAGE TO ETTORE BASTIANINI — GOP 745 — a duet taken from Irving Berlin's musical ANNIE GET YOUR GUN is reproduced, originally recorded in Vienna (and not Berlin as it was erroneously reported) in June of 1960; this also appeared together with the studio recording of Act II of DIE FLEDERMAUS (IL PIPISTRELLO), conducted by Herbert von Karajan

With the compact disc devoted to FRANCO CORELLI — Melodram 26020 — excerpts are taken from the CARMEN in Palermo (8 Feb. 1959) which include the duet *Sei tu! Son io!* sung by Franco Corelli and Giulietta Simionato

The Martini and Rossi concert of 20 Dec. 1954, with Ferruccio Tagliavini, conducted by Pietro Argento, is part of the anthology INCONTRI MEMORABILI—Cetra CDMR 5006

The Martini and Rossi Concert of 26 Nov. 1956, with Giuseppe Di Stefano, conducted by Nino Sanzogno has been partially reproduced in the compact disc "THE BEST OF THE MARTINI AND ROSSI CONCERTS" — Memories HR 4419/20 — and exists in its entirety in the anthology INCONTRI MEMORABILI — Cetra CDMR 5015

Tapes Also Exist of the Following Performances

Beethoven — NINTH SYMPHONY — The slender volume known as "The Furtwängler Sound" published by the Wilhelm Furtwängler Society U.K. in 1982, edited by John Hunt, mentions a tape of Beethoven's Ninth Symphony performed at La Scala on May 28, 1949, with Simionato, Cecil, Prandelli and Siepi, conducted by Furtwängler. This tape could be part of a private Milanese collector's archive.

Bizet: CARMEN — 21 Aug. 1953
With: Corelli, Rizieri, Protti

Donizetti — LA FAVORITA, RAI — 26 Nov. 1952
With: Poggi, Silveri, Bruscantini, Fort. Cond. Gavazzeni.

Verdi — LA FORZA DEL DESTINO, Rio de Janeiro — 2 Sep. 1954
With: Penno, Tebaldi, Silveri, Neri. Cond. De Fabritiis.

Index of Names

Exclusive of names contained in prefatory matter and in the concluding sections of the book (Debuts, Repertory, Chronology, Discography)